95

STALIN'S WAR
AGAINST THE JEWS

The Second Thoughts Series
Edited by Peter Collier and David Horowitz

STALIN'S WAR
AGAINST THE JEWS

The Doctors' Plot and the Soviet Solution

Louis Rapoport

THE FREE PRESS
A Division of Macmillan, Inc.
NEW YORK

Collier Macmillan Canada
TORONTO

Maxwell Macmillan International
NEW YORK   OXFORD   SINGAPORE   SYDNEY

The Free Press
A Division of Macmillan, Inc.
866 Third Avenue, New York, New York 10022

Collier Macmillan Canada, Inc.
1200 Eglinton Avenue East
Suite 200
Don Mills, Ontario M3C 3N1

Printed in the United States of America

printing number
1 2 3 4 5 6 7 8 9 10

Library of Congress Cataloging-in-Publication Data

Rapoport, Louis.
  Stalin's war against the Jews : The doctors' plot and the Soviet
solution / Louis Rapoport.
      p.   cm. — (The Second thoughts series)
  Includes bibliographical references.
  ISBN 0-02-925821-9
  1. Jews—Soviet Union—History—1917- 2. Jews—Soviet Union
—Persecutions.   3. Stalin, Joseph, 1879-1953—Views on Jews.
4. Soviet Union—Ethnic relations. I. Title. II. Title: Doctors'
plot. III. Series.
DS135.R92R36 1990   90-3101
947′.004924—dc20   CIP

To the memory of the Lischinsky family,
who perished among the millions

Abram had a keen sense of great but restrained malice coming through the howling of the storm. Abram did not have time to protect himself. Something hard and black flashed before his face like a bird, and then a furious, scalding pain cracked his jaws, brain, and teeth, and it seemed to him that his entire head had burst into flames.

—MIKHAIL BULGAKOV, "The Raid," trans. Carl R. Proffer

Contents

Preface

On January 13, 1953, the Soviet government announced to the world that nine Kremlin doctors, six of whom had identifiably Jewish names, had medically murdered two of Joseph Stalin's closest aides in 1945 and 1948 and were now involved in a vast plot conducted by Western imperialists and Zionists to kill the top Soviet political and military leadership. The announcement stunned the world, for it was obvious that Stalin was about to unleash another terror, along the lines of the great purges and show trials of the 1930s, which had consumed millions of lives.

For the next six weeks the Soviet media pounded away at the supposed "fifth column" in the USSR, with constant references to Jews who were being arrested, dismissed from their jobs, or executed for "economic crimes" or "spying."

Only a few of the over two million Jews of Russia, survivors of the recent Nazi onslaught that had exterminated three million other Jews in Soviet territory, realized that they were about to be shipped in cattle cars to concentration camps in the Gulag empire. The great majority remained completely loyal to the totalitarian regime, and were ashamed and frightened by the heavy Jewish slant to the revelations of treason, conspiracy, sabotage, and "wrecking."

The barracks in Siberia and Kazakhstan and Birobidzhan were ready and waiting for the Jews, whether loyal Communists, commissars, ex-ambassadors, war heroes, intellectuals, doctors, or criminals. There were to be only a handful of exceptions who would not be deported, such as Lazar Moiseyevich Kaganovich, the last Jew in the Soviet hierarchy and one of Stalin's most sinister executioners.

The aristocrats of Soviet Jewry, such as the famous writer-journalist Ilya Ehrenburg and violinist David Oistrakh, were asked to sign a letter—to be published on the front page of *Pravda*—appealing to the Father of All the Peoples to deport the Jews to the Far East territories in order to protect them from the Peoples' righteous anger. Scores of the most famous Soviet Jews signed; but four refused, including Ehrenburg, who up until then was the complete Stalinist lackey, and a survivor of what he grimly termed "the lottery."

The alleged mastermind of the Doctors' Plot, according to the charges on *Pravda*'s front page, was Solomon Mikhoels, a man who had already been dead five years to the day these charges were published. A Yiddish actor and stage director of international renown, Mikhoels during and after World War II had been the ostensible head of Soviet Jewry, so anointed by Stalin and secret police chief Lavrenty Pavlovich Beria, who placed him in charge of the Soviet government's Jewish Anti-Fascist Committee. Although Mikhoels was murdered on the personal orders of Stalin on January 13, 1948, Stalin saw no problem in tying him to the alleged 1953 plot, which, like the notorious early twentieth century *Protocols of the Elders of Zion,* presupposed an apocryphal Jewish plan to take over the world.

Mikhoels's deputy as chairman of the Jewish Anti-Fascist Committee, the "ruling council" of Soviet Jewry from 1942 to 1948, was the famous Yiddish poet Itzik Solomonovich Feffer—a colonel in the Red Army and a secret agent of the security organs. Feffer, who helped arrange the murder of his friend, was himself liquidated along with a score of other leading Jewish intellectuals a few months before the announcement of the Doctors' Plot. The squalid role of Feffer, friend of Paul Robeson and many other prominent American Communists and fellow travelers, is fully explored in this book for the first time.

Mikhoels's first cousin, the eminent Kremlin physician Dr. Miron Vovsi, was also singled out as one of the leaders of the alleged plot. Two of Vovsi's colleagues died under torture during interrogation about their fellow doctors and other "conspirators." Vovsi himself outlived Stalin by seven years, but eventually died of injuries he suffered in prison.

Besides the planned public execution of the doctors and the mass deportation of the Jews—both of which were preempted by Stalin's sudden death—the dictator's intricate strategem included the deportation of half a million Georgian Mingrelians to concentration camps in the wilds of the Soviet empire; a vast purge of the Communist party, Presidium, and security forces; and a general letting of blood—possibly even a third world war.

One of the foundation stones of communism is the myth that socialist rule and proletarian consciousness automatically eliminate nationalist conflicts. Marxism and the nationality question are integral elements in the shaping of the Doctors' Plot, from Lenin's early pronouncement that the Jews are not a nation, to Stalin's actions as commissar of nationalities, the deportation of eight nations during the 1940s, and the 1952 "Jewish conspiracy" to detach the Crimea from the USSR.

Jewish "bourgeois nationalism," and the negation of Jewish nationality, was of central importance in the formation of Marxist-Leninist dogma. This issue accounts for the systematic liquidation of Jewish culture under the Bolsheviks, and the extermination not only of Zionists but also of Communist true believers with Jewish origins. Central figures in this book like Mikhoels and the leading Yiddish poets and intellectuals were loyal Communists who were murdered because they identified with the Jewish people. The Kremlin's Jewish doctors were also loyal Communists.

Stalin's plan for the extermination of his real and imaginary enemies was the only great conspiracy he ever contrived that did not succeed—and only because "God told him to depart from his rib cage," as Alexander Solzhenitsyn put it in *The Gulag Archipelago*. Stalin's death in late February or early March 1953, probably speeded along by one or more of his closest associates, was the surprise dénouement of this consummate actor's most elaborate scenario. The Doctors' Plot came to a sudden halt with his death, and one month later the doctors were released and the Soviet government admitted for the first time that it had fabricated a conspiracy.

Yet this watershed event remains largely unexplored, though many facts about the Stalin plot are now being revealed for the first time in the era of glasnost. Without an understanding of the pogrom atmosphere of 1948 to 1953 that culminated in the Doctors' Plot, it is impossible to comprehend the subsequent exodus of a large part of Soviet Jewry in the 1970s, which was resumed in 1989 under Gorbachev and reached a stampede level just as the 1990s began.

A close study of this period reveals that from about 1948 until his death in late February or early March 1953, Stalin became increasingly fixated on the Jews, following in a different way the path taken by his erstwhile partner, Hitler. Stalin, of course, was on record as condemning anti-Semitism, terming it a vestige of chau-

vinistic "cannibalism"; and communism in principle was opposed
to all forms of racism. But in reality the Jews suffered far more
under the "anti-racist" Bolsheviks than they had under the openly
anti-Semitic czar Nicholas II. And even though for many years
Stalin was much more restrained and devious than Hitler in using
anti-Semitism as a political weapon, he succumbed openly and uncontrollably to the passion in his last days.

Although the application of psychoanalytic theory to historical
interpretation is often problematical, if it is regarded as only one
element in the wider landscape of political action it can shed light
on the subterranean impulses that govern so many actions. Paranoia is an integral element in the etiology of anti-Semitism, epito-
mized by the *Protocols* forged by the czarist secret police and by the
Doctors' Plot as fabricated, staged, and directed by Joseph Stalin.

A strong histrionic element runs through the story of Stalin and
his Doctors' Plot. His daughter, Svetlana, spent her life with her
father offstage, but she sensed the theatricality of it all, the Shake-
spearean spirit. "It's dark behind the scenes," she wrote in *Twenty
Letters to a Friend.* "You can see the audience applauding. . . .You
can see the actors too, playing their roles as czars, gods, servants,
and extras. . . .But what an interesting place it is to watch! It's
where the makeup men, the prompters and the costume people
have their being. They wouldn't change their lives for anything. No
one knows better than they that all of life is an enormous theater."
For the Jews, it has too often been the theater of cruelty.

Louis Rapoport
Jerusalem
July 1989

Acknowledgments

My requests to visit the Soviet Union to conduct research there were refused in 1987 and 1988, possibly because of an unflattering series of articles about the treatment of Soviet Jews in the pre-glasnost days of 1986, which were syndicated by the *New York Times*. On three later occasions I was denied a visa at the last minute. I greatly appreciate the Soviet government's reversal of those decisions in February 1989, which enabled me to attend the opening of the Solomon Mikhoels Jewish Cultural Center in Moscow. The moving spirit behind the center, Isi Leibler of the World Jewish Congress, and his aide, Alec Ranoschy, were most helpful in arranging the trip, as was the Simon Wiesenthal Center.

Fortunately, a great deal of material about the Doctors' Plot can be found in archives in Israel, the United States, and England, as well as in private archives in the USSR. Several relatives of the central figures involved, who have emigrated from the USSR during recent years, were witnesses to the events and shared their memories with me. I have also had assistance from relatives and others who remain in the Soviet Union, and some who are in the process of leaving. I greatly appreciate the help of the last surviving physician involved in the Doctors' Plot, the nonagenarian Dr. Yakov Rapoport (no relation to me) and his daughter, Natalia.

Thanks also to ethnographer Mikhail Chlenov of Moscow, Professor Alexander Drushchinsky of Tbilisi, Viktor Mushegian of Tbilisi, Aharon Ben Daniel of Gori, and David Yoffe of Leningrad.

The old Stalinist Alexander Chakovsky, former head of the Soviet Writers' Union, and *Izvestia*'s Washington correspondent, Leonid Koriavin, provided valuable insights from the Soviet point of view. My special thanks for many hours of their time to Natalia and Nina Vovsi-Mikhoels, who are the daughters of Solomon Mikhoels and close relatives of Dr. Miron Vovsi, the senior Jewish doctor involved in the Kremlin plot. I am also indebted to the family of the slain Jewish poet Peretz Markish: Esther Markish and her writer son, David.

Dina Beilin, who possesses a keen understanding of the Soviet system, has always been generous with her time and suggestions, as has Martin Gilbert. Thanks also to Natan Sharansky, and to his mother, Ida Milgrom, for access to her husband Boris Shcharansky's memoir of the period, and to Yehudit Kollik for her assistance in translations and gleanings from the Soviet press. Thanks also to Ina Rubin, Aryeh "Lova" Eliav, Ilia and Ruth Serman, Mikhail Beizer, Aryeh Levavi, Solomon and Roald Nezlin, Lev Ovischer, Felix Kandel, Etel Kowenskaya, Vladimir Lifshitz, Mikhail Agursky, Mikhail Kollik, Paul Robeson, Jr., Morris Shappes, A. B. Magil, and Simon Chertok.

Hebrew University chancellor Abraham Harman, among the last one can safely call both a gentleman and a scholar, was instrumental in obtaining a research grant for my project. The Carnegie Fund for Authors was also helpful. Professors Edith Frankel, Mordechai Altschuler, and Adam Ulam have been most generous with their time. Dr. Herman von Prag of New York was also generous with his time and help.

Thanks also to those who have aided my research through correspondence, including Harrison Salisbury, George Kennan, Robert Conquest, Professor Robert Tucker, S. Badasch, Zhores Medvedev, (the late) Mary McCarthy, and Harry Schwartz.

Anne Crawford at the Public Record Office in Kew, Surrey, helped preserve my sanity when I arrived in England only to find the PRO closed for two weeks' annual inventory; I'm most grateful for her courtesy and assistance. Denise Glick, archivist at the Joint Distribution Committee in Manhattan, was attentive and helpful, as was Sally M. Marks and David Pfeiffer of the National Archives Diplomatic Branch in Washington. John Butler and Mary Dyson at the National Records Center in Suitland, Maryland, were also most kind. Thanks also to Marek Web at the YIVO archive in New York, Yoram Mayorek at the Zionist Archives in Jerusalem, Sarvely Dudakov at the Hebrew University's East European Library, and the directors of the Yad Vashem archives, for granting partial access to the Ehrenburg papers there.

The advice and guidance of Peter Collier and David Horowitz, Laura Wolff and Adam Bellow, my editors at The Free Press, have been of great value in this project. I appreciate the careful fine tuning of Edith Lewis and copy editor Amy Litt of The Free Press. Thanks also to my agent, Helen Rees.

Lastly, but most honored: my wife, Sylvia, and our children—Ehud, Adi, Avigal, and Gavriela—for their patience, encouragement, and understanding.

CHAPTER 1

The Ossetian Connection
Stalin's Iron Roots

There is no evidence that the so-called Man of Steel, Joseph Stalin, contracted the disease of anti-Semitism from his Georgian surroundings. In fact, Iosif Vissarionovich Djugashvili's wooden cradle was rocked in one of the few lands where Jews had lived in relative security for centuries, though anti-Semitism was far from unknown among the Christians, Muslims, and other religious believers of the Caucasus.

He probably *was* infected by an incipient anti-Semitism in his own home at a very early age: perhaps from his drunken, brutal father, who liked to put his wine-drenched fingers into his infant son's mouth; perhaps from his mother, who consecrated her son to the Orthodox Christian church and who believed implicitly in the legend that the perfidious Jews had murdered the "Messiah." Georgia and the entire Transcaucasus were, in any case, only a small part of the vast Russian empire, where anti-Semitism was endemic.

Stalin was born on approximately December 21, 1879,[1] in the town of Gori: set magnificently in a small, temperate valley where the towering northern Caucasus and southern Caucasus come to an abrupt divide. It is an area where many ancient peoples have fought and shared the land, where Greeks and Romans, Mongols and Turks, Persians and Russians have ruled, and where Jews have lived for at least 2,500 years. And through the ages, the Jews there remained relatively unmolested, even for some time after the advent of the Communists.

Iosif (Joseph) was the son of an alcoholic shoemaker, Vissarion Ivanovich Djugashvili, and of a cleaning woman and sometime whore,[2] who became pious when finally gifted with a child who survived. Ekaterina (Catherine) Georgievna Geladze's first three children, all boys, had died soon after birth, and little Joseph was regarded as a godsend. Catherine, known as Keke, had prayed to St. Joseph for a healthy son, and that was why she named her only child after Jesus' father.[3]

An old synagogue is located just a few hundred yards down a winding lane from the small house on Cathedral Street where Stalin was born, nestled below the dark ruins of the ancient fortress that dates from the Byzantine era. At this synagogue on muddy Cheluskinzev Lane, the Djugashvilis' Jewish neighbors prayed at every dawn and every sunset for the coming of the Messiah and the restoration of the Jews in the Land of Israel. The Jews of Georgia had repeated these prayers for over two millennia. At Ony, seventy miles away, a ninth-century synagogue is built on the ruins of another which predates the birth of Jesus by some 500 years. But the Jews' Caucasian connection can be taken back even further, into the realm of myth.

According to tradition, after Noah's Ark came to rest on Mount Ararat in neighboring Armenia, Noah's sons—Shem, Ham, and Japheth—fathered the peoples of the earth. The Caucasus Mountains and the area to the south became the home of the Japhetic peoples. In the dawn of human history, they were joined by scattered descendants of Shem, who settled throughout Georgia and the rest of the Transcaucasus. The numbers of Shemites probably increased with the dispersions of the Israelites that followed the destruction of the First Temple in 722 B.C.E. and the Romans' destruction of the Second Temple in the seventieth year of the Common Era.

A large Jewish community thrived in the ancient Georgian capital of Mtskheta, just outside the modern capital of Tbilisi (Tiflis), which became Christianized in the fourth century during the reign of King Mirian, son of a Persian monarch. The Georgian language is Semitic, and some have speculated that the Georgians may have been one of the Ten Lost Tribes carried off by the Assyrians. What is known is that Judeo-Christian civilization, blending with Asian cultures such as the Turkish and Persian, deeply influenced Georgian culture.

Although Stalin almost never mentioned his childhood, and there is no testimony that he was personally acquainted with Jews in Gori, it is obvious to any visitor to the town that such encounters must have taken place in this ancient settlement, where Georgians, Jews, Armenians, Persian-related Ossetians, and a handful of Russians lived in close geographic proximity (if ethnic semi-isolation) from one other. In one of the rare remarks Stalin did make about his childhood, he told his close associates that his father drank himself into penury, often pawning his belt for drinking money.[4] Most pawnbrokers and many tavern-keepers at that time were Jews, and Vissarion's addiction certainly brought him into contact with them.

Jews in the Gori of today say that their grandparents knew the Djugashvilis, and that the family were not Georgian, as is popularly thought, but that they were in fact Georgian-speaking Ossetians. In the Caucasus, that means a great deal.[5]

Like the Jews, Ossetians have been in Georgia and the Caucasus for a long time. Numbering approximately a quarter of a million in Stalin's youth, the Ossetians were a people of Iranian-Japhetic origin, who later mixed with the conquering Scythians, an ancient Persian-related people known for their savagery and worship of fire (to many minds, Stalin would come to epitomize the Scythian spirit). Most of the Ossetians made their home in the 15,000-foot-high icefields in the middle of the Great Caucasus, where the Titan Prometheus stole fire from heaven and was chained to a rock by the Olympian gods while vultures tore at his liver. Karl Marx would refer to the central and northern Caucasus, where the Ossetians lived, as the "knees" of the Russian empire.

The fire-worshipping tribe, living among the knife-edged massifs where yellow-eyed tigers roamed, called their capital Dzaudzhikau, ages later to be renamed Ordzhonikidze after one of Stalin's associates. Most Ossetians spoke a dialect called Iron and lived in a district of the same name—poetically fitting for an area where the Iron Age began, and for the region's most famous son, who chose the name Stalin, meaning Man of Steel. The name Iron is derived from "Iran," according to Ossetians.[6]

Some of the Ossetians, also known as Alans, became Jews after the Caucasus was conquered in the early Middle Ages by the Jewish Khazars. In 1245 Plano Carpini reported the presence of Jewish Ossetians in the northern Caucasus,[7] but there was no trace of them in recent centuries. Traditionally, the Georgians protected their Jewish neighbors against Ossetian attackers, though there were never massive pogroms in Georgia. Although most Ossetians became Muslims, there were many Christians among them. But even seventy years after the Bolsheviks took power, Ossetian groups reportedly retained "many pagan traditions."[8]

Over the centuries Jewish merchants and colonizers left their imprint throughout the temperate climes of the Transcaucasus, while the "big powers" of the day conquered and ruled the area, one after the other. Georgia itself frequently turned to the Russians for help, as in 1492, when the ruling Bagratid dynasty obtained the czar's assistance against Turkish and Persian rival invaders.

But Georgians and other peoples of the Caucasus also fought long and fiercely against Russian hegemony; the czars only managed to fully conquer the vast, mountainous region toward the middle of the nineteenth century, around the time when Stalin's father was born.

The Christianized Ossetians were the only Caucasian people who consistently welcomed Great Russian hegemony, possibly providing a clue to Joseph Djugashvili's passionate desire to assimilate.[9] Stalin's national origins would certainly influence his attitude toward the approximately one hundred nationalities dominated by the Great Russians. The mature Stalin sometimes thought of himself as an Asiatic and was never able to shake off his thick Georgian accent, but he completely identified with the Russian majority. In this respect he can be likened to the Corsican Napoleon, who came to personify France, or to Hitler, the Austrian "savior" of Germany.

Stalin's Russification would become evident in his treatment of his fellow Caucasians when he became the first Soviet commissar of nationalities: in his decimation and deportation of eight nationalities in the 1940s—when he generously gave the Ossetians a large area of the confiscated homelands of other Caucasian peoples—and in his policy toward the Jews. For the prophet of centralism believed that only the ethnic Russians were trustworthy; the minorities were all unreliable, or even hostile. In this context, the persistent stories that Joseph Vissarionovich Djugashvili was at least half Ossetian are significant, although whether Stalin's Ossetian connection was paternal or maternal remains an open question.

Innumerable biographers have quoted Stalin's childhood friend Joseph Irmashvili's appraisal that the "undeserved, frightful beatings" administered to Stalin by his alcoholic father "made the boy as grim and heartless as was his father." People who had any power over "Soso" (a diminutive of Joseph) reminded him of his brutal father, and "soon he began to hate everyone who had any authority over him."[10] Stalin later took revenge for these beatings on his own children—whom he brutalized and lashed—and on humankind in general.[11]

The stocky, mustachioed Vissarion Djugashvili left his family when Joseph was five or six and returned some five years later. He was stabbed to death in a drunken brawl when his son was about eleven. Vissarion's epitaph could have been taken from a line in Mikhail Lermontov's classic tale about the Caucasus, *A Hero of our Time*: "You may be sure that the end will be bad: it is always so with these Asiatics: they get tight on buza, and the knife play starts."[12]

Stalin's mother, whose physical features could be considered typically Ossetian, raised her only child singlehandedly, keeping him in the local theological school—where, of course, there were no Jews—with the fervent prayer that he would rise from his humble origins to become a priest.

Throughout his boyhood Joseph witnessed racial strife between Armenians and Azerbaijanis, Georgians and Armenians, Ossetians and Georgians.[13] There was a particular acrimony between the latter two; Ossetians regarded the Georgians as lazy bohemians, while the Georgians called the Ossetians worshippers of work and thieves who had stolen their land.[14] But Joseph must have learned early on—perhaps around the age of six or seven when he received his first lessons in the Russian language—which of the many peoples he encountered was the most important.[15] Power was in Great Russian hands.

The Jews were at the bottom of the heap. A founder of modern Zionism, the Russian Jew Moses Leib Lilienblum, writing in the wake of the pogroms of 1881, declared: "We are aliens, not only here, but in all of Europe, for it is not our fatherland. . . . We are Semites among Aryans, the sons of Shem among the sons of Japheth."[16]

One son of Shem who would not agree with this diagnosis, Lev Davidovich Bronstein, was born in Kherson province in the Ukraine two months before the birth of Joseph Djugashvili a thousand miles to the south. The man who would later call himself Leon Trotsky, and would become Stalin's great nemesis, was born on October 26 according to the Old Style Gregorian calendar—November 7 according to the New Style calendar—the same date thirty-eight years later on which he would lead the Bolshevik coup d'état. Trotsky never liked to dwell on his Jewish origins or to think in terms of "racialism." But in his biography of Stalin—which he was completing in Mexico in 1940 when an NKVD agent assassinated him on Stalin's orders—Trotsky briefly mentioned the reports that Djugashvili was an Ossetian. While this imputed heritage was "scarcely necessary for the purpose of explaining Stalin's moral stature," Trotsky proceeded to make racialist comments of his own about the superiority of northern to southern peoples. Then he dropped the subject, saying, "But we must not venture too far afield into the unprofitable region of national metaphysics."[17]

=====

There were two doctors, or "medical men," among the approximately 7,000 residents of Gori in the last decades of the nineteenth century, one of whom was said to have been a Jew.[18] It is possible that Joseph Djugashvili was treated by this very physician when he almost died of smallpox at the age of seven. The disease left his face permanently pockmarked. Stalin's crooked left arm was the result of another childhood infection, which almost killed him. He would later tell his sister-in-law, Anna Alliluyeva, that he didn't know whether he had been saved by his healthy constitution or by the ointments smeared on him by "the village quack."[19]

The youthful Stalin was both an industrious student and an arrogant bully at his Gori grammar school. He finished at the top of his class in 1894 and was recommended to the prestigious Theological Seminary in Tiflis (Tbilisi) the Georgian capital, some fifty miles away—considered the best high school in the entire Transcaucasus.[20]

The Tiflis seminary (now a museum of Georgian art) occupied a modern, four-story building that stretched along a full block of Pushkin Square. Its several hundred students included many fierce Georgian nationalists and foes of the czarist regime, among them a small number influenced by the relatively new social democratic movement.

The teachers and administrators were all Orthodox monks who ruled the institution through strict discipline, constant threats, and the use of intricate conspiracies. The students considered most of these officials, like the rector Germogen and Seminary Inspector Abashidze, to be jesuitical monsters. In 1931 Stalin told the writer Emil Ludwig that he had rebelled "against the outrageous regime and jesuitical methods prevalent at the seminary," and he condemned their "sordid" methods of "spying, prying, worming their way into people's souls and outraging their feelings."[21]

Although Djugashvili did rebel against certain methods and teachings, his mentors undoubtedly influenced the bright teenager in many ways. In the seminary the weaving of conspiracies was raised to an art, collaboration with the secret police was encouraged, and hatred for Jews was simply a part of the fabric of life.[22] In fact, Stalin's teachers and seminary administrators like Abashidze were among the founding members of the most anti-Semitic movement in the Russian empire, the infamous Black Hundreds.[23]

In the years just before and after the turn of the century, the Black Hundreds inspired pogroms in Moldavia and the Ukraine in which hundreds of Jews were slain. The group was active in 1902 in helping to suppress the oil workers' movement in Baku, the Caucasus oil port of 25,000 people, at the same time that the young Stalin was provoking violence at the Rothschild plant there.[24] The Black Hundreds later assassinated two Jewish members of the second Duma, and promulgated the czarist secret police forgery that came to be known as the *Protocols of the Elders of Zion.*

Thus Joseph Djugashvili came of age just as Russian anti-Semitism was reaching a fresh peak—at a time when the tutor of Czar Nicholas II, Constantin Petrovich Pobedonostsev, procurator of the Holy Synod, predicted that his country's "Jewish problem" would be solved by the killing of one-third, Christianizing one-third, and banishing the remaining third forever.[25] The czar and members of his family were charter members of the most viciously anti-Semitic groups and helped finance the publication of the *Protocols.* Stalin, an avid reader, certainly was exposed to the prevalent anti-Semitic literature in the Theological Seminary and possibly to early versions of the *Protocols.*

The alleged minutes of the secret meetings of the principal Jewish conspirators who aimed at world domination were published in different forms, first by the reactionary anti-Semite Pavel Krushevan in 1905, and in subsequent years under the new title: "He Is Near, at the Door . . . Here Comes Antichrist and the Reign of the Devil on Earth."[26] Czar Nicholas made enthusiastic marginal notations of his own on his copy of the *Protocols:* "What depth of thought! . . . What foresight! . . . Everywhere one sees the directing and destroying hand of Judaism."[27] The tract answered all of his questions: Jewry aspires to world domination through control over the international banking system and through socialist subversion. Under the Soviets, the terminology would change to "Jewish bourgeoisie," "Zionists," and "cosmopolitans," but the message would be the same: some Bolsheviks held that the Judaic belief in the Messiah was inculcated so that Jews would always aspire to mastery over all humankind.[28]

"Whether he read it or not, Stalin believed in the *Protocols of Zion,* in the Jewish cabal," claimed Aryeh "Lova" Eliav, a former Israeli diplomat who served in Moscow in the 1950s;[29] and an Israeli historian, Yehoshua Gilboa, also saw a link between the Protocols and the Doctors' Plot.[30]

The precedents of such conspiratorial allegations against the Jews began long before the *Protocols,* the blood libels in medieval Europe, the autos-da-fé of the Inquisition, or the Jews' expulsion from Spain. Stalin was probably no more anti-Semitic in his early youth than millions of others. But the seeds of all-consuming hatred were there, and they would be nurtured in the coming years.

CHAPTER 2

Up from the Underground

Stalin Rises from Provocateur to Commissar

In May 1899 nineteen-year-old Joseph Djugashvili was expelled from the Tiflis Theological Seminary for continuing to read forbidden literature. His crime was that he had exchanged the New Testament for newer ones: he was reading Dostoevsky, Darwin, and especially Karl Marx, the apostate German Jew whose philosophy had already seduced an important segment of the European and Russian intelligentsia well before Stalin's birth.[1] For Marx, the proletariat became the new Chosen People.

The dissolution of all nationalities, as well as classes, in the utopian state was part of the bedrock of Communist doctrine. But Marx, whose parents were both descended from illustrious rabbinical lines,[2] showed particular venom for the Jews and for the religion that had preserved them through the millennia. "Money is the jealous God of Israel, beside which no other God may stand," he wrote.[3] Equating the universal dominion of money with the "Jewish spirit," Marx sought to throw the capitalists out of the Temple, liberating society from Judaism. Long before the alleged Jewish plot discerned by Dostoevsky and the author of the *Protocols of the Elders of Zion,* Marx inadvertently encouraged the anti-Semitic myth that Jews controlled the world's money markets. He portrayed the Rothschild banking family as the personification of cancerous capitalism, as would countless other socialists, and in his correspondence made occasional remarks of an incipiently anti-Semitic nature, as when he expressed admiration of ancient Egypt for expelling "the nation of lepers."[4]

If Marx was the Communist prophet, Vladimir Ilyich Ulyanov,

born in 1870, was his Russian St. Paul. The man who became Lenin was not at all a personal anti-Semite, in the manner of Marx or Stalin, but he did preach that it was essential for the Jews to disappear—through total assimilation. And Communists of most stripes agreed that the Jewish problem did not exist as an independent issue; once capitalist oppression was overthrown, all people, including the downtrodden Jews, would be free and equal. The bloody outrages against Jews in 160 towns and cities at the turn of the century were abetted by the government; and the U.S. ambassador in St. Petersburg, John W. Foster, reported to the State Department that "the acts which have been committed are more worthy of the Dark Ages than of the present century."[5] Jews were expelled from Moscow, denied jobs, and strictly confined to the Pale of Settlement in southwestern Russia and Poland where they had been forced to live since 1762.

In stark contrast, the political Zionist movement, which began developing in Russia and Central Europe around the time of Lenin's birth, was based on the principle that the Jews were a nation, that all the Jews could never and should never assimilate, that they were strangers in a strange land and needed a country of their own.

In the three decades before the Revolution of 1917, growing numbers of young Jewish revolutionaries flocked to the new religion of communism, seeing it as a means of delivery not only from their own constricted status as Jews, but for all humankind. These were the educated, secular equivalents of those Jews who had followed previous false Messiahs—such as Shabtai Zvi in the seventeenth century, or much earlier pretenders like David Reuveni. The very high proportion of Jews in the forefront of the movement in Russia was, however, also directly linked to the fact that aristocracy and peasants shared a mutual antipathy toward Jews, considering them Russia's main source of bedevilment. Although many Russians and other peoples of the empire were not anti-Semitic—Jews have always had defenders there, including Tolstoy, who believed that the Jews were the pioneers of liberty and the emblem of eternity—the majority thought otherwise, and various Russian writers fostered this perception, portraying Jews as poisoners, spies, and traitors.

The Jews of European Russia, confined to a Pale of Settlement since the eighteenth century, were further restricted under Czar Nicholas I's new code of laws issued in 1833. Jews were then barred from settling along the western borders, because they were considered a "security risk" and a conduit for smuggling. By 1843 Jews were totally banned from frontier districts—as would be the case during the latter part of the Stalinist era.

In the early 1880s Czar Alexander II, the great emancipator of the Russian serfs, eased some of the restrictions on Jews, and for the first time a few Jews were allowed to attend Russian schools. Throughout the empire, Russification—the primacy of the Russian language and culture—was the order of the day in schools from Siberia to the Crimean peninsula. At the same time that Joseph Djugashvili was studying at the Tiflis seminary, the Jewish-born Lev Bronstein (later Leon Trotsky) was attending St. Paul's high school in Odessa; and like Stalin, he welcomed the idea of Russification, lightly dismissing his narrow ethnic origins. But unlike Stalin, he looked more to the West for intellectual succor.

The assassination of Alexander in 1881, in which indirect Jewish involvement was cynically played up by the authorities, led to a period of renewed persecution that did not ease until the Revolution in 1917; indeed, it subsequently worsened during the civil war. In this period of great historical change, the reaction of most Russian Jews was to choose neither socialism nor Zionism, but to emigrate. Periodic mass pogroms, mostly in the Ukraine, resulted in thousands of deaths and sparked the emigration of some two million Russian Jews to the United States, 200,000 to the United Kingdom, and 60,000 to Palestine over the first two decades of the twentieth century.[6]

But Jewish nationalism in Russia was not confined to the Zionist movement. In 1897 a number of Jewish socialists founded the Bund, or General Jewish Workers' League, to agitate among Jewish workers. The Bundists held that each nationality in the vast "prison of nations" that was the Russian empire would control its own ethnic identity within the future democratized state. The Jewish proletariat, in Marxist terms, also had national concerns which required an autonomous structure.

Lenin believed that the Bund's cultural nationalism would harm the revolutionary cause. The Bund was pushed to withdraw from Lenin's Social Democratic Labor party at the Brussels congress in July 1903 because of its nationalist positions, including the formation of self-defense units during the Ukrainian pogroms.[7] The Bundists had demanded the right to elect their own central committee and to frame policy affecting Russian Jewry. The twenty-four-year-old firebrand Leon Trotsky spoke even more vehemently than Lenin against the Bund. Trotsky lashed out at them viciously, in one of the rare occasions he ever spoke about Jews or referred to himself as one. Along with Julius Martov, David Axelrod, and other socialists of Jewish origin, Trotsky argued for assimilation, following Marx and Lenin in the belief that the Jews had no future as a people.[8]

Like Lenin's followers, the Bundists also opposed Zionism, rejecting the idea of an independent Jewish state in Palestine or anywhere else. Hebrew was degraded as the language both of a calcified religion and of a reactionary nationalist movement. Others saw no contradiction in being both socialist and Zionist, and these Russian Jews played an instrumental role in the eventual creation of a Jewish homeland in Palestine.

A community of interest existed between Zionists and those anti-Semites who, like Dostoevsky, demanded the expulsion of the Jews. The spread of the new nationalism at the end of the nineteenth century led some anti-Semites to stress the "rootlessness" of Jews, who could be neither swallowed nor assimilated and therefore must be expelled. On the other hand, most socialist revolutionaries of Jewish origin, like Trotsky, shared the assimilationist ideas of liberal bourgeois Jews and were reluctant to perceive the true nature of anti-Semitism. Instead, they subscribed to Lenin's dogmatisms, as in February 1903 when he derided the Zionist "fable about anti-Semitism being eternal." Lenin held that "the idea of a separate Jewish people is reactionary in its political meaning, prevents assimilation [of the Jews by the Russians] and promotes the 'mood of the ghetto.'"[9]

The persistence of the Jewish nation was a constant irritant to Marxists, though they believed that Jews could not have assimilated in the past because of ghettoization and repression. Marxists like Trotsky, Martov, and the German-Jewish revolutionary Rosa Luxemburg loathed nationalist passions, and, like Marx, transposed their loyalties to the global proletariat.[10] They ignored the fact that the Jews were a separate nationality whose culture was not confined to the Judaic religion; and this flaw was a major factor in the resurgence of anti-Semitism under the Communists.

In 1901 Stalin, then using the underground name Koba, was still an obscure and shady activist in the remote Caucasus. Some of his comrades suspected that he was a double agent and provocateur, and there was a question of where the jobless young revolutionary got money to live on. He admitted to his associates in Tiflis, Batum, and Baku that he had denounced fellow students in the seminary, but excused his actions with the claim that these false accusations would make them better revolutionaries. Stalin probably was recruited and trained by the czarist secret police between July and December 1899, a "missing period" in his life.[11]

In his first recorded speech in 1900, the youthful agitator exhorted unarmed workers and organizers to risk their lives in confrontations with the police. He was visibly excited by violence. His friend Irmashvili, recalling a May Day 1901 clash between 2,000 workers and Tiflis police, wrote: "The blood that had flowed during the demonstration had intoxicated him."[12]

Stalin identified with Lenin and those like-minded people who called themselves *Iskra*-men, after Lenin's revolutionary newspaper *Iskra* (The Spark), first printed in Germany in December 1900. Stalin knew that his lack of education hampered him from contributing to *Iskra,* so he settled for the local Georgian-language paper called *Brdzola* (The Struggle), where his first essay, "The Russian Social Democratic Party and Its Immediate Tasks," appeared in December 1901. In an expression of solidarity with all the oppressed peoples of the Russian empire,[13] he put the "Russian peasantry" at the head of a list of social classes being strangled by autocracy. Next came "town-dwellers, petty employees . . . petty officials . . . lower and even middle bourgeoisie . . . the oppressed nationalities and religions . . . the Poles and the Finns," and lastly, "the unceasingly persecuted and humiliated Jews, deprived even of those miserable rights that other Russian subjects enjoy."[14] The Jews were low down on his list, and only after them did Stalin mention the Georgians, a good part of whose middle class was Jewish.

Stalin was constantly intriguing against his comrades, including his political tutor, Sylvester Dzhibladze; and a revolutionary court banished the suspicious agitator from Tiflis at the end of 1901. He went to Batum, the big oil town 220 miles away, where he helped spark a bloody demonstration at the Rothschild plant in which fifteen workers were killed.[15] The liturgical language of his boyhood school and of the Tiflis seminary echoed in a leaflet he wrote eulogizing the fallen workers: "All honor to you whose brows are adorned with the crowns of martyrs."[16]

Stalin identified himself as a follower of Lenin's Bolsheviks—the "hards," as they were at first called—and a foe of the other main faction of the Russian socialist movement, the "soft" Mensheviks. The split had occurred at the 1903 Brussels congress, where the young Trotsky played a prominent role, and where the Bund was forced out of the movement. The Bund was crushed for advocating recognition of the Jews as a nationality analogous to the Poles and for the even more serious deviation of calling for a federative party system in contrast to Lenin's demand for a highly centralized apparatus. Trotsky at that point sided with the Mensheviks, castigating Lenin as a Jacobin.[17] None of the leaders as yet had heard of Joseph Djugashvili, who would remain obscure for years to come. But in the backwaters of the Caucasus, the seething mind of the young Stalin learned to equate the word "Menshevik" with the word "Jew."

Stalin's first recorded contacts with Jewish revolutionaries were in 1901, though it is certain that he met "movement Jews" much before then. Tiflis Jews were among the prominent democratic socialists rounded up by the czarist secret police, the Okhrana, possibly with Stalin's help, on the night of March 21.[18] His own first arrest, and mild sentence of exile in Siberia, came in 1903 and may well have been merely a cover devised by the secret police.[19]

In 1904 Stalin sought out a Jewish revolutionary from Tiflis named Lev Borisovich Rosenfeld, who, though even younger than himself, had already acquired a reputation as a theorist and gifted orator. At twenty-one Rosenfeld, who would assume the name Kamenev (Man of Stone), had already spent time in Moscow's Butyrka and Taganka prisons for socialist activity, met with Lenin in Paris, and become his disciple and a leader of the Iskra-men back home. Kamenev's girlfriend and future wife was Olga Bronstein, Trotsky's sister. Stalin would one day become coeditor of Pravda with Kamenev, and would defend him after the revolution against charges that he had been an Okhrana agent. But now, in 1904, he asked and received Kamenev's help in finding him a "shelter from the police"—although whether he actually needed one is doubtful.[20]

Stalin's main activity at this time was to undermine the Mensheviks in the Transcaucasus. They were in the great majority among revolutionaries in the region, numbering in the thousands, while there were only a few hundred Bolsheviks. Most of the Mensheviks were Georgians, with many Jews among them. A high percentage of the Bolsheviks, in contrast, were Ossetians, including many illiterate peasants. Both factions were rife with undercover agents and double agents, especially among the Ossetians, who had a long tradition of involvement in police work.[21]

The Jew who would play the most eventful role in Stalin's life, and in the Soviet Revolution, was Trotsky; and Stalin's enmity toward him—even years after he had finally been murdered— would become an integral element in his eventual solution to the "Jewish problem."

On one point about Trotsky, there is no disagreement: he was brilliant, probably a genius. While still in his late teens in Odessa, he displayed extraordinary talent as a mathematician, linguist, theorist, and writer. Such qualities often engender not only envy but hatred—especially in other talented people whose gifts appear mediocre by comparison. Alexander Pushkin had treated this theme in his play *Mozart and Salieri,* which all educated Russians knew very well. Instinctively, Stalin, inarticulate and relatively uneducated, despised his contemporary long before he ever set eyes on him.

The young Bronstein, who later took the name of one of his Russian prison guards, registering his nationality as Great Russian, fell under the spell of Marx, Ferdinand Lassalle, and Eduard Bernstein: the men of Jewish origin who laid the foundations of communism and socialism. But he did not want to think of them as Jews. For Trotsky, like many of his fellow Jewish revolutionaries, felt total revulsion for the Jewish past. In historian Salo Baron's words, it bordered on "outright self-hatred, and greatly contributed to the revolution's destructive methods in dealing with the established Jewish institutions."[22] Trotsky believed that Zionism was doomed to failure and called its founder, Theodor Herzl (1860–1904), a "repulsive figure" and "shameless adventurer."[23]

The cataclysmic events of 1905, the "dress rehearsal revolution" that followed Russia's military defeat by the Japanese months earlier, seemed to pass Stalin by. Trotsky, in contrast, was a major player in the aborted revolution, which began in January. The spark that set it off was the peaceful march on the czar's Winter Palace in St. Petersburg led by Father Gapon, a prison chaplain and Okhrana secret agent. The czar's troops panicked, fired on the huge throng, and killed hundreds in what would become known as Bloody Sunday. Trotsky returned from European exile to lead the revolution with his pen, his organizational skills, and his fiery speeches. He was the moving spirit of the Soviet of Petersburg, the hub of the revolution—a role he would successfully repeat twelve years later. Thus, while Stalin in his provincial den remained almost invisible, in Russia's center a Jew had become the star of the revolution.

The Trotsky-supported Mensheviks remained the main revolutionary force throughout the Transcaucasus, and Stalin's mission—on the orders of the Bolsheviks or the Okhrana, or both—was to destroy them. One useful and effective weapon was anti-Semitism. Stalin had already attacked Georgian and Armenian nationalists in the region by comparing them to the despised Jewish Bund. Now, whenever he addressed small groups of men, he constantly pointed out that most Mensheviks were Jews. Before he had ever met Lenin, he told Georgian revolutionary Razden Arsenidze:

> It exasperates Lenin that God sent him such comrades as the Mensheviks. Just look at this rotten crowd: Martov, Dan, Axelrod—nothing but uncircumcised Yids! And that old bitch Vera Zasulich, too! All right, go work with them. You'll find that they won't fight, and there is no rejoicing at their banquets. They are cowards and shopkeepers! The workers of Georgia should know that the Jewish people produces only cowards who are useless in a fight.[24]

Stalin's use of anti-Semitism at this time was partly pragmatic, partly personal. But as various sources attest, it would become obsessive only much later. "He never liked Jews," his daughter Svetlana would write in her memoirs, "though he wasn't as blatant about expressing his hatred for them in those days [the mid-1930s] as he was after the war."[25]

In December 1905 Koba, as Stalin was still calling himself, attended his first national gathering of revolutionists, at Tammerfors, Finland. As a representative of the small and relatively insignificant Bolshevik faction of Georgia, and as someone with no oratorical or theoretical gifts, he was hardly noticed. Here he met Lenin for the first time (probably introduced by Kamenev) though Lenin did not know who he was or remember his name afterward. Trotsky—the man already regarded as Lenin's intellectual equal—had just been imprisoned in the fortress of Peter and Paul for leading the first Soviet. In prison Trotsky pondered the lessons of 1905 and worked out his theory of "permanent revolution." Undoubtedly Stalin did not lament the absence of this Jew whose name was on everyone's lips.

Stalin, who would become leader of the Great Russian chauvinist movement—in the guise of "socialism in one country"—opposed Trotsky and his followers, advocates of an international movement. Stalin correctly viewed Trotsky as representing a westernized ideology which did not fit into Russia's closed conspiratorial revolutionary world. The Jews Grigory Zinoviev and Kamenev (whose mother was not Jewish and who therefore was not Jewish according to Judaic precepts) rose to the top of the Bolshevik party and became leaders of the "internationalist" faction, seeking to foster revolution in the West in order to support it in Russia. This would become a "Jewish conspiracy" in Stalin's eyes. In the great struggle between Lenin's two disciples, Stalin would style Trotsky as "Judas Iscariot," Lenin's betrayer.[26]

One of the many revolutionaries of Jewish origin whom Stalin met at the conference in Finland was Semyon (Solomon) Lozovsky, the future Soviet deputy foreign minister, who would be executed with a score of other well-known Jews in the buildup to the Doctors' Plot in 1952. Stalin also met Mikhail Borodin (né Gruzenberg), who would become famous in the twenties as an aide to Chiang Kai-shek; he also became editor of the *Moscow News* and another Stalin victim during the days of the Doctors' Plot. At the conference, Lozovsky proposed that the local organizations of the Mensheviks and Bolsheviks merge as a preliminary step toward total reunification of the two factions. The motion was accepted, probably to Stalin's dismay. But his own election to a conference planning committee counted as his first success on the national level.[27]

Stalin met Lenin for the second time in 1906 at the Social Democratic party Fourth Congress in Stockholm, where the Bolsheviks suffered a setback at the hands of the Mensheviks. He later remarked contemptuously that Martov, Axelrod, and the others "did not in the least look like real victors," and said that he admired Lenin's "hatred for snivelling intellectuals."[28]

In 1907 Stalin attended another party conference in London, sharing a room with a delegate from Poland, Maxim Wallach— later Maxim Litvinov, and a future Soviet foreign minister. Described by Lenin as possessing the "virtues of a clever and adroit Jew," Litvinov was one of the few old Bolsheviks whom Stalin would allow to die a natural death.[29]

The London conference failed to resolve the differences between the two Russian revolutionary camps. Stalin's presence there became a minor issue because he did not represent the required 500 party members in Russia and therefore could not vote with the other delegates. Trotsky would later wonder why Stalin was in

London, and hint darkly, "He must have had other tasks. Just what were they?"[30] Many of Stalin's biographers have also wondered at Lenin's sudden sponsorship of the obscure Caucasian at the London conference. One possible explanation is that Stalin was already involved in "expropriations"—bank robberies to finance the revolutionaries—and that Lenin wished to reward his services. The Menshevik Jews, led by Martov, and the Georgian veteran revolutionary Noi Zhordania objected when Lenin tried to push through a consultative status for the tough young Bolshevik from Georgia. Martov, referring to Stalin, exclaimed, "Who are these people? Where do they come from?" Such a remark could never be forgiven by a person of Stalin's temperment.

Shortly after the conference, Stalin's anti-Semitism emerged again in a reference to the preponderance of Jews in the Menshevik faction. Stalin related a "jest" he said he had heard that "the Mensheviks were a Jewish faction while the Bolsheviks were truly Russian, and hence it would not be amiss for us Bolsheviks to instigate a pogrom in the Party." Trotsky, writing his biography of Stalin in 1940, expressed astonishment that Stalin got away with the "retelling" of such a reactionary "joke."[31] In the wake of the slaughters of Jews in 1905 by the Black Hundreds and others associated with the secret police, the joke was especially tasteless.

When he faced his czarist judges in 1906, Trotsky spoke out against the Black Hundreds and their government protectors. But he nevertheless explained away the traumatic pogroms of 1903 and 1905, agreeing with Lenin that anti-Semitism was not immutable and that the final victory of the masses would end the Jewish problem once and for all.[32]

———

In the decade following the events of 1905, Lenin built his party with the help of men like Nikolai Bukharin, Kamenev, the Lithuanian Jew Jacob Sverdlov, and the Jew Zinoviev. Stalin meanwhile quietly rose through the ranks, mainly by doing Lenin's dirty work, directing such bank robberies as the 1907 Erevan Square outrage in Tiflis, in which many bystanders were killed or maimed. Stalin was expelled that year from the Tiflis party organization (for creating his own apparatus within the organization and for his divisive behavior), a fact Martov would try to use against him immediately after the revolution.[33]

From mid-1907 and for the next six years, Stalin came and went in the cities of the Transcaucasus, including Baku, which had been a Persian city for one thousand years. Sometimes he traveled under a Persian name and with a Persian passport. Arrested, jailed, and exiled several times, he always escaped with ease and traveled without hindrance by the authorities.[34] Stalin became a prominent Bolshevik only in 1913, when Lenin once again drew him out of obscurity.

At that time Lenin's party was in danger of collapse over the thorny nationality problem. Without an acceptable theory, the Bolsheviks could lose allies: Polish, Ukrainian, Jewish, and other social democrats whose support was vital. Most of Lenin's chief theorists and writers were Jews, Poles, or Great Russians, like the brilliant Nikolai Bukharin. Though Lenin could not recall to mind the name Djugashvili, he knew the man, and chose "that admirable Georgian" to draft the major essay on the nationalities question.

One factor that had pushed this question to the fore was the 1913 trial of a Kiev Jew named Mendel Beilis, who was accused of the ritual murder of a thirteen-year-old Russian boy. The obvious frameup, abetted by top czarist officials, created a worldwide outcry. It also furthered Lenin's attempts to deal with "the poison of nationalism." Meanwhile, Trotsky became aware of the depth of the "Jewish problem" for the first time, observing that the trial was redolent of medieval blood libels.[35]

The nationalities essay would prove to be Stalin's one and only important piece of writing. He could not and did not write it alone, of course. He was intellectually handicapped by his inability to read the important German literature on the subject, and his writing style was turgid and pedestrian, with a marked liturgical tone. Bukharin, Marxist intellectuals Alexander Troyanovsky (a future Soviet ambassador to the United States) and his wife, Elena Rozmirovich, and Lenin himself did much of the work, though Stalin's heavy hand is obvious throughout. Trotsky would later ridicule Stalin's clumsy writing here and in other instances, but he refrained from commenting on Stalin's dozens of unfavorable references to the Jews. Trotsky thought Stalin's approach to the nationality question was "theoretically correct."[36]

Stalin wrote the essay in Vienna at Troyanovsky's home, but it was in a Jewish Menshevik's home that Trotsky and Stalin met for the first time. They disliked each other instantly, with Trotsky later remarking on the grim and uncouth Bolshevik's evil "yellow eyes."[37]

In "Marxism and the National Question" Stalin maintained that the rights of nations was not an isolated question, but part of the general problem of the proletarian revolution. In a footnote he described Zionism as "a reactionary nationalist trend of the Jewish bourgeoisie," in which "the Zionists endeavored to isolate the Jewish working-class masses from the general struggle of the proletariat."[38] Indeed, in Part I of the 12,000-word essay, Stalin focused on the Jews in order to define what is *not* a nation.

Community of language, Stalin wrote, is a primary requisite for nationhood. Furthermore, "people cannot live together for lengthy periods unless they have a common territory." The Jews fit neither of these requirements. But even these were not enough to define a nation, he said. Even the Georgians before the abolition of serfdom in 1861 "did not, strictly speaking, constitute one nation, for, being split up into a number of disconnected principalities, they could not share a common economic life; for centuries they waged war against each other and pillaged each other, inciting the Persians and Turks against one another."[39] The Georgians had only emerged as a nation in recent decades, after they were bonded together economically.

Driving his point home, Stalin continued:

> It is possible to conceive people possessing a "national character," but they cannot be said to constitute a single nation if they are economically disunited, inhabit different territories, speak different languages and so forth. Such, for instance, are the Russian, Galician, American, Georgian and Caucasian Mountain Jews, who do not, in our opinion, constitute a single nation.[40]

Stalin assailed the Austrian Social Democratic theoretician Otto Bauer (Bukharin probably researched and translated the relevant passages). Bauer had spoken of the Jews as a nation, although admitting that they had no common language. Stalin dismissed this idea: "What 'community of fate' and national cohesion can there be, for instance, between the Georgian, Daghestanian, Russian, and American Jews, who are completely disunited, inhabit different territories and speak different languages?"

If there was anything common to the Jews, Stalin continued, it was "their religion, their common origin and certain relics of national character." "But," he asked, "how can it be seriously maintained that petrified religious rites and fading psychological relics affect the 'fate' of these Jews more powerfully than the living social, economic and cultural environment that surrounds them?" Bauer was nothing more than a "mystical . . . spiritualist."[41]

Stalin's essay was edited by Lenin, as Trotsky pointed out, but the editing is often very poor, with his views on the Jews repeated three times. He called the Jews a "paper 'nation'" and said that the Social Democratic party "can reckon only with real nations, which act and move, and therefore insist on being reckoned with."[42] This passage not only seems to have escaped Lenin's editorial pencil, but is obviously pure Stalin, without any of Bukharin's cool intellect in evidence, either. In Stalin's mind, the Jews were not a people to be reckoned with; they were nothing more than a bothersome tribe.

The essay took note of the fact that the czarist regime incited nations against one another, causing "massacres and pogroms."[43] *Pogrom,* the Russian word for "devastation," was usually used to describe the massacre of Jews.[44] But Stalin, consistent in denying that the Jews had any independent status, used the term to describe the killing of workers in "The Caucasus and South Russia."[45] He also remarked that pogroms could only happen in a "semi-Asiatic country" like Russia, and never in a European country like Germany—he was not much of a prophet.[46]

In this key essay, which still influences to some extent contemporary Soviet policy regarding subject peoples, the Bolsheviks guaranteed the right of any nation "to arrange its life on autonomous lines. It even has the right to secede." A big "but" was attached. "But this does not mean that it should do so under all circumstances." And Stalin used the example of the Transcaucasian Tatars—a nation he would deport in its entirety to Siberia and Kazakhstan thirty years later—suggesting that they might fall under the spell of their Muslim religious and political leaders, the mullahs and beys, and be persuaded to act against the interest of "the toiling strata of the Tatar nation."[47] Much of Stalin's fire in this essay was directed at the Jewish Bund: "We must declare our decided opposition to a certain very widespread, but very summary manner of 'solving' the national problem, which owes its inception to the Bund."[48] Part V of the essay is subtitled "The Bund, Its Nationalism and Its Separatism."[49]

Bauer was basically correct in stating that it was impossible to preserve the existence of the Jews as a nation because they had no territory of their own, Stalin wrote. But it was not "the whole truth."

The fact of the matter is primarily that among the Jews there is no large and stable stratum associated with the soil, which would naturally rivet the nation, serving not only as its framework but also as a "national market." Of the five or six million Russian Jews, only three to four per cent are connected with agriculture in any way.

The rest were engaged in trade and industry, and dispersed in the towns, leading to their assimilation, he said.

The abolition of the Pale would only serve to hasten this process. The question of national autonomy for the Russian Jews consequently assumes a somewhat curious character: autonomy is being proposed for a nation whose future is denied and whose existence has still to be proved![50]

After thus characterizing the Bund's "shaky" position in its 1905 congress, Stalin went on to attack Bund and Austrian Social Democratic calls for Jewish national autonomy. In any case, this would be—and Stalin underlined the words—"national cultural autonomy." He said that there could be no territorial political autonomy for the Jews, since the Jews lacked any definite, integral territory.[51] Stalin not only assailed the idea that the Jews were a nation, he also attacked the Bund's stand on the question of the marking of the Sabbath and the use of Yiddish.[52]

In no other forum, or at any other time or place, did Stalin go into such detail about how he, and his mentors, viewed the Jewish people. Neither Lenin nor Bukharin bothered to tone down his obvious hatred not only for the Bund but for many things Jewish.

In retrospect, a most disturbing line in the essay was Stalin's prediction that "the Bund is heading for separatism," since forty years later Stalin would accuse Soviet Jewry of attempting to detach the Crimea from the Soviet Union.[53]

Stalin also discussed the question of regional autonomy in the Caucasus, asking what should be done with the Ossetians. He said that the Transcaucasian Ossetians were becoming assimilated by the Georgians and the Ciscaucasian Ossetians, while some were being assimilated by the Russians. Nowhere does he refer to his own national origins.[54]

Stalin concluded that national cultural autonomy would be a "senseless reactionary escapade in the Caucasus."[55] But the really striking aspect of Stalin's discussion here is not the Marxist differentiation between regional, national, and cultural autonomy, nor the sentiment that "national equality in all forms (language, schools, etc.) is an essential element in the solution of the national problem." Rather it is Stalin's unusual focus on the Jewish element as a major roadblock on the way to the socialist utopia.

The Bund also dominated Stalin's concluding remarks. He termed it an obstacle to worker unity, and a persistent cause of disharmony and disorganization within the ranks of the Russian Social Democratic party.[56]

Thus, in Stalin's early thinking on the "Jewish question" in relation to the ideal socialist order, a fatal distinction emerges. The solution to the national problem was either to be the pernicious way of the Jewish party, with its claims to some form of autonomy, or the Bolshevik international solidarity of the workers. The distinction would bear fruit in later years, when the Jewish nationalistic trend perceived in Stalin's 1913 essay would come to be equated with treason against the Soviet state.

CHAPTER 3

The Struggle Against "Judas"

Stalin's Rivalry with Trotsky

In January 1913, around the time when the thirty- three-year-old "K. Stalin" was directed to write his essay on the nationality question, he went out of his way to attack Leon Trotsky. In a letter to the *Social Democrat* Stalin described him as a "noisy champion with faked muscles" and excoriated him for preaching unity between the Mensheviks and Bolsheviks. No longer totally obscure, Stalin was now a member of the first Bolshevik Central Committee, elected the previous year, and his words carried some weight. This was only the first, relatively benign volley in a long and increasingly vicious struggle between the two.[1]

In late February 1913 Stalin was arrested in St. Petersburg, and in July he was sent into Siberian exile with one of Lenin's associates, Yakov (Jacob) Mikhailovich Sverdlov, a Jew who would become the first Soviet president. The two young revolutionaries had nothing in common, as they immediately learned during their enforced stay in the town of Turukhansk. Stalin soon came to despise his gentle cabinmate, six years younger than himself—a "cosmopolitan" adept at many languages and an esthete. In the small exile community, they reportedly became romantic rivals for the affections of a fellow revolutionary, actress Vera Alexandrova Delenskaya of the Moscow Art Theater. Apparently she chose the happily married, sophisticated Jewish intellectual over the brooding, uncouth Caucasian.[2]

Stalin, in any case, was not very interested in women, though his first marriage (in 1904 to a simple Georgian woman, Catherine "Keke" Svanidze) had been a happy one, according to Irmashvili—

mainly because the young Keke was totally subservient to her husband. They had a son, Jacob, who would be cared for by his mother's family after her sudden death in 1907. At the funeral Stalin told Irmashvili, his one childhood friend, "This creature softened my stony heart. She is dead, and with her my last warm feelings for all human beings have died."[3]

According to Trotsky, in his biography of Stalin, it was at this time that Stalin "revealed himself as an anti-Semite, resorting to coarse Georgian expressions against the Jews" in conversations with other exiles.[4] These political exiles disliked and distrusted him, especially after he violated their common code by befriending a policeman named Kibirov, one of the many Ossetians who served as Russian guards and constables. Stalin told the other exiles in the Arctic Circle hamlets that his friendly relations with the Ossetian policeman would not deter him from doing away with the man as a political enemy, if the time came.[5] He had apparently terminated his arrangements with the czarist secret police a year earlier, after Lenin again blessed him by co-opting him into the party leadership following a conference in Prague.[6]

In the four years leading up to the Revolution of 1917 Stalin spend much of his time trapping and skinning wild beasts and living a sort of monastic life in stark Siberia, which he loved, in contrast to his feudal southern birthplace. "He loved Russia, not Georgia," his daughter Svetlana would write.[7]

There were many Jews among the revolutionary exiles in Siberia. When World War I broke out in 1914, many more would come. The czar contemplated sending most of Russia's Jews to join the political exiles. The proto-Fascists of the Black Hundreds urged Nicholas II either to deport the Jews to the harsh Kolyma region, just below the Arctic Circle, or to destroy them physically.[8] The czar's commander-in-chief, Grand Duke Nicholas Nikolaevich, issued a military ordinance accusing all Jews located along the front of treason and calling for their banishment. All the rich and important Jews, as well as the rabbis, must be seized and deported to the interior, ordered the grand duke. The mass evacuations began in March 1915; 600,000 Jews were uprooted, many of them sent to Siberia.[9]

Lenin saw the war as a great opportunity, creating a more direct path to revolution, and continually preached the slogan "Turn the imperialist war into a civil war." He denounced those European socialists who took patriotic national stands, and, along with Zinoviev, called for "revolutionary defeatism." Trotsky, in Paris, called for "neither victory nor defeat," but revolution. Inside Russia many Bolshevik leaders believed Lenin's "unpatriotic" position would cut them off from popular support; and when Kamenev and other leading Bolsheviks were jailed and charged with treason, they dissociated themselves from Lenin. This split led to raging debate within the Bolshevik movement. But Stalin, in Siberia, in the same area where Kamenev was exiled after his trial, hedged his bets until the death-knell of the czarist regime and the exiles' return to St. Petersburg in March 1917.[10]

Kamenev and Stalin arrived in the capital days after the popular uprising that forced the czar to abdicate and led to the the formation of a liberal provisional government. The émigré party leaders had not yet returned, and Stalin and Kamenev, the senior men on the spot, took over the editorship of *Pravda,* the party organ. The Bolsheviks, and all other parties, were legal now.

Stalin became the de facto head of the party for three weeks, until Lenin's arrival on April 3 from Switzerland in the famous German-supplied "sealed train." Lenin, declaring that the Russian revolution was the beginning of a worldwide socialist takeover, jotted down his platform for the Bolshevik revolution, a ten-point scheme that became known as the April Theses and that was to pave the way for the "dictatorship of the proletariat." He called for immediate revolution, dispensing with the interim cooperation with a bourgeois regime laid down by orthodox Marxism. The war had to be stopped, as a means of bringing down the new democratic government, with his iron men ready to fill the vacuum. He attacked those Bolsheviks who "show [ed] confidence in the Government" and who sought unity with the loathsome Mensheviks. Lenin called for "not a parliamentary republic . . . but a republic of Soviets . . . abolition of the police, and the army and of officialdom," as well as "land to the peasants" and nationalization of banks and industry. He said the party should change its name to the Communist party, and proposed an international organization that would be the prototype of the Third International.[11]

Kamenev, Mikhail Ivanovich Kalinin, and others who represented the old, as opposed to the new, Leninism called for a more cautious and moderate approach. They grumbled that the new program was Trotskyism, not Leninism.[12] Stalin, who before the April Theses supported Kamenev and the old-line Bolsheviks calling for cooperation with the government, now followed dutifully after Lenin.

Stalin also began to distance himself from the internationalist trend of Jews like Kamenev and Zinoviev, who held that Russian socialism could only be built if the Revolution succeeded in the West, as well.[13] These controversies would last throughout the year of the Revolution, breaking out again during the succession struggle that followed Lenin's death. In Stalin's eyes, the issue would become transformed into another aspect of "the Jewish problem." Svetlana Alliluyeva believed that the origin of her father's anti-Semitism "stemmed from the years of struggle for power with Trotsky and his followers, gradually transforming itself from political hatred to a racial aversion for all Jews bar none."[14]

In late April 1917 Stalin was elected to the new nine-member Central Committee. Although there were many more Jews among the Bolsheviks' Menshevik rivals in the nation, Jews were also well-represented among what Stalin called the "truly Russian" Bolsheviks. Jews were among Lenin's top men: Kamenev, Zinoviev, and Sverdlov.

Trotsky arrived in St. Petersburg (which had been renamed Petrograd) on May 4, already regarded with suspicion by both Mensheviks and Bolsheviks. In one of his first speeches, he said that Russia "had opened a new epoch, an epoch of blood and iron."[15] Three days later he met with Lenin and heard more about the heated controversy with Kamenev—Trotsky's brother-in-law—who was leading the Bolshevik faction and accusing Lenin of having abandoned Bolshevism for Trotskyism and "permanent revolution." Trotsky consoled himself with the fact that Lenin had adopted his view that the proletarian dictatorship must be the main aim of the Russian revolution.[16] Lenin and Trotsky were close on many issues, and Lenin persuaded him and his followers to join his party.

Chaos reigned in the streets of the capital, with tides of people moving up and down the main thoroughfares. All-night meetings were held in every neighborhood, and, in the words of the leftist American journalist John Reed, "Mysterious individuals circulated around the shivering women who waited in queue long cold hours for bread and milk, whispering the Jews had cornered the food supply."[17]

Power was there for the taking, and Lenin was prepared to do just that. Kamenev and Zinoviev adamantly opposed his plan for a coup d'état, and Lenin demanded that they be expelled from the party for their "betrayal" of armed struggle. Many Bolsheviks, including Stalin, also resisted Lenin's plan, but Stalin soon changed his views and became an eager advocate of a coup d'état. Kamenev and Zinoviev would never be completely forgiven, and within a few years many of the Menshevik and Bolshevik Jews would be grouped together as part of "Judas-Trotsky's gang of wreckers and Fascist diversionists."[18]

Stalin played a relatively minor role in the events surrounding the October Revolution, as evidenced by contemporary reports, including John Reed's.[19] The Jew Trotsky, on the other hand, was second only to Lenin among revolutionary leaders of national prominence; and the whole world knew his name.

=====

Trotsky and his Red Guards seized power in Petrograd on October 26 (November 7 by the new calendar), Trotsky's thirty-eighth birthday. Stalin was virtually invisible, a "gray blur" in the eyes of many of the leaders. When the new order was introduced, Trotsky, the man of the hour, became commissar of foreign affairs in the fifteen-member Council of People's Commissars, and soon would take on the job of war minister as well. In contrast, Stalin's post, as head of the People's Commissariat for Nationality Affairs, was minor indeed. On Lenin's recommendation, Stalin's 1913 essay had become a policy document of Bolshevism—and it was only fitting that the Communist party's foremost expert on nationalities should be placed in charge of designing the fate of scores of nations, including a large part of the Jewish nation, Russian Jewry.

There was little for Stalin to do initially, as the world's first Communist government struggled to cope with civil war, intervention by foreign armies, an economy in ruins, and staggering social problems. Yet the nationalities question was important, not only in Marxist-Leninist theory but also in the practical life of the Russian empire and its museum of peoples. Lenin made generous promises to the nationalities, as well as to the workers and peasants—pledges that were extremely libertarian only in theory.[20]

One of the first departments Stalin set up was the Central Commissariat for Jewish National Affairs (YEVKOM), soon made up of Jewish sections of the Communist party, the Yevsekztia. Its mission was to liquidate all Jewish national and religious institutions while fostering the dictatorship of the proletariat. From December 1918 to August 1919 Stalin and Samuel Agursky, co-head of the Jewish Commissariat, signed decrees banning the teaching of Hebrew, suppressing religious instruction, and abolishing all Jewish organizations such as the central office of the Kehillot (or the central bureau of Jewish communities), the Jewish war veterans' organization, ORT (a vocational training group), and the OZE, a health organization. For Jews were persistent in their efforts to organize Jewish life in accordance with Jewish tradition, which was perceived as a direct challenge to the Soviet pattern of centralization.

Agursky, once active in the Bund and the anarchist movement, had returned to Russia from the American Midwest when the Revolution broke out, and he volunteered his services to de-Judaize Russian Jews. He thought Stalin was a "very modest man" and did not lose his illusions about him even during the purges of the late 1930s, when Agursky was accused of being part of the "Jewish fascist underground."[21]

The Yevsekztia considered all Jewish organizations incompatible with Marxism, if not outright counterrevolutionary, and activists were rounded up and imprisoned. The Jewish Bolsheviks were the most fanatical advocates of suppressing Jewish parties—no matter how anti-Zionist, such as the Bund. The main Jewish enemy was the "bourgeois-clerical-Zionist" camp: Judaism, Zionism, the Hebrew language. At one and the same time, the Bolsheviks granted grudging recognition of the Jews as a nationality while taking the rights of a nationality away from them. For the sine qua non of the Communist revolution remained the dissolution of all nationalities, and the Jews were at the head of the list.

In December 1919 Stalin hailed the demise of the Jewish organizations in an article in the nationalities newspaper he ran from 1917 to 1919, *Zhizn Natsionalnostei:*

> The Jewish toiling masses in the RSFSR [Russian Soviet Republic] have their Socialist fatherland, which they are defending at the front with the workers and peasants of Russia against the imperialism of the [Western] Entente and all its agents. The Jewish question no longer exists in Soviet Russia. Jewish workers and toiling masses have all civil and national rights. Jewish culture has no longer any obstacles to development. We need no other countries. We lay no national claim to possession of Palestine.[22]

The Bund escaped the fate of the Zionists and the Orthodox Jews, being absorbed into the Communist party.

Although there was a great outpouring of support for the Bolsheviks among Jewish intellectuals, the broad masses of Jews were
not at all enthusiastic. But many young educated Jews, including
the majority of the Bundists (as opposed to the Jewish anarchists),
identified completely with the Bolshevik revolution at a time when
they were involved in their own personal emancipation, their own
social and cultural awakening. Another former Bundist who now
joined the Bolsheviks, Lev Mekhlis, would become Stalin's secretary and one of the most despised men in Soviet history. In his last
days he would become a figure in the plot to deport Soviet Jewry to
concentration camps.

The Revolution that had freed the Jews from the Pale of Settlement and that included the first enactment of juridical measures
against pogroms and the anti-Semitic movement also led to a cultural break with Jewish tradition. Almost overnight, intermarriage and assimilation became the goal of increasing numbers of
newly liberated Jews. Immediately after the Revolution, many
Jews were euphoric over their high representation in the new
government. Lenin's first Politburo was dominated by men of Jewish origins: Trotsky, the leader of the Petrograd coup and founder
of the Red Army; Kamenev, and Zinoviev, Lenin's righthand man
despite "the betrayal." Sverdlov was now the president of the
Party's Central Committee, and Karl Radek, Maxim Litvinov,
A. A. Yoffe, and others all held prominent positions. With the
exception of Litvinov, they all registered their nationalities as
Great Russian, not Jewish. In spite of their quasi-humanistic
preachings about the "Jewish problem," the Jewish Marxists
were, in the view of a Russian Zionist contemporary, a group of
bullies, "intolerant of the hunger for national freedom, the attachment to cultural traditions, which others felt. Liberators of the
world, they repressed with ridicule and the weight of numbers
those whom they called the minority, but who happened to represent the actual majority of the Jewish people."[23]

There would always be Jews who loved Russia despite her cruelty to them. Under Lenin, Jews became involved in all aspects of
the Revolution, including its dirtiest work. Despite the Communists' vows to eradicate anti-Semitism, it spread rapidly after the
Revolution—partly because of the prominence of so many Jews in
the Soviet administration, as well as in the traumatic, inhuman
Sovietization drives that followed. Historian Salo Baron has noted
that an immensely disproportionate number of Jews joined the new

Bolshevik secret police, the Cheka, "perhaps in subconscious retaliation for the many years of suffering at the hands of the Russian police." And many of those who fell afoul of the Cheka would be shot by Jewish investigators. Even at the height of Stalin's anti-Jewish campaign from 1948 to 1953, the anti-Semitic dictator would use some Jews against their people. And Jewish secret policemen would work against other Jews into the 1980s, entrapping those who identified with Israel and the Jewish people.[24]

In keeping with the antinationalist "internationalism" of Marxist-Leninist theory, the first head of the Cheka, founded on December 20, 1917, was a Pole. Felix Dzerzhinsky laid the foundations of the terror state with Lenin's guidance. "The Cheka is not a court," Dzerzhinsky said. "We stand for organized terror. The Cheka is obligated to defend the revolution and conquer the enemy even if its sword does by chance sometimes fall upon the heads of the innocent." Dzerzhinsky was indeed a scalpel in the hands of Lenin, whom Gorky once characterized as a remorseless experimental scientist working upon the living flesh of the Russian people. In a 1917 conversation with Raphael Abramovich, the Jew who was a leader of the Mensheviks, Dzerzhinsky said that one way to force political and social change was through the extermination of some classes of society. Zinoviev added: "We must carry along with us ninety million out of the one hundred million Soviet Russian population. As for the rest, we have nothing to say to them. They must be annihilated."[25]

A major impetus to the systematized terror was provided on August 30, 1918, when a young Jewish woman, Dora Kaplan, wounded Lenin in an assassination attempt. Kaplan was a member of the Socialist Revolutionary party, a milliner in a factory who had once been imprisoned for trying to kill a czarist official. Stalin and his chief lieutenant, Kliment Yefremovich Voroshilov, a former locksmith from Lugansk, sent a telegraph message to Sverdlov urging "open and systematic mass terror against the bourgeoisie and its agents" as the only proper response to Kaplan's act.[26] Lenin appreciated such ruthlessness, and he promoted Stalin accordingly.

Trotsky himself was not lacking in this respect. In the subsequent "crackdown" organized by Trotsky, Dzerzhinsky, Stalin, and Zinoviev, it was said that as many as 10,000 people were executed, many of them Jews. Jews had also been prominent in the antiauthoritarian anarchist movement, and these political oppo-

nents were exterminated on a grand scale by Trotsky's commander, Mikhail Tukachevsky. Trotsky would become known as
"the butcher of Kronstadt," the man with an iron hand who suppressed the Kronstadt sailors' anarchist rebellion against the Bolsheviks in 1921.

The nationalist revolts that set off the ensuing civil war were
dealt with every bit as ruthlessly by Lenin, Stalin, and Trotsky. A
week after the Revolution, Lenin and Stalin had laid down "The
Declaration of the Rights of the Peoples of Russia," whose four
points included "the right . . . to free self-determination, even to
the point of separating and forming independent states," as well as
that of national minorities to determine their own development.
But these principles were found wanting when the Ukraine, "Little
Russia," erupted in chaos with reactionary, separatist forces at the
fore, and anti-Bolshevik governments sprang up all along the
empire's vast frontiers—including Georgia, which declared its independence and kept it for three years.

In Georgia, the Mensheviks were in the great majority, and the
Georgians and Jews who made up that socialist faction were highly
nationalistic. Many Ossetians in Georgia joined the Bolsheviks, "to
spite the Georgians and Jews."[27] The Ossetians were engaged in a
merciless massacre of neighboring Chechens, a nation which Stalin
during World War II would put into wagons and deport into the
Russian wilderness. Old Stalin enemies were at the helm of the
Menshevik government in Tiflis, "infected by local nationalism," in
Stalin's words. He called Georgia a springboard for imperialist
aggression.[28] From January to March 1921 Stalin brutally crushed
Georgian independence with the help of Trotsky's Red Army, in-
stalling one of his closest and coarsest lieutenants, the Russified
Georgian Sergo Ordzhonikidze, as the dictator of Georgia. The
Ossetian capital in the northern Caucasus would be renamed after
him.

Pogroms against the Jews reached new peaks in the Ukraine and
western Russia during the civil war period. Five rival armies criss-
crossed the Ukraine, and all of them, even Nestor Makhno's anarchists, killed thousands of Jews, though the Red Army and
Makhno's forces were by far the most protective of the Ukraine's
large Jewish population.[29] War, famine, and disease were the most
powerful forces. Thousands of cases of cannibalism were reported
in the Volga and Bashkiria regions; and as the countrywide chaos
deepened, the Jews were increasingly blamed. The old czarist and

Black Hundreds' motto was repeated endlessly, "Kill the Jews and save Russia!"[30]

Throughout the civil war period, Stalin attempted to undermine Trotsky's military authority and replace him as Lenin's closest disciple. The most famous confrontation was at Tsaritsyn, the future Stalingrad. Sending a message to Lenin asking for special military powers in the south, Stalin, the shoemaker's son, cast the first stone by denigrating Trotsky as follows: "If only our war 'specialists' (the shoemakers!) had not slept and been idle."[31] Stalin was among old friends there, including Voroshilov and Semyon Mikhailovich Budenny—two former sergeants and future marshals—and Ordzhonikidze. The four men, all of plebian stock, despised the intellectual revolutionaries and ex-gentry whom Trotsky had made officers of the new Red Army. Lenin tried to take the middle ground, placating both of his disciples—though new evidence suggests that Lenin actually offered Trotsky the eventual leadership of the Communist party. Trotsky, however, reportedly declined on the grounds that his Jewish origin would give their enemies an opportunity "to say that our country is being ruled by a Jew." He thus unwittingly paved Stalin's way to ultimate power, while revealing the extent of Soviet anti-Semitism.[32]

In the 1920s anti-Semitism crept into Party propaganda, but Trotsky remained "usually reticent on the subject," as even the sympathetic writer Isaac Deutscher would point out.[33] For many years Stalin used his anti-Semitic weapons surreptitiously, dropping dark hints and playing on the general suspicion, fear, and hatred of the feverish "Talmudists" who filled the party's top ranks. He quietly and patiently composed a list of those he would eliminate; and anyone, Jew or otherwise, who had ever slighted him was doomed. Near the top was Lenin's friend and Marx's biographer David Ryazanov, a Jew who at a meeting of Party theorists in the old days had once contemptuously interrupted Stalin: "Koba, don't embarrass people. Theory is not your strong point." Years later the historian would be arrested on Stalin's direct orders and shot like a stray dog.[34] Another future victim was Jan Sten, a Marxist philosopher who tutored the nationalities commissar and emerging Party strongman in the early 1920s, trying unsuccessfully to help him master Hegelian dialectics. Sten predicted that his pupil's intense hatred for the Jewish people would one day lead him to mount trials of Jews that would "put the trials of Dreyfus and Beilis in the shade."[35]

But Stalin had no trouble working with Jews like Agursky, or with one of Voroshilov's friends who would eventually become a top Stalinist lieutenant and executioner: Lazar Moiseyevich Kaganovich. Kaganovich—who would still be haunting Moscow in the Gorbachev era, in his apartment on Frunzeskaya Boulevard—was born on November 22, 1893, in the Ukrainian village of Kabany. His brother Mikhail, four years older, joined the Bund and later the Bolsheviks. Lazar, a steely-eyed young man who had been the school bully, converted to the Bolshevik cause after hearing Trotsky speak in 1911 and gained a reputation for ruthlessness before he was twenty. He became close to Voroshilov in the early days of the Revolution, sleeping on an adjacent cot in the Smolny Institute, where the deputies to the Constitutional Assembly had gathered and where Trotsky had orchestrated the Bolshevik coup d'état. He fought in the civil war and rose quickly in the Party, mainly because of his brilliant administrative skills. With his broad-brush black mustache, he looked like a Jewish version of Stalin, the Caucasian Bolshevik fourteen years his senior who had replaced Trotsky as his hero. Previously he had cultivated an intellectual look, like Trotsky or Aleksei Rykov; now he patterned himself after his new master, who did not like intellectuals. Kaganovich was Stalin's mirror image, wearing a similar workers' cap and shiny leather boots. Together the two would one day direct forces of extraordinary scope and power.[36]

Stalin's struggle with Trotsky intensified as Lenin's health deteriorated after an illness at the end of 1921. In May 1922 the fifty-two-year-old Soviet dictator was crippled by a stroke, unable to speak or write, and though his health would fluctuate over the coming months, it became obvious to all that his days were numbered.

Many believe that Stalin speeded Lenin's death along, in the first of many "medical murders" that would culminate in 1953 with the charges that Jewish doctors had murdered Soviet leaders.

Stalin had been chosen general secretary of the Central Committee on April 3, 1922, to coordinate the overlapping work of the burgeoning bureaucracy. According to Trotsky, it was on this occasion that the ailing Lenin expressed his misgivings about his protégé, saying, "This cook can only serve peppery dishes."[37] Lenin thought Stalin's rude manner was a symptom of a deeper ailment. In his famous "Testament" he would tell members of the Central Committee that Stalin had concentrated enormous power in his hands, "and I am not sure whether he will always be capable of using that authority with sufficient caution."[38]

Stalin kept close tabs on Lenin's staff, especially his cooks and doctors, and particularly on his chief physician, the Jew Mikhail Yosifovich Auerbach. When Stalin visited the invalid Lenin in Gorky in 1923, the two men joked about the doctors who had ordered the dictator to stop talking about politics in order to preserve his ebbing strength.[39]

Lenin himself had established a special Kremlin medical service because the leading Bolsheviks overworked themselves and often ignored their health. He insisted on prescribed periods of rest and medical treatment. The special hospital was supposed to prevent ailing leaders from falling into the hands of a doctor who might be an "enemy of Soviet power." But as historian Adam Ulam noted, "This praiseworthy solicitude had, as his own case vividly demonstrates, the most unfortunate result of making a sick person's regimen and treatment subject to the Politburo's approval."[40]

It will probably never be known if Stalin poisoned Lenin; the reports recorded in various memoirs are more in the realm of conjecture than fact.[41] But Stalin did worsen Lenin's condition by deliberately insulting his wife, Nadya Krupskaya, in order to upset the stroke victim and bring on another attack. In his own old age, Stalin himself may have fallen victim to a similar strategem.

Stalin certainly knew of Lenin's "second thoughts" about him and was aware of the steps he took to make Trotsky his deputy and heir apparent. In Lenin's so-called Testament, the dying dictator judged his disciples like the biblical patriarch Jacob weighing the sins and merits of his sons. Despite his critical remarks about Stalin, he said he was one of the ablest men in the Politburo. Trotsky was the ablest man of all, Lenin said, but overly self-confident. Referring to the October 1917 betrayal by Zinoviev and Kamenev, Lenin excused them, saying that it mattered no more than Trotsky's "non-Bolshevism." Bukharin was praised as "the favorite of the whole Party." The Testament—with a codicil condemning Stalin's "rudeness" and suggesting his removal as general secretary—was known by all the Party leaders, but it was not made public until Khrushchev's denunciation of Stalin in 1956.[42] Notably, three of the five "sons" were of Jewish origin.

Nine doctors took part in Lenin's autopsy, and though they detected the possible presence of poison—the main indication being that blood vessels of his impressive brain were calcified—the poisoning of Lenin remains a speculative conclusion. But reports of the medically induced death of another Soviet leader a year later appear to be solidly grounded in fact.

M. V. Frunze, a foe of Trotsky who replaced him as leader of the Red Army in 1924, showed that he was his own man soon after he assumed the post of commissar of war. In doing so, he offended both Stalin and the Chekists. Stalin told his secretaries that Frunze might be a potential Bonaparte, hinting that he was planning a coup.[43] Trotsky himself would say that Frunze was too close to Zinoviev, and too zealous in protecting the army from the incursions of the secret police—the same crime for which Marshal Tukachevsky would be executed during the Great Terror.[44]

Frunze had long suffered from stomach ulcers, but was recovering when the Politburo, at Stalin's direction, ordered him to undergo surgery in October 1925. Frunze told his wife that he was puzzled by the order, since the operation was pointless. Within hours he would go into convulsions after "an allergic reaction" to the anesthetic, which brought about heart failure. Soon afterward the case became the subject of a story, published in *Novy Mir* by the distinguished Jewish writer Boris Pilnyak, "The Tale of the Unextinguished Moon," about an army commander who is forced to undergo an unnecessary operation on the orders of "Number One, the unbending man." During the operation, the doctors murder him.

Pilnyak learned of this case from a senior secret police official, Yakov Savlovich Agranov. Stalin liquidated both men in 1938.[45]

In the light of what we know about the medical trials during the great purges for the alleged poisoning of prominent Soviet leaders, and the similar charges brought against the Kremlin doctors in the 1950s, the Frunze case, and that of Lenin, become highly relevant. A modus operandi emerged, akin to the methods employed by the Borgias, the Caesars, and the pharaohs.

The Kremlin polyclinic and pharmacy would expand under Stalin, who ordered all members of the Politburo, the Central Committee, and the Central Executive Committee, as well as the secret police and army hierarchy, to undergo medical checks and treatment there. Possession of the little red booklet that ensured attention at the hospital was a sign of great privilege in Soviet society, where good doctors and medicine were in short supply. From its inception and for the next thirty years, most of the staff—the best doctors in the country—were Jews. Stalin's own life was reportedly saved by a Jewish doctor named Rozanov, who operated on him at Moscow's Soldatensky Hospital after an appendicitis attack in November 1919.[46]

In the 1920s Stalin's personal corps of physicians included Drs. Weisbrod, Moshenberg, and Lev Grigorievich Levin. At one time, the chief Kremlin pharmacist reportedly was Genrikh (Henry) Yagoda, a Jewish toxicologist who would succeed V. Menzhinsky as chief of secret police in 1934. The poison expert was widely believed to have achieved his meteoric rise by carrying out the medical murder of his predecessor.[47] Under the Soviets, doctors, like everyone else, did what they were told. They became used to acting "on instructions," which often involved sending people to prison camps instead of recuperation resorts.

Another case two years after Frunze's death lends weight to the belief that the Soviet leadership consistently used medicine as a weapon in various ways. In 1927 Trotsky's close friend and ally Adolf Yoffe, the Soviet diplomat famed since the Brest-Litovsk treaty ending Russian involvement in World War I, committed suicide after the Medical Committee of the Central Committee refused to allow him to go abroad for treatment of tuberculosis and recurring nervous crises. He had also been refused medicine from the Kremlin pharmacy.[48] Though typical of Stalin's spitefulness and sadism, it was mild enough in comparison with what was to come.

======

The collective leadership that emerged in Lenin's dying days was headed by the Jew Zinoviev, a loquacious, mean-spirited, curly-haired Adonis whose vanity knew no bounds. He was a lustful ladies' man, though his colleagues thought of him as effeminate and cowardly: his stand against the seizure of power in October 1917 had stemmed mainly from personal fear. Despite his scratchy, high-pitched voice, he was considered a great orator, and his comrades nicknamed him "the blabbermouth." The second triumvir, Kamenev, was more of a diplomat; his stand in 1917 had been motivated not by cowardice, but by caution. Stalin was the third, while Trotsky remained a *Luftmensch* high above the fray.

Stalin in his early forties was a low-slung, short man with hairy ears, a low forehead, sallow pockmarked skin, and fat nicotine-stained fingers (the poet Osip Mandelstam compared them to fat little worms). Though he was only five feet four inches tall, he was always portrayed as a large man with a high forehead; he would not pose for pictures with tall people. He loathed Trotsky's looks, and

Zinoviev's, too, especially their high foreheads, which in popular lore bespoke intelligence. Many who knew him referred to his dirty fingernails, his decay-blackened teeth, his yellow eyes giving him the aspect of an old, battle-scarred tiger. But what was obvious to all was that the short man puffing loudly on his pipe had an "immense, diabolical shell as a tactician," brilliant and terrifying.[49]

Throughout the early twenties Stalin built his political machine methodically, centralizing power in the Secretariat. Zinoviev tried to halt the process, but he and Kamenev worked closely with the third triumvir to emasculate Trotsky. The intricacies of the shifts in power in the Kremlin between 1923 and 1929 have filled many volumes, but suffice it for our purposes to say that Trotsky was already a defeated man by 1924, and that the eventual switch to his side by Zinoviev and Kamenev came far too late to do them any good. For they, too, were doomed from the start; and Stalin, their greatest enemy, knew why: they were Jews. Winston Churchill also perceived the real reason that Trotsky lost the struggle with Stalin: "He was still a Jew. Nothing could get over that. Hard fortune when you have deserted your family, repudiated your race, spat upon the religion of your father, and lapped Jew and Gentile in a common malignity, to be baulked of so great a prize for so narrow-minded a reason!"[50]

When Stalin destroyed the so-called Left Opposition in the 1920s, he let it be known that the opposition was led by Jews, and that the struggle was between Russian socialism and aliens. Trotsky himself remarked on this far too late, saying in his 1940 biography that Stalin had pretended to be neutral in the 1920s as the number of anti-Semitic caricatures and doggerels increased in the Party press—until finally matters went so far that Stalin was forced to come out with a published statement which declared, "We are fighting Trotsky, Zinoviev and Kamenev not because they are Jews, but because they are Oppositionists." It was absolutely clear to Trotsky, however, that Stalin was in fact "broadcasting throughout the entire Soviet press the very pregnant reminder, 'Don't forget that the leaders of the Opposition are Jews.'" Such a statement "gave carte blanche to the anti-Semites," Trotsky wrote. Trotsky had noted in 1926 what was going on—but he confined his protests in a letter to Bukharin and did not "go public." On March 4, 1926, he underlined his distress: "Is it possible that in *our party,* in *Moscow,* in *Workers' Cells,* anti-Semitic agitation should be carried out with impunity?"[51]

Stalin took up the cause of "socialism in one country" not simply

as a cudgel to oppose the Jewish revolutionaries who followed
Trotsky's internationalist preachings, but because he was in essence a Great Russian nationalist. But just as his 1913 essay on
Marxism and the nationality question could have been subtitled
"The Truth about the Bund and Jewish 'Nationalism,'" so too did
the "Jewish question" underline Stalin's highly successful doctrine
calling for the building of socialism in one country—Russia—first.

Although the "cult of personality" was only beginning in the late
1920s and had yet to take on its ultimate stratospheric proportions,
statues of Stalin already were being erected in his native Caucasus;
and poets were comparing him to the Supreme Being. Soon there
were no more constraints, and in the vast portion of the earth
under Stalin's rule, he began to produce death on a staggering
scale.

Between 1929 to 1932, from five to ten million people were
directly exterminated, starved, or frozen to death in Stalin's program of collectivization and "de-kulakization": his first effort at
the "transformation of the human element." The objects of this
genocidal action, the "rich" peasants known as kulaks, were often
associated with Jews in the Russian subconscious, as exemplified
by Dostoevsky's remark in *The Diary of a Writer:* "Indeed, we
take no pride in our kulaks and we do not set them as examples for
imitation, and on the contrary, we agree wholeheartedly that both
[Jews and kulaks] are no good." The Jews, with their "sempiternal
gold pursuit," had exploited and "ruined" the Russians with
vodka, Dostoevsky had said, and if they were the majority and the
Russians the minority, "Wouldn't they slaughter them to the last
man, to the point of complete extermination, as they used to do
with alien peoples in ancient times, during their ancient history?"[52]
Lenin and Stalin both said that the kulaks were not human, just as
Hitler and the National Socialists tried to dehumanize the Jews.
Even the writer Maxim Gorky denounced the kulaks, hoping that
"the uncivilized, stupid, turgid people in the Russian villages will
die out . . . and a new race of literate, rational, energetic people will
take their place." Intellectuals could always be relied upon to compose such revolutionary prose for use against a target nationality
or class, or to embellish their leaders' crude characterizations—for
Stalin simply called these peasants "scum."[53] The kulaks were
depicted in films and cartoons as hideous Jew-like, bearded money-
grabbers. Even the great Jewish film director Sergei Eisenstein
helped foster this image.

But rational arguments were not needed for this genocidal work, as Hitler proved in his war against the Jews: the idea that only a class war against the kulaks would allow the Party to mobilize the rest of the peasantry was "almost entirely fantasy."[54] The rationalization for the liquidation of "hostile human resources" was economic, but it could just as well have been political, or for "security," as the case against the Jews would be framed twenty years later. Although habitual lies had become an integral part of the Soviet system from the beginning of the Revolution, the distinction between what the Communists really believed and what they said was entirely obliterated during this period. As George F. Kennan would put it, "From the time of their seizure of power . . . the Russian Communists have always been characterized by their extraordinary ability to cultivate falsehood as a deliberate weapon of policy."[55]

The system of mass deportations began with collectivization, what Stalin termed a "revolution carried out from above." Three million peasants and their families were deported to the harsh climates of the north, while hundreds of thousands of others were sent to die in the growing Gulag. Entire villages were wiped out, and three to six million people starved to death. Some scholars have estimated that as many as twenty-two million deaths were caused by Stalin's policies in the early 1930s.[56]

Some of the strongest protests against Stalin's "revolutionary" program came from worldwide Jewish organizations, which only confirmed his belief that the Jews were among the worst of his many enemies. The Soviets fought back by creating new icons. One of the most cherished saints in Soviet history—until the demystification thaw of glasnost—was Pavlik Morozov, a fourteen-year-old boy who was murdered by his kulak parents in 1932 after he had denounced them as enemies of the state. This model of Communist morality embodied the spirit of denunciation. The phenomenon turned into a sweeping conflagration engulfing the entire Soviet Union of the 1930s; it would be reignited against Jews in the late 1940s and even more so in the early 1950s, spurred by the "revelations" of the Doctors' Plot.

CHAPTER 4

The Great Purge
Show Trials and Medical Murders

When Lady Astor visited Moscow in December 1931 and bravely asked Stalin, "How long will you keep killing people?" he answered that "the process would continue as long as was necessary" to establish the Communist society.[1] Under Lenin, the Bolsheviks had openly announced, "We are exterminating the bourgeoisie as a class."[2] The wheels that Lenin and Trotsky had set in motion only accelerated under Stalin. The difference was simply one of scale. The process would come to a climax with the Great Terror of the 1930s, known as the *chistka* (a cleansing or evacuation of the bowels).

The event generally believed to have sparked the purge was the assassination on December 1, 1934, of Sergei M. Kirov, Stalin's second in command: an energetic organizer and orator whose talents had provoked the leader's jealousy. But the bloodbath of the thirties may have been inspired two years earlier, as Stalin's murderous impulses accelerated with the suicide (or slaying) of his second wife, Nadezhda Alliluyeva, the mother of two of his three children, Vasily and Svetlana.[3]

On the night of November 7 or 8, 1932, the fifteenth anniversary of the Revolution, Stalin vilified and cursed his beautiful and sensitive wife at an all-night party held at Kliment Voroshilov's dacha. The colorless Voroshilov and his Jewish wife, Catherine, a Communist organizer in her youth, were good friends of Nadezhda Alliluyeva's, as were the Jewish wives of Vyacheslav Molotov and Kaganovich, Paulina Zhemchuzina and Maria.

The argument may have been set off when Alliluyeva, once Lenin's private secretary, dared to voice some criticism of the policy of collectivization and de-kulakization. She was known to be deeply upset about the expropriations dooming the peasants. One rumor had it that the argument was sparked by the presence at the party of "voluptuous, curvaceous" Rosa Kaganovich, sister of Stalin's associate Lazar Kaganovich and supposedly the dictator's "Jewish mistress." On the other hand, there is serious doubt about her very existence, as Svetlana Alliluyeva, Stalin's biographer Adam Ulam, and others have averred.[4]

After an obscene torrent of abuse, Nadezhda Alliluyeva fled in disgust back to the Kremlin, accompanied either by Voroshilov or by Molotov's wife, who had also been at the banquet. After her companion left, Nadezhda Alliluyeva, crying hysterically, told her housekeeper she would be either poisoned or killed in an "accident."[5] Stalin returned, furious, and another quarrel ensued. The next morning, Nadezhda was found dead, a pistol in her hand. Finger marks were visible on her neck, according to one version of the story.[6]

Stalin's longtime associate Abel Yenukidze, who found the body, would be liquidated in 1937, accused of trying to poison Stalin.[7] Stalin also destroyed the doctors who signed his wife's autopsy report, including Professor A. V. Rusakov and Minister of Public Health Dr. A. F. Tretyakov. Dr. Ivan Kuperin, of the Kremlin Health Board, survived. He would likewise eliminate the doctors who signed the death certificate of his close aide Sergo Ordzhonikidze, who reportedly killed himself in 1937.[8] This modus operandi would repeat itself throughout the purge trials, and in the Doctors' Plot fifteen years later, when physicians or officials who signed the death certificates of prominent figures who had died unnaturally were themselves arrested and conveniently died.

"Stalin was not really a normal man," wrote George Kennan. "Like Ivan the Terrible, he was the captive of a personal devil within his own soul."[9] While Ivan became completely mad after the death of his beloved wife, Stalin never lost his senses, but he reportedly went into deep mourning, and his persecution mania intensified; as many as ten million deaths in the next six years attested to that fact.

That he may have taken comfort in the arms of a Jewish woman appears improbable in the light of what is known of him. In her memoirs Svetlana Alliluyeva wrote:

Nothing could be more unlikely than the story spread in the West about "Stalin's third wife"—the mythical Rosa Kaganovich. Aside from the fact that I never saw any "Rosa" in the Kaganovich family, the idea that this legendary Rosa, an intellectual woman (according to the Western version, a doctor), and above all a Jewess, could have captured my father's fancy shows how totally ignorant people were of his true nature; such a possibility was absolutely excluded from his life.[10]

Svetlana said that her father paid little attention to women. But what she appears to stress in this passage is that he would certainly never sleep with a Jewish woman.

Throughout this period, Lazar Kaganovich accumulated increasing power as a remarkable administrator who soon became known as the Iron Commissar. Kaganovich's extraordinary organizing skills, which included planning mass terror under Stalin's direction, would be noted by his protégé and future enemy Nikita Khrushchev: "If the Central Committee put an ax in his hands, he would chop up a storm. Unfortunately he often chopped down the healthy trees along with the rotten ones."[11] Kaganovich himself was fond of employing the Bolshevik axiom "When the forest is cut down, the chips fly," a saying that was used to rationalize the murder of millions. Kaganovich was also known for his vow against alleged class enemies and saboteurs: "We'll break their skulls in."[12] In 1932, when he was in charge of suppressing a strike by Kuban Cossacks during collectivization in the Ukraine, he transferred whole Cossack settlements to Siberia—a mere rehearsal for the transfer of eight entire nationalities in the forties. Khrushchev, who participated in many of these events and whose own hands were not unsullied, termed Kaganovich "unsurpassed in his viciousness."[13]

Kaganovich eventually held more key posts in the power structure than anyone except Stalin and perhaps Lavrenty Pavlovich Beria. He steamrolled his way through the Moscow underground, building the world's most beautiful subway in record time and showing no mercy to the 70,000 workers who toiled around the clock to do so. He demolished the huge Church of Christ the Savior and replaced it with the Palace of the Soviets. As commissar of heavy industry during the war years, he chose his brother Mikhail as his deputy and controlled everything from the vast fuel and steel industries to chemicals and building materials. But he made his real mark during the Great Terror, when he became Stalin's scythe. In Khrushchev's estimation, Kaganovich had always been "a detestable sycophant, exposing enemies and having people arrested right and left."[14] All the while, he would finger a string of amber "worry beads," which became a sort of Bolshevik rosary during the time of the "cleansing," fashionable among high officials.[15]

Kaganovich had been drawing up lists of enemies since the mid-twenties, when he served as Stalin's chief of Central Personnel and Assignments. The lists were the heart of the bureaucratic machine. Both Kaganovich and Stalin, sharing a deep-rooted hatred for intellectuals, alphabetically enumerated thousands of enemies. Many of those so doomed had Jewish names, for Kaganovich particularly despised the educated Jews of his native Ukraine (after the abolition of czarist-era quotas, Jews constituted half the university students there). These lists would become a hallmark of the Terror, and of the future mass deportations. In his zealous pursuit of peoples' enemies, Kaganovich would be second only to the successive chiefs of the secret police during the Terror: Yagoda, N. Yezhov, and Beria.

Thousands of Jewish revolutionaries helped to spearhead the Terror machine with a messianic fervor. One of them, Matvei Berman, had helped to institutionalize slave labor as early as 1922 (it was the refined philosopher Lenin, not the coarse Stalin, who created the Gulag concentration camps to accommodate the growing numbers of imprisoned enemies of the people and to liquidate them in huge numbers). As Arthur Koestler put it in *Darkness at Noon*, "Death was no mystery in the movement; there was nothing exalted about it: it was the logical solution to political divergencies."

Other Jewish Chekists who rose to the top included Aron Soltz, long known as "the conscience of the Party," and Naftali Frenkel, a Turkish Jew whom Solzhenitsyn would characterize as "the nerve of the Archipelago, which stretched across the nine time zones of the vast country."[16] It was Frenkel who refined Berman's use of prisoners as slave laborers. In 1932 Stalin put him in charge of the construction of the White Sea–Baltic Canal, which took the lives of some 200,000 prisoners, and later he worked under Yagoda, the first and last Jewish head of the Cheka. Most of the chief overseers of the Canal were Jews. Solzhenitsyn described them as "six hired murderers each of whom accounted for thirty thousand lives: Firin—Berman—Frenkel—Kogan—Rappoport—Zhuk." However, a great many other Jews with these same family surnames were among the victims of communism, living in frozen holes in the ground throughout the vast Gulag empire, as Solzhenitsyn also reported.[17]

Soltz, who had once shared a hideout with Stalin when he was still known as Koba and who became one of his key men in the Central Control Commission in the 1920s, would be one of the few high-ranking Jews to escape execution during the purge; instead he was incarcerated in an insane asylum, and only released after he had actually lost his sanity.[18] But thousands of other Jewish Chekists would be executed during the Great Terror, including the men at the top, such as secret police chief Yagoda, the principal Soviet poisoner in the years 1934–36, chief of operations K. V. Pauker, and the Berman brothers, Boris and Matvei.[19]

In the 1930s Lev Inzhir, a Jew, became chief accountant of the Gulag's thousands of industrial enterprises and building sites, stretching from Dickson Island and Spitzbergen to Kamchatka and Central Asia. The Gulag became a kind of nation unto itself, a world with its own classes, laws, customs, rulers, and language. Inzhir, the all-powerful clerk, was kept busy with figures on transit points, rail depots and harbors, human and other freight transfers, lengths of terms, mortality rates. Whole nationalities would fall victim to this system, and it had amply displayed its efficiency when the plan to send Soviet Jews into mass exile was being formed, only to be aborted by Stalin's sudden death in 1953.[20]

The idea of the Great Purge probably germinated in Stalin's mind for years before he unleashed the wave of show trials, mass terror, arrests, and executions. It is certain that Stalin himself ordered Kirov's assassination[21] and used it in the same way that Hitler used the Reichstag fire. Within hours of the killing, Stalin, who publicly appeared to be in deep mourning for his lost comrade, issued a warrant for wholesale executions, signed by his faithful friend Abel Yenukidze, which directed investigative agencies to "speed up the cases of those accused of the preparation or execution of acts of terror," instructed judicial bodies not to impede the execution of death sentences, and directed "the organs"—the sexual nickname for the secret police, which caused snickers along with fear—to "execute the death sentence against criminals . . . immediately after the passage of sentences."[22] Ironically, Yenukidze, who had found Nadezhda Alliluyeva's corpse, was signing his own death warrant, along with millions of others. The pattern of an ever-expanding ring of alleged plots constantly being "revealed" would be repeated in the 1953 charges against the Kremlin doctors.

Stalin started the death list by dividing a sheet of paper down the middle and filling up the two columns with the names of the first traitors to be arrested, beginning with his erstwhile partners in the ruling troika, the Jews Zinoviev and Kamenev. Hundreds of thousands of other Jews would be among the estimated seven to ten million fatalities. Stalin used the Soviet press and mass rallies to whip the Russian people into a frenzy. They screamed for the blood of the Trotskyites, of the sons of the old regime, of the followers of Bukharin, of citizens who had relatives living abroad, of old Bolsheviks and Chekists who were "not sufficiently vigilant," of the many traitors in the armed forces.[23] Feverish public denunciations and the so-called unmasking of peoples' enemies swept the country. In Moscow 180,000 Party members were rounded up as enemies of the people, and 40,000 in Leningrad. Like Ivan the Terrible, Stalin liquidated members of his own family, including the brother of his first wife, Alexander Svanidze, who had raised Stalin's first-born son, Yakov, in his own home.[24] Svanidze's wife, Maria, an opera singer from a wealthy Georgian Jewish family, was imprisoned and died of a heart attack five years later upon hearing that her husband had been shot. Almost the entire staffs of *Pravda* and *Izvestia* disappeared; 30,000 Red Army and Navy officers were purged, 5,000 of them shot; marshals, generals, secret police chiefs, and ambassadors were killed alongside some of the most prominent authors, directors, critics, and actors in modern history.

Introducing himself to a foreign visitor, Stalin, toying with his Dunhill pipe, would bow slightly and say in the humblest tones, "Stalin." He was the favorite of the international intelligentsia, including prominent Jewish writers like Lion Feuchtwanger and Romain Rolland, who refused to believe that Stalin had committed any crimes or that he was tainted with the slightest bit of anti-Semitism. George Bernard Shaw praised him to the skies, and H. G. Wells, who visited him in 1934, wrote during the escalating purges: "I have never met a man more candid, fair and honest, and it is to these qualities, and to nothing occult and sinister, that he owes his tremendous undisputed ascendancy."[25] To Russians, he had become the *vozhd* (the supreme leader). He chose his victims, laid his plans minutely, wreaked his implacable vengeance, and then went to bed, feeling that there was nothing sweeter in the world. In a famous 1936 speech, in the midst of the Terror, Stalin said: "Life is better and gayer now," a line repeated constantly by the Soviet media.

The cosmology behind all the purges, show trials, and plots de-

Joseph Stalin was born Iosif Djugashvili on December 21, 1879, in the small Georgian town of Gori (*above*). His father was a shoemaker of Ossetian descent. His mother, Ekaterina (*below left*), did washing and baked bread in the homes of the rich. *Below right*, a child who may be the young Stalin (marked with a double *x*) is pictured with a group of Gori schoolchildren. (*Sovfoto*)

At 15, Stalin entered the Tiflis Seminary where, instead of becoming a priest, he joined the revolutionary movement. He was expelled for leading Marxist study groups, but may have also informed on other students. Stalin pursued his revolutionary career in the cities of Georgia and the Caucasus, but is thought to have also been an agent of the Okhrana, the czarist secret police. *Left*, Stalin when he entered the Seminary. *Below left* and *right*, police photos of Stalin taken in 1900. (*Sovfoto*)

Stalin's private life was stormy and unstable. *Above left*, a rare photo of Nadezhda Alliluyeva (*AP/Wide World*), his second wife and Lenin's former secretary. She bore him two children: Svetlana (*above right; AP/Wide World*) and Vasily (*right; Sovfoto*). Svetlana, Stalin's favorite, displeased him by marrying a Jew, as did his elder son, Yakov. Nadezhda died in the Kremlin on November 8, 1932, under mysterious circumstances, and while the official claim was suicide, there were reports that Stalin shot her in the heat of a quarrel.

Stalin became Lenin's protégé around 1911. At Lenin's request he wrote an essay on the "nationalities question" which expressed an early antipathy toward Jews. This famous photo (*above*) was supposedly taken at Gorky during Lenin's final illness, but in the Soviet Union is widely thought to be a composite. Stalin's main rival in these years was Leon Trotsky (*below*), a Jew whose reputation as a bold leader and brilliant theorist grated on Stalin even before they met. Lenin's testament, long hidden, stated that Stalin was "coarse" and should be carefully excluded from holding too much power. (*Sovfoto*)

Jacob Sverdlov (*right*), a Jew who became the first Soviet president, spent some time in Siberian exile with Stalin. The worldly, multilingual intellectual was just the sort of "cosmopolitan" that Stalin most suspected and disliked. (*Novosti from Sovfoto*) After the revolution, when Stalin became commissar of nationalities, he chose Samuel Agursky (*below, center, first seated row, in suit and tie*), a one-time member of the Jewish Bund, to head his campaign to wipe out all traces of Jewish religion, politics, and culture in the Soviet Union. (*YIVO Institute*)

Above, Stalin at the Bolshoi ballet with his Kremlin associates in 1936: *right to left*, Lazar Kaganovich (the highest-ranking Jew in the Soviet Union); Ordzhonikidze; Mikoyan; behind him Yezhov, head of the secret police; Bubnov (in the background); Stalin; Voroshilov; Molotov; Kalinin; Shvernik; Andreyev. Many were killed in the purges; some had Jewish wives, whom Stalin sent to the Gulag one by one. (*AP/Wide World*) *Left*, Lavrenty Beria, Yezhov's successor and one of the worst killers in Soviet history. (*Bettmann/Hulton*)

In 1925, Marshal Frunze (*above, left, with Budenny and Voroshilov*), Trotsky's successor as Red Army commander, was ordered by Stalin to undergo unnecessary surgery. His resulting death was undoubtedly a "medical murder." The deaths of Politburo member V.V. Kuibyshev (*below left*) and writer Maxim Gorky (*below right*) during the purges of the thirties were attributed to two Kremlin doctors, Levin and Pletnev. Levin, a Jew, was executed. (*Sovfoto*)

Russian writer Isaac Babel (*left*), a Jew who rode with the Cossacks during the civil war and later served in the Cheka, or secret police, was arrested at the peak of the Great Terror and executed around 1940. (*AP/Wide World*)

Theater director Vsevolod Meyerhold (*below*) was among many prominent Jewish artists and cultural figures, including poet Osip Mandelstam, who were executed at the same time. (*Sovfoto*)

signed by Stalin portrayed the *vozhd* and his people as beset with internal and external enemies, bent on assassination by poisoning, conspiracy, sabotage, and counterrevolution. He staged the show trials literally as dramatic performances; it did not matter if the victims were real people or stand-ins, for they were all well-rehearsed actors in a spectacular play. No one was certain if it was Rykov or Bukharin or Kamenev on the stand, or doubles made up to look and sound like them. It was hard to believe that the Bolshevik leaders could actually have committed such absurd crimes as they confessed to, but confess they did; and their confessions were widely believed.[26] Stalin, the chief purported victim of the myriad conspiracies, was never called to the witness stand and did not publicly attend any of the trials—though some correspondents thought they saw pipe smoke curling up from behind a curtain at the Bukharin trial. Nevertheless, his presence, like that of an invisible director, was continually felt at the macabre spectacles. The old Bolsheviks had been ritually recanting since the 1920s, but now—prompted by Stalin—they ended "by confessing apocalyptic sins."[27]

The big show trials were repeated in tens of thousands of local Soviet schools, universities, factories, collective farms, and other institutions. The purges—considered as a sort of Passion Play—thus became as much a part of Russian society as the Holy Week dramas performed at Oberammergau in Germany. Their theatrical aspect was noted in the memoirs of Victor Kravchenko, a Soviet official who defected to the United States in 1944 and was subsequently murdered by the NKVD: "Sitting in the Institute auditorium, I was strangely aware of the immediate scene as just a tiny segment of a super-drama, with millions of men and women as the actors, one-sixth of the earth's surface as the stage."[28]

Like *War and Peace*, the trials employed a huge cast of characters. Lazar Kaganovich played the little Stalin, condemning untold numbers to death for "suspicious behavior" or for allegedly plotting against the dictator's life.[29] There was plenty of gold braid in these dramas. In 1937 one of the leading Soviet generals, Yona Yakir, a Jew, sent Stalin a letter from his prison cell pleading his innocence in the alleged conspiracy led by Marshal Tukhachevsky. Stalin wrote on the margins: "Scoundrel and a male whore." Yakir was also labeled a "fiend," along with many others being tried. Kaganovich appended his own comments under Stalin's: "For the traitor scum . . . . one punishment—the death sentence."[30]

Yakir, son of a Jewish chemist in Kishinev, had been the only professional soldier to become a full member of the Central Committee. He was totally loyal to the Soviet cause and to Stalin: his last words before execution were, "Long live Stalin!" Yet this Jewish Communist stalwart, along with two other Jewish generals under Chief of Staff Tukhachevsky, was accused of conspiring with the Nazis, a patently anti-Semitic charge. The wife of physicist Alexander Weissberg, a ceramicist arrested in April 1936, was accused of surreptitiously incorporating swastikas in the patterns on the teacups she designed, and also "plotting to kill Stalin." The swastika charge was typical of the absurd accusations made against many Jews before the Hitler-Stalin romance.[31]

Just prior to his arrest, General Yakir had visited in prison the civil war hero and recent divisional commander of the Kiev area, General Dmitri Shmidt, once the swashbuckling son of a poor Jewish shoemaker. Shmidt, who would be shot in secret in May 1937, had been associated with Trotsky in the 1920s and was very close to Yakir. He had signed his own death warrant at the 1927 Party congress by insulting Stalin, who never forgot a slight. In a half-joking manner, Shmidt had gestured toward his big curved sword as he cursed Stalin, saying he would lop his ears off one day. Stalin blanched, saying nothing.[32] Nine years later, when Yakir visited his old friend in his dank cell, he was shocked at how thin and gray he had become within a few short months. "He looked like a Martian," Yakir told friends. Soon afterward Shmidt "confessed" under torture that Yakir was involved in plotting a military coup to overthrow the Stalin regime.[33]

The accusations that Soviet Jewish generals cooperated with the Nazis were part of a revival of Russian nationalism as a central element of Stalinism, and punctuated the increasing willingness of the dictator to use anti-Semitism as a weapon. The idea of widespread Jewish plotting with Hitler was no more absurd than the charges that thousands of top army, Party, and police officials were allegedly conspiring to detach parts of the Soviet Union and unify them with Turkey, Japan, or Iran. Similar charges would be brought against the entire Jewish nation in Stalin's attempt to replay the Great Terror in the 1950s. But it would be Stalin, not Tukhachevsky or Yakir, who would sign a nonaggression pact with Hitler, a man who, like himself, had risen from humble origins, seized power and used it ruthlessly. They admired one another, with Hitler calling Stalin "a tremendous personality, an ascetic who has taken the whole of that gigantic country firmly in his iron grasp."[34]

Officially, Stalin opposed anti-Semitism. In a short answer to an inquiry about anti-Semitism from the Jewish Telegraphic Agency in 1931, Stalin, the Great Russian chauvinist par excellence, sounded like a distinguished anthropologist appalled by the backwardness of humanity. In his single officially recorded comment on the subject, he wrote: "National and racial chauvinism is a vestige of the misanthropic customs characteristic of the period of cannibalism. Anti-Semitism, as an extreme form of racial chauvinism, is the most dangerous vestige of cannibalism." He said that anti-Semitism lands working people "in the jungle," and added with shocking blandness that "under USSR law active anti-Semites are liable to the death penalty."[35] Interestingly, Stalin's letter was not published in the Soviet Union itself until almost six years later, at the height of the Great Terror,[36] when euphemisms like "Trotskyite" and "internationalist" were being used to condemn thousands of Jews.

As the purge fever developed, Kaganovich, who, among his many key posts, was also commissar of transport, shipped hundreds of thousands to their deaths. Like Adolf Eichmann, he oversaw the train schedules and governed the movement of massive human cargos. Kaganovich made sure that even the rail engineers and managers lived in terror, ordering the arrest and execution of many top rail officials and experts.[37] In 1937–38, when millions of Soviet citizens were killed, the innumerable death warrants were short and to the point: "To NKVD, Frunze. You are charged with exterminating 10,000 enemies of the people. Report results by signal. Yezhov [the chief of the NKVD]."[38]

Many of the victims of the main show trials were men of Jewish origin who had been at the forefront of the Revolution and were instrumental in the creation of the first Communist state: Trotsky (in absentia), Zinoviev, Kamenev, Radek, Rykov. Stalin had been toying with Zinoviev and Kamenev for years, first sending them into Siberian exile and then allowing them to return, accepting their recantations and then imprisoning them again. Zinoviev believed his greatest political mistake was abandoning Trotsky in 1927,[39] but neither he nor Kamenev said anything about the anti-Semitism that underlay the attacks on Lenin's three Jewish tribunes.

Many of the prosecution witnesses and agents provocateurs used against these Kremlin Jews were Jews themselves. Some of the main instruments of the Terror were also of Jewish origin: M. I. Gay, who headed a special secret police department; A. A. Slutsky and his deputies Boris Berman and Shpiegelglas, who were in charge of terror and espionage abroad; and NKVD operations chief

Pauker. None of these mass executioners survived the purges. Slutsky was given cyanide in February 1938. Pauker disappeared in March 1937, one of 3,000 secret police officials executed that year,[40] although just three months earlier Pauker had brought great pleasure to Stalin, giving a drunken performance at a Kremlin banquet for the heads of the secret police. A Hungarian Jew, Pauker had performed as a comic actor in Budapest in the years before the Revolution. Now, at the December 20, 1936, banquet, the NKVD operations chief, supported by two other Chekists playing the parts of prison guards, mimicked Zinoviev's last moments, when he was dragged to his execution. Pauker, assuming a heavy Jewish accent, kept raising his hands and crying, "Hear O Israel, our God is the one God." Stalin roared with laughter.[41]

According to accounts of Zinoviev's actual execution, he had collapsed in fear and hysteria, screeching at the top of his high-pitched voice as he was dragged into a killing cell in the Lubyanka cellar, where an NKVD lieutenant shot him in the head.[42]

When the Terror was instigated, Stalin's chief hangman was Yagoda, the Jewish former pharmacist who kept a special chest in his office filled with vials of poison, which he dispensed to his agents whenever the occasion required. Medical assassinations, at which Stalin had become adept, would become a focal point in one of the main purge trials involving Yagoda himself, for Stalin's chief poisoner ended up in the dock along with countless others.

The third round of major trials involved Bolshevik pioneers, a number of Kremlin doctors, and the now humiliated former head of the secret police, a Gothic curtain-raiser for the Doctors' Plot fifteen years later, since all of the accused were implicated in the murders of prominent Soviet figures, and in the Stalin government's presentation of the incredibly complex plot, there were frequent references to the Jewish mastermind Judas-Trotsky.

Two Kremlin doctors were in the dock with Yagoda, charged with poisoning four men: the great Soviet writer Maxim Gorky in 1936; his son, Maxim Peshkov, in May 1934; Yagoda's predecessor as secret police chief, Vyacheslav Menzhinsky, in May 1934; and Politburo minister V. V. Kuibyshev, a strong supporter of Kirov's, in January 1935.

The more famous of the two doctors was Lev Grigorievich Levin, a Jew born in 1870 who had been physician to both Lenin and Stalin and their families since 1920. He served in the Kremlin hospital, on the staff of the secret police medical services.[43] Levin was "not an ideologue" or a conspirator in any way, simply a "devoted physician," according to a prominent Soviet diplomat, Alexander Barmine.[44] But Levin may well have been one of Yagoda's chief poisoners, acting on direct orders from Stalin's notorious secretary Alexander Poskrebyshev.[45] Stalin, since the days of Lenin's illness, had known how to use the Kremlin doctors, and some of them undoubtedly were murderers; others consistently lied in their autopsy reports about the "natural deaths" or "suicides" of various Soviet personalities.

The other prominent Kremlin doctor on trial was Dmitri Dmitriyevich Pletnev, a Russian, born in 1872, who was regarded as Russia's leading heart specialist. He had treated many Soviet leaders, including Stalin's close associate Ordzhonikidze. But it was Dr. Levin who had been one of the three Kremlin doctors who signed the official autopsy report on Ordzhonikidze in 1937, saying he had suffered from angina pectoris and "died of paralysis of the heart." This report was dictated by Stalin himself. Viewing the body, he wondered aloud, in front of the doctors: "What an odd disease. Man lies down to rest, has a heart attack."[46] All those who signed—Levin, I. Khodorovsky, S. Mets, and Commissar for Health G. Kaminsky—would soon be liquidated.[47]

During the trial for his alleged complicity in the killing of Gorky and Kuibyshev, the elderly Dr. Pletnev was exposed as a "rapist." According to a letter of public denunciation from one of his many "victims," which was published in the Soviet press during the sensational show trials, the elderly physician had bitten the victim's breasts and performed other unspeakable acts while treating her: "Be accursed, sadist, practising your foul perversions on my body!" she wrote. "Let terror and sorrow, weeping and anguish be yours as they have been mine."[48] Pletnev, apparently a psychiatric expert as well as a great heart specialist, was said to have been foolish enough to set down in writing his belief that Stalin was a paranoid-megalomaniac. (In 1927 another Kremlin psychologist, Vladimir Bekhterev, was reportedly overheard saying that Stalin was paranoid, whereupon Stalin had him poisoned.[49])

Stalin despised doctors as invaders of the body, and shared with Hitler his contempt for the "Jew science" of psychoanalysis. Solzhenitsyn, in his description of Stalin in *The First Circle*, captured the fear he engendered, and Stalin's phobia about doctors: "Stethoscopes trembled in the hands of the most famous men in Moscow medicine. They never prescribed injections for him. (He himself had ordered all injections stopped.)''[50] As Stalin biographer Robert C. Tucker has observed, Stalin's plot-ridden mind was a textbook example of a paranoid delusional system imposed on an entire society: the paranoid unites real and imagined people, organizations, and encounters in a malevolent "pseudo-community."[51] The apparently eternal phenomenon of anti-Semitism can also be seen as a form of mass paranoia—aggressive destructiveness under the spell of a delusion.[52] Thus Jews and doctors were wedded in Stalin's mind—even when the doctors were Russians or other non-Jews.

In addition to Levin and Pletnev, two other doctors, A. I. Vinogradov of the secret police hospital and Khodorovsky, head of the Kremlin Medical Administration, were implicated; but both died, or were killed under questioning.[53] A fifth doctor, Ignaty Nikolayevich Kazakov, "confessing" his involvement in the medical murder of his patient Menzhinsky, told Stalin's main prosecutor, Andrei Vyshinsky, that the murdered Cheka chief suffered from angina pectoris and bronchial asthma. Dr. Levin had allegedly ordered Kazakov to administer heart stimulants, including strophanthus, and Menzhinsky died soon afterward. Strophanthus given in large doses is a deadly poison, the same drug African Pygmies use to poison their hunting arrows.

Dr. Levin confessed at the trial that he had indeed ordered Kazakov to poison Menzhinsky so that Yagoda could take over the secret police.

The "doctor-poisoners" (a label that would later be used again in 1953) had kept the tubercular Maxim Gorky in an overheated room and then taken him into the freezing cold, repeating this torture until the writer died, the court was told.[54] Prosecutor Vyshinsky said that Levin and Pletnev had given Gorky overdoses of digitalis, a powerful cardiac stimulant and diuretic derived from the purple foxglove.[55] Thus the Soviet people heard on the radio that the beloved Gorky's murderers had been greatly respected doctors, who would now pay the ultimate penalty for their crimes.[56] But the terrorized and degraded doctors were nothing but scapegoats.

Dr. Levin also confessed to purposeful medical negligence in the death of Kuibyshev, who had suffered from a heart condition. Yagoda himself spoke only a few words during his brief testimony: "I gave Levin instructions to bring about the death of Alexei Maximovich Gorky and Kuibyshev, and that's all."[57] If there was any truth to this, then it was certainly on Stalin's orders. Levin was also accused of conspiring with Bukharin in the assassination of Kirov, and of trying to poison Yagoda's successor as secret police chief, N. Yezhov.

Throughout the medical trial, Vyshinsky tried to widen the net, implicating in Gorky's medical murder not only Yagoda but also the brilliant Bukharin, as well as Rykov, Lenin's onetime deputy. And of course, any connection to Trotsky, however tenuous, was ruthlessly exploited. Lev Kamenev, the son of a Jewish doctor and the husband of Trotsky's sister, Olga, was implicated in yet another alleged doctors' conspiracy to kill Stalin in 1935. In a bizarre twist, Kamenev was connected to this plot through his brother, the painter Rosenfeld, whose doctor wife worked at the Kremlin hospital. The painter testified against his famous brother.

A commission of five doctors served as expert witnesses against Levin and Pletnev. Two of them, Professors Shereshevsky and Vladimir N. Vinogradov, both of whom would be arrested in the future Doctors' Plot, said they had no questions for Dr. Levin because, as they put it, "everything is quite clear."[58] Three other future figures in the Doctors' Plot—M. Vovsi, B. B. Kogan, and V. Zelenin—were among the prominent physicians to denounce Levin and Pletnev.

The elderly Dr. Levin was sentenced to death and immediately executed. Dr. Pletnev two years younger and a Russian, was sentenced to only twenty-five years in prison "because of his old age." According to one report, he outlived Stalin by a few months. Journalist Brigitte Gerland, who was in a Gulag camp in Vorkuta from 1948 to 1953, said that Pletnev was the camp doctor and had confirmed Trotsky's thesis that Gorky was poisoned because he wanted to leave the USSR and return to Italy, where he had lived for many years. Gorky and two of his male nurses were all given poisoned sweetmeats, Pletnev said. The doctors who signed Gorky's death certificate, including himself, all knew the true cause of death.[59]

═══

One fact that emerged out of the era of the "cleansing" was that Stalin had become insanely possessed by his hatred of Trotsky, and millions died in order to wipe out his memory. The bodies of thousands of little Trotskys were drenched in paraffin, and left to burn deep into the night in the remote vastnesses of the Soviet Union. Peasants in the Siberian forests near Vorkuta, north of the Arctic

Circle, noticed the strange warmth radiating from certain bogs and ravines, unaware that large numbers of alleged followers of Judas-Trotsky were buried there. Stalin even detested and envied the Talmudist's high (and thus presumably intelligent-looking) forehead: in drawings and paintings and in film portrayals, Stalin's low forehead was always transformed into a high one. Trying to wipe out all traces of his archenemy, Stalin hunted down innumerable followers and associates—real and imagined—and killed the members of Trotsky's family one by one. The vendetta continued long after a Stalin agent finally split open Trotsky's leonine head on August 20, 1940.

During the Great Terror, Stalinist agitators had stirred up anti-Semitic prejudice and brought it to a climax. Ironically, while the world's attention was focused on the anti-Semitic legislation and persecution of Jews in prewar Nazi Germany, Stalin was actually exterminating some 500,000 to 600,000 Jews among the ten million victims of the purges. The ratio of Jewish victims was probably the highest among all the Soviet nationalities.[60]

This genocide continued through the forties, whether the Jews were loyal Communists, Zionists, or totally apolitical. "An entire generation of Zionists has died in Soviet prisons, camps and in exile," wrote Dr. Julius Margolin, who was kept in various concentration camps in the Baltic–White Sea region from 1940 on. He also said that no one in the outside world, not even fellow Zionists, made any effort to save them.[61]

The high number of purged Jews did not go unnoticed in the USSR itself. As an old czarist officer told his cellmate, "At last the dreams of our beloved Czar Nicholas, which he was too soft to carry out, are being fulfilled. The prisons are full of Jews and Bolsheviks."[62]

But Communist propaganda in the 1930s, aided by many of the world's leading thinkers, succeeded in masking these gargantuan crimes against humanity. In the year before the pact with Hitler, Stalin continued to call many of his Jewish victims "agents of the Gestapo." Most of the leading intellectuals of France, England, and the United States remained uncritical even when Stalin turned over to the Nazis German-Jewish Communists who had taken refuge in the socialist fatherland. Hitler said of Stalin: "He is as cruel as a wild beast, but his baseness is human."[63] The two had that in common. They were also the two worst persecutors of the Jewish people in the thousands of years of their troubled history.

CHAPTER 5

Rescue Denied

Stalin and Hitler
Sacrifice the Jews

As Joseph Stalin's purge was winding down, Adolf Hitler was preparing an equally massive terror. Stalin's terror was carried out mostly during peacetime, yet the toll in human life was on a scale rivaling that of Germany's murder of innocents during World War II. Despite everything the two dictators had in common, they were infected with different strains of anti-Semitism; and for every Jewish "Trotskyite" or "saboteur" that Stalin killed, Hitler would exterminate ten, without resorting to euphemisms.

Stalin's sins of both omission and commission during the war cost the lives of at least one million Soviet Jews in addition to the 500,000 to 600,000 who died in prison or were slain as a result of the purges. The Holocaust, in which one-third of world Jewry would be exterminated, also speeded up the process of Jewish national liberation in Palestine. Simultaneously, three million Soviet Jews were placed in increasing jeopardy as Stalin's anti-Semitism grew obsessive in the postwar era.

A year before World War II began, Stalin's chief poisoner and head of the Soviet concentration camps, Henry Yagoda, was executed along with Bukharin, Rykov, Dr. Levin, and the other defendants in the last public purge trials. Jews were still functioning cogs in the machinery of repression, but most had been liquidated along with Stalin's other victims. A fitting commentary was the dynamiting into dust of a granite colossus of Yagoda bestriding the entrance to the White Sea Canal.[1] In a message to Kaganovich and other members of the Politburo, Stalin declared that Yagoda, who had once been the most dreaded man in the Soviet Union other than Stalin himself, had committed a grave crime: he was "four years behind" in the task of "unmasking the Trotskyite-Zinoviev bloc."[2]

In his last days Stalin, like a serial murderer, would revert to similar charges against his current managers of state security for not being "vigilant," while Kremlin doctors had supposedly been conspiring since the war days to destroy the Soviet leadership.

In one of the last acts of the four-year-long Terror, Yagoda's successor, N. Yezhov—"the mailed fist," who killed even more people than had his predecessor and whose brief, blood-soaked reign became known as the *Yezhovschina* (the period of Yezhov)— was executed in his turn. Stalin then appointed vulture-faced Lavrenty Pavlovich Beria, a fellow Caucasian, as the new chief of the Soviet secret organs. The thirty-nine-year-old Beria, a vegetarian, seemed like a gracious liberal compared to his two predecessors. He was selective in his killing, usually measuring out death in batches of thousands instead of tens of thousands. But though he reined in the Great Terror for Stalin, his moderation went only so far. In the belief that a Soviet prison was neither a resort nor a boardinghouse, he made conditions much more severe: for example, in innumerable dank cells the wood planks where prisoners slept were removed, leaving only the floor without mattress or blanket.

Throughout his life rumors persisted that Beria was at least half-Jewish, but this has never been substantiated. He was born on March 29, 1899, in the village of Merkheuli (a few miles inland from the Black Sea), most of whose inhabitants were members of the small, ancient tribe of Mingrelians. Beria's mother came from the village of Tekle, inhabited mainly by Jews and their kin, the Karaites. One author cites a paternal connection to the Jews, linking the name Beriah to the biblical tribe of Ephraim.[3] These rumors would become relevant during the last days of both Stalin and Beria, for the Mingrelians and the Jews would be the two peoples singled out by Stalin for deportation in 1953, and Beria was under attack for the same kind of "negligence" that cost Yagoda his life.

When Beria took over as director of the secret police, with its 1.5 million agents, there were few prominent Jews left in the hierarchies of the Party, the military, or the security organs. Hardly any Russian Bolsheviks were left either—perhaps one in ten. Few tears would be shed for them. One of those Bolsheviks left for Beria to finish off was Béla Kun, a Jew: the cruel tyrant of the 1919 Communist revolution in Hungary and later Stalin's chief of terror in the Crimea. In prison since 1937, Kun (né Kohen) was tortured until he went black in the face, and was finally put out of his misery on November 30, 1939.[4] Stalin also purged all the heads of the Jewish Sections who had worked so hard under his personal guidance to suppress organized Jewish life. Almost all remaining Jewish cultural institutions—including 750 schools where Yiddish was the language of instruction—were shut down between 1934 and 1939.[5] Stalin's chief suppressor of Jewish life and culture, Samuel Agursky, was thrown into a dungeon and accused of being part of a "Jewish Fascist underground," some of whose alleged members, such as Moishe Litvakov and Esther Fromkin, were executed.[6]

But the worst omen for Soviet Jews, and for the Jews of neighboring Poland (who constituted 10 percent of that country's population and nearly half of Warsaw's) came on May 3, 1939. Stalin abruptly fired Foreign Minister Maxim Litvinov, a Jew who had held this post for nearly a decade, and replaced him with the "Aryan" V. M. Molotov. Hitler and Stalin understood each other well, and in the last week of August the Stalin-Hitler pact was signed, including a secret annex dividing up Eastern Europe between them. Germany launched World War II on September 1, and the Soviet forces crossed the frontier sixteen days later to claim Stalin's share of Poland.

One of Stalin's first gifts to the Nazis after the signing of the pact was to turn over some 600 German Communists, most of them Jews, to the Gestapo at Brest-Litovsk in German-occupied Poland, the city where the Bolshevik Jews Trotsky and Yoffe had signed the treaty with Germany ending Russian participation in World War I. One of the Communists handed over to the Nazis was the composer Hans David, who was gassed at Majdanek, like many of the other six hundred.[7] From September 1939 to the following July, two million Jews from the three Baltic states, eastern Poland, Bessarabia, and Bukovina came under Soviet rule. There were many Zionist and religious Jews among them, and these knowledgeable Jews had an immediate impact on some of the three million Soviet Jews with whom they came in contact, raising the consciousness of a community whose Jewish roots had been torn out by the czar's successors. The new Soviet Jews, for their part, soon understood more about the society that swallowed them: Jewish community leaders were shipped to Siberia; and all Zionist, Bund, and Jewish religious organizations and schools were shut down. Soviet Jewish army officers were instructed to win over the local Jewish population. In the Polish town of Glinianyi, for example, a Jewish captain told the assembled community that the Soviet state would protect them: "Jews, your Messiah has finally arrived."[8]

Beginning in February 1940 in the Soviet-occupied zone of Poland, Beria's NKVD arrested and deported about one million Polish refugees, half of them Jews. Many died en route to Siberia, as had happened during World War I, when the czar deported hundreds of thousands of East European Jews to the same location. Arthur Koestler would describe the Stalin-Beria event as "mass-deportations on a scale hitherto unknown in history" and called it the "chief administrative method of Sovietization."[9]

Beria's lists were divided into several categories, including one for "The Jewish National Counterrevolution," which included Zionists and anti-Zionist Bundists alike. Among the arrested Polish Jews were Menachem Begin, a young Zionist leader, and two socialist revolutionaries with an international reputation: Henryk Ehrlich and Viktor Alter, the founders of the Polish Bund, that country's largest Jewish party. Other categories included anarchists, Trotskyites, aristocrats, clergymen, merchants, Social Revolutionaries, "cosmopolitan elements," and, of course, many Communists.

In the spring of 1941, enormous quantities of Russian food and raw materials were shipped in the opposite direction from the human cargo: from Soviet-occupied Poland to German-occupied Poland, as the friendship treaty seemed to be in full flower. The Jews in the Soviet zone were told nothing about the mass atrocities taking place a few miles away.

In the spirit of the Stalin-Hitler pact, all Soviet organs deliberately remained silent about the genocidal slaughtering of the Jews by the Nazi conquerors of Poland between September 1939 and June 1941, when the Nazis invaded the USSR. The silence continued even after Hitler invaded his former partner's empire. Stalin thus paved the way for the extermination of 1.5 million unsuspecting Jews in White Russia and the Ukraine. In July 1941, a month after the invasion, a Wehrmacht report stated:

> The Jews are strikingly ill-informed about our attitude towards
> them and about the treatment Jews are receiving in Germany
> or Warsaw. . . . Although they do not expect to be granted
> equal rights with the Russians under the German
> administration, they do believe that we will let them alone if
> they apply themselves diligently to their work.[10]

In the small town of Kerostia, near the Ukrainian capital of Kiev, the uncle of Soviet Yiddish poet David Hofstein and other elders of the Jewish settlement went out to meet the invading Nazis with the traditional bread and salt.[11]

Consistently, Jewish victims of mass executions were called "Poles" or "Ukrainians" in the Soviet press and radio reports, and there was no hint of the special extermination tasks of the SS troops accompanying the German army. The millions of Soviet troops who attended constant lectures and indoctrination sessions throughout the four years of the war heard not a word. As Soviet historian Roy Medvedev wrote: "Not once . . . was one lesson or one lecture devoted to anti-Semitism, its role in Nazi policy, or the Nazi murder of almost the entire Jewish population of Europe."[12] No step was made to counter Nazi propaganda, which contributed to the high rate of collaboration with the Nazis of the Russians, Ukrainians, and Tatars against their Jewish neighbors. Nazi propaganda, which relentlessly hammered away at the "war of Jewish intrigue," found a receptive population almost everywhere, but especially in the Ukraine. Stalin was in step with the times.

Even two years after the invasion, when the Ukraine was liberated, the Soviets continued to conceal the extent of the Nazi crimes against the Jews. The most infamous example was Babi Yar, the ravine of Kiev where 40,000 to 50,000 Jews were massacred in early 1942. As usual, the Soviets reported atrocities against "Ukrainians" or "Russians," but not Jews. Soviet writer and war correspondent Vasily Grossman reported that the Germans had exterminated the whole Jewish nation in the Ukraine, a million people, but this fact was studiously ignored by the Soviet press.[13] The Soviet policy of officially repressing news of the extermination had tragic consequences for the Jews, which obviously could have been avoided.[14] One excuse that is offered for these "omissions" was that the Soviets did not want to fuel Nazi propaganda linking Bolsheviks and Jews. And Stalin and his government, like the other Allies, did not want the war to be seen as a defense of the Jews. But a more likely reason is that Stalin tacitly approved of Hitler's "Final Solution," and that most of the Jews in the cities, towns, and hamlets of western Russia were purposefully left for the kill.

Hitler, hysterically obsessed by the Jews, was willing to enfeeble Germany's war effort in order to continue murdering Jews to the last moment. But Stalin was still in control of himself and would not be consumed by anti-Semitic hatred until near his end. His Jewish nemesis, Trotsky, had finally been exterminated. But other Jews, important or insignificant, continued to annoy him, sometimes through his children, whom he rarely saw. When Stalin's estranged first-born son, Yakov ("Yasha") Djugashvili, was taken prisoner by the Germans at the beginning of the war in June 1941, Stalin ordered the arrest of Yulia, his Jewish wife, for "plotting" and "to find out what was behind it." Their three-year-old child, Gulia, Stalin's first grandchild, was left parentless.[15] Stalin refused to acknowledge the "disgrace" of Yasha's capture and abandoned him to his fate—suicide in 1942. "The Jewish wife," as Stalin always referred to her, had led his son to surrender, he believed.[16]

Stalin also broke with Svetlana, his only daughter, when she fell in love with a Jewish screenwriter in 1942–43, Alexei Yakovlevich Kapler. Svetlana's naive perceptions of her father changed radically when Stalin sent Kapler to prison. He declared that his daughter's suitor had been "infected" by Zionism and was a "British spy."[17] Stalin slapped Svetlana around, tore up her love letters and photographs of Kapler, and sputtered: "Writer! He can't write decent Russian! She couldn't even find herself a Russian!"[18]

Kapler got off relatively easily given the charges. Another Soviet Jewish writer, Zelik Akselrod, was executed on June 26, 1941, for "manifesting Jewish nationalism" when he protested the closure of a Yiddish newspaper in Vilna, Lithuania.[19] His fate was shared by thousands of other victims of the post–Grand Terror Soviet campaign against "bourgeois nationalists," alleged Trotskyites, and assorted enemies of the people.

In the wake of events in Poland, the fate of the majority of Soviet Jews could be readily foreseen. Yet no special measures were taken to evacuate Jews at a time when the Soviets managed to evacuate massive numbers of "security" prisoners, the populations of whole towns, and 1,364 giant factories from European Russia to safety across the Urals.[20] "The Soviet administration did not display direct action in evacuating the Jews. . . . it openly hampered it," according to historian S. Schwartz.[21]

The able-bodied Jewish men—500,000 of them—were in the Red Army. Of these, 200,000 would die in the fighting. Some 160,000 were awarded medals and orders.[22] About fifty top Soviet generals were Jews.[23] While Soviet anti-Semites claimed that Jews were draft dodgers, taking refuge in remote Tashkent, Jews served in the army at a much higher ratio than that of any other Soviet nationality.[24]

The bloody purges had destroyed most of the Soviet officer corps and left Russia defenseless. When the Germans invaded, the "sublime strategist of all times and nations," as Stalin called himself, stayed at his vacation retreat, refused to take phone calls, and reportedly drank himself into a stupor. After the war he would refer to the rapid Soviet retreats in terms of the ancient Persians: the Parthian or Scythian tactic of "strategic retreat" against the Romans.[25] An interminably long two weeks after the invasion, on July 3, 1941, as the Nazis advanced on Leningrad and Kiev, Stalin uttered his first words to the nation. In slow, calm tones he appealed to "my brothers and sisters," saying that "everything of value" must be shipped to the rear, all rolling stock, every cow and pound of grain.

Meanwhile, Soviet propaganda was successful in convincing American correspondents like Corliss Lamont that a million Jews had been safely evacuated to Uzbekistan. And there may indeed have been half a million Jews or more among the twelve to fifteen million evacuees who qualified as industrial personnel or loyal Communist party members. But the Jewish nation did not qualify as a category that was especially endangered. Although it is an exaggeration to accuse the Soviets of totally abandoning three million Jews, certainly most Jews were left to their own devices against the Nazis; and hundreds of thousands undoubtedly could have been saved had they been warned or helped to flee to the east.[26]

Of five million Jews in the USSR, two million were exterminated by the Nazis. Yet Foreign Minister Molotov's May 1942 diplomatic note on Nazi atrocities did not mention Jews.[27] Throughout the occupied areas, their neighbors, with a few exceptions, looked on either uncaringly or approvingly as death entered every Jewish home.

═══

What was left of organized Soviet Jewish life had been destroyed by Stalin at the end of the purges, but with the outbreak of the war it became immediately apparent that a new body was needed to harness Jewish energies for the Soviet war effort, and to help camouflage the Soviet abandonment of the Jews, as well. In a way, the organization which came into being in 1942 as the Jewish Anti-Fascist Committee (JAC) was a new form of the postrevolutionary YEVKOM and the Yevsekztia, with the aim of tightening control over all Soviet Jews. But the JAC's most important task was to help push the Soviet propaganda effort abroad for the opening of a second front, and to appeal to world Jewry to aid the USSR against the common enemy. At the same time, the JAC was ordered to disseminate news about the atrocities against the Jews to foreign media, while blocking out and covering up the news on the home front.

The JAC, whose officers and activists were the most prominent Jewish Communist artists and officials in the USSR, would be decapitated by Stalin in 1948, but its ghost would figure prominently in the 1952–53 murders of the Jewish intellectual elite, the so-called Crimea Affair, and the Doctors' Plot, as well. Among the JAC's leading figures were its chairman, the great actor-director Solomon Mikhoels, who was made the unofficial "head of Soviet Jewry"; the well-known Yiddish poet Itzik Solomonovich Feffer, a Stalinist, JAC deputy chairman, and secret police functionary; the eminent Yiddish poet Peretz Markish; Deputy Foreign Minister Solomon Lozovsky; Molotov's wife, Paulina Zhemchuzina; famed writer-journalist Ilya Ehrenburg; film director Sergei Eisenstein; Lieutenant General Jacob "Yankel" Kreiser, a hero of the defense of Moscow; violinist David Oistrakh; Lena Shtern, the most honored Soviet woman scientist; Kremlin Hospital senior physician Miron Vovsi, Mikhoels's cousin and head of the Red Army's Medical Division; and Dr. Boris A. Shimelovich, head of the Botkin Hospital, one of the world's largest. Most of them would later be included in the vast Jewish-Zionist-American-British "conspiracy" that Stalin would eventually "reveal" to the world.

Khrushchev said that the JAC may have been Stalin's idea. Given the dictator's past involvement in "Jewish affairs" with Samuel Agursky, this may indeed have been the case. But Khrushchev also speculated that the JAC might have been Molotov's creation, because Paulina, the foreign minister's wife and a government minister in her own right, was prominent in the JAC.[28] Others said it was Beria's suggestion. But anything that touched on international politics had to be approved by Stalin himself; and it would have been entirely out of character for Molotov to initiate such a bold step without prior clearance "from above."

Stalin may have taken the idea from proposals made by the Polish Jews Henryk Ehrlich and Viktor Alter, who were among the most eminent leaders of the international socialist movement. Both these men would be executed on Stalin's personal orders, like Mikhoels in 1948 and other JAC leaders in 1952. These slayings took on a different coloring than Stalin's murders of innumerable other prominent Jews and gentiles before the war: the later killings were more in the spirit of Hitler's extermination of Jews as Jews, and were a portent of Stalin's plans for most, if not all, of Soviet Jewry.

Even in the midst of the carnage of war, the Soviets' arrest of Ehrlich and Alter was considered a story of international importance, for Ehrlich had been a member of the Petrograd Soviet in 1917, and both men were former leaders of the Comintern, as well as founders of the strongest and largest Jewish party in Poland, the Bund. Ehrlich and Alter forged strong ties with American, French, and English trade unions: David Dubinsky, head of the International Ladies Garment Workers Union, was a close friend and supporter, for example. But they incurred the wrath of the leader of the world's "progressive forces" because they were Jews and Bundists, and they had dared to criticize the show trials.

Shortly after falling into Soviet hands in September 1939, the two men were thrown into Moscow's huge Butyrka prison and personally interrogated by Beria. But after Hitler betrayed his partner, the imprisoned Bundists expressed their wish to help the Soviets in the common struggle against the Nazis. The opportunity came in September 1941, when the two were freed during the general amnesty for Polish prisoners and allowed to go to Kuibyshev, where the Soviet government had moved when Moscow was threatened. Some of the other freed Polish Jews, like Begin, went to Palestine—and therefore survived.[29]

Because of the two leaders' ties with the American trade unions, Beria approved in principle a suggestion that they organize a Soviet-based Jewish anti-Hitler committee. Ehrlich would be the president, Alter the secretary, and Mikhoels would be a member of the committee's presidium and chief representative of Soviet Jews.[30] The two Polish Jews suggested that representatives of the Allies and of the Jews of occupied countries be included in the committee, as well. They met with Mikhoels, and poets Feffer and Markish—the three Soviet Jews who would head the JAC once it had been stripped of the international elements suggested by the Polish Jewish leaders.[31] After discussing drafts of their proposal with Beria in his capacities as the commissar of the interior and head of the security police, Ehrlich and Alter then addressed themselves to Stalin himself. It was not an act of temerity on their part; Beria had told them that only Stalin could make the final decisions.[32]

Stalin was annoyed by the presence in Kuibyshev of these two former leaders of the Second International, and was not kindly disposed when their letter was put among his daily work papers. He wrote two words across their written plea: *Rasstrieliat oboikh*, "Let them both be shot."[33]

On December 4, 1941, three months after they had been released from Soviet prison during the "Polish amnesty," Ehrlich and Alter got a phone call at the desk of the Grand Hotel from a secret police official named Khazanovich, a Jew, summoning them to an urgent meeting after midnight. "Lavrenty Pavlovich Beria wants to see you and Ehrlich immediately," Khazanovich told Alter. "He has received from Moscow an answer to the letter you sent to Yosef Vissarionovich."[34] This was a typical NKVD trick, which was constantly replayed, as in the Mikhoels case six years later. Since all government offices were buzzing after midnight, in keeping with Stalin's own practice of working at night, their suspicion was not aroused by the hour of the rendezvous; and the two Polish Jewish leaders were used to meetings with Beria and his officials. But they never returned from this encounter. They probably were shot that night—certainly no later than January 1942,[35] though their execution would not be officially acknowledged until over a year later.

Their disappearance set off a storm among leftist and socialist friends of the Polish Bund and eminent figures around the world, including Clement Attlee, Albert Einstein, and Reinhold Niebuhr.[36] The Polish ambassador to the USSR, Professor Stanislav Kot, in a conversation with Andrei Vyshinsky, Molotov's deputy foreign minister, was one of many who formally protested against the imprisonment of the Bund leaders. Kot said it was imperative to release them, warning: "Just think what a hullabaloo the American Jewish organizations will raise over these arrests." Vyshinsky, who as prosecutor of the purge trials had been the voice of doom for numerous other revolutionary leaders, told Kot coldly, "It has been established that they were working on behalf of Germany." Kot, astonished, responded: "That is quite incredible! Jews holding such important positions, yet you say they are German agents!" Vyshinsky's answer was simple: "And yet Trotsky turned out to be a German agent."[37]

In the fall of 1942, long after Alter and Ehrlich had been secretly executed, Stalin told visiting Wendell Wilkie that their case would be "resolved in a satisfactory manner."[38] The execution of the two men was not admitted by the Soviets until February 1943, when

Foreign Minister Molotov sent a message to American Federation
of Labor leader William Green, through Ambassador Litvinov in
Washington, saying they had been executed in December 1942 as
"agents working for German interests." Molotov asserted that
Ehrlich and Alter had appealed to Soviet troops to conclude an
immediate peace with the Nazis.[39] It was yet another example of
the campaign started in 1936 to link Jews of the Soviet sphere with
the Nazis. The furor over Ehrlich and Alter would not die down
until the JAC came into being, and its officials—with the help of
American Jewish leaders—smothered the issue for good.

The JAC and all the various other Soviet anti-Fascist commit-
tees—for women, scientists, and other groupings—were directly
under the supervision of SOVINFORMBURO, whose deputy chief
was Lozovsky, the old Bolshevik Jew who was also the chief Soviet
spokesman during the war. Like his former boss, Litvinov,
Lozovsky was a sophisticated, Western-influenced man, popular
with the foreign correspondents in Moscow. But he was subservient to the drunken Alexander Sergeyevich Shcherbakov, a towering fat man who was the most xenophobic and anti-Semitic
member of the Politburo other than Stalin himself. Shcherbakov
had been one of the chief purgers in the 1930s, and Khrushchev
would recall him as "a poisonous snake."[40] The coarse, treacherous
official was a Stalin favorite, and many saw him as a leading con-
tender to succeed the Soviet dictator. But he died in May 1945, at
the age of forty-four. In 1953 Stalin would blame the Jews for his
"medical murder," along with the 1948 death of Shcherbakov's
brother-in-law, Andrei Zhdanov, who was once Stalin's second in
command, just as Kirov had been.

The JAC's most eloquent spokesman, Ilya Ehrenburg, like
everyone else loathed Shcherbakov. Ehrenburg, born in Kiev in
1891, had become the USSR's leading publicist in the thirties, but
never truly identified with his Jewishness until the war, when he
stirred his country with anti-German polemics. Though he knew he
was a Jew, he thought it essential to Sovietize the Jews, believing
that assimilation was the only answer. However, Shcherbakov's
blatant anti-Semitism unsettled Ehrenburg, as did his attacks on
the intelligentsia. Like Stalin, Shcherbakov liked to torment what
he called "frightened little intellectuals," such as Ehrenburg.[41]

Intellectuals, Jews, and everyone else had reason to be frightened; anyone who had lived through the Great Terror and then
associated himself with such an enterprise as the JAC had to as-

sume that it was implicitly dangerous, since such a committee by its nature might foster close contacts with foreigners. Hundreds of thousands of Soviet citizens had recently been imprisoned or executed because a relative lived abroad, or because they had visited Europe in the 1920s, or had fought in the Spanish Civil War.

Once the JAC was finally set up, an artist became its guiding spirit: Solomon Mikhoels, the creator of the Moscow Jewish Theater, where Marc Chagall had painted sets, murals, and the great actor-director's expressive face. But Mikhoels was much more than a fine performer and theatrical director. The Communists held that it was the duty of the creative intelligentsia to bring the word to the people, to act as instruments of Party and state policy. Many Soviet artists accepted the need to serve the state, cognizant of the fact that artists have always had a special calling. Stalin only took this to its logical conclusion; and though he never met Mikhoels personally, he placed on the imaginary throne of Soviet Jewry this eminent actor whose Yiddish King Lear and other roles had won international critical acclaim.

Mikhoels was born as Solomon Mikhailovich Vovsi on March 16, 1890, in Dvinsk, Latvia. He was one of nine brothers whose Orthodox Jewish family spoke Hebrew as well as Yiddish and proudly traced their lineage to Vophsi, mentioned in the Bible (Nm. 13:14) as the father of one of the twelve spies representing the Tribes of Israel whom Moses sent, according to the commandment of the Lord, to reconnoiter the Promised Land. Their report frightened the Jews of the Exodus, who were too scarred by enslavement to undertake the tasks of a free nation and therefore had to die out—the Generation of the Desert. It was somehow appropriate that Solomon Vovsi Mikhoels would not only represent the millions of Jews in the Soviet desert, but also would come to symbolize the fate of most Soviet Jews: he would be murdered, like millions of others. Mikhoels's close relative, Dr. Miron Vovsi, would become the main Jewish culprit in Stalin's script for the Doctors' Plot.

For six years from Mikhoels's appointment as JAC chairman in 1942, Soviet Jewry increasingly looked upon the beloved actor as not only a great artist but also their spokesman and intermediary with the Soviet power structure. Mikhoels grew to relish his role: "An actor could become a tribune," he once told a friend.[42]

The JAC's deputy chairman, poet Itzik Solomonovich Feffer, was a very different kind of Soviet Jew, much more in the tradition of those who had helped shape totalitarian terrorism. Feffer, born in Kiev in 1900 and a Party member from age nineteen, was a devoted Communist, a Red Army colonel, and an operative of "the organs." In his poem "I am a Jew," he declared that he drank "happiness from Stalin's cup" and praised Kaganovich, "Stalin's friend." Though Feffer boasted of his rabbinic ancestry, his poems jeered at Judaism, while celebrating the slave-labor society. He immortalized the show trials of "traitors, spies and assassins. . . . we shoot you down like mad dogs." He cursed the names of the executed Jewish general Yakir and Chief of Staff Tukhachevsky, "Trotskyist scum. . . . Death to the assassins, even today!"[43] There is no doubt now why Beria chose him as second in command at the JAC—to watch everyone else, and denounce them at the appropriate moment.

Other than Ehrenburg, the most famous of the many Jewish writers associated with the JAC was Peretz Markish, a brilliant poet who identified deeply and passionately with his people. But in some ways Markish was a typical Soviet intellectual, coldly indifferent to the murder of millions in the name of "historical necessity" or the class struggle even while feeling tormented by the executions of individuals he knew, his artistic colleagues. Markish, born in 1895 in the Pale of Settlement, received a traditional Jewish education among poor, pious Jews who dreamed that the Messiah would come to rescue them. The strikingly handsome "Adonis of the Yiddish world" headed the Jewish section of the powerful Soviet Writers' Union in 1934, and was a winner of the Order of Lenin. As one of the leaders of the JAC, he wrote poems celebrating Jewish resistance to the Nazis. He always hated Feffer, who was a very minor poet in comparison, and regarded him as an intriguer.[44] They would die as differently as they lived, though both were executed together, in the same dungeon with other JAC members seven years after the war.

In mid-1943, a few months after the Soviet Jewish Anti-Fascist Committee was formed, Mikhoels and Feffer were dispatched on a seven-month-long mission to the United States, partially in order to offset the damage caused by the furor over the Ehrlich-Alter affair. It was a pivotal event in the JAC's history. Some historians have written that the trip had Stalin's "personal blessings" at a time when only a tiny number of Soviet diplomats, propagandists like Ehrenburg, and NKVD operatives were allowed out of the USSR.[45] But reports that Stalin himself came to bid Mikhoels and Feffer farewell were untrue.[46] Markish was furious that Feffer had been chosen over him to accompany Mikhoels, and suspected that "the organs" were behind the decision.[47]

They arrived in July 1943 and soon became the toast of leftist America. They were feted by the Soviet embassy, by American Communists like black singer Paul Robeson, by fellow travelers like Lillian Hellman, by establishment Zionists like Rabbi Stephen Wise and Nahum Goldmann, by Albert Einstein and Chaim Weizmann, and by old friends like Marc Chagall. Writer Howard Fast, long a Stalin supporter, recalled meeting Feffer:

> He won our hearts. A tall, handsome man wearing the uniform of a colonel in the Red Army, he appeared to be a symbol of what the Soviet Union had pledged in the way of wiping anti-Semitism out of Russia; for Feffer was a Jew, a beloved poet in the Soviet Union, an army officer, and a man who in every word he spoke breathed the love of his fatherland.[48]

While a few American Jewish anti-Communist socialists boycotted the mission, the more typical reaction was that of the World Jewish Congress and its co-founder, Nahum Goldmann. Goldmann and the WJC were instrumental in turning the Mikhoels-Feffer mission into a success.[49] According to documents in the Zionist Archives in Jerusalem, Goldmann, in his frequent talks with State Department officials, took an undeviatingly pro-Stalinist stand. He insisted, for example, on the necessity of suppressing the Ehrlich-Alter affair. He told Loy Henderson, head of the State Department's Russian desk, that "our condition" for the Mikhoels-Feffer visit was that "the Alter-Ehrlich murders be kept off the agenda."[50] Ironically, when Mikhoels and Feffer met the same fate as Alter and Ehrlich a few years later—even though the wartime pro-Stalinism had been replaced by Cold War politics—the murders of Soviet Jewish leaders would not be any higher up on the agendas of world Jewish leaders like Nahum Goldmann.

Rabbi Stephen Wise, the proud leader of American Jewry who headed an array of Zionist and Jewish organizations, denounced all the critics of the Mikhoels-Feffer mission, calling them "Jewish Trotskyites."[51] By thus libeling all Jews who protested against the execution of Ehrlich and Alter, Wise acted in the spirit of those who wished not only to cover up the murder of the Polish Bund leaders, but also to portray Jews as traitors who helped the Nazis.

Mikhoels tried to sidestep questions about Ehrlich and Alter, but never reverted to such Stalinist language as Wise's—and of course, he was not an American rabbi whose family lived in the safety of a great democracy, but a highly vulnerable Soviet Jew. Mikhoels did appear uncomfortable whenever he was faced with inquiries about the fate of the two Polish Jewish leaders. He said that among the Jewish refugees in Russia, "there were certain individuals who, by their attitude, helped Nazism."[52]

Feffer, on the other hand, appeared self-confident and in total possession of the truth in assuring his audiences that Ehrlich and Alter were really Nazis, who deserved nothing less than what they got. He was also diligent in the other major cover-up behind the Mikhoels-Feffer mission, presenting "personal testimony" that the Soviet government had saved "huge masses" of Jews from Nazi extermination. American Jews believed him and the Communist-front organizations which helped put on the mass meetings, such as a July 8, 1943, rally of 45,000 at the Polo Grounds in New York. FBI informants told the State Department that the mission was "one of the greatest propaganda successes for the Soviet Union" and that the applause the Soviets were winning on the Jewish question would enhance "recognition of Communist leadership on many other questions."[53]

Mikhoels performed especially brilliantly, attracting huge audiences and raising large sums for the hard-pressed Russian people.[54] Both he and Feffer, wearing his uniform as a Red Army colonel, made a deep impression on the important people they met: Chaim Weizmann, the Zionist leader who had been cut off from his fellow Russian Jews for over twenty-five years, termed his three-hour talk with them a great privilege and an emotionally moving experience. The future first president of Israel said that though both men were cautious and highly noncommittal, they showed interest in the Zionist cause—damning praise in this case.[55]

Mikhoels did love Zion. He would tell his friend Abraham Sutskever, the poet and partisan hero, that "when I flew to America in July 1943, I kissed the air when we passed over Palestine."[56] The actor knew very well that if such a statement reached the wrong ears, he could be killed or disappear in the Gulag.

At the midpoint of the Mikhoels-Feffer trip, in September 1943, the two JAC leaders reached an aid agreement with officials of the American Jewish Joint Distribution Committee, popularly known as "the Joint." The Joint had had a long and often controversial relationship with Soviet Russia, and reference to its previous activities is necessary in understanding the part it came to play in the hatching of Stalin's last plot. The organization's leadership, representing the American Jewish aristocrats of German origin, could not have imagined that ten years after the Mikhoels-Feffer mission the Joint would be accused of being a spy front that helped Mikhoels and other members of the JAC in the interrelated Crimea Affair and the Doctors' Plot.

The Joint, which had come into being three years before the Russian Revolution, was founded by extremely wealthy and highly assimilated American Jews such as the Warburgs, Schiffs, Kuhns, Loebs, Lehmans, and Marshalls. All were anti-Zionist, especially the biggest individual donor, Julius Rosenwald.[57] They were not interested in furthering the nationalist goals of Zionism, and therefore spent more money on aiding Jewish settlement in Russia than in Palestine—some $28 million between 1917 and 1938 (equivalent to about $300 million in today's terms).[58] The Joint aided tens of thousands of deported Jews and Jewish POWs in Siberia in 1919–20, helped fight the cholera epidemic during the civil war, and built dispensaries, hospitals, and maternity homes. In 1924, at a time when a few hundred Russian-born Jews had organized themselves into kibbutzim to work the soil of Palestine, the Soviets set up KOMZET, a commission for the settlement of Jews on the land, primarily in the Crimea and the Ukraine. The Joint helped fund these farm projects in Russia.

In 1934 the Joint became involved in a Stalin-approved plan to make Birobidzhan in the remote Soviet Far East a Jewish Autonomous Province. The Soviets wished to resettle many thousands of Jews in the huge, barren territory on the borders of Mongolia and Japan-occupied Manchuria, to industrialize the sparsely populated region, and to discourage Japanese imperial ambitions. Yiddish was to be the official language of the province; and Soviet propaganda hailed Birobidzhan as the true promised land, a Bolshevik counterweight to the Zionist-Jewish national home in Palestine. But Birobidzhan never attracted more than a handful of Jews; only 23,000 remained there by 1941, and they were from the least successful sector of Russian Jewry. The Joint became involved in the Birobidzhan scheme in the belief that Russia was the only European country prepared to take Jews in from prewar Poland, Germany, and other countries that did not want their Jews. But those Soviet officials who favored mass Jewish immigration into the USSR were all to fall victim to the Great Terror.

The purges also reduced the Joint's staff in the USSR, from 3,000 to 100, and it became unthinkable for a foreign organization to continue working in the Soviet Union much longer. The connection between the Joint and the USSR was broken off completely in 1938. Two years later, at the time of Ehrlich and Alter's arrest, the Soviets tortured another prominent Polish refugee, Dr. Yehoshua Gottlieb, journalist and former member of the Polish Parliament, and alleged that he was part of a conspiracy orchestrated by the Joint. He was accused of "Zionist espionage" against the USSR on personal instructions of Chaim Weizmann and David Ben-Gurion. Gottlieb died in a Pinsk prison after an uninterrupted interrogation of several days.[59]

Despite such experiences and the obvious dangers of philanthropic work in the USSR, Joint executives tried to pry open the door once again in the wake of the Nazi invasion, setting up a nonsectarian committee to send medicine and medical equipment to the USSR.[60] The Jewish agricultural colonies in the Ukraine and Crimea which the JDC had helped finance were totally destroyed by the Nazis, and hundreds of thousands of Jewish refugees faced a desperate plight.[61] During their mission abroad in 1943, Mikhoels and Feffer renewed the Soviet Union's contacts with the Joint, appealing for its aid. It is not clear to this day who suggested this initiative. But given what we now know about Stalin's methods, one can almost hear the little clicks in his brain: the Joint, Crimea, spies, doctors, Mikhoels, Markish, Lozovsky—the Jews. . . . These contacts would be the basis for Stalin's inclusion of the Joint in what he would perceive as the interconnected great conspiracies of 1952–53. In the end, no effort was made by the Soviets to rebuild the Jewish settlements destroyed by the Nazis, even one that proudly carried the name Stalindor.[62]

The JAC's secretary, Shakno Epshtein, in writing about the committee's achievements, cited especially the "successful outcome of the negotiations of Comrades Mikhoels and Feffer with the 'Joint,' the latter having begun to put into effort its decision to help through the Red Cross the evacuated population regardless of nationality." In fact, the Joint had clashed with Mikhoels and Feffer over how to dispense refugee relief, though it eventually gave in to their demands. Some of the American Jewish groups affiliated with the well-endowed Joint asked that its funds be used to help Jewish refugees exclusively, but the two JAC envoys turned them down because they knew that the Soviet leadership would never agree to such "particularistic" treatment. Mikhoels and Feffer prevailed; the Joint bent over backward to reopen the Soviet door, not suspecting the depth of Stalin's enmity.[63]

The Jewish Anti-Fascist Committee turned into a major enterprise by mid-1943, working out of a two-story building on Moscow's Kropotkin Street, where it moved after the Nazis were pushed back and the government had returned to the Soviet capital. Its staff of eighty included about forty Yiddish writers, whose various activities included the publishing of a newspaper: a Yiddish version of *Pravda* called *Einikeyt* (Unity). Its foremost duty was to enlighten "the Jewish popular masses in all countries about the great historical accomplishments" of the Soviet era, according to an article describing the committee's activities by Epshtein, the group's publicist.[64]

In addition to the newspaper, the members of the Soviet Jewish organization wrote and staged plays; produced four weekly radio broadcasts—aimed especially at the United States and England; published works chronicling active Jewish resistance of the Nazis (such as Markish's "For the People and the Fatherland"); searched for missing persons, setting up information centers to help relatives of Nazi camp inmates; and gathered material for what came to be called *The Black Book*, a massive contemporary journalistic effort to capture the horrifying details of the extermination of 1.5 million Soviet Jews.

Epshtein in his press releases and articles did not refer to Holocaust-connected work, or to the "foreign" role of the JAC. He skirted the raising of funds for the Soviet war effort and the activating of world Jewry to help the Soviet cause by lobbying for the immediate opening of the second front.

Both Ilya Ehrenburg and fellow JAC member David Zaslavsky, an establishment Soviet journalist, constantly claimed in their famous news reports that the Jews were being saved by the Russians and Ukrainians. These writers were definitely instructed to refrain from writing about the extermination of the Jews, and they followed orders faithfully. Only committee member Vasily Grossman alluded to the local peoples' hostility to the Jews in a novel.[65] There were two exceptions to the rule of silence: *Einikeyt* did describe the extermination of the Vilna Jews and the Kiev Jews.[66] But the news came far too late to make a difference; the Nazis had been pushed back by then, and almost all the Jews in the areas they occupied had been exterminated. In the last months of the war,

Zaslavsky, who made his name in *Pravda* and *Izvestia*, wrote in the JAC newspaper that "the Red Army saved the Jewish people at the most critical hour of its history."[67] Another JAC activist, the Yiddish poet David Bergelson, tried "persistently to prove that the Soviet authorities did all they could in order to save the Jews from annihilation."[68] The JAC did what it could to prevent the truth from emerging—that Stalin had helped his erstwhile partner by acquiescing in the extermination of the Jews.

One critically important development came out of the JAC: Soviet Jews, for the first time, could speak of "the Jewish nation," which none of the Allies yet recognized. Bergelson, in an article published in March 1944, wrote about the struggle of "the Jewish people" against Hitler's genocide machine. He said that hundreds of thousands of Jews of many countries "have fought and are fighting also for the honor of the Jewish people, in order to safeguard its future as a people."[69] Such a development could only heighten Stalin's suspicions about the Jews, and challenge the cornerstone of his faith: his 1913 essay denying that the Jews were a nation.

Mikhoels and Feffer wound up their seven-month mission in February 1944, and upon their return Mikhoels reported directly to Molotov to brief him about their accomplishments.[70] He presented Molotov with a mink coat for Stalin, a gift of American furriers, who had also given similar coats to Mikhoels and Feffer. It was at this meeting that Mikhoels raised the question of the Joint aiding the resettlement of Jews in the Crimea. But it is not clear whether the question of a Jewish autonomous republic in the Crimea was discussed within the Jewish Anti- Fascist Committee at this time, or after the deportation of the Tatars from the Crimea in May 1944, or only after the war.

What is known is that Mikhoels wished to expand the activities of the JAC, and probably went beyond the committee's mandate by approaching Soviet officials about individual Jews or by addressing cultural and national issues.[71] For example, when the Red Army liberated the Crimea, Mikhoels tried to intervene in the deportation of the Karaites, a sect which, like the Samaritans, split from the Jewish people some 2,000 years ago.[72] The Crimean Karaites were ethnic Tatars.

Many of the Crimean Tatars had collaborated with the Germans. But the decision by Stalin and the Politburo to deport the entire nation of over 200,000 was probably reached because the Soviet government regarded the Tatars as an unreliable Turk-related ethnic group, and they wished to transform the Crimean peninsula into a strategic base for Soviet expansionism.[73] Mikhoels was apparently upset by his failure to persuade government officials not to deport the Karaites.

But the JAC was still in good standing, as evidenced by the committee's mass rally in early March 1944 in the Kremlin's Trade Union Hall of Columns, where the show trials had taken place. Over 3,000 people crammed the room to hear Mikhoels, Feffer, Ehrenburg, and others talk about Babi Yar and the extermination of millions of Jews. Ehrenburg, a brilliant survivor in the tradition of the great Jewish historian of Roman times, Flavius Josephus (who joined the enemy rather than be exterminated, and wrote his history of the Jewish war), warned the audience obliquely of "contamination" from "microbes of anti-Semitism."[74] He had seen close-up the results of the Nazis' handiwork, and knew very well—though he did not and could not report it—that the local Russian, Ukrainian, and Tatar populations either abetted the massacres of the Jews or ignored them. He could foresee the results of a rejuvenated Russian hatred of the Jews, and the prospect frightened him. He knew of the continuing deportations of whole peoples by his patron, Stalin, and was made aware by the Holocaust that his own people were among the most vulnerable in the Soviet museum of nationalities.

The deportation of nations was the logical extension of the Marxist-Leninist position on the national question. In Stalin's preface to his essay on nationalities, he had said that "the high mission" of socialism was to resist nationalism, and he called for "particular firmness," especially around the border regions.[75] Stalin was always worried about the border areas, where the Jews were concentrated. It was a Pan-Slavic reflex reaction. Dostoevsky, who had said that the Jews were intent on the "conquest of the world," warned about the Jewish presence in border regions.[76] The last Romanov czar and his family had deported hundreds of thousands of Jews from the border areas to the distant Siberian wilderness. Now, a quarter of a century later, Stalin also acted against several "border peoples."

In the summer of 1940, before the Nazi-Soviet war, Stalin had ordered the deportations of about one million refugees from Poland, most of them Jews. A large number of Jews along the border of the Ukraine were deported to the Urals and Siberia soon after the Nazi invasion, under Khrushchev's direction, while the highly vulnerable mass of Jews in and around Kiev were left to be slaughtered.[77]

Although Stalin matched or bettered Hitler in liquidating various categories of people, this was not the case in terms of genocide against nations. Hitler exterminated between five million and six million members of the Jewish nation, three million Poles, hundreds of thousands of Gypsies. In the deportations of eight nations by Stalin during the war years, "only" one million deportees died.[78] Both dictators used cattle cars and cattle trucks to move their human cargos. Of the nearly one million Polish Jews sent to the Urals and Siberia—a journey of four to six weeks under terrible conditions—between one-fifth and one-third perished, according to a Joint Distribution Committee bulletin in June 1943.[79]

The Soviet deportation figures after the Polish Jews were shipped to the east may not have been as impressive as the Nazi statistics, but they were staggering nevertheless: 382,000 Volga Germans in August–September 1941; 75,000 Karachai in October–November 1943; 134,000 Kalmyks in December 1943; 42,000 Balkars, 407,000 Chechens, and 92,000 Ingushi in February 1944; 202,000 Crimean Tatars in June 1944; 200,000 Meskhetians in 1944; 200,000 Greeks in 1949.[80] The deracinated Chechens of the Caucasus, a traditional enemy of their Ossetian neighbors, died in great numbers. They were a forest people transported to the sandy steppe in Kazakhstan or to Siberian wastelands, where they could not sink new roots; and they died in droves. One of the men Stalin reportedly charged with deporting the Chechens was an Ossetian Colonel, G. A. Tokaev, who led military and NKVD secret police units into deportation areas a few weeks before the operation.[81] It was a military undertaking, carried out mainly by motorized infantry. Deportees were allowed to take 50 to 100 kilograms of property and food.[82]

In addition to the eight nationalities, there were massive deportations of Kurds, Gypsies, Koreans, Finns, Russified Bulgarians, Estonians, and others.[83] Thousands were sent to prison camps, or perished during the three to four weeks it took to reach Kazakhstan. Exiled nations soon formed half of Kazakhstan's population. Others were sent much further, to Birobidzhan or northeast Siberia. Numbers of Jews were always among the new arrivals in these areas.

Voroshilov supervised the Crimean deportations in May–June

1944, a month after the German withdrawal, apparently with a great deal of brutality and bloodshed.[84] Some of these deportees were given five to fifteen minutes to collect their things before they were taken away; others were given as many as twelve hours. Many were told to leave their homes with only the bare essentials, to form up in columns, and to march to the nearest rail stations. Others were transported to rail stations in trucks, where they were made to sit cross-legged, like prisoners. The special troops of Beria's secret police were put on alert and only informed hours before the secret operation to deport all the Tatars. The Chekists were told that the Muslim Tatars were being punished "for their collaboration with the enemy and for planning to hand over the Crimea to Turkey as an autonomous province," according to a former secret police official.[85] Jews, eight years later, would be charged in secret with a similar separatist conspiracy.

Apart from the publication of the deportation decrees of the Chechens and Ingushi and the Crimean Tatars in *Izvestia* on June 26, 1946, no mention was made of these deportations anywhere in the USSR until after 1956.[86]

The Volga Germans and other nationalities—"divisionists and spies"—were deported to Kazakhstan and Kirgizia.[87] The Kalmyks, a Mongol people who followed the Buddhist religion, were deported from the Volga region where they had lived for two centuries. Most of them perished along the Yenisei River in Siberia.[88]

Every Soviet people, including the Jews, knew that Stalin could reactivate the deportation apparatus at any time. After the war two million displaced Soviets, including soldiers who had fought in Andrei Vlasov's collaborationist army, were handed over to Stalin by Anthony Eden. They were herded into freight and cattle cars and sent to oblivion in the Gulag.[89] Once there, the inmates were shuffled between the huge units of the prison and labor camp complex. Beria's Gulag included a special transportation department with elaborate timetables, special bases, and supply depots. Beria himself had gained experience in such mass transport when he and Kaganovich deported the whole tribe of Kuban Cossacks from the sunny Caucasus to Siberia in the early 1930s.[90] Families were automatically separated, with husbands, wives, and children placed in often distant camps.

Both Stalin and Hitler showed the world what modern transportation could achieve. Transporting millions of people meant organizing a massive system employing top engineers, scheduling

experts, construction specialists and security personnel. Once they
built the system, it could almost run by itself. It could be put into
operation at any time, against any people—as long as they were
less numerous than the Ukrainians.

The obscure Ossetians were among the big winners in the deportations, with Stalin giving them most of Ingushetia, the land of the
Ingush people. Four of the eight nations Stalin uprooted and deported had been the Ossetians' neighbors—Chechens, Ingushi,
Karachai, and Balkars—strengthening the suggestions that Stalin
was at least part Ossetian. In general, Georgia was inordinately
favored when the lands of the deported nations were parcelled out.
Although these events were not reported in the Soviet media,
people heard about them by word of mouth, and it was possible to
read between the lines when the Central Committee issued a decree on February 10, 1948, criticizing the Chechens and Ingushi for
their behavior in the 1917 Revolution while heaping praise on the
Ossetians and Georgians.[91]

After the war Greek Soviet citizens would be accorded the same
treatment as Soviet Turks. Just as the Tatars had been accused of
plotting to detach the Crimea from the USSR and join it to Turkey,
in 1949, when 200,000 Greeks were deported, they were charged
with a nationalist plot to detach a large part of the Ukraine to
create a Greater Greek Republic.[92] Three years later the Jews
along the border areas would face similar fantastic charges, and
less than a year after that all Soviet Jews would be threatened with
this weapon of mass terror.

═══

In the postwar period the Russian people, who suffered terrible
losses in their struggle against the Nazis, appeared indifferent to
the sufferings of Jews in the Holocaust, or, for that matter, to the
terrible wartime toll of Poles or Yugoslavs. Hitler's treatment of
the Jews won sympathy for the Jewish people in the West, but in
Poland and Russia, Jews returning to their homes were beaten and
scores were killed. Stalin's own anti-Semitic disease appeared to
worsen. As Khrushchev put it: "Suddenly after the war, Stalin was
seized by a fit of anti-Semitism."[93] At Yalta in 1945 Stalin told FDR
that Jews were "profiteers and parasites."[94]

Anti-Semitism in the postwar era became "the militant official
ideology, although this was concealed in every way possible,"
Stalin's daughter wrote.[95] A quota system was revived in universi-

ties and throughout the bureaucracy. Stalin not only supported the new wave of anti-Semitism, but "he even propagated a good deal of it himself. . . . it now spread throughout the width and breadth of the land with the speed of a pestilential plague."[96]

In the wake of the Holocaust, Russian Jews, almost all of whom had lost members of their immediate family, were shocked into a new level of awareness about their Jewishness. One prominent JAC member, the poet and partisan hero A. Sutskever, gave an emotional speech to a packed JAC meeting following his testimony at the Nuremberg trials: "Our greatest revenge would be realized if Jerusalem were to become ours." The audience's reaction was a mixture of fear and joy. He could have been referring to the Soviets, as well as the Nazis. There was a frozen silence, and then, thunderous applause.[97] The risky speech must have sent chills down everyone's spine. They lived in a country where two million to three million people were arrested after 1940 for reporting late to work, a crime punishable by up to five years in a slave labor camp.[98]

The JAC continued to be a major operation in the immediate postwar period, occupying many offices staffed by specialists, department heads, writers, secretaries, and clerks. It had evolved into the chief organ of Soviet Jewry. The American fellow traveler B. Z. Goldberg, whose organization had hosted Mikhoels and Feffer during their mission, compared it to the American Jewish Congress.[99] The fact that it took on the trappings of a general Jewish organization would be part of the "evidence" of subversiveness that was cited when the committee was closed down at the end of 1948.

Another black mark was the collaboration of American Jewish organizations with the Soviet committee to prepare *The Black Book* of eyewitness reports about the murder of 1.5 million Soviet Jews. The documentary book was to appear in Russian, English, and Yiddish editions. According to Ehrenburg, the book, which he co-edited with the brilliant writer Vasily Grossman, was set in type and was to be published at the end of 1948; but the government suppressed it suddenly. The printing plates were destroyed, and *The Black Book* never saw the light of day in the Soviet Union.[100] It was incendiary material, and Ehrenburg knew it: "Let this book burn like fire. Let it call for retribution," he wrote in a letter to the prospective co-publishers.[101]

Ehrenburg, who personally collected innumerable documents and eyewitness reports about the extermination, did manage to publish excerpts from the first part of the book in the Yiddish magazine *Znamya* (The Banner) under the title "Murderers of Peoples." Although it was obvious that this title referred to the Nazis, it could be taken to mean the Soviets as well. For the Communist party, led by the first commissar of Nationalities, had committed genocide against whole nations, as well as against the bourgeoisie, "rich" peasants, and much of that class known by the Russian word *intelligentsia*.

CHAPTER 6

An Actor's Tragedy
The Murder of Mikhoels

The many great Soviet artists who lived in Stalin's shadow could never explain why he spared some of them—such as Mikhail Bulgakov, Dmitri Shostakovich, Sergei Prokofiev, Boris Pasternak, Sergei Eisenstein, and Ilya Ehrenburg (the last three of whom were of Jewish origin)—and destroyed others: Isaac Babel, Vsevolod Emilievich Meyerhold, Mandelstam, Mikhoels, Markish, Pilnyak, Der Nister (all of them Jews). Well-known writers and artists could vanish at any time for no comprehensible reason. But some artists had more of a sense of their doom than others.

Though Solomon Mikhoels was raised to such an exalted position, somehow he knew that he would not be among the winners of "the lottery," as both Ehrenburg and Khrushchev termed life under Stalin. He sensed that instead, he would meet the fate of his close friend Isaac Babel, with whom he had made the appropriately entitled silent film *Jewish Luck*.[1] Babel, a gentle man who wore very thick spectacles that magnified a pair of sad eyes, was generally regarded as one of the great Russian writers of all time. In "The Story of My Dovecote" he summed up Jewish history in a few warm and lighthearted lines that suddenly turned to hardness in describing the stark terror of a pogrom. Like Ehrenburg, Babel had dreamed of Jewish assimilation. He had even served in the secret police, and admired the steeliness he found in special units of both the police and the army. He knew Yagoda, the Jewish pharmacist who became Stalin's secret police chief, and he often visited the Jewish wife of Yezhov, Yagoda's successor and one of the worst killers in human history. Despite his gentleness, Babel envied the Cossacks, the czarist special forces who later fought for the Revolution. The Cossack cavalry, with whom he rode during the civil war, helped to forge the classless society into which even a sensitive, myopic Jew could be thoroughly assimilated, he believed. But despite such yearnings, Babel insisted on writing about Jewish life, and he was far too individualistic to survive in Soviet society.

Mikhoels always had Babel's fate in front of him, as well as that of another good friend, Vsevolod Emilievich Meyerhold: Constantin Stanislavsky's student and Sergei Eisenstein's mentor—generally regarded as the most influential theater director of the modern era. The end of this totally assimilated Jew had begun in January 1938, when the government announced that the famed Meyerhold Theater was being closed because of its "alien" nature. Soviet critics had said that Meyerhold distorted Alexander Pushkin—Russia's Shakespeare, who had been turned into a Soviet holy of holies—drawing characters from his own "Jewish psyche" instead of truly portraying the great writer's intentions. Days after Meyerhold was arrested in June 1939, his wife, the famous actress Zenaida Reich, was found slain in their Moscow apartment, her eyes gouged out and her throat cut. But Meyerhold simply could not bring himself to believe that it was Stalin who was behind his persecution, and he remained an honest Communist till his execution in February 1940.[2]

Mikhoels was not as blind as Meyerhold, nor was Peretz Markish; they played the game as long as they could, without any illusions. Like Mikhoels and Markish, most of the intellectuals associated with the Jewish Anti-Fascist Committee would be executed or imprisoned in the years and months immediately preceding Stalin's last conspiracy. The impending destruction of the JAC in 1948 and most of its leaders in 1948–1952 would serve as a microcosm of Stalin's plans for the arts and Soviet society in general, a stage setting for Stalin's end-game.

The words "intellectual" and "Jew" were synonymous in many minds, particularly Stalin's. In the postwar era, as in the thirties, the whole social structure was to be purged, not merely the intelligentsia and the Jews. However, the Jews, in Stalin's mind, were a primary enemy because they were Western-oriented, too open to foreign influences, and therefore loyal to a different divinity than the Communist state—even if they professed conversion to the Marxist-Leninist faith and died with praise of Stalin on their lips, like General Yakir or Meyerhold.

In the postwar battle against Soviet intellectuals, the key word became "cosmopolitanism," a euphemism connected to Jews and

those gentiles who had become "infected" by Jewish ideas. A Soviet joke circa. 1949 was: "If you don't want to be known as an anti-
Semite, call the Jew a cosmopolite." The inner response of many
Jews in the professions and the intelligentsia to the postwar repression was, "What are we supposed to do now, go back to run-
ning taverns and trading furs?"

As in the field of Soviet medicine, the Jews were over-
represented in the arts and intelligentsia, and in outsized numbers:
approximately 12 to 15 percent of the painters and theater critics,
poets and professors, composers and mathematicians, were of Jewish origins. In some fields, such as film, the proportion was even
higher.[3] An estimated 70 percent of all the intellectuals and artists
attacked by the Soviet media during the postwar "anti-cosmopolitan" campaign were Jews.[4] Such treatment was both an indication
of how far the Jews had advanced in Russian society under the
Communists and how precarious their position was.

Stalin, the consummate actor-director, personally interfered in
many of the arts. He was particularly interested in the film world,
and vetted every Soviet film produced at Mosfilm's two studios in
the capital or Lenfilm's studio in Leningrad. He was not pleased by
the fact that there was a highly disproportionate number of Jews in
the Soviet film industry, as in the other arts: for example, directors
Sergei Eisenstein, Mikhail Romm, Mark Donsky, Leonid Lukov,
and Yuli Reisman; actors and actresses Faina Raneskaya, Mark
Berness, Daniel Segal, Solomon Mikhoels, and Benjamin Zuskin;
scriptwriters Vasily Grossman (the novelist-journalist) and
Yevgeny Gabrilovich; and cinematographer Boris Volchok.[5] One
such Jew was his daughter Svetlana's ill-fated wartime lover, Alexei Kapler. Kapler, who wrote the scripts of such popular Soviet
war films as *She Defends Her Native Land,* had also been a member
of the Jewish Anti-Fascist Committee.

In the spring of 1944, three years after Kapler was sent to the
Gulag, Svetlana married Grigory Morozov, a Jewish student at the
Institute of International Relations. Although Stalin opposed the
marriage and refused to ever meet the young Jewish intellectual,
he gave in to Svetlana's wish. He felt she was "one of those literary
types" and that she "wanted to be a bohemian." He told her, "To
hell with it. Do as you like."[6] Following the birth of Stalin's grandson, named Joseph after both Stalin and Grigory's father, Stalin
provided for the family on the condition that Grigory continue
never to set foot in the Kremlin. In 1948, a year after the couple

separated for personal reasons, Stalin ordered the arrest of Joseph Morozov, Grigory's father, and later told Svetlana: "That first husband of yours was thrown your way by the Zionists." When she protested that the younger Jews couldn't care less about Zionism, Stalin answered sharply, "No! You don't understand. The entire older generation is contaminated with Zionism, and now they're teaching the young people, too."[7]

Stalin and the thousands of subordinates made in his image felt that Soviet literary circles, like the film world and the other arts, were also dominated by Jews, a clique bent on keeping Russian writers down.[8] The work of Jewish poets, painters, filmmakers, critics, actors, and playwrights "smelled of garlic," according to popular Soviet thought, meaning "too Jewish—Mediterranean." (Apparently, these writers did not know of Stalin's love of garlic, which is a staple in Georgia.)

The intelligentsia, which had been among the strata of Soviet society devastated in the purges, quivered as Stalin's personal anxieties intensified in the years after the war. He had ordained, for example, that death was an inappropriate theme for Soviet art—probably because of his own fear of death and his interest in promoting studies of longevity.

Shostakovich in his memoirs remarked that artists and intellectuals had sometimes defecated in their pants or passed out in front of Stalin. All but a handful were intent on pleasing him. Composer Vano Muradeli, for example, wrote an opera in 1947, *The Great Friendship,* with a plot featuring the Ossetians. Shostakovich, who was one of those who held that Stalin was an Ossetian and not a Georgian, noted that not long before Muradeli wrote his obsequious opera, Stalin, who despised the Chechens and Ingushi, had loaded the "two nations into wagons and took them to the devil."[9]

Although Stalin always kept a hand on the pulse of the arts, he made his heir apparent, Andrei Zhdanov, the czar of Soviet culture in the period from early 1946 until Zhdanov's premature death in 1948—the most important of the purported "medical murders" that would be blamed on the Jews in 1953. It was Zhdanov, the founder of the Cominform (the central "information bureau" of several Communist parties), who had first announced the declaration of Cold War against the West; he was the spokesman for Stalin's doctrine that the world was divided into two great camps which would inevitably collide.

As soon as Zhdanov was put in charge of "the problem of art" at the beginning of 1946, he attacked Russia's leading poet, Anna Akhmatova, declaring that she "adulates the West" and that her brilliant work was "too personal." She was nothing but a typical writer of vacuous poetry devoid of ideas and alien to the Soviet peoples, said Zhdanov and the other arbiters of art. Stalin took an interest in the case and personally wrote a noxious resolution, issued by the Central Committee on August 14, 1946, attacking Leningrad "cultural saboteurs" like "the female writer Akhmatova," the "decadent drawing-room poetess."[10]

Zhdanov's two-year reign of cultural terror against the intelligentsia was named after him: the *Zhdanovshchina* (period of Zhdanov). It was a part of Stalin's slow and deliberate postwar buildup to the next big purge, and the dictator's spotlight would move from the arts to other fields—medicine, science, philosophy, linguistics, economics, the universities, the army, the Party, the secret organs—until all of Soviet society was "cleansed." But Stalin always had a megalomaniac's view of his relationship to the arts. He also wanted to be recognized as the greatest critic of all time, telling Shostakovich how to compose, Pasternak how to write, and Eisenstein how to make a movie. At times Stalin felt he was the rebel archangel incarnate, son of the morning, the artist par excellence.

The cultural campaign against the Jews was launched in early 1946, when the prominent Russian writer Nikolai Tikhonov wrote an article entitled "In Defense of Pushkin," which appeared in *Sovetskaya Kultura*. Tikhonov attacked Jewish critic Isaac Nusinov, whom he termed "a vagabond without a passport"—another way of saying "rootless Jew." Nusinov, he said, was trying to "Westernize" the greatest Russian poet, to take his Russian soul from him, like a vampire. "Anti-patriotic" theater critics were attacked in *Pravda* in late 1948 and in January 1949, identified as "rootless cosmopolitans" whose work was deeply repulsive and inimical to Soviet Man. *Pravda* asked how someone with the last name of Gurevitch or Yuzovsky could form an idea of the national character of Russian Soviet Man?[11] The fact that half of Soviet Jewry had just been exterminated elicited no sympathy for the Jews. If anything, the opposite was true.

"I could see anti-Semitism growing all around me," Dmitri Shostakovich said of this period. "Despite all the Jews who perished in the camps, all I heard people saying was, 'The kikes went to Tashkent to fight [far from the front].' And if they saw a Jew with military decorations, they called after him, 'Kike, where did you buy the medals?''[12] Shostakovich, deeply influenced by Jewish folk music, was one of many gentiles among the intelligentsia who respected Jewish culture and one of the few to pursue it despite official disapproval. None of his "Jewish Cycle" works were performed until after Stalin's death.

On December 21, 1949, when Stalin turned seventy, many of the paintings and sculptures at the Tretyakov Art Gallery in Moscow depicted him as a schoolboy with his books, or as the master strategist of World War II standing beside the huge globe of the world he kept in his office. In Soviet eyes this was true art, socialist realism, and many leftist Western intellectuals supported what Arthur Koestler, referring to a Bertolt Brecht play, called "glorification of the anti-Christ."[13]

Stalin kept a tight rein on his "culture czar." Zhdanov usually consulted with him before he closed down magazines, forced famous composers to confess to past sins (he told Prokofiev and Shostakovich that the most important element in music was a melody that could be hummed), demanded socialist realism in all the plastic arts, and proscribed numerous writers, poets, and theater critics.

Stalin himself did most of the talking when he and Zhdanov met with film genius Sergei Eisenstein in early 1947. Eisenstein was one of the few members of the Jewish Anti-Fascist Committee who died naturally, though his heart condition probably was not helped when Stalin grilled him intensively a few months before the director's final cardiac arrest. He was the only member of the JAC in the arts who met Stalin personally, and it was a wrenching experience for this son of a converted German Jew.

When Eisenstein's brilliant screenplay for *Ivan the Terrible* was published in 1943, it was clear that the film would be made in two parts. Part 1 was released at the end of 1944, and its author, widely recognized internationally as one of the leading artists of the century, was applauded by the Soviet government and awarded the Order of Lenin. However, Part 2, *The Boyars' Plot*, ready for release in 1946, ran into serious trouble with the authorities, and was the object of a biting attack by the Party.[14] It was said that Stalin himself had delivered the ultimate judgement: "Can it!"

On February 24, 1947, Eisenstein and actor Nikolai Cherkasov, who played Ivan, were summoned to the Kremlin for a chat with Stalin himself. Stalin questioned Eisenstein closely, sucking furiously at his pipe. Zhdanov and Molotov threw in their comments, as well, but it was clearly Stalin's show. Stalin knew everything about Ivan the Terrible; he identified with Ivan more strongly than with any other historical personality, including his other heroes, Peter the Great and Boris Godunov. And he thought that no Jew, no matter how great a filmmaker, would ever know as much as he did about Ivan.

Stalin did not lose his temper, but talked to Eisenstein as any teacher would lecture a bright but errant pupil. Stalin said that Ivan the Terrible's major mistake was that he failed to liquidate the five remaining great feudal families: "Had he wiped out these families, there would have been no Time of Troubles." Looking at Cherkasov, whose photograph as Ivan hung in his office, Stalin said, "But . . . there God stood in Ivan's way."[15] Stalin wanted Ivan to be portrayed as a great and wise king, in no way mad, whereas Eisenstein had portrayed him as a slightly effeminate waverer "something like Hamlet."[16] Stalin was saying that there should be no hint that Ivan was a paranoid personality, or that there was anything sexually ambivalent about him. He praised Ivan as the vanquisher of the Tatars, the people Stalin had recently deported from the Crimea, and claimed that Ivan "did not let foreigners in—he safeguarded the country against penetration by foreign influences."[17] He scolded Eisenstein for his portrayal of the *oprichniki,* Ivan's "secret police chiefs," who, he complained, had been shown as a band of degenerates. Stalin said that "during their dances [they] look like cannibals and remind one of Phoenicians and Babylonians."[18]

Immediately after this encounter in the Kremlin, Eisenstein wrote a long article in *Culture and Life* magazine, confessing that he completely misinterpreted Ivan's great role in Russian history, which had made the film "worthless and vicious in an ideological sense." He wrote that the focus should have been on "Ivan the Builder, Ivan the Creator of a new, powerful, united Russian power." Shostakovich, who also had to listen to Stalin's ideas about art, condemned Eisenstein in his memoirs as a Stalinist lackey, who, like the poet Vladimir Mayakovsky, "added his babble to the magnification of the immortal image of our leader and teacher." Eisenstein, wrote Shostakovich, "had no conscience at all, but he did have fear, a lot of it."[19]

The intelligentsia—especially the Jews—had every reason to be afraid, and in January 1948 they were given a dark hint of the shape of things to come. The *Zhdanovshchina* was moving from criticism to murder, the same process that had occurred during the purges. The first target was the man who symbolized the Jewish spirit in the arts, and was one of the most beloved leaders of Russian Jewry in its long and tormented history.

In 1946 and 1947, as the *Zhdanovshchina* intensified, Solomon Mikhoels found his greatest solace in the theater complex under his direction, in acting, and in his continuing involvement in the Jewish Anti-Fascist Committee. He was also a warm father to his teenage daughters and a loving husband to his second wife, Pototzskaja, a sensitive daughter of the Polish nobility who started the unique Progressive High School (Gymnasia) in Moscow. But theater was his first love. Prokofiev had once told Mikhoels that "the only rescue is in work," and he tried to submerge himself in his activities at GOSET (the Russian acronym for the Moscow Jewish Theater). But Mikhoels was a little like the protagonist of Sholom Aleichem's "The Bewitched Tailor," who starts out a cheerful, simple man but becomes the target of a practical joke and ends up mystified, terrified, and finally destroyed.

Mikhoels identified passionately with King Lear, his most famous and acclaimed role.[20] Like Lear, his understanding grew as the last illusions withered away and his end approached. People regarded this homely, extraordinarily expressive actor as every inch a king, a Jewish king who knew the darkness of the soul but who was constantly straining toward the light.

The Yiddish *King Lear,* with its long pauses and overdramatic rendering, had something of the flavor of a *purimshpiel:* an earthy skit Jews perform to mark the rescue of their people from an ancient plotter who tried to exterminate them. Indeed, Mikhoels's first exposure to the world of Yiddish theater had been encounters with *purimshpielers,* groups of amateur actors who performed at the Purim carnival throughout the Pale of Settlement. Mikhoels would retain a *purimshpieler's* spark of spontaneity even in the darkest of times.[21]

Stalin never summoned Mikhoels to perform Lear for him; this was a myth repeated for forty years and detailed in numerous books about Soviet Jewry or Soviet theater. Nor did Stalin call him "my wise King Solomon," as the story would have it. In fact, they never met. Mikhoels had told his daughters, "I do not want his

honey and I do not want his sting.''[22] He was not like his friend
Meyerhold and so many others who believed that the Yezhovs and
Berias, not an unknowing Stalin, were to blame for the continuous
nightmare. He knew the Man of Steel, though he never encountered him face to face.

The JAC in the immediate postwar era gave Mikhoels hope that
Russia's isolationism was coming to an end. But Mikhoels became
worried about the increasing viciousness of the new anti-Semitic
campaign against "cosmopolites," and hinted as much to his
friends and fellow JAC artistic personalities: Ehrenburg, Markish,
and Benjamin Zuskin—the great actor and Mikhoels's co-director
at GOSET. All four of these loyal Communists had been trauma-
tized by the Nazi extermination of three million Soviet Jews and
the Stalin regime's murders of so many of their friends and associates. None of them could really believe that socialist Jews like
Ehrlich and Alter had been Nazi agents. In varying degrees all of
them were "non-Jewish Jews," secular socialist humanists, but
somehow they knew that this was no answer to "the Jewish problem" either.

Ehrenburg once stayed up all night at Mikhoels's apartment on
Tverskoi Prospekt arguing about the future of the remaining two
million Soviet Jews, repeating his long-held position that the only
way to survive was to disappear—assimilate. Mikhoels agreed in
principle, but countered that the Jews had to guard tradition and
roots.[23] Stalin may not have been aware of the differences between
these two prominent Jews; nor would it have made a difference
when he decided which one would live and which would die. Though
he never met either man—he spoke to Ehrenburg only once, on the
telephone—he did know a great deal about both of them from
various sources. Stalin distrusted everyone who had been exposed
to life outside the Soviet Union. This included Ehrenburg—the
most traveled—Mikhoels, and even Feffer, though the devoted
Stalinist poet had been sent on the long wartime JAC mission by
the secret organs, undoubtedly with Stalin's personal approval.

Stalin was not interested in hearing about Mikhoels's great artistic accomplishments. In 1946 the secretary of the powerful Soviet
Writers' Union, Abolgasem Lakhuti, a Persian political émigré
who was long a Stalin favorite, wrote one of his frequent fulsome
letters to the dictator, saying: "Stalin the Great Gardener knows
the scent of every flower, but one fragrant blossom has perhaps
been overlooked—Mikhoels's marvelous Yiddish theater." He rec-

ommended that Stalin visit GOSET. The author was duly ordered never to write to Stalin again.[24]

But there were often mixed signals. Soon after the end of the war, both Mikhoels and Benjamin Zuskin were awarded Stalin Prizes for *Freilechs,* a play based on the Jewish folklore of small provincial towns. Stalin himself approved the selection of winners for all of the prestigious and generous annual prizes in his name. It was no protection, however: scores of Stalin Prize winners were executed or disappeared in the Gulag.

When Ilya Ehrenburg watched GOSET's production of *Freilechs* in 1946, he was gripped by fear as he remembered the mass killing sites he had seen just a year before, where the Nazis had murdered millions of people like the characters in this play. Perhaps the fearsome memory was also a chill of presentiment. Ehrenburg, writing his memoirs in the 1960s, would say: "How could one have imagined that soon Mikhoels would be killed in a deserted spot outside Minsk, and Zuskin would be shot in Lubyanka's cellar?"[25] But this comment was pure dissimulation; he had already seen the Soviet murder machine on the rampage in the 1930s, and knew as well as his fellow Stalin Prize winners Mikhoels, Markish, and Feffer that the Nazis could not be blamed for the killings of Ehrlich, Alter, Babel, Meyerhold, and countless other Soviet and East European Jews who were not so famous.

Under Soviet rule, there were always messages between the lines; this type of communication had become an art form in itself. The deeply hidden message of *Freilechs* was *Am yisrael chai* (The Jewish People lives), despite the innumerable attempts over the centuries to extinguish them. The fact that the play's two stars and co-directors won official praise for their electrifying performances showed just how deeply the message was hidden. To a seasoned eye, "Zuskin and Mikhoels went in tandem. Zuskin was the body of the Jewish people and Mikhoels the spirit, whether they played Lear and the Fool or two children from the shtetl."[26] The two swam against the current during the *Zhdanovshchina,* when actors played their parts according to government directives. Somehow, the creative spirit possessed by a few artists managed to persevere. But only up to a point.

It would have been entirely out of character for Stalin to attend the Moscow Jewish Theater, or to order up a Shakespeare performance by Mikhoels or anyone else: he loathed Lear, and Hamlet and Macbeth as well. He did give a nod of sorts to the illustrious

Moscow Art Theater founded by Stanislavsky, where he asked the famous question: "Why is this necessary—playing *Hamlet* in the Art Theater, eh?"[27] "Everyone knew about Stalin's question directed at the Art Theater," Shostakovich wrote in his memoirs, "and no one wanted to risk it [staging *Hamlet*]. Everyone was afraid. And *King Lear?* Everyone knows that our best Lear was Mikhoels in the Jewish theater, and everyone knows his fate. A terrible fate."[28]

Stalin had his own ideas about theater, as he did about film, linguistics, economics, gardening, and most other subjects. Many writers and historians have noted Stalin's theatricality, his sense that all the world was his stage. "The stage manager was at the same time the leading actor," Adam Ulam wrote in his biography, adding that in the midst of the Great Terror, "Stalin exhibited most strikingly his consummate acting talent." Robert Tucker remarked on his "extraordinary histrionic ability," and George F. Kennan called him "a consummate actor." Indeed, the Doctors' Plot itself would be described as "political stagecraft . . . the final act of Stalin's career."[29]

With his typical skill at deception, Stalin the director crushed Mikhoels's theater. The lights would be dimmed so slowly that the audience did not realize for some time that GOSET, Mikhoels, and eventually all of Soviet Jewry were being blacked out. The Moscow Jewish Theater had been packed every night in 1946 and the first half of 1947. The theater built around Mikhoels's great talent was a major enterprise occupying three buildings and operating on an annual budget of three million rubles. It buzzed with activity. There was a long waiting list to get into the theater's acting and directing school, and to join the troupe of sixty actors. But in the months leading up to Mikhoels's death at the beginning of 1948, the actors played to empty houses. One member of the GOSET troupe, recalling those days a decade later, said: "No, the public did not die out. . . . But the theater they killed. Took a knife and slaughtered it."[30]

At the end of 1947, a few weeks before Mikhoels was murdered, Jewish theater people celebrated the birthday of the late Yiddish writer Mendele Mocher Sforim ("Mendel the Bookseller") in the Hall of the Polytechnical Museum in Moscow. It was packed, with people even sitting in the aisles. Mikhoels opened the evening with a short speech; then he and Zuskin played a few scenes from *The Voyages of Benjamin III*. In his opening remarks, Mikhoels said of

Benjamin that at the start of his voyage seeking the Promised Land he asked a stranger, "Which is the way to Eretz Yisrael?" "And just at this time Comrade Gromyko has given us an answer to that question," Mikhoels said, referring to the strong Soviet support at the United Nations for the partition of Palestine and the establishment of a Jewish state.

The crowd roared in approval. "It was as if he was telling them all to go to Israel," Nina Mikhoels would recall. "Everyone was jumping from their seats, clapping madly, and for over ten minutes." Mikhoels went very pale, perhaps because he did not expect such a reaction. He was terribly worried. Afterward he rushed down to the radio station which was supposed to broadcast the performance. "They informed me that they had lost the tapes and therefore the program would not be broadcast," Mikhoels told his daughter Natalia. He took it as a bad sign. Only much later did the sisters come to believe that their father's appearance that night might have sealed his fate.[31]

They were unaware of another, much more ominous event that took place around the same time. Mikhoels and Feffer were summoned to the Kremlin to meet with Molotov and with Kaganovich, then the vice-president of the Council of Ministers. The two Politburo members at first discussed the government's attempts to revive the Birobidzhan region as a Jewish republic, but then suggested that the JAC leaders send a letter to Stalin requesting that the emptied Crimea, the "pearl of Russia," become the Jewish republic.[32] The switch was significant, a tempting and sinister carrot dangled by Stalin's henchmen as part of the trap that would come to be known as the Crimea Affair. Stalin laid his traps all around his victims, who sometimes helped ensnare themselves. This one would be sprung four years after Mikhoels's death.

===

To this day, there are conflicting accounts of Mikhoels's last twenty-four hours and the exact circumstances of his death. But what seems certain is that Itzik Feffer had a direct hand in the murder of his friend.

On January 11, 1948, Mikhoels and theater critic Vladimir Ilich Golubov-Potapov went to Minsk, the Belorussian capital which still lay in ruins from the Nazi devastation. Their mission, at Stalin's behest, was conveyed through his secretary, the infamous Alexander Poskrebyshev. The two men were told that they were to judge plays performed at the Jewish State Theater (housed in the ornate former central synagogue) for a possible Stalin Prize. The timing seemed strange, given the heightening campaign against "cosmopolitans."[33]

Just before Mikhoels went to Minsk, he called Feffer and asked him to fill in for him for a few days as chairman of the JAC, something he had done on many such occasions in the four years since their mission together to the U.S.A. The poet agreed readily. Mikhoels had never liked Feffer, but had reached a modus vivendi with the poet who was so beloved by Communist true believers of Jewish origin. Markish, on the other hand, still could not stand the sight of him.

On the day after Mikhoels arrived in Minsk, hours before his death, he telephoned his wife and daughters from the Intourist hotel and told them that he had been astonished to spot Feffer in Minsk that very morning, eating breakfast in the hotel restaurant. He said that Feffer, supposedly filling in for him in Moscow, was reading a newspaper and had pretended not to see him. Apparently they did not talk. After touching on the incident, Mikhoels changed the subject and his family thought no more of it. It was their last conversation.[34]

There were tens of thousands of Itzik Feffers in Soviet Russia, for he was a typical Chekist intellectual. "I'm a quiet guy and hardly a villain," Feffer once declared demurely in one of his many anti-Judaic poems. "My honesty has no great appeal; /I'm never known to put on tefilin [phylacteries], /I'm never known to wheel and deal."[35] But the balding, bespectacled, middle-aged poet undoubtedly played a villain's role in the death of the great actor and leading personality of Soviet Jewry.

During the late afternoon of January 12, Mikhoels was paged in the Minsk hotel lobby and told that a phone call awaited him. The caller summoned him to "an urgent meeting," possibly with local party chief Ponomarenko, either at an office or at someone's private home. Such urgent meetings were a standard device employed by the secret police apparatus, as had been the case with Ehrlich and Alter. Mikhoels, regal in the mink coat that had been given to him during the war by American fur trade unions, walked out the door with Golubov chatting behind him. (Feffer also had one of these coats, as did Stalin; Mikhoels had given the third coat to Molotov, asking him to pass it on to "The Boss," which he did.[36]

Nothing more was heard of the two men until they were found

the next morning, allegedly the victims of a "hit and run" car accident—a favorite secret police device.[37] Their bloodied corpses were discovered near the war-torn city's rail terminal, covered in snow.[38] The setting could not have been more ironic. Before the Nazi invasion, Minsk had been the home of the largest Jewish community in White Russia. Just over four years had passed since the Germans slaughtered 19,000 Jews there in two days, and a total of over 100,000 in the city altogether.[39]

The murder of two more Jews, however prominent, might seem insignificant in comparison to such deeds. Stalin's quiet campaign against the Jews was still specific in its targets, not systematic and all-inconclusive, as was Hitler's program. But the seeds for another Jewish bloodbath had definitely been planted.

Stalin's direct involvement in the double murder was reported to the world twenty years afterward by his daughter, Svetlana:

One day, in father's dacha, during one of my rare meetings with him, I entered his room when he was speaking to someone on the telephone. Something was being reported to him and he was listening. Then, as a summary of the conversation, he said, "Well, it's an automobile accident." I remember so well the way he said it: not a question but an answer, an assertion. He wasn't asking; he was suggesting: "an automobile accident." When he got through, he greeted me; and a little later he said: "Mikhoels was killed in an automobile accident." But when next day I came to my classes in the university, a girl student, whose father had worked for a long time in the Jewish theater, told me, weeping, how brutally Mikhoels had been murdered while traveling through Belorussia in a car. The newspapers, of course, reported the event as an "automobile accident."

He had been murdered and there had been no accident. "Automobile accident" was the official version, the cover-up suggested by my father when the black deed had been reported to him. My head began to throb. I knew all too well my father's obsession with "Zionist" plots around every corner. It was not difficult to guess why this particular crime had been reported directly to him.[40]

On the morning after the corpses were discovered, January 13, a Minsk official telephoned Mikhoels's daughters and informed them that their father had died that way in an accident. The word spread immediately, and the family's apartment was soon filled with friends and relatives.

One of the mourners was Yula Fictengolds, niece of Lazar Kaganovich—the only Jew left in the Politburo—and daughter of his brother Mikhail, another high-ranking Soviet official, who had just been imprisoned. (Soon afterward Mikhail Kaganovich would be ordered by Stalin to commit suicide or be executed, and Lazar would sanction the death of his brother without a sign of remorse. Mikhail was accused of having "helped the Nazis.")

Yula Fictengolds was connected to the Mikhoels family through her husband, a violinist who was a friend of Natalia Vovsi-Mikhoels and her composer husband, Moshe Veinberg. In their many visits together, Yula had never mentioned her uncle to the young couple—not until that day.[41]

She beckoned Natalia and her husband to the bathroom, the "safe room," where Soviet people felt it was not too hazardous to talk; every other wall in Moscow did, in fact, have ears. The faucets were all turned on and the toilet flushed while they whispered to each other. Yula said, "My uncle sends his condolences, and he requests that you never ask details about what happened to your father." That was all.

Neither Natalia nor her husband really comprehended what Kaganovich's niece was telling them. They did not understand what was behind her words until much later.[42]

In the afternoon of that January 13, an anonymous caller rang up the Moscow Yiddish theater and said: "Mikhoels is dead; the leading Jew of the Jewish theater was killed; now it is the turn of all Jews."[43]

In the rush of events following the actor's tragic end, Mikhoels's widow and daughters completely forgot the strange encounter in Minsk between Mikhoels and Itzik Feffer. Only afterward would they recall the incident, and begin to wonder why Feffer had appeared so suddenly in Minsk when he was supposed to be in Moscow at the head of the JAC, why he had kept it a secret, why he did not pay a condolence call during the week of mourning.[44] Of all the people writing about Mikhoels after his death, Feffer was the only one to constantly repeat the official version of death by an auto accident.

It was not prudent to ask questions in the USSR about anything, let alone about someone who had vanished, or died suddenly. A friend of Mikhoels who was an officer of the secret police—one Lev

Sheinin, who was also a member of the Jewish Anti-Fascist Committee—tried to make inquiries into the actor's death. But Sheinin, who had been a detective and writer of crime novels, disappeared suddenly and was not heard of again until 1956, when he was released from a prison camp.[45]

Moscow was rife with rumors that Mikhoels had been a victim of foul play. Two days after the "accident," the Jewish wife of a prominent general, Sergei Trofimenko, told Esther Markish that Mikhoels had been murdered. The actor had spent much of his last day in Minsk at the Trofimenko house, Irina Trofimenko said, swearing Markish's wife to secrecy.[46] Two weeks after the murders, an American embassy official in Moscow sent an airgram to the U.S. secretary of state about "the recent and sudden death" of Mikhoels, which, "although probably not an important political event in itself, has roused a remarkably large crop of rumors in Moscow."[47] The death of "one of the most prominent Jews in the USSR" received a great amount of "eulogistic press coverage," the report said, but of course there was no mention in the media of the conflicting rumors about the circumstances of the alleged accident, which made it "difficult to report exactly how Mikhoels met his death."[48]

The obituary published in *Pravda* on the freezing morning of January 14, 1948, lamented the death of "one of the greatest actors of all time," singling out his performances as tragic King Lear and as wise Tevye in Shalom Aleichem's "Tevye the Milkman," the story later popularized as *Fiddler on the Roof.* The obituary lauded his Soviet patriotism, his Lenin and Stalin prizes, and said "The image of this great, admirable Soviet artist will rest forever in our hearts." It was signed by fifty-eight Soviet writers and artists. But in the media's copious coverage on January 14, not a word appeared about the circumstances of his death.

The bodies of both Mikhoels and the Jewish theater critic, placed in zinc caskets, were brought by train from Minsk straight to GOSET on Mala-Bronnaya Street, five minutes' walk from the Mikhoels's home near Moscow's inner circle (the city is built in a series of rings that expand from around the Kremlin); but the families were told to stay put for a few hours, until the work on the bodies could be completed.

Mikhoels's smashed frizzy-haired head, highlighted by what Markish called "a kingly pate"—a big bald spot in the center—was patched up for the funeral by Professor Boris I. Zbarsky, the famed expert who had embalmed Lenin. He applied makeup thick enough to cover a particularly deep gash on the actor's left temple. It was all arranged so that no questions would arise when Mikhoels's corpse was displayed later that day in an open coffin strewn with flowers.[49]

Zbarsky, a Jew, would soon be sent to a prison camp. The other men who had seen Mikhoels's face before it was cosmetically repaired would all be either imprisoned or executed. One of them was the actor's first cousin, Dr. Vovsi, of the Kremlin Hospital, who, five years later to the day, would be named as one of the chief "murderers in white coats" involved in the Doctors' Plot. Another doomed witness was Zuskin, Mikhoels's upstairs neighbor in the thespians' building on Tverskoi Prospekt and his best friend.[50]

Thousands of people were waiting outside the theater to pay their last respects to Mikhoels. The line stretched from Mayakovsky Square to the Tass building on Tverskoi. Though the temperature was far below freezing, the mourners, many of them clad in sheepskin coats and felt boots, queued for hours. Among the huge throng were hundreds of Jewish students who had been deeply moved by Mikhoels's performances on the stage where his body now lay in state.

Inside GOSET the guard of honor, composed of actors standing around the corpse, was changed every few hours. The coffin, holding that distinctive thick-set body which had always radiated unbounded energy, was titled upward. Mountains of flowers filled the theater. It was not a funeral according to Jewish custom, but an adaptation of alien rites, Russian and Soviet. The victim's second wife, Pototzskaja, and her stepdaughters—Natalia, nineteen, and Nina, fifteen—weeping together over the corpse, were comforted by Dr. Vovsi and other close relatives and friends.

It was said that Professor Zbarsky's work was not up to his usual standards, and perhaps it was intentional. Family members noticed that Mikhoels's hands were clenched in tight fists; the right hand appeared to be fractured, and a blue mark under his eye could be discerned beneath the makeup. A strange, frightening smile was frozen on his mouth. But the actors' relatives attributed it all to "the accident."[51]

Thousands filed past the casket, including Mikhoels's friends and colleagues from the JAC such as Paulina Zhemchuzina and Ehrenburg, who eulogized him from the GOSET stage as "a comrade to those who fell in the war." Peretz Markish strode up to the podium to read his long threnody entitled "S. Mikhoels—An Eternal Light at his Casket," in which he cast Mikhoels as another of the Jews exterminated in the Holocaust, and, knowingly, prefigured his own fate—liquidation in the dungeon of Lubyanka Prison: "Clear through the heart of all your people went your misfortune: /In their graves by arising honor you the millions six, /As you by falling did honor them amidst ruined Minsk."[52] A few whispers ran through the audience, for a number of people already were suspicious about how the actor died, although it would not become obvious to everyone until later in the year.

But Markish's poem, which he had written in a frenzy throughout the night, more than hinted at murder. In addition to comparing Mikhoels's fate to that of the thousands of other Jews massacred in Minsk by the Nazis, the poem used the word "murder" twice in different contexts.[53] Markish said that when you saw what had been done to Mikhoels, when you looked at his wounds, you could see the fate of all his people.

Markish's dirge would prove to be the last nail in his own coffin, which he correctly sensed was already being prepared.[54] "Markish understood everything," Mikhoels's daughter Natalia would recall. "This poem was the main reason for his arrest a year later."[55]

Zuskin followed Markish to the podium, saying, "Mikhoels's death is a great loss; he cannot be replaced. But we know at what time we live, and in what country we live." He said it in a positive, comforting way, as if Stalin's Russia were heaven on earth, as if there were no darkness in the polar atmosphere. It was yet another message between the lines.[56]

At 5:00 P.M., on the roof of a building near the theater, an old Jew started to play on his violin the ancient Hebrew melody of the *Kol Nidre* prayer, the dramatic opening of the service on the Day of Atonement. *Kol Nidre* is a central motif of Judaism, an expression of the links that bind the Jewish people together. Since the time of the Inquisition, it has been an unstated vow against false gods and those who attempt to convert the Jews, whether the attempt be made by gentiles or by apostate Jews such as Paul, Torquemada, Marx, or Trotsky.[57]

The moving violin music played by the fiddler on the roof could be heard inside the theater, in a scene befitting the death of Tevye, or of Lear. As Markish wrote in his tribute to the murdered actor, "Now and here you need no wig. /A royal cloak—is even more unneeded, /To see that you are indeed King Lear /Who his crown for wisdom bartered."

CHAPTER 7

The Crimea Affair

A Separatist "Plot"

At almost the same moment that Stalin was ordering the murder of the chief representative and personification of over two million Soviet Jews, he was recognizing the state of Israel that was being created by 600,000 others in Palestine. There was only an apparent contradiction in following this dual course; and in the end Mikhoels, Israel, and the Zionist conspiracy would all come together.

Without doubt, Stalin personally followed up on his directive to kill Mikhoels with orders to prepare a "case" against the dead man—and to destroy most of the other JAC officials, including Itzik Feffer. Stalin, who thus kept the dead actor under his microscope while methodically formulating his "cure" for the Jewish problem, was moving simultaneously against two central, interrelated Jewish targets: the Moscow Jewish Theater and the JAC, over both of which Mikhoels had presided.

In late January 1948, shortly after the mourning period for Mikhoels ended, two Chekists came to the family's apartment and asked for his American mink coat, which he had worn on the night of his death, saying that mink hairs had been found at the site of the accident in Minsk and that they needed the coat for evidence. They acted as if they were simply looking for a hit-and-run driver. In the presence of the secret policemen, Natalia Vovsi-Mikhoels picked up the phone, called Feffer, and asked him to bring his matching fur coat so that the police could check it, as well. The two officers, taken aback, left hurriedly.[1]

When Feffer arrived at the apartment, unable to look the widow or Mikhoels's two daughters in the face, he alternately stared at the walls and the floor. The family expected him to relate details of his last meeting with Mikhoels in Minsk, but he was silent. The longer his silence continued, the more suspicious the three women became. But they were afraid to ask him why he had appeared so suddenly in Minsk. And they were even more afraid that they would hear the truth.[2]

Within days of Feffer's visit, the Moscow Jewish theater was renamed after its departed guiding spirit. But Mikhoels's family noticed that every month after that, the letters of the actor's name on the marquee got smaller and smaller. The gradual shrinkage lasted from January to October 1948, when the name Mikhoels disappeared altogether. It was only then that Mikhoels's daughters realized what the slow fade meant. Natalia could not understand how they had blocked out the reality, had refused to recognize that fewer and fewer callers were coming to the apartment, that no friends telephoned them anymore.[3]

Attendance at the theater was now reduced to a trickle. People did not want to enter any building where a Black Maria (a secret police van) was parked in front. The government subsidy was cut off. Some Jews continued to buy tickets to support the theater but did not dare attend. All the actors feared arrest.[4]

At the beginning of September 1948, Feffer, who had succeeded Mikhoels as head of the JAC, appeared for the first time at the Mikhoels apartment since his strained visit in late January. This time he was accompanied by two unidentified men wearing similar coats and hats, obviously from "the organs." Feffer asked Natalia for all of Mikhoels's correspondence with people abroad. She had none, she told him; and the three men left without searching the apartment. Later in the day she went up to Benjamin Zuskin's apartment and related what had happened. He called Feffer and asked him what it was all about. Feffer replied only that *der alter* (the old man), a reference to Mikhoels, was to blame for everything. Zuskin, angry and astonished, slammed down the phone.[5]

On September 4, 1948, Zuskin walked down one flight from his fourth-floor apartment in the thespians' building, knocked on the Mikhoels family's door, and asked to make a phone call. Natalia was shocked by his appearance. He had gone completely pale and his eyes were bulging. He told them he had just been informed that he would not be allowed to leave for Leningrad, where the Jewish theater troupe, including his actress wife, Eda Berkovskaya, was performing. He had signed an official document vowing not to leave Moscow.[6]

Within days, Zuskin was ordered to go to the hospital "to be treated for insomnia." He summoned a relative to watch his twelve-year-old daughter. As soon as he was admitted to the hospital an injection was administered, and while he slept MGB (Ministry of State Security) men came, took him from his bed, and brought him to the Lubyanka prison. The Jewish theater troupe returned from Leningrad on December 31 1948, to find that their director had "disappeared."

In early December Feffer went to the offices of the Jewish theater in the company of no less a personage than V. S. Abakumov, the notorious minister of state security since 1946 and Beria's top deputy. Together they rifled the desks in the GOSET offices and confiscated what remained of Mikhoels's papers.[7]

A great fear swept through the Jewish artistic community. No one visited Zuskin's wife and daughter, or the Mikhoels family. MGB agents took up eight-hour shifts next to the Mikhoels family's apartment night and day, with a second agent checking to see that the first never fraternized with the family.[8] Scores of other Jewish artists were kept on a tight leash, under constant surveillance.

In April 1949 a group of officials arrived at GOSET, informed the actors that the theater was dissolved, arranged some severance pay, and suggested that they find other jobs. Everything was shut down, including the actors' studio, where Nina Vovsi-Mikhoels was studying. As one member of the troupe would recall, "The State Yiddish theater, the pride and showcase of Soviet Yiddish culture, ceased to exist."[9]

Mikhoels's name also ceased to exist, until January 13, 1953, five years to the day after his murder, when his name would be resurrected as the supposed Mephistopheles behind the Doctors' Plot. The memory of his service to Stalin, his assimilationist efforts, his loyalty to the Communist cause though he was never a member of the Party, his artistic genius—everything real would be ignored. Like Trotsky's, his name would now become synonymous with Judas.

=====

Another prominent Soviet figure who died in 1948 was Andrei Zhdanov, Stalin's second in command. Zhdanov, despite his successes in the campaign against Jewish cosmopolitans and subversive culture, was out of favor in the months preceding his death, apparently because he was too "moderate" in his position on philosophy and science: he opposed the notorious T. D. Lysenko, whose drive to take over Soviet science was backed by Stalin. Although Zhdanov was credited with launching the anti-cosmopolitan campaign and purging all the remaining Jews from the Leningrad Central Committee, he was being blamed for contributing to the split with the Yugoslav communist leader, Tito.[10] His protégés Alexei A. Kuznetsov and Nikolai A. Voznesensky were arrested sometime in 1948.

Stalin knew that Zhdanov was an alcoholic who suffered from recurrent heart attacks. In the last months of his life, Zhdanov could not control his drinking. It was a pitiful spectacle, Khrushchev said. At Stalin's nightly banquet table, the dictator's associates were all encouraged to get drunk, but he ordered Zhdanov to drink nothing but fruit juice (Tito's aide, Milovan Djilas, also remarked on Zhdanov's drinking of orange juice at the saturnalias). Khrushchev surmised that Zhdanov drank himself to death at home: "This same vice killed Shcherbakov, and it certainly hastened Zhdanov's death to a considerable degree."[11] The Kremlin's Jewish doctors in 1953 would be blamed for these two deaths.

Despite Stalin's paternalistic-seeming ban on Zhdanov's drinking, he helped drive him to an early grave—using the same coarse tactics that he had employed during Lenin's illness. Stalin, fully aware of the state of Zhdanov's heart, had been openly contemptuous of his heir apparent in the months leading up to his death. Stalin's daughter recalled a banquet in late 1947 at which her father sat scowling at Zhdanov, angered by his silence at the dinner table: "Look at him, sitting there like Christ, as if nothing was of any concern to him! There—looking at me now as if he were Christ!" The blood left Zhdanov's face and beads of sweat appeared on his forehead.[12]

Rumors of Zhdanov's ill health reached Western intelligence in a convuluted form: it was Stalin, not Zhdanov, who was reported to be "very seriously ill" in a secret British dispatch on February 16, 1948. A Czech official had received information that a specialist was called in to examine a large number of men looking like Stalin, so that he would not know which one was the real Stalin. The British official discounted it as one of the usual stories about Stalin and his doubles.[13] What actually happened around the time of the British report was that ten to fifteen of the best Soviet internists were summoned individually to examine the medical records, including electrocardiograms, of "Comrade X." This was a standard method of treating the Kremlin leaders. The doctors in this case would not learn till years later, when several of them were arrested, that the patient was Zhdanov. They may very well have thought it was Stalin's health they were being queried about. Every one of the doctors was asked if the anonymous patient's heart condition was acute. They all made the same diagnosis: the patient had a chronically bad heart, but there was no acute infarction and no imminent threat, although he would be likely to have a myocardial infarction—a coronary—sometime in the future. One of the doctors, Binyamin Nezlin, recommended that the patient be sent for a long rest.[14]

Although it seems probable that the British intelligence report confused Stalin's health with Zhdanov's, there is a strong possibility that Stalin, too, was ailing in 1948, both from high blood pressure and mental strain. Stalin's paranoia certainly accelerated from 1948 on, and the autopsy report on Stalin in March 1953 "showed that he suffered from a brain disease, arteriosclerosis, that began at least five years before his death," according to the chief pathologist of Moscow during those years, Dr. Yakov Rapoport, who was among the doctors arrested in January 1953.[15] Dr. Rapoport's associates, who performed the autopsy, all told him after his release from prison that "Stalin had been ill for a very long time. It definitely affected his brains and increased his paranoia." Stalin's temper "definitely changed. [His] anger [was] often directed against the Jews, and paranoia [was] a way of releasing this anger."[16]

In his last years, Stalin and his associates spent much more time at his Kuntsevo dacha than at the Kremlin; and at nightly drinking and gorging parties, which lasted usually from 10:00 P.M. to 4:00 or 5:00 A.M., he was the genial patriarch presiding over a terrified table.[17] Because Stalin stayed up so late, all Soviet officialdom was expected to be at their desks deep into the night in case he might phone them. In every Soviet city the lights of government buildings blazed in permanent White Night. The dictator's bizarre habits were thus reproduced on a mass level.

No writer has captured more revealingly than Djilas the atmosphere of the nocturnal gatherings late in Stalin's life. At one of Stalin's lengthy dinners, where Tito and Djilas were present, the host tauntingly expressed his perception—a correct one—that anti-Semitism existed among all peoples, not only the Russians. Stating that his Yugoslav guests were anti-Semitic, he asked why there were so few Jews in Yugoslavia's Communist leadership. Djilas answered that there were very few Jews in Yugoslavia and that most were middle-class, adding that the only prominent Communist Jew was Pijade, a member of their Central Committee and translator of *Das Kapital.* "In our Central Committee there are no Jews!" Stalin interrupted, with a reproachful laugh. "You are an anti-Semite, you, too, Djilas; you, too, are an anti-Semite!" Djilas interpreted Stalin's "jests" and his taunting laughter as an expression of his own hatred for the Jews, and as a provocation.[18] With the stench from the Nazi extermination camps still hanging in the air of Eastern Europe, Stalin's words were deeply disturbing to the intellectual Yugoslav Communist leader.

Tito himself was formally excommunicated from the Communist movement at a meeting of the Cominform on June 28, 1948, presided over by Zhdanov in his last public appearance. Zhdanov died of heart failure on August 31 at age fifty-two, amid persistent rumors that Beria's agents had poisoned him.[19]

There has always been a certain community of interest between Zionists and anti-Semites. Many Russian and East European anti-Semites of Stalin's time shared the belief of most Zionists that the Jews "should all go to Palestine." Stalin, in becoming the first world leader to recognize the new state of Israel, was not, of course, moved by sentiment or by agreement with Zionist aims. Rather, as an adept practitioner of *Realpolitik,* he was seeking to provide an anti-British bastion in the Near East. For 1948 was a year of political turbulence for the Soviets, marked by the intensifying Cold War, the Marshall Plan and Truman Doctrine, the revival of the Comintern in the guise of Zhdanov's Cominform, the Berlin blockade, and Tito's defection.

On May 15, 1947, the Soviet ambassador to the United Nations, Andrei Gromyko, spoke sympathetically of the calamities the Jews had experienced and the "aspirations toward Palestine of a considerable part of the Jewish people."[20]

Stalin not only recognized Israel, he helped arm the country through his Czech satellite. In contrast, the Americans and British had banned any military help to the new state as it battled for survival against several Arab armies.[21] Although Stalin did try to make inroads among the Arabs, he also had hopes, albeit short-lived, of gaining a Communist foothold in Israel. The "organs" considered Israel to be one of the best listening posts in the world because of the close family ties existing between American and Israeli Jews. So the secret police sent numerous Soviet Jewish agents to Israel as future moles.[22] They had no trouble gaining acceptance among the Jewish population of 600,000, at least 100,000 of whom had emigrated to Palestine from Russia before and immediately after the Revolution. In fact, eight of the sixteen ministers in Ben-Gurion's cabinet, including Golda Meyerson (Meir), were Russian-born, as was President Chaim Weizmann.

The Soviet romance with Israel would come to an abrupt halt a few months after it began, as evidenced by a January 1949 pamphlet by the Soviet economist T. A. Genin, proclaiming that the aims of Jewish nationalism and Zionism "are similar to the aims of reactionary capitalism and American imperialism."[23] Conspiracy-laden language linked Zionism with capitalist spies, and it would be employed effectually in Stalin's grand design against the Jews.[24]

A highlight of the "honeymoon" period with Israel occurred in May 1948 when the JAC, in one of its last actions, sent a telegram congratulating Weizmann on the establishment of the state. Such positive feelings were no longer in evidence by July of that year.[25] But diplomatic relations remained "correct," and Israel's first ambassador to the Soviet Union, Golda Meir, arrived in Moscow on September 2, the day when the capital was totally shut down for Zhdanov's funeral.

The Israelis did not seem to realize the extent of the chill, or how furiously Stalin viewed the huge Jewish turnout to welcome the Israeli mission six weeks later on Rosh Hashanah, October 16. Isaac Deutscher, in his Trotskyist mind's eye, imagined Stalin watching the demonstration from his Kremlin window (a physical impossibility) and speculated that he decided there and then that the Jews were an unstable element. "Reckoning with the possibility of a conflict with the U.S.A., or even a war between Russia and the West, he started to persecute the Jews," Deutscher wrote, ignoring Stalin's forty-year-long record of consistent anti-Semitism, including the murders and campaigns against "cosmopolitans" that began much before Golda Meir's appearance in Moscow.[26]

But the turnout of some 50,000 Soviet Jews to welcome the Israeli envoy undoubtedly did confirm Stalin's belief that the Jews could not be assimilated. He ordered the arrest of Jews who could be identified from photographs taken of the event.[27]

The sea of Jews who came out to greet Ambassador Meir showed that the Communist regime had failed in its thirty-year effort to wipe out Zionist sympathies. American intelligence was also interested in the fact that Zionism was enduring under the most severe conditions: A confidential U.S. memorandum, for example, dispatched from Moscow on January 13, 1948, reported that one-third of the nearly 2,000 Jews in the Byelorussian town of Mozir were confirmed Zionists. The Americans' Soviet Jewish informant also said that he and his friends were extremely interested in the Jewish state forming in Palestine, but because of the absence of regular communications with Zionists in the USSR and abroad, "his group . . . was uncertain about the best method to follow for immigrating there."[28]

Golda Meir also did not know what course to follow concerning Soviet Jews who wished to immigrate to the new Jewish state. According to a still-persistent rumor, she presented Stalin's men with a long list of Soviet Jews who wanted to go to Israel, the great majority of whom were thereupon either executed or imprisoned.[29] But Ambassador Meir's longtime aide Lou Kadar, who arrived in Moscow with her in September 1948 and remained there for fifteen months, attests that "she never gave any list to anyone—it is just a big lie."[30] Aryeh Levavi, the third-ranking diplomat in the first Israeli delegation, also said that the list was "a fairy tale."

But Levavi did recall an incident which could have inspired the rumors, and which certainly endangered some Soviet Jews:

> We had a very out-of-date list of Soviet Jewish institutions and collective farms—most of which had been wiped out during the war—and we naively sent out a mailing of some fifty brochures about Israel to these addresses. Golda got an angry summons to the foreign ministry, where she was told that such distribution of printed material was not acceptable in the framework of legitimate diplomatic activity.[31]

What is certain is that any Soviet Jew who wrote to the Jewish Anti-Fascist Committee inquiring about Israel was arrested.[32] The JAC received "thousands" of such self-incriminating letters.[33] Any Jew who inquired at a Soviet office about volunteering to fight for Israel, the new "Soviet ally," was later arrested as a Zionist.[34] To express admiration for Israel was evidence of bourgeois nationalism, which carried an immediate ten-year sentence to "out there."

On September 21, 1948, nine months after the murder of Mikhoels and less than three weeks after the arrival of the Israeli

diplomats in Moscow, a vicious attack on Zionism appeared in
Pravda, penned by Ilya Ehrenburg. Ehrenburg, the best-known
member of the JAC, apparently wrote the article on orders from
the editors of the Communist party organ. It was probably vetted
by Stalin himself, who still thought of himself as the chief editor,
having been co-founder of *Pravda* in 1912. Ehrenburg, addressing
himself to "the Jewish Question," Israel, and anti-Semitism, attacked the "nationalists and mystics among the Jews. It is they
who drew up the Zionist program." He said that the only common
bond between a Tunisian Jew and a Jew in Chicago was "the tie
forged by anti-Semitism." He quoted Gorky, Lenin, and of course
Stalin's bit of self-knowledge: that anti-Semitism, as the extreme
form of racial chauvinism, is the most dangerous survival of cannibalism. The article was a clear warning to Soviet Jews, who "all
regard the Soviet Union as their homeland," Ehrenburg said.
"They are not looking to the East."

But the answer by Soviet Jews was the massive turnout three
weeks later for Golda Meir at the Moscow Synagogue on the Jewish New Year. Their act of mass bravery was unique in the annals
of the Stalin years—a defiant slap at the writer and his masters,
according to Ambassador Meir, who had been exasperated by the
Ehrenburg article. She felt it denied the existence of a Jewish
people and was a warning to Soviet Jews to stay away from the
Israeli delegation.

A few weeks after the piece appeared in *Pravda,* Golda Meir met
Ehrenburg for the first time at a reception at the Czech embassy.
"He was quite drunk," she reported, "not an unusual condition for
him, I was told—and, from the start, very aggressive."[35] Ehrenburg spoke to her in Russian. "I'm sorry, but I can't speak Russian," she said. "Do you speak English?" Ehrenburg looked at her
"nastily" and replied, "I hate Russian-born Jews who speak English." She answered, "And I'm sorry for Jews who don't speak
Hebrew or at least Yiddish!"[36] That was the extent of their dia-
logue. Aryeh Levavi recalled that Ehrenburg was "defiantly
drunk. . . . He rattled off what he had to say—'You are a servant of
the United States,' formulas like that—and then moved away."[37]

If Golda Meir felt repulsion for Ehrenburg, she was captivated
by another famous Soviet Jew, Paulina Zhemchuzina. Molotov's
wife was the best-dressed and most worldly of the Soviet government wives. The one-time factory worker and party activist had
seen the West—Paris, New York, Berlin—and after her friend

Nadezhda Alliluyeva's death she had become Moscow's "first lady." She was a member of the Central Committee and also minister of fisheries. Stalin told his daughter that Paulina had been a "bad influence" on her ill-fated mother, that she had somehow led her to commit suicide.[38] Because of her active role in the JAC, Stalin thought she was "mixed up with the Zionists" and was spying on her husband.[39] He was probably also suspicious of her brother living in the United States: Samuel Carp, a Bridgeport, Connecticut, millionaire who had left Russia in 1911 and who was the conduit for $50 million in Soviet trade with the United States.[40] Paulina's feelings for Stalin were quite different. She thought he was the greatest genius in all history. She crumbled diced garlic into her soup, in the Georgian manner, because Stalin always ate it this way.[41]

Her last public appearance before Stalin shipped her to the Kazakhstan wilderness was at a lavish official party for Moscow's diplomatic corps at the Molotovs' mansion on November 8, 1948. She was eager to meet the recently arrived first ambassador from the state of Israel, and her first words to her were in Yiddish: *Ich bin a yiddishe tochter* (I am a daughter of the Jewish people).[42] Paulina blessed Israel and its people: "May things go well with you. If all will be well with you, things will go well for Jews in the whole world."[43]

Golda Meir was accompanied by her daughter Sara and by Mordechai Namir, the Russian-born Israeli diplomat, who described the confrontation with the fiftyish Soviet "first lady" in his memoirs as "a real Jewish human meeting, one that informed the heart." He said that when she wished Israel and Jews everywhere well-being, "tears streamed from her eyes."[44]

Three weeks later, on November 29, Namir met Ehrenburg again at another diplomatic party. When Namir invited him to visit Israel, he responded:

> "Of course I'll visit—but not now. Today a visit would appear to be a political act. . . . The state of Israel must understand that there is no Jewish problem in this country anymore, that the Jews of the USSR should be left in peace, and all efforts to seduce them to Zionism and repatriation should be stopped. This will evoke sharp resistance from the [Soviet] authorities, as well as from the Jews."[45]

Ehrenburg still defined himself as a Russian writer, though his passport stated that he was not a Russian but a Jew. Early on, he had embraced the new Communist Russia, believing in the path of the October Revolution and genuinely feeling that Russia was the New Jerusalem. Despite everything he had learned from the Great Terror, from the experience of his friends like Babel, he continued trying to Sovietize the Jews, believing that assimilation was the only answer.

But in the months after the murder of his friend Mikhoels, Ehrenburg did try to act against the growing anti-Semitism among Soviet writers fostered by the campaign against the "cosmopolitans." Ehrenburg was told by the famed novelist Alexander Fadeyev, head of the Soviet Writers' Union, that Stalin had personally ordered the campaign against the Jewish drama critics for "slandering the Soviet character." During a 1949 meeting of the Writers' Union, a list of names was read out of people no longer fit to be members; all the names were Jewish. Ehrenburg apparently put a stop to it by asking why his name was not on the list.[46] This was an effective move, since Ehrenburg still commanded a certain respect—really fear: no one could be sure whether he was still being protected by Stalin himself. Ehrenburg reportedly took issue with the powerful novelist Tikhonov, the dramatist Vichnievsky, and the novelist Leonov (the latter had accused him of "Judaizing the press").[47]

Until Stalin's death, Ehrenburg was one of the few Soviet citizens allowed to meet foreigners. Few of them were charmed by the tousle-haired *artist*-publicist with burning Picasso eyes; he looked a bit like Picasso himself, his friend and fellow Communist. He was constantly smoking, letting the ashes spill down over his English herringbone tweed vest in one of many studied gestures.[48] American ambassador George Kennan met Ehrenburg two or three times at highly formal official receptions. But "it was simply impossible for anyone of higher rank in the American Embassy to have anything resembling normal social relations with any Soviet citizens at all." It was "a terrible time," Kennan would recall, an "atmosphere of terror and uncertainty."[49]

All the foreigners in Moscow, including the Russian-born Israelis, could obtain only the most fragmentary information about what was going on around them. Mordechai Namir remarked on the fear of Soviet Jews to approach any member of the Israeli delegation, or any other foreigner for that matter. His own mother, whom he had not seen since before World War II, did not have the courage to get in touch with him though she knew her son Namerovsky was Namir, the Israeli consul in the Soviet Union. When he visited his birthplace, the city of Kherson, he recognized a relative, but she fled in a hurry when their eyes met.[50]

Some seven months after the Israeli diplomats arrived in the USSR, at a Shavuot holiday service at the Moscow Great Synagogue, a thirty-year-old man followed the departing envoys and whispered in the ear of Aryeh Levavi, "Do you know what our real situation is, or don't you? They are strangling us." He repeated himself several times and would not leave until the Israelis indicated that they understood the situation.[51] But more typical was the reaction of the Russian who asked Levavi where he bought his shoes. "Abroad," answered Levavi, and the man ran away in terror. Levavi had another chance encounter, with one of the players at the Park Kultura outdoor chess tables. "Do you care for a game?" the man asked Levavi, who answered "yes" just as two of the secret policemen who regularly followed the diplomat arrested the chess player and took him away, "probably straight to Siberia." They undoubtedly assumed the encounter was a "spy drop."[52]

====

In November and December of 1948 the Stalin regime crushed the last vestiges of the Jewish Anti-Fascist Committee. Peretz Markish and the others—including Feffer—knew their end was near. Truckloads of state security agents were sent to shut down the JAC's Yiddish-language version of *Pravda* (called *Einikeyt*) and the Yiddish-language publishing house Der Emes (The Truth).

Hundreds of prominent Jewish cultural figures were imprisoned or executed at this time, and tens of thousands of other Jews of all classes were arrested or deported. Among them were the top officials of the Moscow Great Synagogue, including Rabbi Shlieffer and synagogue president Chabrutsky, who, like Feffer, was a known secret police collaborator. The two men had held several receptions for the Israeli diplomats at the synagogue.[53]

There were unverified reports of a massacre of Jewish workers from the Stalin Automobile Works who were taken from the Lubyanka prison to a pasture outside Moscow and told to "run." The engineer Edinov was shot in the head, while several others were torn to pieces by police dogs. One engineer who fell into a gully lived to tell the tale.[54] Mass deportations of Jews to Siberia took place throughout late 1948 and early 1949 from the Ukraine,

Eastern Galicia, Bukovina, Bessarabia, and the Baltic states. "Some 30,000 Jews were deported from the city of Lemburg, alone. Very little information about this forced exodus has reached the outside world," said a report submitted to Secretary of State Dean Acheson by the New York-based Jewish Labor Committee, whose officers included socialist activist David Dubinsky. These figures were speculative by definition, and definitely were inflated; but they do provide an indication of the extent of the operations that were mounted to arrest and deport tens of thousands of Jews in this period. *New York Times* correspondent Harrison Salisbury also mentioned rumors of mass arrests and deportations. Numerous letters from American Jews to relatives in the USSR during the period were returned with the notation "addressee unknown."[55]

But the five foreign correspondents and Western diplomats in Moscow, living in their terrified isolation, could only theorize. They knew nothing specific about the repression. The Israelis, for example, only heard in late 1948 that Mikhoels's death had probably been murder.[56] *Pravda* did not mention the raids on the JAC. Namir, in a cable to the Israeli foreign ministry in early December 1948, noted: "The plaque of the Jewish Anti-Fascist Committee has been removed. I think that the institution has ceased to exist." He further reported that *"Einikeyt* doesn't appear anymore."[57]

He did not know that many of the most prominent Jewish poets, actors, and writers who had so loyally produced Stalinist propaganda also did not appear anymore. They were picked up one by one. Molotov's wife, the highest-ranking Jewish woman in the USSR, vanished in early December. She had been close to Mikhoels, not only as an activist in the JAC but also as a personal friend. And she had also been a key promoter of the idea of establishing a Jewish autonomous province in Crimea.

JAC chairman Itzik Feffer was arrested around the same time.[58] Two of the leading Yiddish writers and JAC members, David Bergelson and Leib Kvitko, were arrested on January 23, 1949. Bergelson, born in the Ukraine in 1884, was considered one of the greatest Yiddish prose writers of all time. He was also a dedicated Stalinist, whose JAC propaganda included such lines as, "Carrying Stalin's name in our hearts, each one of us must be ready at any moment to sacrifice his life. . . . It's an exalted name—Stalin!—he will save the world."[59] Kvitko, whose books appeared in twenty-two languages, had helped fellow JAC members, the journalists

Ehrenburg and Grossman, to compile *The Black Book;* the two war correspondents would be among the few JAC members to survive.

On the day Bergelson and Kvitko were arrested, the outstanding poet Mikhail Golodny (né Epshtain), age forty-five, was run down and killed by an official car in Moscow—dying like Mikhoels, his friend and associate in the JAC.[60]

Markish, head of the Jewish section of the Soviet Writers' Union, had expected arrest since late 1947, when his superior at the union, the novelist Alexander Fadeyev, told him that certain individuals were sending denunciations to the Central Committee, accusing him of Zionism. Fadeyev named names: JAC officials Feffer and Shakno Epshtein were among the writers who signed the denunciations.[61]

When the agents came for Markish on January 27, 1949, his wife Esther screamed. One of the secret policemen said, "Come now, no need to get excited. Our minister just wants to have a talk with your husband." Among the documents the secret policemen seized in the apartment were Markish's threnody to Mikhoels in Boris Pasternak's translation from Yiddish to Russian, and a copy of Markish's proposal to cede the confiscated land of the Volga Germans to the Jews. Seals were placed on two of the four rooms in the apartment; no one but agents of the organs would ever be allowed to enter them.[62]

Among the many JAC members arrested in the same week in January was Markish's friend Lena Solomonovna Shtern, the Soviet Union's most famous woman scientist, dubbed "Einstein in skirts." She was the discoverer of "Soviet penicillin," which saved millions of lives during the war, and was the only female member of the Soviet Academy of Sciences. Just before her arrest, she had had an angry argument with Georgi Malenkov over the "Jewish quota" at her medical institute.[63]

Among the arrested in early 1949 was a Dr. Yerusalimsky, a highly respected elderly physician who had treated government officials and was close to several of the Kremlin doctors. He was questioned closely about his famous colleagues. Yerusalimsky's interrogators accused him of donating valuable Russian paintings to the new state of Israel through that country's recently arrived envoys.[64]

Word of the arrests spread among Jewish intellectuals in a manner caught by a Soviet Jewish "joke" from the period about "a typical telephone conversation":

"Please, may I speak with Abramovich?"
"He's not at home."
"Is he at work?"
"No."
"Is he out of town?"
"No."
"Did I understand you right?"
"Yes."

Shortly after Markish was taken, the Jewish section of the Writers' Union which he had headed was liquidated. Many Jewish writers—such as Alexander Bezymensky, Nokhem Oyslender, and his wife Mira Khenkina—denounced Markish and the others, welcoming the shutting down of the JAC as a nest of spies. At a general meeting of the Moscow section of the Writers' Union, the Jewish poet A. Kushnerov was supposed to justify the closing of the JAC before his distinguished colleagues. He had to be vigorously tugged to the podium, where he burst into tears, unable to speak. Kushnerov, who had lost his only son in the war, died soon afterward. His wife was arrested and sent to the Gulag.[65]

When Stalin told his Politburo associates at their nightly banquet that most of the members of the Jewish Anti-Fascist Committee had been arrested as part of an espionage ring, the usually stone-faced Molotov trembled and asked, "What will become of Paulina Semionovna?" Stalin pierced him with a mocking stare and addressed the others: "What a question! Vyacheslav Mikhailovich still doesn't know how the Soviet government deals with imperialist spies!" Molotov later called Khrushchev to ask his advice about Paulina; none of them knew if she had been shot or only imprisoned. At a meeting of the Central Committee Plenum, all voted to remove her except for Molotov, who abstained.[66] Everyone, including the Molotovs' only child, thought she was dead.[67]

═══

The entire leadership of the Jewish Anti-Fascist Committee, with the notable exception of Ilya Ehrenburg and a few others, was under arrest; but word that many of the leading Jewish writers and intellectuals had vanished got out to the West only three or four months later. Ehrenburg's continued survival surprised no one. Some regarded him as little more than another Feffer. But most Soviet Jewish intellectuals continued to think of him as someone who, though a stalwart of the ruling regime, was determined to stay alive for a higher purpose—to bear witness, or to keep the Jewish flame alive. Esther Markish and Nadezhda Mandelstam were among them who would regard him in this way.

In February 1949, shortly after Peretz Markish and the others were arrested, Ehrenburg bravely visited the stricken Markish family—Esther, her sons Simon and David, and daughter Olga. He told them that he knew of the arrests but had had nothing whatsoever to do with any of them. Esther believed him completely.[68] Peretz Markish had always "thought very highly of Ehrenburg, though he was cowardly; whoever was not, was killed," Markish's younger son, David, the future writer, would recall.[69]

Beginning in February 1949, Ehrenburg was not allowed to publish anything. *The Black Book,* the chronicle of the extermination of millions of Soviet Jews which he had compiled with Vasily Grossman and other members of the JAC, was permanently shelved, suppressed on Stalin's orders. Ehrenburg's name was deleted from critics' reviews. He was sure that he would be arrested next, and mulled over the fates of his murdered or missing friends. He felt bent in slavery, like trodden grass, and waited for the knock on the door. Until Stalin's death, Ehrenburg kept a small bag packed in readiness for his arrest, a practice among intellectuals that had become part of Soviet daily life since the purges. He wrote a letter to Stalin asking if he had done something wrong. Malenkov wrote back, saying there was nothing to worry about. Apparently the regime still needed its foremost publicist.

From 1949 until Stalin died, the major Soviet Communist propaganda front was the World Peace Council, which called for a ban on nuclear, chemical, or biological warfare; and this is what occupied most of Ilya Ehrenburg's time. By 1950, when he was in his late fifties, he was often "troubled" in his mind and felt life slipping away. He recorded in his memoirs that the "peace movement," led by people he admired like Joliot Curie, was his salvation; he was absolutely certain that Stalin did not want war. He called for peace not only with "the America of Paul Robeson and Howard Fast but also for peace with the America of Mr. Truman and Mr. Acheson. We live on one planet. However, it has plenty of room on it for adherents of different social systems." Even as he mouthed the platitudes of the peace movement, he continued to attack "the imperialists." At a time when Stalin's campaign against the Jews began accelerating, Ehrenburg warned against another Holocaust—one conducted by the U.S.A. and abetted by American

Jews. "American Jewish capitalists support a policy which is preparing a new Auschwitz," he told a Hungarian Jewish weekly in December 1947.[70]

But one of the primary tasks of Ehrenburg (and the handful of other Soviet intellectuals and artists allowed to travel abroad) was to deflect questions about what had happened to all the famous personalities connected with the now-defunct JAC or the Mikhoels theater.

The novelist Alexander Fadeyev led the Soviet delegation to one of the Soviet-backed peace affairs in the late spring of 1949, a meeting of the Cultural and Scientific Conference for World Peace at the Waldorf Astoria Hotel in New York. American writer Mary McCarthy asked Fadeyev directly what had happened to a number of Soviet writers. Where was Der Nister (The Hidden One), author of the classic novel *The Family Mashber?* Where was Peretz Markish? Bergelson? The famous Itzik Feffer? Howard Fast would recall that Fadeyev "not only gave his solemn word as a Soviet citizen that all the named writers were alive and well, but he brilliantly ticked off the titles and descriptions of the work that each particular writer was engaged upon."[71] Fadeyev talked about his visits with them and related their wry reactions to the capitalist slanders about their persecution. Fast believed him, noting that he learned only much later that all these writers were actually dead or being tortured in dungeons while Fadeyev spoke.[72] Unlike Fast, Mary McCarthy "certainly did not believe Fadeyev's response." Why Howard Fast did not seek further information was obvious in her estimation: "Having been still a Stalinist at that time, he [Fast] would not have been interested in the fate of any out-of-favor writers."[73]

The gentile McCarthy was among the minority at the function who were concerned about the fate of the Yiddish writers, while Soviet sympathizers like Norman Mailer and Arthur Miller, the great American Jewish writers, proudly posed with Fadeyev and remained remote from the controversy about writers in the obscure Jewish language. Ehrenburg, when asked about his friends' fate, was glib about it.[74] Often during his trips to "peace congresses" abroad, he refused to grant interviews to Jewish journalists inquiring about his missing colleagues. His Communist friends, like French poet Louis Aragon, formed a protective wall around him and helped him to evade his interlocutors. But the journalists in London, in Buenos Aires, in New York, kept asking: "What has become of Moscow's Jewish writers?" Ehrenburg, when cornered in London on one occasion, said, "Markish? Bergelson? But I never knew these writers; I don't know anything about them."[75] He lied about them even after Stalin's death.[76]

"I knew about many crimes, but it was not in my power to stop them," Ehrenburg was to say tersely in his voluminous memoirs.[77] Undoubtedly, he and his family and his remaining friends would have been killed or imprisoned in Siberian camps if he had said too much. But that was not the case with American Communists like Paul Robeson, who had a famous meeting with Feffer in Moscow in 1949 to prove to the world that all this talk of arrests was nonsense. It was one of the most sinister cover-ups in left-wing intellectual history.

The growing demands in the U.S.A. and Europe to know what had happened to the Soviet Jewish intellectuals had become increasingly embarrassing for fellow travelers and prominent Communists in the West. So Robeson, during a long visit to Moscow, kept asking Soviet officials to arrange a meeting with his old friend Feffer, whom he had hosted, along with Mikhoels, for seven months during the 1943–44 JAC mission to America. The officials kept putting Robeson off while they fattened up Feffer in his cell. Agents brought a suit and tie and a Jewish salami from Feffer's daughter's apartment to his cell in the Lubyanka. Feffer, still the loyal Chekist, reportedly agreed to fool Robeson, and a meeting was set up. Various inaccurate versions of this meeting were published over the years; Robeson would only allow the true story to come out posthumously.

Feffer came to Robeson's room at the Metropole Hotel (which was obviously bugged) unaccompanied and acting quite normally as they conversed in Russian. The agents waited below. According to Paul Robeson, Jr., his father "quickly noticed that Feffer's comments were at variance with his gestures. . . . with the aid of a few handwritten words and phrases (which the singer later destroyed) Feffer 'told' him a terrible story in this way."[78] After Feffer had indicated to Robeson that Mikhoels had been murdered on Stalin's personal orders and that many JAC leaders were under arrest with little hope of being saved, Feffer "drew his finger across his throat [as in an execution]. . . . When Feffer rose to leave, he and Robeson embraced like brothers; both of them had tears in their eyes, because they knew they were seeing each other for the last time."[79] Feffer was taken straight back to the Lubyanka, from which he would never emerge.

Robeson, who sang at Moscow's ornate Tchaikovsky Hall around this time, spoke emotionally about the great Jewish writers and artists living in Soviet freedom, about his close personal relationship with Mikhoels and Feffer, and about the joy of meeting Feffer again. He sang his last song, a Yiddish hymn of the Jewish resistance fighters by Hirsh Glick, first translating the lyrics into Russian:

> Never say that you have reached the very end,
> When leaden skies a bitter future may portend.
> For sure the hour for which we yearn will yet arrive,
> And our marching steps will thunder: *we* survive![80]

There was a complete hush over the audience of three thousand, then a flood of emotion, with people throwing their arms around each other, weeping.

When Robeson went home, he continued to misrepresent the reality of life in the Soviet Union. Apparently Robeson, Howard Fast, and others who knew what was going on felt that "quiet diplomacy" was the best way to help their friends. Robeson made his son vow not to make the story public until after his death, "because he had promised himself that he would never publicly criticize the USSR."[81] The singer-actor who had become as much a leader for black Americans as actor Mikhoels had become for Soviet Jews was covering up not only the murder of Mikhoels and the arrest and imminent death of his Jewish writer friends, but the clear signs of an anti-Semitic campaign that spelled impending genocide. While at the same time proclaiming that American blacks were being "exterminated" by the U.S. government, the great singer was telling the monthly magazine *Soviet Russia Today* in August 1949 that he had met Jews from all walks of life during his recent trip to the USSR and heard not one word of complaint from any of them. "How could there be anti-Semitism in the Soviet Union?" Robeson asked his interviewer, Amy Schechter.[82]

Robeson and Fast were typical American Communists, believing completely in Stalin. As the longtime Communist polemicist A. B. Magil would put it in his old age: "It was inconceivable to us that people who dedicated their lives to socialism would frame other people, let alone be anti-Semitic. We didn't believe in camps, in the executions—it was impossible for us to believe. Communism was the true path."[83]

Composer Dmitri Shostakovich, who posed with Fadeyev, Normal Mailer, and Arthur Miller during the 1949 Soviet-sponsored peace conference in New York, would recall: "The Americans don't give a damn about us and in order to live and sleep soundly they'll believe anything. . . . Robeson went back to America where he told everyone that the rumors about Feffer's arrest and death were nonsense and slander. He had been drinking with Feffer personally."[84]

Robeson would not help Feffer, and no one else could. Somewhere along the line, like thousands of secret police agents before him, Feffer's luck had run out. What is certain is that he knew too much, and Stalin and his henchmen did not need him anymore. Feffer's wife was taken soon after her husband.

After Stalin's death, Howard Fast did try to save Feffer's reputation, while impugning Ehrenburg's. Fast claimed that Feffer, upon hearing that his friend David Bergelson had been arrested, tried to save him: "Feffer pleaded with Ehrenburg and the story goes that Ehrenburg refused. Ehrenburg stood high and well with Stalin. The story also goes that Feffer cried out to Ehrenburg, 'Then I'll do it alone—and when they arrest me and kill me, my death will be upon your soul for as long as you live.'"[85] This story was not only out of character for Feffer, it simply could not have happened: Feffer was arrested at least one month, and possibly two months, before Bergelson. But a good American Communist, even an ex-Communist, would have trouble accepting the fact that the Yiddish poet and Red Army colonel Itzik Feffer was no hero, but a villain, as well as a victim. American Communists thought he was a Jewish god in his Soviet uniform; at Camp Kinderlin in upstate New York, where American Communist intellectuals and fellow travelers sent their children every year, they named cabins after Feffer. At a 1981 New York memorial gathering of old Communists and fellow travelers to honor the "martyred Soviet Yiddish writers," Feffer was once again the main hero. But one American fellow traveler, B. Z. Goldberg, would say that Feffer performed about-faces immediately on cue. Goldberg recalled that a month after Mikhoels's death, he got a letter from Feffer and Lozovsky asking for all clippings, information, and memorabilia relating to Mikhoels's 1943–44 visit to the U.S.A. in order to "immortalize his memory." This was pure Cheka business, and Goldberg knew it.[86]

Pro-Soviet groups like that headed by Goldberg did bring up the subject of the missing poets in 1949 and later, but always accepted explanations such as the one Fadeyev had given at the Waldorf conference, or that of Molotov when he came to New York to address a UN session. When Goldberg and others asked him about Feffer, Molotov responded: "Would the American ambassador in Moscow know if a particular person had been arrested in Chicago?"[87]

————

While Stalin's emissaries held peace conferences and dodged embarrassing questions about the Jewish writers, war talk was in the air. The Chinese Communist intervention in Korea in 1950 led some American and European experts to believe that a wide war, even a world war, was imminent. Intelligence analysts assigned to the task of figuring out what went on in Stalin's mind seemed to take in stride Stalin's growing obsession with linguistics at this critical moment in human history.

As the deification of the rapidly aging Stalin intensified during the celebrations of his seventieth birthday in December 1949, he was increasingly referred to as the Great Philologist (as well as the Genius of Economics, the Great Gardener, the Transformer of Nature, and the Best Friend of Soviet Gymnasts). In the same year when he arrested all the major writers and poets in the Yiddish language, Stalin reasserted the superiority of the Russian language to all others in the Soviet mosaic of nationalities. Stalin believed that languages competed with one another, and that the stronger always devoured the weaker. Certainly, he himself had done his utmost to devour the Jewish tongues, first destroying the Hebraicists in the USSR—under Lenin's direction—and now the Yiddishists, who had been so much more acceptable to Communism. Stalin hated the "loser languages" and often mimicked a Jewish accent, Khrushchev noted, in the mocking manner of "thick-headed, backward people who despise Jews." He was adept at it.[88]

As a youthful revolutionary, Stalin had studied Esperanto, and briefly flirted with the idea of adopting it as the universal Communist language before he became a total Russophile. At the Sixteenth Party Congress, Stalin had declared that all existing national languages would fuse into one common tongue, in complete accordance with a basic tenet of Marxism-Leninism.

The Russian language was on the march. In a 1949 article entitled "Linguistics in the Stalinist Epoch," Academician I. I. Meshchaninov and Professor G. P. Serdyuchenko hailed the pre-eminence of the "great, rich and mighty" Russian language over all others in the USSR and quoted Comrade Stalin's characterization of the Russians as "the most outstanding nation of all the nations that make up the Soviet Union."[89] But while Stalin always heaped praise on the language he spoke with a thick Georgian accent, his own linguistic "investigations" concerned the languages of the Caucasus, particularly languages associated with the subgroup of Indo-European (Aryan) languages known as Indo-Iranian. He pursued these researches until days before his death. In his last conversation with a foreigner, Indian diplomat K. P. S. Menon, on February 17, 1953, Stalin startled the Indian intellectual by peppering him with linguistic questions about the Gujarati-speaking Bhils of the subcontinent, whose language belongs to the same subfamily of Indo-European (Aryan) languages as Ossetic, the Persian-related tongue.[90] Stalin also asked him about the language of Pakistan. When Menon said that Urdu had developed as "a language of the camp" in India—a bastardized mix of tongues—Stalin said, "In that case it cannot be a real national language."[91] Under such a criterion, Yiddish—a mixture of German and Hebrew—could hardly qualify as a legitimate language in Stalin's eyes, and a Mikhoels or a Markish or even a Feffer could only be perceived as a cultural subversive. Throughout 1949–51, Russification intensified not only in the USSR but in the East European satellites as well.[92]

On May 9, 1950, *Pravda* published a linguistics bombshell, a thirteen-column attack—or about half the issue—on the hitherto canonized father of Soviet linguistics, the late Professor Nikolai Y. Marr (1864–1934), who had specialized in the languages of the Caucasus and who had determined that Georgian was a Semitic language. American diplomats cabled the State Department that this was no tempest in a teapot, but a major development, since linguistics and all related social sciences were synthesized in an all-embracing framework of dialectical materialism aimed at serving government policy.[93] The debate was not over Marr's Japhetic language theories, but about his beliefs concerning "the class nature of language," which clashed with the standard Marxist doctrine of "primitive communism" and the ideal of a homogeneous, "classless" tongue. Stalin himself entered the controversy on June 20, 1950, in a huge *Pravda* article: his first major published state-

ment about anything at all in four long years, indicating the importance of the subject in the Soviet world.[94] It was here that he stated
that when two languages compete, one always emerges the "victor," as in "all cases of contact of Russian with other languages."
On August 2, 1950, Stalin followed up with three long epistles to
Pravda, in which he condemned "literal-minded scholars and
Talmudists."[95]

Stalin seemed to be clearing the ground for his next giant stride,
which could devastate his country and the whole world in the new
"epoch of the domination of socialism." The Talmudists would
have to be eliminated. That was the real message behind these
lessons in linguistics, and it was driven home a year later in remarks by P. F. Yudin, former editor of *Cominform Journal,* on
"The Anniversary of Stalin's Observations on Linguistics."[96]
Yudin declared that in the light of the world situation, the USSR
must strengthen the organs of the state, the intelligence apparatus, and the army against "capitalist encirclement."

The further tightening of totalitarian control was recommended
in yet another article on linguistics, published in *Voprosy filosofii*
(Problems of Philosophy), a mass-circulation publication of the
Academy of Sciences. As the Yiddish writers were being tortured
in Moscow prisons, A. E. Mordvinov condemned "bourgeois nationalists" who fostered their foreign tongues "in order to alienate
their peoples from the Russian language and from Soviet culture."[97] It was a linguistic death sentence, couched in scholarly
Marxist jargon.

═══

The main "charge" against the former leaders of the Jewish
Anti-Fascist Committee took years to formulate, and focused on
their alleged attempt to make Crimea a Jewish autonomous republic and a springboard for Western imperialist adventures. Markish
was the only one not tied to the "Crimea Affair," but was accused
of "bourgeois nationalism" associated with his proposal to turn
over the deracinated Volga Germans' lands to the Jews.

The roots of the alleged Crimea plot went back to the early years
of the Revolution, and even before. Calls for the Crimea to be a
Jewish homeland were first voiced in the early part of the nineteenth century, when a Decembrist revolutionary of Jewish descent, Grigory Peretz, spoke of the need to liberate Russian and
even European Jews and settle them on the distant Black Sea

peninsula. At the turn of the twentieth century, the Jewish Bund proposed creation of a Jewish autonomous republic in the Crimea. One Jewish Communist leader of the 1920s, Moishe Litvakov, called Crimea the true Promised Land: "The Crimea is our Palestine . . . for surely you can't compare the Jordan to the Dnieper."[98] And in 1923 the Bund's implacable enemy, Stalin, proposed the same thing: Twenty years before he emptied the Crimea of its Tatar population, and thirty years before he invented the Crimea Affair, two of Stalin's aides, Mikhail Kalinin and Mikhail Koltsov, had publicly called for turning the Crimea into a Jewish republic.[99]

There were some 40,000 Jews on farms in the Crimea during the 1920s, or 6 percent of the Crimea's population; and the Soviet regime favored it as an area for Jewish settlement until the early 1930s, when settlement in barren Birobidzhan was promoted. In addition to the Jewish settlers, there were also indigenous Crimean Jews, called the Krimchak, a non-Ashkenazi Jewish people like the Georgian, Bukharan, and Mountain (Tat) Jews in the nearby Caucasus. James N. Rosenberg, a wealthy lawyer who had visited the American Jewish Joint Distribution Committee's agricultural colonies in the 1920s, became the Joint's main advocate of pro-Soviet policies and promoted the Crimea as a postwar haven for East European Jewish survivors. It was Rosenberg who brought about the Joint's meetings with Mikhoels and Feffer in New York in September 1943, in which the two JAC envoys had secured financial aid for the Soviets. But a Joint Distribution Committee memorandum a year later said that the organization felt "it was premature to approach the Soviet government re any plans for resettlement of Jews in the Crimea."[100]

The JAC leaders and many other Jews believed they would somehow be rewarded after their experience as Hitler's primary victims and the great effort by Soviet Jewish fighters to defeat the Nazis; General Jacob Kreiser of the JAC was among the leading Red Army officers who recaptured the Crimea in April–May 1944.[101] The Muslim Tatars, in contrast, had been regarded as Nazi collaborators, so why shouldn't the Jews inherit their land? The Holocaust and the postwar difficulties the Jews experienced further convinced some of the JAC leaders that Stalin would allow a mass Jewish settlement in the Crimea. There was even talk among the Jewish writers that Mikhoels would be chosen to head the new Jewish republic, and Mikhoels reportedly dropped hints to his theater troupe that something big was in the works for Soviet

Jewry.[102] Crimea seemed a natural choice for the Jews, while government-favored Birobidzhan on the remote border of Manchuria was an artificial product of bureaucratic thinking, a place urban Jews would never choose to live.

The Joint proceeded to negotiate with the Soviets beginning in April 1945, offering to help rehabilitate the Jews returning to their farms in the Crimea. An exchange of letters continued over the coming months, mostly concerning the amount of start-up funds that would be required.[103] All of this would later be used as incriminating evidence of a conspiracy.

As previously mentioned, Molotov's wife, Paulina, was instrumental in getting her husband to pursue the subject of Crimea on behalf of the Jewish Anti-Fascist Committee. After speaking with JAC leaders, she had set up the fall 1947 meeting of Mikhoels and Feffer with her husband and Kaganovich, in which Kaganovich had made the ominous suggestion that the JAC leaders put their Crimea proposals in the form of a letter to Stalin.[104] No such meeting could have been held in the first place without Stalin's blessing.

Stalin and his men sometimes believed their own lies: it made sense to them that the imperialists, preparing for war, were setting up a fifth column in the USSR, mainly Jews. Perhaps Mikhoels and Feffer had been "recruited" by the Joint Distribution Committee and the American government during their visit to the U.S.A.; and if the JAC was asking Stalin for the Crimea, it was also probably negotiating with the Americans at the same time to set up a puppet government there, as a first stage in the dismemberment of the USSR. The Israeli diplomats' naive mailing of Zionist brochures to the destroyed Jewish collective farm settlements in the Crimea in late 1948 could only have reinforced Stalin's beliefs.

When Stalin and other members of the Central Committee got Mikhoels's JAC letter formally requesting the Crimea for the Jews, it was tantamount to a death sentence for the JAC leaders and "led to a catastrophic deterioration in the position of all Soviet Jews," according to a former secret police official. The Second Chief Directorate of the secret service issued reports to its agents that Mikhoels and other members of the Jewish Anti-Fascist Committee were campaigning to get the Crimea for the Jews. The Chekist view was that Ilya Ehrenburg had "refused to play any part in the business and even opposed it, and by so doing appears to have saved his position and his life."[105] This may have been true: Ehrenburg had termed the whole idea "prattle."[106] Peretz Markish was asked to sign the proposed letter but thought it a provocation; the territory belonged to the deported Tatars, he said, and he wanted nothing to do with it.[107]

Stalin had discerned or concocted alleged secessionist conspiracies since the early 1920s; and as Adam Ulam has written, they formed a fairly accurate picture of Stalin's nightmare chart: "It was clear that he was concerned that Soviet border regions would gravitate toward the neighboring states."[108] But the element of paranoia took Stalin way beyond "concern." As Khrushchev said about the Crimea Affair, Stalin "let his imagination run wild. . . . He was struck with maniacal vengeance."[109]

He struck out not only against Mikhoels, Lozovsky, Markish, Feffer, and the other JAC leaders, but at other "enemies" as well. The execution of the Politburo's leading economic expert, Zhdanov's protégé Voznesensky, may have been ordered after he had suggested in a letter to the dictator that Leningrad be made the capital of the Russian federation, an idea which Stalin interpreted as separatism.[110] After Zhdanov's death his followers in Leningrad and Moscow were purged and many executed: some 3,000 Communist party members were slain.[111] "Plots have been uncovered," Stalin told Khrushchev.[112] Some saw the affair as part of the succession struggle of Malenkov and Beria against Khrushchev, or more likely, another Stalin plot to keep potential successors at each other's throats and away from his.

On January 13, 1950, two years to the day since Mikhoels had been liquidated and three years to the day before the Doctors' Plot would be announced to the world, the Presidium of the Supreme Soviet, in reaction to "popular demand," reinstituted the death penalty for crimes of treason. Of course, it was only a legality to restore the death penalty (which had been abolished in May 1947), for summary executions went on unceasingly throughout Stalin's long rule. But now "spies" and "traitors" could once again be publicly executed. Yet in many respects, it seemed a superfluous bit of legislation, since Voznesensky had just been secretly executed; hundreds of lesser figures were also being exterminated; and the Jewish writers and artists would be secretly murdered in 1952. One possible explanation is that the restoration of the death penalty was a signal that Stalin was preparing much wider purges in the near future, against a much larger number of people, including the Jews and hosts of other traitors.

He chose not to use the revived death legislation against the

Jewish intellectuals in 1952. The officially approved leadership of the Soviet Jewish community was small in number and could be eliminated by the usual methods. The Jews, meanwhile, were gradually being "written out" of Soviet society in 1950–52. For instance, when the new edition of the *Great Soviet Encyclopedia* was published in 1952, the listing under "Jews"—their history, culture, language, and religion—was reduced to two pages, from fifty-four in the previous 1932 edition. The operative sentence in this shrunken entry was that "the Jews do not constitute a nation." It was an ominous portent: the eight deported nationalities had disappeared entirely from this second edition of the encyclopedia.

The firing of Jews as a "prophylactic measure" during this period more than decimated Soviet institutions. University faculties, hospitals, and laboratories in 1952–53 lost as much as half their staffs.[113] One important indicator of the removal of Jews from all sectors of Soviet society was in the Red Army, which once had an egalitarian reputation celebrated by Communist Jewish writers from Babel to Fast. Between 1948 and 1953, 63 Jewish generals and 260 colonels were thrown out.[114] This was true of the entire security, intelligence, and media network. At the Law Faculty of Moscow State University, where 30 percent of the students had been Jews in the immediate postwar period, the atmosphere was "of jail, arrests all the time—you didn't dare to complain about the food or anything else."[115] The Jewish professors at the law school, where Mikhail Gorbachev began studying in 1950, were arrested or fired. The Ministry of Higher Education reinstituted a quota on Jews, who were now officially "unreliable" elements.[116] Thus it went, throughout every profession. Communist Jewish activists were ordered by the People's Commissariat of State Security to strike up a conversation with a fellow Jew to gauge his bourgeois nationalist allegiance to the "world Jewish people." Soviet Jews prepared for another nightmare while trying to keep up appearances: a common Jewish expression was, "We pinched our cheeks and made them rosy."

＝＝＝

Minister of State Security Abakumov called Dr. Lena Shtern in from her Lubyanka cell for a chat a few days after her arrest in January 1949. "We know everything!" he roared at her. "Come clean! You are a Zionist. You were bent on detaching the Crimea from Russia and establishing a Jewish state there." Shtern shrugged her shoulders, "This is the first I've heard of it," she said. "Why, you old whore!" Abakumov shouted. Shtern, dismayed, retorted: "So that's the way a minister speaks to an Academician."[117] For the next three years she was kept in her fetid prison cell, and she never saw any of the other arrested former members of the JAC during that time, until just before the "trial."

A few of the arrested JAC members were kept at Moscow's vast Butyrka prison, but most were held at the KGB (then MGB) private prison, the mammoth Lubyanka in the heart of the capital. One reason Shtern never saw any of her fellow detainees was that the long corridors at the Lubyanka, and at the other huge Moscow prisons, Lefortovo and Butyrka, were closed niches, little black boxes where no prisoner would encounter another prisoner or an informer being led down the hall; prisoners were shoved hastily into a niche to avoid any confrontations. Torture rooms, including the "Dentistry Department," were on the Lubyanka's fourth floor. Execution cells were in the basement—windowless three-by-six-foot rooms with black walls marked by white quicklime spots, applied there to cover remnants of blown-out brains. The Lubyanka, an eight-story building that looked down with a glassy stare at the nearby Maly Theater and the Foreign Ministry, was a Baal with a gaping mouth that consumed thousands of human sacrifices. It was just one of ten huge buildings in the area occupied by the MGB, under the Ministry of State Security, and the MVD, which administered the Gulag under the Interior Ministry. Around the corner at 24 Kuznieckii was the Information Hole, where thousands of people waited in line in 1937 to seek word about arrested loved ones. In 1949 the line usually had about a hundred people at any given time. A man in MGB uniform was at the other end. He would look at a list and invariably say, "No, nothing known; ask in another two weeks."

Among the approximately twenty Jews associated with the JAC who were arrested and executed were two other women besides Lena Shtern: Feffer's secretary, Mira Zheleznova, and the American Chaika Watenberg, a former journalist and translator for the JAC.[118]

Lozovsky was the highest-ranking government official among the arrested. The old Bolshevik member of the Central Committee and former deputy to Shcherbakov, Litvinov, and Molotov was well-known and liked by Western correspondents. Khrushchev, who referred to the JAC as "the Lozovsky committee," called him "an energetic person and sometimes almost annoyingly persistent."[119] Among the other arrested men besides Markish, Feffer, and Lozovsky were the poet David Hofstein[120]; the writer Der Nister (the mysterious Cabbalistic mystic reportedly died in the Lubyanka hospital in 1950); Zuskin; Bergelson; Leib Kvitko; Shmuel Persov; the literary critic Isaac Nusinov; Botkin Hospital chief Dr. Boris A. Shimelovich, the JAC treasurer; literature professor Leon Talmi; Academician Eli Spivak, of Kiev; Professor Michael Greenburg; Professor Yehezkel Dobruchin; journalist Nahum Levin; trade union leader Yusefovich, and Chaika Watenberg's husband.[121]

In early May 1952 Lena Shtern was brought to a Lubyanka interrogation room where she met a demoralized, sickly Itzik Feffer. "Well, Lena Solomonovna," Feffer said, "no use trying to deny it. You know only too well that you were involved in an underground Zionist organization." She thought he had gone completely mad, as he repeatedly said: "Admit it! Admit it! Admit it!" Later that month she saw Zuskin, who was half out of his mind; the bloodied Dr. Shimelovich; Markish; and Bergelson, grown old and feeble.[122]

At the *in camera* "trial" later in May, only the judges and the defendants took part. Peretz Markish, though he had been tortured like all the others, defiantly declared: "I am absolutely innocent, and all the others are innocent. You are Fascists and killing us because we are Jews." Shtern, the only one among the defendants to survive, described the trial for the Markish family in November 1955. She said Peretz Markish had been eloquent and courageous in attacking his tormentors and those who pulled their strings.[123] Only Feffer, a true believer to the end, pleaded guilty, Shtern said. Following a tactic developed during the great purge trials, the whole case was built around him "exactly because he was a big Communist and anti-Zionist."[124] Shtern said that Lozovsky also described Feffer as nothing more than "a witness for the prosecution."[125] All the Jews were sentenced to twenty-five-year jail terms, Shtern added, but Stalin then overruled them, saying, "No, kill them all—except Lena Shtern." They were secretly condemned to death on June 18, 1952.[126] Shtern, who was given a five-year term in exile, was probably spared because she was the Soviet Union's foremost expert on longevity, a subject dear to Stalin's aging heart.[127] In addition to the charges centered around the Crimean Affair and general charges of bourgeois nationalism and contact with foreigners, one accuser testified that the JAC writers had "collaborated" with the two Polish Bundists, Ehrlich and Alter, who first came up with the proposal to set up the Jewish Anti-Fascist Committee.[128] Details about the trial released by the Gorbachev regime in 1989 revealed that two scientists, Itzik Goldshtein and Grigory Greenburg, gave damning testimony after they had been tortured. The only defendant who did not break under torture was Dr. Shimelovich. Itzik Feffer was the only defendant to testify against the others. But he repudiated his testimony at the very end, telling the court he had lied because his old friend Abakumov had threatened to torture him.[129]

The executions of the Jews were carried out on August 12, 1952, in two Moscow prisons, the Lubyanka and Butyrka, at a time when Soviet sympathizers in the U.S.A. were claiming that Julius and Ethel Rosenberg, the atomic spies, were victims of an American anti-Semitic conspiracy. Stalin, in one blow, removed most of the remaining JAC activists, the intellectual leadership of Soviet Jewry. Assassinations of writers and artists have been described as "genocide of the spirit," an attempt to destroy the entire culture and literature of a people. It is true that the national idea is preserved by poets and intellectuals. But there were much more direct reasons for Stalin's action. The JAC might have been a dangerous focal point of information gathering, of organizing, or even of resistance to his eventual plans for the Jews.

CHAPTER 8

The Slansky Trial
A Prologue to the Doctors' Plot

No profession in the Soviet Union was more "Jewish" than medicine, and it not surprising that the general purge of Jews from all sectors of Soviet society after 1948 should have been most extreme in the vital field which had been greatly influenced by Jews for thousands of years.[1] It was not extraordinary that Stalin would focus on Jewish doctors as being at the heart of a vast, sinister conspiracy to destroy the New Covenant embodied by Russian communism.

Jews had always had a reputation for possessing great medical knowledge, and they had served as court physicians throughout Europe, North Africa, and Asia for as long as could be remembered; the most famous was the philosopher Maimonides, doctor to the sultan of Egypt in the twelfth century. The practice of medicine had always attracted Jews in large numbers, which in turn generated attacks by anti-Semites exploiting a widespread distrust and hatred of the profession in general. In medieval Europe there were frequent campaigns against Jewish physicians accused of maliciously causing the death of their Christian patients.[2]

The Doctors' Plot had its precedents in Russian history. The first Jew to settle in Moscow was Master Leon, a famed Italian physician summoned to the Russian capital from Venice in 1450 by Ivan the Terrible's grandfather, the Grand Duke Ivan III. In 1490, when Ivan III's son became dangerously ill, Master Leon treated the patient using hot cupping-glasses, a method that would still be in use in Russia in modern times. He assured the ruler that his son would be cured, regrettably adding, "Otherwise you may put me to death." The heir to the throne died on the Ides of March in 1490, and Master Leon was beheaded outside the Kremlin walls in Red

Square, as it was called centuries before the Revolution.[3] The grandson of Leon's killer, Stalin's greatest hero, expelled Jewish merchants alleging that they had imported "poisonous medicines." Stalin, on the other hand, had used the most infamous Jewish poisoner of all time, the ex-pharmacist Henry Yagoda, as his chief executioner in the early years of the Great Terror. But he did not trust doctors in general, and Jewish ones in particular.

Paranoids often focus on doctors as their main tormentors, as in Freud's textbook case of Daniel Paul Schreber, the nineteenth-century German jurist who came to believe that his psychiatrist was the source of all his misery. The paranoid characterizes his or her enemy as having special powers over publishing or banking or the arts, or—especially—medicine. Paranoia was a condition shared by Stalin and his sixteenth-century predecessor, Ivan. Stalin believed doctors kill more people than generals do, and he found Jewish doctors particularly threatening. In his memoirs Shostakovich relates the story of the world-renowned Soviet psychiatrist Dr. Vladimir Bekhterev, who, at age seventy, was called to the Kremlin to assess Stalin's mental condition and dared to pronounce him sick, perhaps even paranoid. The doctor died straightaway, and his friend, the surgeon Grekov, was certain that Stalin had poisoned him.[4]

In the last two decades of czarist rule, Jewish entry into the professions, especially medicine, made tremendous strides, and both St. Petersburg and Moscow soon had a disproportionate number of Jewish doctors.[5] This trend accelerated after the Revolution; and the doctor soon held a special place in Soviet society, in addition to his universal role as a healer of humanity's ills: with a few words on a sick-leave slip, he or she—large numbers of women were encouraged to enter the profession under Soviet rule—could ease the life of an urban factory worker or a collective farmer, or of one of the tens of millions of prisoners in the slave labor camps. Such authorizations for tardiness or absence for medical reasons were no small thing in a society where hundreds of thousands of people were imprisoned for being late to work.

There were approximately 215,000 doctors in the USSR in 1951.[6] Some 35,000 were Jews.[7] A growing number of them served as medical staff in the Gulag, snipping off bushels of frostbitten fingers and toes, treating the main ailments—trophic starvation, scurvy, and destruction of the flesh tissue—and performing countless autopsies in that vast gray netherworld.[8] In the biggest prison camps and huge transit camps like Taishet, prominent Jewish physicians from Moscow and Leningrad headed departments of internal medicine, psychiatry, orthopedics, or ophthalmology in the prison hospitals.[9] Solzhenitsyn has written that those who worked in the Gulag medical sections "never knew hunger there,"[10] but he felt a mystical attachment to one of the Jewish doctors, Boris Nikolayevich Kornfeld, who sat by his bed one night in the surgery ward and told him fervently about his conversion from Judaism to Christianity—something bound to please the pan-Slavic spirit, no matter how privileged camp doctors appeared to be. Kornfeld, "gentle and well-mannered," told the future Nobel laureate that "there is no punishment that comes to us in this life on earth which is undeserved," which meant that Stalin's camps and the Nazi extermination of the Jews were divinely ordained. The next morning, the good doctor and Christian convert was dead, murdered by some criminal who smashed his skull with a plasterer's mallet.[11]

Conditions varied dramatically within the vast camps—some as big as European countries—and across huge territories like Kolyma. Not all the doctors in the camps led well-fed lives, Solzhenitsyn's assertion notwithstanding. Prisoner-doctors could be treated well in one facility and tormented in another, according to Eugenia Ginzburg, who spent twenty years in the Gulag, where she married a doctor-prisoner.[12] Sensitive observers like Ginzburg began to notice a change in the camps beginning in 1949—the gathering menace of a renewed wave of horror. They noted the growing numbers of new prisoners arriving in Kolyma from the mainland, "but it was taboo to speak of it."[13] She thought 1949 was the twin brother of 1937, "advancing on our land, on the whole of Eastern Europe, and, before all else, on the places of prison and exile." Freed prisoners like the Zionist Averbach, who had moved close to Moscow, were being shipped back to remote areas and then rearrested.[14] By 1950 many families of ex-prisoners, living in exile, were being split up. Several of Ginzburg's friends, such as Dr. Kalambet, a physician from Belichye, hanged themselves.[15]

Doctors were high up on the extermination list in 1949 which Stalin, "the Georgian Serpent, yawning with repletion and boredom, was drawing up at leisure."[16] Dr. Shimelovich, director of Moscow's mammoth Botkin Hospital, had been one of the most privileged men in Soviet society before the JAC leaders were rounded up. But he had engaged in risk-filled occupations, such as coordinating the JAC's contacts with foreign physicians during and immediately after the war and handling the campaigns abroad to raise medical aid for the Red Army.[17] His friends thought of him as "a warm Jew, fond of singing liturgical songs he remembered from a synagogue choir in his youth."[18] Publication of the famed doctor's name would be banned, until January 13, 1953, when *Pravda* announced the Doctors' Plot to the world and linked Shimelovich to Mikhoels, the seditious actor-mastermind behind the giant conspiracy.[19] Famous foreign doctors and scientists who were Jews fared badly in the Soviet media: Freud was proscribed; and Einstein's theory of relativity was termed "counterrevolutionary obscurantism."

Dr. Shimelovich and Dr. Lena Shtern, both of whom had been arrested in January 1949, were at the top rung of Soviet medicine. But the "first circle" was the corps of Kremlin doctors. Most of them would be arrested in 1952, but two of them were held as early as the fall of 1950.

The three-story Kremlin Hospital where the elite doctors worked was located in Moscow's innermost ring at the beginning of Kalinin Prospekt near the Lenin Library and close to Red Square. There were no identifying signs or any other indication of the building's function, but a heavy militia presence was enough to tell passers-by to avert their eyes.[20]

Foreign Communist dignitaries were treated here alongside Kremlin leaders like Zhdanov. In Stalin's last years the Kremlin doctors attended to the medical needs of the French Party leader Maurice Thorez, the Bulgarian dictator Georgi Dimitrov, and Marshal Choi-Balsan of the Mongolian People's Republic. Dimitrov's death in July 1949 may have been on Stalin's orders, because the old revolutionary was said to be drawing close to Tito.[21] Dimitrov's death certificate was signed by one of the most prominent Kremlin physicians, Professor P. I. Yegorov, who had been among five doctors, none of them Jews, who had signed Zhdanov's death certificate a year earlier.[22] Yegorov lived in an apartment building at 57–65 Novoslobotskaya Street shared by several other Kremlin doctors, including M. B. Kogan and Alexander M. Grinshtein. All would be blamed for Zhdanov's "medical murder," among others.

Soon after Zhdanov's death at the end of August 1948, Lydia Timashuk, an obscure X-ray technician on the Kremlin Hospital's large and eminent staff, examined Zhdanov's electrocardiograms on her own and wrote one of her regular reports to the security organs, expressing her suspicions that Zhdanov's illness had been misdiagnosed. Timashuk, who was only a technician though she did possess the lowest qualifying medical degree, was a mediocrity with a seething ambition, full of hatred for the Jewish woman who headed the hospital's electrocardiography department, Sophia Karpai. She was also said to have a grudge against Dr. M. B. Kogan because he had refused her request to upgrade her medical degree.[23] Timashuk was *sek-sot* (*sekrety sotrudnik*, a secret informer), in direct contact with Mikhail Dmitriyevich Ryumin, Minister of State Security, S. D. Ignatiev's deputy but unlike his boss regarded as one of Beria's men. Ignatiev, who had replaced Beria's supporter Abakumov, was actively purging Beria's men in the security services in 1952, and was in charge of fabricating evidence against the doctors.

"Minka" Ryumin—ex-accountant, former SMERSH (World War II Counterespionage) interrogator under Abakumov, and now chief of MGB Investigation Branch at the Ministry of State Security—was a short, cherubic little man with a rosy complexion who moved like a cat.[24] He was "absolutely immoral, cynical, aspiring to power and career-seeking," in the opinion of an official Soviet journalist writing in the era of glasnost.[25] He was also very busy from 1948 on, telling one of his chief aides about a "serious, difficult investigation of the Jewish Anti-Fascist Committee," which had been infiltrated by spies and traitors bent on detaching the Crimea from the USSR and turning it over to Israel.[26] Now this "case" was being expanded, under instructions "from above," and it was starting to assume momentous proportions though several of the principals had already been executed. Ryumin had a file of many letters from Timashuk, who may very well have believed that some kind of conspiracy was afoot,[27] though her reports speaking of dozens of medical murders through counter-medicines and deprivation of oxygen were a tissue of inventions.

The first Kremlin physician to be arrested in the brewing affair was Professor Yakov Etinger, who was seized in early 1951, about two years before the public government denunciation of the Doctors' Plot. Etinger was from the Vitebsk region in western Russia, between Moscow and Minsk. He was full professor and chairman of the Department of Internal Medicine at the Stalin Medical Institute—the Second Moscow Medical Institute (in the USSR, medical faculties are divided into institutes). A colleague would recall him as "an extremely bright, great diagnostician and internist who was often called in to consult on the cases of the highest ranking people in the country."[28] "He could be given electrocardiograms to examine without being told who the patient was. Unfortunately, he had a loose tongue, foolishly talking too much about politics, offering his opinions—not good."[29] One of his patients had been Shcherbakov, who died of cirrhosis of the liver in May 1945.

Even some family friends did not know of Etinger's arrest until the summer of 1952. Mikhoels's daughters, for example, learned about it at the summer dacha of their relative Dr. Miron Vovsi in the Moscow suburb known as Forty-two Kilometers (*Sorok vtoroy kilomietor*) in June 1952. Many prominent Soviet Jews rented the small wooden houses situated on the Kazan line for the summer months, including a number of Kremlin doctors, such as Etinger, M. B. Kogan, and Dr. Vovsi, Mikhoels's first cousin and chief physician of the Red Army during World War II.[30]

The second Kremlin doctor to be arrested was the woman whose success had so aroused Lydia Timashuk's enmity, Sophia Karpai, the leading electrocardiologist in the Soviet Union, coauthor with Dr. Binyamin Nezlin of the textbook *Electrocardiogram Analysis*. Karpai, a talented contralto and still a stunning beauty at age forty-five, was arrested in the summer of 1951.[31]

Dr. Etinger, like all of the JAC people except for Dr. Shimelovich, broke under torture. Karpai was the only Kremlin doctor who did not cave in despite night-and-day interrogation in Lubyanka that extended on and off for two years. According to a colleague arrested in the later stage of the Doctors' Plot, "she was exceptionally strong and brave in prison," where her hair turned gray and she became asthmatic and seriously ill.[32] Both Etinger and Karpai were accused of deliberately falsifying the diagnosis of Zhdanov's electrocardiogram.[33] Over the next eighteen months Karpai's coauthor, the cardiologist Binyamin Nezlin, and his brother, Dr. Solomon Nezlin, as well as other important Moscow physicians not directly connected to the Kremlin Hospital, would also be arrested in connection with the Zhdanov electrocardiogram.

Etinger, and the third eminent Kremlin Hospital doctor to be arrested, M. B. Kogan, would both die in prison long before the January 13, 1953, announcement of the Doctors' Plot. They were either executed or died under torture. They may have assisted the security organs in preparing the case against most of the top doctors at the Kremlin Hospital—from fourteen to twenty in number—as well as implicating other important physicians, such as Moscow's chief pathologist, Dr. Yakov Rapoport.

The arrests of the first of the Kremlin doctors in 1951 came at a time when Stalin's mental illness was becoming more apparent to his subordinates. Stalin's personal doctor, the famed cardiologist Professor Vladimir N. Vinogradov, a Russian who was then almost seventy, had been permitted to see his patient only rarely. Now he could not get near him at all, for he was about to be arrested with the other leading Kremlin physicians.

In Stalin's room at his Kuntsevo dacha, he kept his medicines in a compartment of a china-filled sideboard. "My father picked out his medicines himself," Svetlana Alliluyeva recalled, "since the only doctor he trusted was Vinogradov, whom he called once or twice a year."[34] But that was no longer the case. For as Khrushchev has recorded, 1951 was also the year that Stalin declared to Khrushchev and Politburo member Anastas Ivanovich Mikoyan, during a vacation in Afon in the south: "I'm finished. I trust no one, not even myself."[35] And certainly not Dr. Vinogradov, who had made the nearly fatal error at Stalin's last examination of recommending that he take a rest. Khrushchev did not have to study Freud to know that Stalin's "extreme mistrust did indicate that he had a serious psychological problem . . . [his] mental condition was progressively weakening. . . . He was declining fast."[36] Stalin behaved, Khrushchev said, as though the devil held a string attached to his main nerve, and "no one knew when the devil would give the string a jerk, sending Stalin into one of his fits of rage."[37]

It was around this time, in 1950, when Stalin's hypertension was getting out of hand, that he mobilized the entire Soviet medical world to search for a miracle cure for his high blood pressure.[38] Simultaneously, he was crushing the very doctors who could have helped him, making them the center of all evil, the personification of the International Jewish Conspiracy.

======

Nature was Stalin's most implacable enemy, for it hid from him the secret of longevity. It constantly reminded him of his corporeality, the inevitability of the grave. Therefore, nature had to be conquered. The Plan for the Transformation of Nature was a program Stalin launched in his last years, not only to change the course of great rivers and to seed protective forest belts, but to prolong his own life.[39] Ironically, just as his fear of death became manic, he grew increasingly wary of doctors, saying that nature was a better healer than any quack.

As Stalin's associates vied with each other in their panegyrics to the leader, he began to think of himself as one of nature's strongest forces, beyond human fallibility. But even at his most psychotic, Stalin retained a certain clarity of mind, and he could not delude himself into believing that any living thing in the world lives eternally. His image, made of thirty-three tons of copper, would stride the Volga-Don Canal, it was resolved by the USSR Council of Ministers in the summer of 1951. Ten thousand other large statues and innumerable small ones were commissioned. But that was a different kind of immortality, like that of the pharaohs.

In hundreds of thousands of kindergartens from Baku to Leningrad to Vladivostock, Soviet children of the early 1950s sang, "We love Comrade Stalin more than Mommy and Daddy. May Comrade Stalin live to be a hundred! No, two hundred! No, three hundred!" Millions of Soviet people prayed, "May Comrade Stalin live forever!"[40]

When he turned seventy on December 21, 1949, his image was eerily projected from a blimp onto converging spotlights above the Kremlin, like the full moon. His hair was nearly all white and he moved more deliberately; but he still worked far into the night, imitated by millions of Soviet officials. He rarely appeared in public, and never granted interviews or spoke on the radio. Portraits showed him looking much younger than his actual years. Stalin tested his courtiers, often saying, "I'm already an old man." They would jump to be the first to reassure him, "No, no, nonsense. You look fine. You're holding up marvelously."[41]

Obsessed as he was with death and the related fear of doctors, he had even ordered the uprooting of the funereal cypress trees around his Black Sea villa at Sochi because the evergreens reminded him of his mortality.[42] Under Stalin, there was a phenomenal concentration of Soviet medical research on longevity. Lena Shtern had escaped the executioner's pistol in August 1952 because of her expertise on the subject. Five months later, the mediocre Lydia Timashuk would be raised up to become the nation's foremost heroine, perhaps because she had started her career on the right foot: in 1939, as a young medical student, Timashuk was noticed for the first time when she proposed a competition on ideas for prolonging Comrade Stalin's life.[43]

As his high blood pressure worsened, he read the Ukrainian professor Bogomolet's studies on rejuvenation, reinforced his bodyguard, put more locks on the doors, and would not tolerate anyone who put a hand inside a pocket.[44] His fears of being poisoned deepened. His favorite dishes would be tested not only by secret police agents and medical staff, but by his companions.

"Every dish had its own appointed taster who would find out if it was poisoned or not."[45] Every morsel prepared by his old cook, Matryona Petrovna, and served by Valentina "Valechka" Istomina was examined first by Dr. Mikhail Dyakov, who himself was under constant observation by Beria's agents.[46] Dyakov, a Stalin prize winner, famed for his work on efficient feeding of animals, died in 1952 at the age of 80.

The Soviet press knew of the leader's pre-occupations and often reported on the longevity of Georgians, Azerbaijanis, and other peoples of the Caucasus. A special gerontological institute was set up to study longevity in the northern Caucasus, an area with the greatest concentration of centenarians in the world. On August 7, 1952, five days before the lives of the Jewish poets and writers were cut short, *Kommunist Tadzhikistana* published a long article about the collective farmers of Azerbaijan and asserted, with typical Soviet hyperbole, that one farmer born in 1809 was still working on his *kolkhoz* at age one hundred and forty-three.[47] In Nicholas Virta's 1948 play about Stalingrad, *The Great Days*, which Stalin himself reportedly edited, the play's hero, Stalin, says he will live to age one hundred.

All of this caught the attention of American intelligence, which was trying to chart the dark waters of Stalin's mind at a point in history when the Cold War, and Communist triumphs in Eastern Europe and the Far East, made a third world war seem a real possibility.[48] It was just at this moment, as he searched for the Fountain of Youth, that "anti-Semitism grew like a growth inside Stalin's own brain," as Khrushchev put it.[49] But it did not make him move any faster; he prepared to go after the Jews and his innumerable other enemies in the same methodical way, laying the groundwork in a systematic fashion.

Another ominous hint that purges on a vast scale were in the works was Stalin's decision to call the Nineteenth Party Congress in October 1952, the first to be held since 1939. Some thirteen hundred delegates representing seven million Party members registered their names under thirty-seven nationalities, including Ossetians and Yakuts—but no Jews.[50] Delegates Kaganovich and the semiretired Mekhlis had made their choice, and the old joke about what Moses and Stalin had in common ("Moses led the Jews out of Egypt, Stalin led them out of the Central Committee") had become literally true, with no exceptions: Lozovsky was dead and Paulina Zhemchuzina was in exile.

Stalin's own appearance at the ten-day congress was low-keyed; and he left it to Khrushchev, Molotov, Malenkov, Beria, Poskrebyshev, and other speakers to indicate the need for a harder line. Molotov warned against warmongers and called for the Soviet people to be vigilant every minute. Malenkov attacked the laxity that could be observed in the Party organization, making it open to the betrayal of state secrets. The fifth column, understood to be primarily the Jews, was served notice when Malenkov said that "capitalist encirclement" was more threatening than ever, and foreign agents were trying "to exploit unstable elements in Soviet society for their own vile purposes." Using similar terminology, Poskrebyshev linked economic crimes, such as those being exposed in Kiev and in the Party organization for the Ukraine as a whole, with espionage and capitalist encirclement. Like Malenkov, he did not have to use the word "Jews," since everyone knew that the purged economic and political officials in the Ukraine were Jews who were about to be executed.[51]

An important incident that occurred during the congress was Stalin's reported offer to resign his post as Party general secretary—the position that he had made the number-one post in the Soviet leadership—and to give the job to Malenkov. This may have been a ruse to test his associates on the eve of a new purge. Or it may have had an even more dramatic meaning: "He wanted to create absolute dictatorship—without any party at all," according to *Izevstia* correspondent Leonid Koriavin, an expert on this period.[51] Major changes were introduced: Poskrebyshev's Secretariat was given more powers, including that of the Orgburo (part of the original Bolshevik apparatus concerned with senior party appointments and administrative structure); the Central Committee was doubled in size; and the Politburo, now called the Presidium, was expanded to include twenty-five full members and eleven candidates, mostly unknowns. Khrushchev and the other Politburo men squirmed in their seats.[53] The move appeared to Stalin's underlings to be another stage in the build-up to a purge. As Khrushchev would put it in his 1956 Secret Speech: "Stalin evidently had plans to finish off the old members of the Political Bureau."[54]

Neither Khrushchev nor Malenkov nor Beria, whispering to each other in the corridors, could figure out who had prepared the list for Stalin of the new, unworkably large number of Presidium members, but they finally concluded that it was the work of that industrious organizer of death lists, Lazar Kaganovich.[55] Stalin was still unusually solicitous to the only man of Jewish origin in the Soviet hierarchy, restraining himself and his associates from making anti-Semitic remarks in front of Kaganovich.[56] Perhaps Kaganovich was the only one of his old associates whom he planned to spare.

It is clear from Khrushchev's own remarks that from this moment in mid-October 1952 until the end of the Stalin era some four months later, the top Soviet leaders knew that if Stalin stayed alive much longer, they would not. Their options were to commit suicide, to remain frozen in fear until Stalin chose to execute them, or to pool their resources and stay alive.

Two days after the Congress, on October 16, Stalin called a meeting of the Plenum of the newly elected Central Committee. He lashed out at his Presidium colleagues, who sat stunned as he chronicled a list of imaginary crimes committed by Molotov, Mikoyan, and Marshal Voroshilov, whom he pointed at with an accusing index finger and called a thick-headed British spy. Beria was attacked too; but Stalin said that it was not too late for the four men to reform themselves. "It all depended on Stalin's fertile imagination, who was an agent, of what imperialistic country from one day to the next," Khrushchev would recall.[57]

After the Plenum meeting, Stalin barred Molotov and Mikoyan from his nightly bacchanals, telling Khrushchev, "I don't want these two coming around anymore." Khrushchev, Beria, and Malenkov conspired with the two outcasts to try to get Stalin to change his mind.[58] These contacts between the two main rival camps in the leadership undoubtedly included hints that a temporary fraternal alliance was desirable; otherwise, Stalin would surely consume them all.

Around the same time, Stalin's "faithful dog" (as Khrushchev called him) Poskrebyshev, head of the newly strengthened Secretariat, fell under Stalin's suspicion. Stalin told Khrushchev: "I caught Poskrebyshev passing secret material. Nobody else could have done it."[59] The secretary, who had been particularly haughty and offensive to Molotov and Mikoyan in the recent days of their disgrace, was himself frozen out sometime in December 1952 and was dismissed in January 1953. His fall was all the more dramatic since he and the Secretariat had just been raised to the heights at the October congress, and he had been designated a key player in the emerging Doctors' Plot scenario.

Poskrebyshev was short, fat, bald, heavy-jowled, with eyes like a bird of prey's. His name, derived from a word meaning bread baked from scraps of dough, was perfectly in character. He had been a director of murder by poisoning for twenty years under his chief, eager to please on every occasion—except once. Poskrebyshev's first wife was Jewish, and Stalin told him in 1949 that he must divorce her.[60] He came home one night and found his apartment empty; his wife had been arrested, just as Molotov's had been. Poskrebyshev came to Stalin literally on all fours—perhaps Khrushchev had this story in mind when he characterized the secretary as Stalin's "faithful dog"—carrying a paper in his mouth that read, "Comrade Stalin, I beg for my wife." Stalin said, "You need a wife? You'll get a new one." When he returned home that night, his future second wife, a Russian, was waiting for him.[61]

On November 7, 1952, after the heavy snowfall at the beginning of the month had turned to ice and dirty slush, the portraits of the Soviet leaders went up for the thirty-fifth anniversary celebration of the Revolution. Beria, three weeks earlier at the congress—and on innumerable occasions beforehand—had always been mentioned fourth after Stalin, Malenkov, and Molotov. Now he was suddenly dropped to sixth place, after Voroshilov and the dapper nonentity Marshal N. A. Bulganin, the two "military men" in the hierarchy. It was a further hint of his impending downfall in the wake of the Mingrelian affair, the Georgian purges, and the ongoing purges in Czechoslovakia and other East Bloc countries.

Stalin, standing on Lenin's mausoleum, presided over the great parade of one million people in Red Square who shouted hallelujahs to the leader. In a rare appearance at the Bolshoi Theater for the November 7 celebrations, he smiled benevolently as the audience sprang to its feet cheering every time his name was mentioned. He seemed totally unperturbed by the worsening political situation: the war between America and China and their South and North Korean allies was raging; in the United States, Dwight D. Eisenhower, the Republican presidential candidate, won the election that very day and vowed to liberate Communist-conquered territories. But behind Stalin's inscrutable grin was the closely held knowledge that a vast internal "conspiracy" was about to be revealed. Besides the tumorous growth of anti-Semitism in Stalin's brain, which Khrushchev had noted, there was a broad, cohesive plan steadily unfolding in the dictator's mind.

======

"When they are pulling out fingernails in the capital, they're cutting off fingers in the provinces," goes the old Russian saying. The new purges intensified a few weeks after the Nineteenth Congress with a campaign to bolster Party discipline, and with a series of death sentences pronounced against textile industry officials in the Ukraine: H. A. Khain, Y. E. Yaroshetsky, and D. I. Gerson—all of them Jews. At the same time that Jews in the Ukrainian Communist party were being purged, many of the top Communist leaders in the Eastern European satellites—most of them Jews—were under arrest and about to be executed. These leaders, who were Jewish by origin only, were now suddenly implicated in a Zionist-American-Israeli-Jewish-capitalist conspiracy.

In the capital of the vast empire in that same month, about a dozen more Kremlin doctors were rounded up to join Drs. Etinger, M. B. Kogan, and Sophia Karpai. But details of the complex and ambitious Doctors' Plot were still being worked out, and the public announcement was seven weeks away. Meanwhile, a dramatic preview of the big event ahead was being staged by the Soviets and their Czech subordinates, in what came to be known as the Slansky Trial, "a pilot model for Stalin's intended top-level purge in Moscow."[62] It was also a rerun of the "medical murder" trials during the Great Purge. The East European trials produced a mass psychosis similar to the one in the USSR itself, with hundreds of thousands of people thrown into prisons and slave labor camps.[63]

In late 1951 Stalin had ordered the Czech president, Klement Gottwald, to jail the head of the Czech Communist party, Rudolph Slansky, as an agent of Israel and the Zionists.[64] It was an ironic slander against the Jewish-born Slansky, who had always been shunned by Israeli diplomats in Prague as the most anti-Zionist and anti-Israel person in the Czech Communist leadership.

Slansky, a tough and talented political organizer and chief spokesman for the advocates of Soviet hegemony over "the people's democracies," was the second in command in the government and President Gottwald's closest adviser. He had long been supported by Lavrenty Beria, who had ruled the Soviet satellite through the Czech secret police. But Beria's power over Czechoslovakia came to an abrupt end when Stalin ordered Ignatiev, Beria's rival, to purge Slansky and Beria's other key men in Prague, accusing them of Zionist and cosmopolitan sins. It was yet another sign of Beria's imminent decline.

Between November 20 and November 27, 1952, fourteen top leaders of Czechoslovakia's Communist party and government, eleven of them Jews, were tried for allegedly plotting with Zionists to murder President Gottwald, overthrow the People's government, and restore capitalism. The indictment read by the public prosecutor tied together Jewish organizations and "Zionist adventurers," Israel and America, "cosmopolitans" and "bourgeois Jewish nationalists," as well as "Trotskyists, valets of the bourgeoisie, and other enemies of the Czech people," all factors in "the great conspiracy against the USSR."[65]

As soon as the trial opened, Prague's 18,000 Jews braced for a pogrom. Jewish houses and shops were smeared with graffiti demanding, "Jews get out!" and "Down with Capitalist Jews!"[66] Important Jewish Communists were still being arrested, including Eduard Goldstucker, the Czech minister plenipotentiary to Israel. A leader of the Rumanian Communist party, Anna Pauker—a rabbi's daughter who became a Comintern chief, Rumania's foreign minister, and a major Marxist-Leninist theoretician—was among many Jews thrown into prison.[67] Radio Bucharest announced: "We also have criminals among us, Zionist agents and agents of international Jewish capital. We shall expose them, and it is our duty to exterminate them."[68]

East European intellectuals joined in the condemnations, including Czechoslovakia's leading writer, Ivan Ulbrecht, who had once written sympathetically about the Jewish people. In a newspaper article, Ulbrecht wrote: "Before the court sit eleven cosmopolitan Jews, men without honor, without character, without a homeland, people only in love with career, private business and money."[69] Over 250,000 Czech Jews had been exterminated by the Nazis just a few years earlier, but the Czech Communists were not going to pay the bill for Holocaust guilt anymore.

Slansky testified on the opening day of the trial and confessed to everything—the involvement of the Rothschilds, David Ben-Gurion, Bernard Baruch, and Henry Morgenthau. He had orchestrated a Zionist plan to destroy Czechoslovakia: "The entire world Zionist movement is in effect the world of imperialists, mainly of Americans," he told the court.[70] Slansky and the others testified that the conspiracy included Jewish Freemasons, the Joint Distribution Committee, Israeli and American spies, and something called "the Truman–Ben Gurion Plan" under which the new state of Israel would become a U.S. military base.[71]

The Czech prosecutors constantly alluded to the Jewish background of most of the defendants and used the anti-Semitic euphemisms of the Communist movement, though all of the Jews on trial were no more Jewish than Marx, Trotsky, Luxemburg, Zinoviev,

Béla Kun, Yagoda, Mekhlis, or Kaganovich. The number-two defendant, Bedrich Geminder, for example, had always tried to conceal his Jewish origins, despised his people, and was devoted to Stalin. Now the prosecutor ridiculed the former head of the Czech Communist party's International Department and said he was "a typical cosmopolitan" who "couldn't properly understand Czech or German." Geminder testified that Slansky had made possible the Joint's "spy operations" and that he had allowed the Haganah— the pre-state Israeli army—to operate in Czechoslovakia.

The accusations against the Joint, which had been engaged in projects in Czechoslovakia until 1950, would be repeated in Moscow six weeks later when the Doctors' Plot was announced. The prosecutors said that the Joint was a "secret branch of the American espionage service" working under the cover of a welfare organization.[72]

As in the famed show trials of the 1930s, everything was thoroughly rehearsed, the script was well learned, and the performances were professional. The former deputy minister of foreign trade, Eugen Loebl, one of the three survivors, would recall that he had to memorize successive depositions as time passed: first, he was a Tito agent, then an Israeli Zionist operative, and lastly Slansky's agent. "I reached a state in which I no longer felt any shame or regret about my lies. I simply lost all sense of human dignity. I was flesh and blood, but I was no longer a person."[73]

The court was told that "the despicable traitor Slansky" (né Zaltzman) came from a wealthy merchant family, had always remained "a lackey of the bourgeoisie" and of "international Zionism," and was directly linked with Israeli diplomat Ehud Avriel.[74] *Rude Pravo*, the Czech version of *Pravda*, described Slansky's "insolent, perfidious eyes" and "Judas-face," and said he was a "trampled snake" and "cannibal," who presumably should get a taste of his own medicine.[75]

Medical murder was once again a central theme, as it had been in the trials of Drs. Levin and Pletnev with Bukharin fifteen years earlier, and as it was to be in the forthcoming Doctors' Plot. Slansky was accused of trying to murder the president by choosing as his physicians persons with a nefarious past, such as "the Freemason Dr. Haskovec." Slansky admitted that he and the doctor had plotted to shorten Gottwald's life so that Slansky could seize power.[76]

Two Israeli citizens who had been imprisoned for a year, the

Solomon Mikhoels, the renowned actor-director—founder of the Moscow Jewish
Theater, a winner of the Stalin Prize, and head of the wartime Jewish Anti-
Fascist Committee (JAC) of the Communist party—became the acknowledged
leader of Soviet Jewry at the start of World War II. *Above left*, Mikhoels plays
with his daughters, Natalia and Nina, in the early 1930s. *Above right*, he appears
as a Yiddish King Lear—his most famous stage role. (*Courtesy Natalia Vovsi-
Mikhoels*) *Below*, Mikhoels clowns with friend and colleague Itzik Feffer, a
Yiddish poet who was co-head of the JAC.

In 1943, Mikhoels and Feffer traveled to the West as Soviet emissaries and met with many prominent Jewish figures, including Albert Einstein (*above*). Both men are wearing the Order of Lenin on their lapels. (*YIVO Institute*) In January 1948, Mikhoels was murdered—beaten to death—on Stalin's personal orders, probably with the connivance of Feffer. Mikhoels' death was a terrible blow to Soviet Jews; he was mourned as a national hero. *Below*, his body lies in state at the Jewish Theater. (*Courtesy Natalia Vovsi-Mikhoels*) A Moscow center for Jewish culture was opened in his name in 1989.

Many foreign writers and artists had contact with their Soviet counterparts during the Stalin era, but almost none raised questions about the fate of Soviet Jews under Stalin. *Above*, a crowd of students hold aloft a banner of American singer Paul Robeson, who visited the Soviet Union during the Stalin era and gave glowing reports on conditions there. During the Communist-sponsored Cultural and Scientific Congress for World Peace held in New York in 1949, novelist Alexander Fadeyev (*below at left*), head of the Soviet Writers' Union, pretended to list the "latest" works of various Jewish writers, though some were already dead. Composer Dmitri Shostakovich (*center*) attended the conference only at Stalin's command. American Jewish writers, including Norman Mailer (*second from left*) and Arthur Miller (*second from right*), made no inquiries about the missing writers. (*AP/Wide World*)

Henryk Ehrlich and Viktor Alter (*left*), two leaders of the Jewish Bund, at a May Day parade in Warsaw, 1936. Respected socialists, the two men first proposed the establishment of a Jewish Anti-Fascist Committee. Both were killed on Stalin's orders. *Below*, a group portrait of Jewish cultural figures associated with Mikhoels (*seated at right*) and the JAC includes Lena Shtern—the only female member of the Soviet Academy of Science—Boris Shimelovich (*next to Mikhoels*), and (*standing, left to right*) poets V. Kushnirov, David Bergelson, and Leib Kvitko. (*YIVO Institute*) A number were killed in Stalin's "Jewish" purge of August 12, 1952.

Above, a broadcast by leaders of the JAC includes several victims of the purges. *Standing at right*, Shakno Epshtein, the JAC secretary who died under mysterious circumstances in 1945; next to him, Mikhoels; seated (*center*), Bergelson; behind him, Feffer; to Feffer's right, Professor Nusinov, killed on August 12; next to him (with glasses) Shimelovich. (*Courtesy Natalia Vovsi-Mikhoels*) Jewish poet Peretz Markish (*below*), a writer with an international reputation, was also killed on August 12. (*YIVO Institute*)

Dr. Miron Vovsi, a relative of Mikhoels, was chief physician of the Red Army and held the rank of general (*above left, in uniform*). As deputy chief of the Kremlin hospital, he was the primary suspect in the Doctors' Plot. (*Courtesy Natalia Vovsi-Mikhoels*) *Above right*, Paulina Zhemchuzina, Molotov's Jewish wife, was a JAC activist and close friend of Mikhoels. The highest-ranking woman in the Soviet government until Stalin ordered her arrest in 1948, she was reunited with her husband—who never dared question Stalin about her fate—only after the dictator's death in 1953. *Below*, Ilya Ehrenburg (*third from left*), whose wartime dispatches made him the best-known Soviet writer, was one of the few prominent Jews to survive the Stalin era. (*AP/Wide World*)

Politburo members A.S.Shcherbakov (*above left*)—a virulent anti-Semite—and Zhdanov (*above right*) died in 1945 and 1948, respectively, either of alcoholism or by order of Stalin. In 1953, during the Doctors' Plot trial, both their deaths were attributed to Jewish doctors in the Kremlin. (*Sovfoto*) The announcement of the "plot" unleashed a wave of anti-Semitic reprisals in Russia, and the secret police forced many leading Jews to sign a letter asking Stalin to deport the entire Jewish population to the East "for safety." Novelist Vasily Grossman (*below*), like many others—including violinist David Oistrakh, historian Isaac Mints, and Nobel physicist Lev Landau—signed the letter. (*AP/Wide World*)

Moscow's chief pathologist in Stalin's last years, Dr. Yakov Rapoport, was imprisoned six weeks after Vovsi's arrest and was released only after Stalin's death. The last survivor of the Doctors' Plot, Rapoport, now over 90, lives with his daughter Natalia (*above*) in Moscow. (*Author photo*) *Below*, the marble pavilion built to enclose the house where Stalin was born in Gori—site of the last remaining statue of Stalin in the Soviet Union. (*AP/Wide World*)

cousins Mordechai Oren and Shimon Ohrenstein, appeared as witnesses at the trial. Oren was a prominent leader of Israel's pro-Stalinist Mapam party, while Ohrenstein had worked as a minor functionary in the commercial section of the Israeli legation in Prague before going into private business, when he was arrested. Oren, who had never been to the USSR, "confessed" that he had met with Jewish physicians there, as well as with the late Solomon Mikhoels, now disgraced as a "Zionist."[77]

Just as Stalin had personally ordered Slansky's arrest, he now ruled that death penalties had to be imposed on Slansky and the others.[78] On December 4, 1952, a few days after the week-long trial ended, eleven of the men were hanged. Three, including the former deputy foreign minister, Arthur London, were given life sentences. London in his memoirs would say that he knew that "the guilty party is Stalin with the monstrous apparatus that he set up. . . . In vain I ask myself: Why, towards what end?" London's non-Jewish wife, Lise, a French Communist true believer, wrote to the court of her happiness that the "gang of traitors," including her husband, were being destroyed. And Slansky's last words were: "I'm getting what's coming to me."[79] Their bodies were cremated in the Ruzyn prison and the ashes stuffed in a potato sack. A driver and two secret police interrogators drove toward the suburbs of Prague, shaking the ashes out the window onto the icy road.

In Moscow Alexander Chakovsky, the editor of *Literaturnaya Gazeta* and an assimilated Jewish author of historical novels about Stalin—called Slansky and the others "toads defiling a crystal spring" who had tried to "transform Czechoslovakia into a foreign branch of Wall Street ruled by American monopolists, bourgeois nationalists, Zionists and all manner of riff-raff steeped in crime."[80] American commentators expressed dismay and revulsion. The *New Republic*[81] tied the charges to the spirit of the *Protocols of the Elders of Zion,* the "warrant for genocide." Israel also compared the Prague affair to the *Protocols.*[82] So did the *New York Times,* which said that the Prague trial's focus on the vast Jewish conspiracy echoed "the infamous *Protocols* . . . again, but in a Stalinist version for which the ground was laid four years ago in Soviet Russia's own campaign against 'cosmopolitanism' . . . whose victims were predominantly Jews." The Slansky affair, the newspaper concluded, "may well mark the beginning of a major tragedy as the Kremlin swings further and further toward anti-Semitism masked as anti-Zionism."[83]

In addition to the long and vicious campaign against "cosmopol-itans" and "Talmudists," the predominant play which the Soviet media gave to the Slansky trial and the Kiev judgments for alleged economic crimes left the average Soviet citizen feeling that the faster the Jews were sent away, the better. The stage was indeed set for a major tragedy, which was about to be launched on January 13, 1953, the fifth anniversary of Mikhoels's death.

CHAPTER 9

The Arrest
of the Kremlin Doctors
A Second Terror in the Making

In the summer of 1952 Stalin summoned the minister of public health, Yefim Smirnov, to his dacha near Sochi on the Black Sea. They walked in the garden and the Great Gardener pointed to the lemon and orange trees and explained how they should be cared for. Then, suddenly, he asked: "Comrade Smirnov, do you know which doctor treated Dimitrov [the Bulgarian dictator who died in 1949] and Zhdanov?" Smirnov answered that the main physician was Dr. B. B. Kogan, the famed cardiologist and internist.[1]

The fifty-six-year-old Boris Borisovich Kogan, a first cousin of the Kremlin doctor M. B. Kogan, who had died under torture or been executed a year earlier (his official obituary gave the date of death as November 26, 1951, and did not mention where or how he died), was the author of over one hundred major books and studies on medical history, bronchial asthma, occupational diseases, myocardial infarcts, and social hygiene. He was the second in command, after Dr. V. N. Vinogradov, Stalin's personal physician, at the Moscow Medical Institution on Perogovskoye Street, and the school's most popular lecturer. A former student recalled him as "brilliant, talented, vibrant and alive."[2] He dressed elegantly, was driven around Moscow by a chauffeur, and hobnobbed with Communist royalty: he was a close personal friend of Dimitrov's.

Stalin told Smirnov that it was "strange" that both Zhdanov and Dimitrov "were treated by the same man and both died."[3] Smirnov reportedly put in a good word for Kogan, telling Stalin: "I was interested in Dimitrov's case record and the medical findings. I make bold to persuade you that Dimitrov himself recommended that doctor to Zhdanov. He thought of him as an educated and tactful man, and a well-qualified specialist." Stalin said nothing, according to Smirnov's rather self-serving account, related thirty-five years afterward. Concerning Stalin's silence, Smirvnov recalled: "I had the feeling that I had failed to convince him. Stalin had always been suspicious, and that trait became simply pathological in him toward the end of his life."[4] Smirnov was relieved of his duties, though not arrested, around the first week of December in connection with the arrest of the doctors.[5]

In mid-October 1952, during a break in the Nineteenth Congress, Stalin read to his inner circle a letter from Dr. Lydia Timashuk claiming that Zhdanov's death was a case of medical murder.[6] He said no more about it until three weeks later, but his associates knew him well enough to realize that he had a plan, and that it was already set in concrete. Adam Ulam, in his outstanding 1973 biography of Stalin, wrote: "Everything we know suggests that there was no clearcut design in Stalin's mind" in the last months of his life.[7] But in the light of the evidence that has emerged in the last few years, it is clear that Stalin certainly did have a master plan for eliminating his enemies, including the Jews, for whom his hatred had by now become obsessive and maniacal. And as his closest associates knew, "once Stalin had made up his mind and started to deal with a problem, there wasn't anything to do."[8]

On November 7, 1952, as Stalin was reviewing what would be his last parade in Red Square, Dr. Miron Semyonovich Vovsi and his family celebrated the thirty-fifth anniversary of the Revolution with their friends, the family of Dr. Yakov Gottlieb. The roars of a million people resonated in the Vovsis' relatively spacious Moscow apartment—three rooms, two of them very small, in a twenty-story building in the Arbat neighborhood a few minutes' walk from Kalinin Prospekt and the Kremlin Hospital.

Dr. Vovsi's twenty-seven-year-old daughter, Lyuba, who came down from Leningrad with her husband, Yasha, and their three-year-old boy for the event, found her father preoccupied and even less communicative than usual, ignoring both his young son, Lyuba's brother, Borya (Boris), and her own little boy. The prominent Kremlin Hospital doctor suggested to Lyuba that they take a long walk.

In the background as they strolled along the Moskva River the roars grew louder as the tanks passed below Stalin's granite presence on the Lenin mausoleum. Dr. Vovsi normally talked very slowly, in measured tones. But now there was urgency in his voice. He told Lyuba suddenly but in a cryptic manner that there was a cloud over his colleague and friend, Dr. Vladimir N. Vinogradov, the director of the Kremlin Hospital and for many years the only Kremlin physician allowed to approach Stalin—on rare occasions. "Vinogradov just celebrated his seventieth birthday four days ago," Dr. Vovsi said. "He received somewhat strange half-congratulations. Dr. Yegorov is also in trouble." Lyuba Vovsi understood that her father was preparing her for some imminent bad news; she left for Leningrad the next day with an uneasy feeling.[9]

Miron Vovsi, therapist and clinician, was a large, balding man with a big nose and pronounced red lips—a family trait. He was every bit as homely as his slain first cousin, Solomon Mikhoels, nee Vovsi, with whom he had served on the now-disbanded Jewish Anti-Fascist Committee. A graduate of the Moscow University Medical Faculty, Dr. Vovsi went on to become a professor at his alma mater, as well as a department chairman and scientific director at the Basmanov hospital, and at the sprawling Botkin, where foreign diplomats were treated along with tens of thousands of Soviet citizens. Vovsi, a pioneer in military medicine, had devised a new classification of angina pectoris and was the author of many major medical works. He held the Order of Lenin "for heroic acts during the fighting for Leningrad," the Red Banner of Labor, the Order of the Red Star, and several other of the highest Soviet medals. During the Great Terror, along with his friend Dr. Vinogradov and the other leading Soviet physicians, he campaigned vigorously for the execution of Drs. Levin and Pletnev and two other Moscow doctors who had been charged with medical murder against top Soviet personalities. Soon afterward he became a consultant to the Kremlin Therapy and Health Board—thus having access to the top Soviet leaders—while serving as the Red Army's chief physician, and from 1950 he was also in charge of a team of researchers at the Institute of Therapy of the USSR Academy of Medical Science. He never once mentioned to any member of his family which patients he treated at the Kremlin Hospital, or what exactly he did there among the collective of four hundred doctors, pharmacists, technicians, and security personnel. But he was a family-oriented man, and not only toward his immediate relatives. He had spent a great deal of time with Mikhoels's daughters ever since their father's untimely death nearly five years earlier.[10]

Vovsi worked closely with Vinogradov, who was the number-one Kremlin doctor and a giant of Soviet medicine. Vinogradov introduced new drugs and methods of diagnosis and treatment, and wrote over seventy works on subjects ranging from hepatitis, tuberculosis, and influenza to syphilis and pneumonia. The USSR's leading doctor held four Orders of Lenin—the most recent one granted on February 27, 1952—in addition to many other honors. This Russian physician, who sported a well-trimmed goatee, was also known for the collection of old icons and paintings which he kept in his cooperative apartment off Zubov Square.

During Professor Vinogradov's last visit to Comrade Stalin he had discovered a sharp deterioration in the dictator's health, according to his friend Dr. Yakov Rapoport, then Moscow's chief pathologist. Vinogradov wrote in Stalin's case record that he was recommending a special diet and total rest, strictly excluding any activity—exactly what Lenin's doctors had prescribed for the Bolshevik messiah thirty years earlier, after his first stroke. Vinogradov did not show this recommendation to Stalin directly; but Beria, who oversaw medical supervision of the Kremlin leaders, informed Stalin of the physician's conclusions. The steel man flew into one of his indescribable rages, screaming at Beria: "Put him in irons! Put him in irons!" For he regarded the recommendation as a clear attempt to depose him. However, Stalin knew he was not in the best of health; and he quit smoking for the first time in fifty years."

On November 3, 1952, a eulogistic article about Vinogradov's work appeared in a Moscow evening newspaper. Only a week later, on November 10, a clear sign that Dr. Vinogradov was in prison or in exile or dead appeared with the new issue of the magazine *Klinicheskaya Meditsina* (Clinical Medicine), on whose editorial board he served. In this issue his name, and that of another arrested Kremlin physician, Dr. Vasilenko, had disappeared. In addition, the magazine contained an article on myocardial infarcts—the disease that killed Zhdanov—by a hitherto totally unknown medical worker, one Lydia Timashuk, whose appearance in the prestigious magazine suddenly thrust her into the nation's top medical circle.[12]

As it turned out, Vinogradov had been thrown into prison on November 9, 1952, charged with deliberately administering wrong medical treatment to Soviet Party and government officials, and "spying for Britain." Stalin wished to paint even the gentile doctors with the brush of "Jewish" intrigue. Minister of State Security Ignatiev, who headed the Doctors' Plot investigation, asked Stalin what should be done with his non-Jewish personal doctor. Stalin reportedly said: "So you don't know what to do? Link him to the Joint. He's a weak character. . . . he'll sign anything for you." (In fact, he readily confessed to whatever he was told to admit.) Ignatiev himself was suffering from heart disease, which was worsened by Stalin's constant abuse, according to Khrushchev, and he "just followed orders."[13]

Dr. Vovsi was arrested on November 11, 1952, the day after the new issue of *Clinical Medicine* was published and four days after his troubled talk with his daughter. The agents who came for him seized him by the arms when he asked to see their MGB identification papers. "Shut up," one of them shouted as he blindfolded the fifty-five-year-old professor, "It's not for your kind to question us."[14] They took him first to the Lubyanka, the MGB headquarters prison, where he was pushed down a long passage, led up and down flights of stairs, and pulled along corridors. In a windowless room, he was told he must not sit down. His tie, belt, and shirt were pulled off, his handcuffs tightened. An agent came in and hit him in the stomach and then beat him around his face.

The first of a long series of interrogations followed, beginning with queries about the late Solomon Mikhoels, interspersed with such questions, assertions, and threats as: "When did you enter the espionage service [the CIA] directed by Allen Dulles? Who are your collaborators?" "Why did Mikhoels change his original Jewish name, Vovsi, to another Jewish name? All you people had different names before." "Who recruited you—where and when?" "We have all the proof. We can make you confess to anything. Your life is hanging by a thread. You had better reach the correct conclusions." The shirtless Vovsi was shuddering from the November cold; and in his pain, Job's words of fear and trembling came to him: "For the thing which I greatly feared is come upon me, and that which I was afraid of is come unto me."

"We can't let our enemies misbehave," the interrogator went on. "You will be punished. Believe me. You will be punished. We'll get rid of you and your filthy race. Hitler was our enemy, but he was right about the Jews, that they are vermin who must be destroyed. We'll bury you and your filthy race ten meters deep. We never let our corn grow too high. We cut it at the right time."[15] He was kept awake day and night, with powerful lamps shining in his face. He was ordered to admit his alleged connections to Hitler's Gestapo during the war years. Vovsi at first defied his interrogators, saying, "You've made me an agent of two secret services [the American and Israeli]; don't try to associate me with the German one—my father and my brother's family were tortured to death by Fascists in Dvinsk." The interrogator sneered at him, "Do not try to use the blood of your relatives for your own aims."[16]

In the first days of his arrest, Vovsi was shown a primary piece of evidence against him, a *lettre de cachet* from the powerful *Literaturnaya Gazeta* editor Alexander Chakovsky. The letter denounced Vovsi and his dead cousin Mikhoels, saying that the two famous Soviet Jews were connected not only by family ties but by treasonous links involving enemies of the Soviet state. Chakovsky supposedly had learned of the Mikhoels-Vovsi sabotage because they all vacationed near one another in the dacha village of Forty-two Kilometers. Dr. Vovsi did not think the letter, coming from such a literary lion, was very imaginative, as he would tell his family years later.[17]

Besides Vovsi and Vinogradov, nine other Kremlin doctors were arrested in the second week of November, among them B. B. Kogan, whom Stalin had inquired about in his garden conversation with Smirnov. When Kogan's son Leonid, a student at the Architecture Institute, returned to the family's large apartment at 4 Kutuzovsky Prospekt late one day shortly after the November 7 celebrations, he heard loud voices coming from the apartment. "A search was on. My father had been taken away, as I understood. The search went on throughout the night: the walls were checked, they searched for weapons, poison and so on."[18]

Meanwhile, poison of a different sort was soon administered to the "doctor-prisoners," as they were called. Those who were not totally cooperative were served a meal of potatoes covered with a bitter-tasting oil laced with scopolamine, an alkaloid drug used as a sedative and hypnotic. A variety of other methods was also employed. The eminent neuropathologist Dr. Alexander M. Grinshtein, a large man in his early sixties who was the leading Soviet expert on organic diseases of the nervous system, got "a taste of his own medicine," in the interrogator's words, when he was tortured with electric shocks. He was beaten brutally and starved, his weight dropping from one hundred kilos to thirty-seven.[19]

Dr. Vovsi was shuttled back and forth between the Lubyanka

and Butyrka prisons, and subjected to Pavlovian methods that were used to extract confessions. He could not stand up to the torture, especially the continual beatings on his shins; eventually the injuries he received at this time would prove fatal.[20] Vovsi told one of his interrogators that he was innocent, a "loyal son of the Party," but that he could not endure further torture. "My health is broken, my strength and energy are sapped . . . . To die in a Soviet prison branded as a vile traitor to the Fatherland—what can be more monstrous for an honest man? And how monstrous all of this is." Vovsi was given pen and paper and ordered to write down all of his contacts with "Zionists." He used his imagination.

One of Vovsi's interrogators was Ignatiev's deputy, Ryumin, who assured the doctor sometime in early January 1953 that he would not need to use his imagination in the coming show trial of Kremlin doctors:

> "You yourself won't need to invent anything. The MGB will provide you with every sentence of your testimony. You will have to study it carefully and to remember without any lapse all the questions and answers which the court will put to you. This case will be ready in a month or two. During this time you will be preparing yourself so that you will not compromise the investigation."[21]

Ryumin then mentioned that Vovsi's wife, Vera, had just been arrested; their small son, Borya, might become an orphan.

> Your future and that of your family will depend on how the trial goes and on its results. If you begin to lie and to testify falsely—that is, to deviate from our instructions—no one but you will be to blame. If you manage to endure what is before you, you will save your head and your children's, and we will feed and clothe you at the government's expense until the day that you die.[22]

Vovsi was told that he would be doing the party and the state a great service by implicating as many conspirators as possible in the plot: if he did so, his life would be spared, and his family would not suffer. MGB guards were stationed outside the doors of Miron and Vera Vovsi's daughter's Leningrad apartment, and the Moscow flats of Mikhoels's daughters. The same treatment was accorded all of the families of the thirteen or fourteen Kremlin doctors held so far.

Only one old friend dared to visit Nina Vovsi-Mikhoels or Natalia Vovsi-Mikhoels, her composer husband, and their young daughter; they were doubly cursed, relatives of two arch-traitors, Mikhoels and Vovsi. The one person who dared run the gauntlet was their non-Jewish Russian friend Tatiana Troyetska, a strikingly beautiful twenty-nine-year-old writer for the mass-circulation weekly *Oganyuk* magazine, who never wavered in her loyalty because "she was more afraid of her conscience than of the secret police."[23] Because of the automatic quarantine on apartments where the plague had struck and the isolation of the few foreigners in Moscow, word of the doctors' arrest did not reach the West until some two months afterward, with the official announcement of the Doctors' Plot.

The torture of the doctors was ordered by Stalin himself. At a meeting with Minister of State Security Ignatiev and his deputy, M. D. Ryumin, Stalin told Ignatiev, "If you don't get the doctors' confessions we will shorten you by a head." Ryumin was told to "beat, beat and beat again the Kremlin doctors until they confess all their crimes."[24] Stalin was "crazy with rage, yelling at Ignatiev and threatening him, demanding that he throw the doctors in chains, beat them to a pulp, and grind them into powder," Khrushchev would recall. "It was no surprise when almost all the doctors confessed to their crimes."[25]

Soon afterward members of the new Presidium received protocols of the doctors' confessions of guilt. It was reportedly on this occasion that Stalin said, "You are blind like young kittens; what will happen without me? The country will perish because you do not know how to recognize enemies."[26]

Khrushchev, in describing the Doctors' Plot in his memoirs, mentioned only the non-Jewish physicians by name. In addition, he described "an elderly doctor" who treated him immediately after the October 1952 congress:

> While he was listening to my heart, he put his ear against my chest. I was touched by his thoughtfulness and his care. I felt terrible at that moment, but not because I was sick. I was tormented because I had already read the testimony against this old doctor, whose concern for my health I found so touching, and I knew that no matter what I said Stalin wouldn't spare him.[27]

But although Khrushchev would term the Doctors' Plot "a shameful business . . . a cruel and contemptible thing,"[28] he deliberately tried to divert attention from the larger implications of the affair, commented Edward Crankshaw, who edited his memoirs. "He treats it as an example of Stalin's nastiness in attacking such innocents as doctors. The unfortunate doctors, most of whom were Jews, were no more than pawns in a major operation directed against Khrushchev's colleagues, an operation which was also intended to involve Soviet Jewry in a wholesale pogrom."[29]

Khrushchev and the others, conspiring to stay alive while Stalin wove his subtle web, had good reason for diverting attention from the true importance of the Doctors' Plot: they themselves were implicated in and compromised by the genocidal scheme then being drawn up. In any case, after March 1953, Stalin's former henchmen would try to dissociate themselves from his criminal acts and to say that he was exclusively responsible.

Again without mentioning the word "Jews," Khrushchev recalled how Russians reacted to cholera outbreaks during his youth, in the years before the Revolution. Anti-Jewish riots broke out among the people of the Donbass, the mining district of the Ukraine. They mercilessly beat Jewish doctors, claiming that they were poisoning their patients. Doctors were accused of throwing some kind of white powder into the wells, Khrushchev recalled, "and now in our time, these same dark powers were rearing their heads again."[30] Stalin biographer Isaac Deutscher also saw the Doctors' Plot as "that truly Russian pogrom, which was to eclipse all the pogroms of the Black Hundreds and all the Beylis [Beilis] trials [for ritual murder] that had taken place in all the Russias of the Tsars."[31] It was an old and proven method, whipping up anti-Semitic hysteria to distract the public from the real social and economic problems of the time. Israeli diplomat Aryeh "Lova" Eliav, who served in Moscow in the 1950s, would say that "whether he read it or not, Stalin believed in the *Protocols of Zion*, in the Jewish cabal."[32]

Soon after the November arrests of the doctors, Marshall I. S. Konev, who held a special position in the army because he was particularly close to Stalin, sent a letter to the dictator claiming that he, too, was being poisoned with "the same medicines used to kill Zhdanov."[33] Stalin was using Konev, a former commissar, as a counterweight to the popular Marshal Georgi K. Zhukov, the World War II chief of staff whom the dictator had kept out of the public eye since 1946. Konev, postwar commander-in-chief of the Soviet ground forces, had become inspector general in 1950. His letter was probably dictated to him directly by his patron.

It was an absurd contention, of course. The top political, military, and secret police officials were always wary of medical treatment, and kept close checks on all the Kremlin doctors and their associates. For example, in 1946 Vovsi's friend Dr. Yakov Gottlieb treated the head of the Azerbaijan Communist party, a favorite of Stalin's named Bagirov, by first injecting himself with a special solution that had aroused the party leader's suspicions before administering it to his patient.[34]

Everyone in the Presidium realized that Konev's charges were a fabrication. The ministers continued to exchange their opinions behind Stalin's back,[35] preparing for the public announcement of the Doctors' Plot.

CHAPTER 10

Assassins in White Coats

The Plot Revealed

Early on the morning of January 13, 1953, a freezing day in the depths of winter, fire broke out or was deliberately set at the Alexei Bakhrushin Museum of Russian Theater on Moscow's Baumanskaya Street, completely destroying the last relics of Solomon Mikhoels's GOSET Jewish theater, as well as the archives of Meyerhold's theater and of the Hebrew Camieri Theater of the 1920s. Mikhoels, Meyerhold, Hebrew theater, and now Yiddish theater had all been murdered by Stalin, and today was the fifth anniversary of Mikhoels's death. Given the well-known Soviet propensity for remembering certain dates in such a telling manner, the destruction of the theater museum was undoubtedly a case of officially inspired arson.

Mikhoels's elder daughter, Natalia, had been walking near her house with her four-year-old daughter Victoria, shadowed as usual by an MGB agent, when someone who knew her passed by. He told her about the fire without looking at her, almost without moving his lips. She walked over to the gutted museum, where she learned that nothing had survived: old posters, documents, programs, photos, memoirs, had gone up in flames.[1]

But there was much bigger news on that freezing day. As the last vestiges of her father's legacy smoldered in the ruins of the museum, the name Mikhoels was published for the first time since it had disappeared in 1948, in an article of ominous importance. Another close relative's name—Dr. Miron Vovsi—figured even more prominently. The news which chilled the blood of millions of people, purported to reveal that the Kremlin doctors, most of them Jews, had murdered top Russian Soviet leaders and had plotted against others—perhaps even Stalin himself.

"Arrest of a Group of Saboteur-Doctors" read the *Pravda* banner over a ten-paragraph Tass report.[2] It was the first time in years that the Soviets had made public any of the massive number of "political arrests" and executions that were carried out on a continuing basis (there had not been a whisper of the recent liquidation of the Jewish artists and intellectuals, for example).

The accompanying front-page editorial, entitled "Miserable Spies and Assassins under a Mask of Professors and Physicians," covered the two righthand columns of *Pravda* and was much longer than the "news" report, which had been edited to fit newspaper requirements. Stalin personally approved both pieces, after blue-penciling his changes.[3]

The affair set off an international blizzard of diplomatic cables and reports, including warnings that the "plot" was a prelude to massive purges and possibly even preparations for a third world war.

"Some time ago agencies of state security discovered a terrorist group of doctors who had made it their aim to cut short the lives of active public figures of the Soviet Union through medical treatment involving sabotage," the news report said. Nine "participants in this terrorist group" were named in the following order: Professor M. S. Vovsi, Professor V. N. Vinogradov, Professor P. I. Yegorov, Professor A. I. Feldman, Professor Y. G. Etinger, Professor A. M. Grinshtein, G. I. Mayorov, M. B. Kogan, and Professor B. B. Kogan.

Although it was not specifically stated that at least six of the nine doctors were Jews, the report repeated those names that were Jewish and said that they were "connected with the international Jewish bourgeois nationalist organization 'Joint,' established by American intelligence for the alleged purpose of providing material aid to Jews in other countries." The report singled out Dr. Vovsi, saying he had confessed that he received American orders "to wipe out the leading cadres of the USSR through the 'Joint' organization, via a Moscow doctor, Shimelovich [who had been executed on August 12, 1952], and the well-known Jewish bourgeois nationalist Mikhoels."[4] Drs. Vinogradov, M. B. Kogan, and Yegorov had proven to be "old agents of British intelligence," the report added.

The report asserted that "documentary evidence, investigations, the conclusions of medical experts, and the confessions of the arrested have established that the criminals, who were secret enemies of the people, sabotaged the treatment of patients and . . . doomed them by wrong treatment."[5] The criminals had confessed that they had killed Comrade Zhdanov by "incorrectly diagnosing his illness, concealing an infarct of his myocardium," and prescribing "a regime counter-indicated for this serious ailment. . . . the criminals likewise cut short the life of Comrade A. S. Shcherbakov by incorrectly employing strong drugs in his treatment. [They] prescribed a regime which was mortal to him and thus brought him to his death." Furthermore, the "criminal doctors sought above all to undermine the health of leading Soviet military personnel, to put them out of action and to weaken the defense of the country."

The top military men listed were three marshals—A. M. Vasilevsky, L. A. Govorov, and Konev—as well as Admiral G. I. Levchenko and General S. M. Shtemenko; all of them were known to be particular favorites of Stalin. Those who were not named as potential murder victims, especially Marshal Zhukov, had the most to fear from Stalin's announcement.

The *Pravda* editorial called the Kremlin doctors "monsters and murderers" who had trampled on the sacred banner of science. The ethnic Russians Zhdanov and Shcherbakov, generally known to the public as leaders of the wartime and postwar campaigns against the Jews, were victims of "this gang of anthropoid animals," who also planned to eliminate the leaders of the armed forces "hence weakening the defense posture of the country. The arrest of the criminals stopped their perfidious plans, and put an end to their monstrous goals." They were paid agents of the Americans, British, and the Joint, the "Zionist spying organization." It was all part of an insane plan by the capitalists, who were "preparing feverishly for another world war."[6]

Key sections of the January 13 editorial commentary called on the Soviet people "to intensify their vigilance in every possible way; to be on the alert for all manifestations of the warmongers and their agents, and to strengthen continuously the Armed Forces as well as the Intelligence Service of our country." A clear warning to Beria and his men came toward the end of the long commentary:

The fact that a group of contemptible degenerates among the "men of science" could act unpunished for some time indicates that some of our Soviet organs and their leaders abandoned vigilance and became infected by gullibility. The Agencies of

State Security did not detect in time the existence of a
saboteur, terrorist organization among the doctors. These
Agencies, however, should have been particularly vigilant,
since history has already known cases of foul murderers and
traitors of the country hiding behind the masks of doctors; like
those "doctors" Levin and Pletnev, who, following orders of
the enemies of the Soviet Union, killed the great Russian
writer, Maxim Gorky, and the prominent functionaries of the
Soviet Government, V. V. Kuibyshev and V. R. Menzhinsky, by
way of deliberate application of improper medical treatment.

The article also mentioned that "Comrade Stalin warned many
times that our achievements also have a dark side." The people
were being lulled and led into a trap, *Pravda* quoted Stalin as
saying, "giving the class enemy a chance to prepare for war
against the Soviet Government." *Izvestia,* the second largest national newspaper, accused officials of the Health Ministry of over-
looking the wrecking activities of the heinous degenerates who sold
out to the enemies of the Soviet Union. A two-column-long editorial
on the paper's front page, similar to *Pravda's* that day, also condemned "certain unstable sections of our intelligentsia who are
infected by the virus of truckling to everything foreign." This
disease was, of course, another reference to the "cosmopolitans,"
the Jews.[7]

Hundreds of Soviet publications in every corner of the empire
splashed coordinated attacks across their front pages; and for almost six weeks hence, on every day until just before Stalin's demise,
the stories about the traitorous Jewish doctors and their Jewish and
Russian accomplices proliferated in every section of Soviet society.
The articles seemed to fall into three categories: stories elaborating
on the alleged role of the Joint and Zionists in spying and wrecking
operations; articles exhorting Soviet citizens to greater "vigilance"
and quoting names—most of them Jewish—of recently unmasked
bourgeois nationalists, spies, and saboteurs; and stories about em-
bezzlement and corruption in various ministries.

Trud, the mass-circulation labor journal, said that "Soviet Justice will crush like a poisonous reptile the criminal band which sold
itself for dollars and pounds sterling," and charged that Zionism
had become the weapon of American and English warmongers.
The monopolists used for their dirty purposes "Jewish Zionist organizations, including the Jewish bourgeois nationalist organiza-

tion Joint."[8] Chakovsky's *Literaturnaya Gazeta* uncovered a subversive cell in the Learned Council of the Moscow Library Institute led by "Abramov, Levin, Fried, Eikenvolts."[9] Cosmopolitan spies like S. D. Gurevich and "displaced persons" such as T. A. Sas who were recruited by Western agents were unmasked almost every day, as the spy mania and recurrent fear of "capitalist encirclement" continued to resonate.[10]

Meditsinski Rabotnik gave a long list of miscreant Jews at the Central Clinic for Legal Psychiatry. The Jewish doctors there had not only refused to apply patriotic Russian psychiatry to their patients, but propagated the false and harmful theories of two fellow Jews, Freud and Bergson. Two other articles in the same issue attacked "an unscientific and harmful book by Professor Rapoport on food and digestion," and the stubborn refusal of two young Jewish doctors, G. Svet and "his girlfriend E. Zalmanson," to accept assignments outside Moscow.[11] Food and poison were, of course, directly linked: the newspaper *Soviet Lithuania* warned against "enemy elements—bourgeois nationalists and Jewish Zionists," who had got their toxic hands on important posts in the Ministry of Milk and Meat.[12]

The cover of *Krokodil*, the Soviet "satirical" magazine, featured a cartoon of a bloodthirsty, dollar-crazed doctor, whose mask had been stripped off by the Hand of Justice to reveal an evil Jew. An article inside mentioned the six Kremlin Jewish doctors first, and then two of the three non-Jews, Vingradov and Yegorov, and said that they "knew how to change the expression in their eyes to give their wolves' souls a human aspect." The doctors were "the personification of baseness and abomination, the same as Judas Iscariot." They had all attended "a well-known school directed by the hypocrite Mikhoels, to whom nothing was sacred and who, for thirty pieces of silver, sold his soul." Then, in a paragraph drawn from the same atavistic source as the *Protocols*, the magazine said: "The black hatred of our country has united in one camp American and British bankers, colonialists, kings of arms, Hitler's defeated generals dreaming of vengeance, representatives of the Vatican, loyal adherents of the Zionist *kahal* [Jewish Community]."[13]

The mass-circulation foreign affairs journal *New Times*, taking its cue from the "doctor-wreckers" case, alleged that Zionists were assisting "American Warmongers" to revive Nazism. Israel was helping the United States to create a fifth column in the USSR in exchange for U.S. support.[14] *Izvestia* tied together the doctor-assassins in the USSR, the "Slansky gang" in Czechoslovakia, and trials of Jews in Hungary, Bulgaria, Poland, and Albania as proof of a widespread American espionage scheme, and demanded "vigilance and more vigilance."[15]

No opportunity would be missed. *Pravda* took advantage of the eighteenth anniversary of Kuibyshev's death on January 25 to emphasize the espionage aspects of his alleged murder and to warn against "alien penetration" and "poisoner-doctors" such as Dr. Levin, executed in 1938, and the band of physicians headed by Dr. Vovsi. Kuibyshev, *Pravda* reminded the nation, had been "villainously done to death by monsters who were disguised as doctors. . . . The foul hirelings of foreign imperialist intelligence agencies brought about his death."[16] Another reminder of the 1930s, and an indication that the purges were already under way, appeared in a major January 14 essay in the Party theoretical organ *Kommunist* by Leningrad party boss Frol Kozlov, who recalled how the Great Purges had rid the Soviet Union of a fifth column, and that this was now being done once again.[17]

But it was in the Ukraine, traditionally the site of the bloodiest pogroms against the Jews, where the new purge campaign appeared to be most intense. A groups of twenty doctors arrested in Zhitomir were called "child murderers" by Ukrainian newspapers. *Pravda Ukrainy* ran a lead editorial about "counter-revolutionary wreckers," such as the three men recently executed in the Ukrainian capital, and commented: "All these Kohains and Yaroshetskiis, Grinshteins . . . the Kaplans and Polyakovs . . . arouse the profound loathings of the people."[18] It was an echo of Sergei Vasiliyev's famous 1949 anti-Semitic poem, "People We Don't Need in Russia," which similarly had listed Jewish names.[19]

The former labor correspondent of *Pravda Ukrainy* in Donetsk, the mining capital of the Donbass region, was a Jewish journalist, Boris Shcharansky, who had been pushed out by an anti-Semitic editor and was now working for the local *Sozialistik Donbass*. Shcharansky, whose younger son Anatoly, the future "Prisoner of Zion" was then five years old, would never forget the atmosphere of fear among the many Jews on the provincial newspaper, and the concurrent excitement of the Communist faithful: the editor-in-chief "couldn't sleep at night because he hadn't come up yet with a list of criminals' names."[20]

A staff meeting of the Donetsk paper was called immediately after the January 13 bombshell. The editor-in-chief, who was among those most pleased by the intensification of the anti-Jewish campaign, told the staff that their mission was to "find all cosmopolitans." He said that "Moscow and Leningrad are working hard on this, and we do nothing." Cosmopolitans were also to be found on the newspaper's staff, he added, and they must be eliminated. All the Jews at the meeting were very quite and fearful; they knew MGB agents were present. The staff was told to write about "bad doctors, bad workers, takers of bribes," and to find as many with Jewish names as possible; their full names and patronymics would be published to show clearly that they were Jews. *Sozialistik Donbass,* on February 26, published a long report by Yuri Chernitzen that the doctors of Donbass had lost all sense of duty, misdiagnosed and maltreated patients, and did not possess proper medical degrees. He mentioned Chief Physician Shapiro of the Donbass Hospital; Professors Weisberg, Mamberg, and Frankel; and Drs. Dubizer, Epshtein, and Sherman. In contrast to the doctors, all of the allegedly mistreated patients had Russian names.

After the article appeared, another newspaper staff meeting was called to praise "the good work by our young correspondent Chernitzen," which had enhanced the paper's efforts to expose the local angle of the nationwide medical plotting. First Secretary Prochakov of the Donetsk Communist party phoned the editor to compliment him on the "useful" exposé, and said that he had ordered every hospital and clinic in the city to study the article and to reach the necessary conclusions. Boris Shcharansky watched the editor snap to attention when the phone call came in and respond to the compliments by saying "I am happy to serve the Soviet Union!" Later that day, at his local clinic, Shcharansky heard one old woman beg to see only a Russian doctor, "because I don't want to see a Jew."

The same reactions occurred in thousands of Soviet cities and towns across nine time zones. Over a period of about forty days, the Soviet media, with their frequent stories about criminal Jewish doctors and numerous medical plots, whipped hysterical anti-Semitism into a mass psychosis. The witchhunt was on against doctor-poisoners, Zionist agents, spies, and wreckers, and every doctor with a Jewish-sounding name was nervous and edgy.

In the Tishin marketplace in Moscow on the day the plot was announced, Ilya Ehrenburg heard a drunk shouting "The Jews tried to poison Stalin."[21] Actress Etel Kowenskaya, a beautiful young Polish Jew who had studied under Mikhoels and now was

playing Desdemona in a Moscow theatrical production of *Othello,*
was told by a fellow actor at rehearsals on the afternoon of January
13, "Don't come in now, it'll only hurt you." When she looked
confused, he asked her, "Didn't you read the papers today?" The
Stalin Prize-winning Russian actor who played Othello, Nikolai
Mordvinov, took her hand, squeezed it, and put it on his heart. She
understood: it meant that he did not believe a word about the
Jewish Doctors' Plot. "It gave me strength," she would recall.[22]

Jewish doctors, nurses, and pharmacists were being exposed, as
primitive superstitious fears of medical treatment swelled like a
noxious boil. In Tashkent, Nadezhda Mandelstam heard a Russian
student claiming that a Jewish doctor had tried to murder the
student's baby. "Similar scenes were played out all over the place;
everyone raved about saboteurs and killer doctors."[23] Many believed that Jewish doctors injected their patients with cancer-
causing agents, or syphilis. All along the Volga, a story spread that
a Jewish doctor had made a dog out of a boy.[24] For a Jewish high
school student like Raisa Palatnik, "it was scary to leave the class-
room and go into the hallway because from all sides you heard,
'You Yids, you poisoned Gorky, you wanted to poison Stalin, you
poisoned all our great leaders.' . . . Even the teachers allowed
themselves such remarks."[25]

Jewish pharmacists, denounced as American agents, were accused of dispensing pills made of dried fleas. The Jewish head of a
Moscow pharmacology institute which supplied medicines to Dr.
Vovsi and other Kremlin physicians collapsed on January 13, which
prevented his arrest; he remained bedridden for the next seven
years.[26] Medical students were forbidden to mention Vovsi,[27] and
his name disappeared from library lists.

In Leningrad it was generally easier for the Jews; there were no
arrests, as yet. But a commission was set up to remove Jews from
medical facilities. Chemist Boris Abramovich Vovsi, a nephew of
the doctor, was dismissed from his assistant professorship at the
Technological Institute in mid-January, in one of many such incidents.[28] When Professor Choldin, the eminent chief surgeon at the
Leningrad Cancer Hospital, was fired, his patients protested vigorously. The hospital director told them he had been ordered to fire
him. But some Russian medical men stood by their Jewish colleagues. Professor Kedrov, a department chief at the Leningrad
Medical Institute and the nephew of writer Andrei Bitov, called the
six Jews who worked under him to his office. "Sit down, please,"

he said, standing behind his desk. "I want to beg your pardon," he said, "as a Russian man and a Russian physician. This 'plot' is shameful, and I will do all in my power to help you." He then bowed them out.[29]

Soon after the announcement, Natalia Vovsi-Mikhoels, as she walked with four-year-old Victoria through a Moscow garden, encountered another young mother, who knew the family. The woman said that the trial of the criminal doctors would take place in a short time, and that it was not good to be a Jew. "All of them are traitors, you know, and your uncle, Dr. Vovsi, was the worst of them, and your father, of course," she said. Victoria then asked her mother, "What is a Jew?" Natalia answered, "I won't say; just that we, our whole family, are Jews, and you are, too."[30]

Even many Russian intellectuals, like the aspiring young poet Yevgeny Yevtushenko, believed the newspaper reports in their entirety, as he recorded in his *Precocious Autobiography*. A fellow poet, whom Yevtushenko had known since their schooldays, waved *Pravda* in his face and said: " See, what did I tell you? Jews, the whole lot of them!"[31] And Sonia, widow of the Russian writer and Stalin sycophant Vsevold Vishnevski, who had died of an illness two years earlier at age fifty-one, went around yelling that her husband had been killed by the saboteur doctors of the Kremlin Hospital.[32] So it was not strange that the revelations about the grand plot electrified the ordinary Russian, who immediately began to think about his local clinic or hospital physician, wondering whether he could possibly be safe, if powerful men like Zhdanov were not. Indeed, the ghosts of Zhdanov and Shcherbakov had been summoned by Stalin to prepare the way for the liquidation of his perceived enemies on a massive scale.

The night before the January 13 announcement, Stalin had attended a performance by Polish artists of the Mazowsze State Song and Dance Ensemble at the Bolshoi, appearing in the Government Box on the left side of the theater and seeming to be in fine spirits. The British embassy in Warsaw, however, reported that a member of the troupe who met Stalin up close described him as appearing "very old and 'gaga.' "[33] But no one suspected that this would be his last public appearance. Three thousand militiamen in navy-blue uniforms and secret servicemen surrounded Sverdlov Square as Stalin and his entourage entered the theater, guided by ushers in black livery and white gloves. A thousand lights and thunderous applause greeted the dictators' appearance. At that moment he must have relished the spectacular drama he was to unveil the next morning—certain that the Doctors' Plot would make the best theater since the three great purge trials of the 1930s, sure to be welcomed by his vast audience.

Diplomats, grasping to pick up any signs of change in the Soviet power structure, always noted who stood closest to Stalin during his rare appearances in public. Because of the Jewish focus of the January 13 announcement, it was noticed, for example, that while the *Herald Tribune* had mentioned Kaganovich as among those attending the Bolshoi with Stalin, the French Communist paper, *L'Humanité,* did not include his name among the attending dignitaries.[34]

But it was not Kaganovich who had cause to be worried. Beria, who also went to the Bolshoi performance, and was listed as attending right behind Molotov and Malenkov, as was customary, could read all the hints about his imminent demise in the *Pravda* articles the morning after the Polish performance. It was obvious that he was a principal target of the Doctors' Plot, and that he would be held responsible for what Stalin had called "lack of security in the Kremlin." He also knew that in the next stage of the "revelations," he might be directly tied to Mikhoels and the other members of the subversive Jewish Anti-Fascist Committee, whose establishment he had recommended in the early days of the war.

A host of enemies was gunning for Beria, and Stalin himself might turn his Medusa gaze upon him at any moment. The army was at the head of the line: the Soviet military chiefs had hated Beria since he had personally tortured Marshal Blucher in 1938. When Stalin made Beria a marshal during the war, the officer corps took it as an insult.[35] In addition, his non-combat NKVD troops had received better rations, housing, and uniforms than did the regular soldiers; and the army commanders despised Beria for planting political spies in every garrison. Of course, many generals hated Stalin, too, but Beria was the scapegoat, even when Stalin exiled the popular commander-in-chief A. I. Antonov to the Caucasus in 1948 after deciding that he was "really a Jew."[36]

Everyone felt that Beria had too much power. Besides controlling a huge army of secret police and the slave nation of the Gulag, he was the chief of the atomic research program, and even had control of the Kremlin's now-discredited health services: he personally supervised the toxicologists who tested every morsel of meat before it entered Stalin's mouth. Inevitably, this led to a rumor that Beria had spiked Stalin's favorite Georgian wine, kinzmaraali, with a special preparation that raised the dictator's already high blood pressure.

After Stalin and Beria were dead, Khrushchev, with help from Stalin's daughter Svetlana and others, tried to place all the blame for the sins of the regime on the Himmler-like sadist, portraying Beria as a sexual pervert and *éminence grise* whose agents had infiltrated Stalin's staff. But some of these allegations have been questioned in recent years, and at least one woman who knew Beria intimately denies that he acted abnormally.[37] In fact, it was Khrushchev's man, Minister of State Security Ignatiev, Beria's new rival and the chief investigator of the Doctors' Plot, whose sexual behavior was unusual. Ignatiev, whom Khrushchev described as " mild, considerate, and well-liked," was especially fond of "male females" from the Gulag concentration camps, who were dressed to impersonate soldiers.

Most experts on the Soviet Union believed that Beria was the principal target of the new purge campaign. Western diplomats throughout Europe sought analyses of the Doctors' Plot from Sovietologists, émigré experts, journalists, fellow diplomats, and other intelligence sources.

Few took seriously the deeper anti-Semitic implications of the plot, portraying it as of secondary importance at most. For example, an American agent in Paris named Dunn noted in a secret report that Laloy of the British Foreign Office "thought worth mentioning" the opinion that the anti-Jewish actions might indicate that a wider purge of Jews was under way "as security measure to eliminate potential fifth column in preparation for conflict . . . Laloy inclined dismiss such speculation in view of fact measures already taken in earlier post-war years by Soviet remove Jews from border areas."[39] But this analysis ignored the continuing attacks against Jews in the Soviet media, as well as the background to the various Jewish-centered affairs culminating in the Doctors' Plot.

The idea that another program of genocide against the Jews was in the making was not mentioned by any of the intelligence reports: American, English, French, or Israeli. Yet the hints were clear enough. The January 13 *Pravda* editorial, while stating that the exploiter classes had long since been liquidated, said there were many vestiges of "private-property psychology and morals" carried by "living people" which had to be eliminated.[40] This was a direct reference to Stalin's official proclamation on the necessity of "the liquidation of exploiter classes."[41]

Four American informants in West Germany—Soviet defectors Vyacheslav Artemiev, Joseph Baritz, Eugene Mylk, and Konstantin Krylov—said that the accusations against the doctors indicated a wide purge extending to both Jews and non-Jews. Krylov, an economist and authority on propaganda, had been predicting for several years that Stalin would use anti-Semitism as a weapon—his "last means of deceiving people"—in preparation for a general war.[42] Artemiev, a former secret policeman, said that up to 25 percent of the MGB's entire force were Jews and that they were all certain to be thrown out, but that this would only be a small part of the great purge throughout the Party and every section of Soviet society which appeared to be in the works. MGB Jews were, in fact, purged at this time: for example, Colonel Gorsky, who handled the British master spies MacLean, Burgess, and Philby; others were arrested, including top secret service officials like Lieutenant General Raikhman.[43]

The senior West German expert on the USSR, Professor Koch, told American intelligence gatherers that the deaths of several important political leaders such as Zhdanov and Dimitrov and a number of marshals and generals had been most convenient for Stalin: "It is not unlikely doctors were therefore accomplices to murder at Stalin's behest."[44] A lengthy January 16 report from the British embassy in Moscow to the Chancery suggested that the Kremlin doctors had probably been treating an ailing Stalin for some time, "but in his pathological condition of mind he may have dwelt with fear and suspicion on the fact that these same doctors had treated Shcherbakov and Zhdanov, both of whom had died."[45] The report added that there may have been some truth to the charge that the Jewish Kremlin doctors had had contact with Jewish organizations in the West.

Israeli diplomats, not surprisingly, were more sensitive to the Soviet media's constant stress on Jews, the Joint, and Zionists, and they collected as many clips and details as possible. But this was the only source of their information in the USSR. Like their Western colleagues, they were working in the dark. As the Russian-born counselor, Zev Argaman, told an American diplomat, he had "almost no contact with the Soviet people."[46] Within the Soviet Union, diplomats relied almost exclusively on press clippings and on scuttlebutt picked up by other diplomats and journalists. They were as ignorant as their Western colleagues about what was happening behind the news reports, including the preparations then getting under way to deport almost all Soviet Jews to concentration camps. Often, narrow national interests prevailed in their minds.

"The main line that passes through all these articles and speeches is of encirclement by strong foreign enemies and the building of a fifth column from within," read a February 10, 1953, dispatch from Israeli envoy S. Eliashiv in Moscow. But "the state of Israel itself is still not a primary, direct target" as it was in "the plainly stated accusations in Czechoslovakia and Poland. . . . Despite this there is a severe, violent anger against Zionists and Zionism."[47]

Meanwhile, a Soviet diplomat at the UN assured his Israeli counterpart that the doctors' case and the growing storm around it was strictly an internal Soviet matter and had nothing whatsoever to do with Soviet policy regarding the Israeli-Arab conflict. The charges of anti-Semitism in the American press were "the wildest exaggeration," according to Soviet envoy Pavel Shakov. Although this certainly wasn't taken at face value, the Israelis simply did not know what was really going on—though they were, as Harrison Salisbury would characterize them, "a most knowledgeable and attractive group. Almost the only people who had a notion of what was happening."[48]

In his February 10 dispatch, the Israeli diplomat in Moscow expressed grave concern over the proliferating reports of alleged Jewish criminals, especially in the Ukraine, Belorussia, and Moldavia, where there were large Jewish populations. The long Israeli report went into detail about one of the espionage arrests announced in *Pravda* in the immediate wake of January 13—that of S. D. Gurevich. The importance of the case was underlined when *Pravda Ukrainy* reprinted the lengthy *Pravda* article in full. Gurevich, who had worked as a journalist and did some translating for the U.S. Information Service, had been raised in a Bund-Menshevik house, the envoy noted. Perhaps his arrest was another sign that the Great Terror was about to be reenacted.[49] The long-extinguished Bund, in fact, was still under attack by its old nemesis, Stalin. Leningrad Party boss Kozlov's January 14 article in *Kommunist* said that those fifth columnists recently purged in Leningrad had been connected with "middle bourgeois nationalist counter-revolutionary" parties such as the Bund, and therefore had been easy prey for foreign intelligence agents.[50]

A German expert on the USSR, Klaus Mehnert, told the Americans that Stalin was playing the anti-Semitic card because the "Hate America" campaign was not sufficiently elemental and primitive to strike the right chord, and that "darker, more archaic, aggressive instincts had to be aroused by Stalin inside Russia in order to deflect hatred from the regime itself."[51]

At least one senior Western diplomat in Moscow at that possible turning point in world history, Britain's Sir A. ("Joe") Gascoigne, a diplomatic Colonel Blimp, believed that the Kremlin doctors probably *were* guilty of political disloyalty. In a long, confidential report to Foreign Secretary Anthony Eden, Gascoigne cited the presence of Kaganovich in the Soviet hierarchy and the prominence of Ilya Ehrenburg and contended that "it would be an exaggeration I think to say, as the B.B.C. recently suggested, that there has been an active 'campaign' against Jews in the Soviet Union."[52] He then reminded Eden that "the Jews in this country have, since the Revolution in which they played a prominent part, been dropped little by little *pari passu* with the consolidation of the regime, to be replaced by Russian nationals. I am not inclined therefore to favour the argument that this must necessarily be the beginning of a violent open and official anti-Semitic purge." But two top diplomats—Foreign Office Northern Department head H. A. F. Hohler and P. Mason, expressed their dismay at Gascoigne's hypothesis, "which indeed seems inconceivable."[53] However, they also rejected the theory that the arrest of the doctors was tied to the Prague trial as the beginning of a concerted anti-Semitic purge in the Soviet bloc: "World Jewry is naturally interpreting the affair in this light, and I see that Israel is to raise the matter in the United Nations. But our view is that we must look primarily for internal motives."

In a January 23 dispatch, an unchastened Gascoigne reported that the foreign colleagues with whom he had consulted agreed with him that the arrests did not necessarily indicate "a violent and bloody purge against the Jews." It was clear, he said, that the Soviets "may well have decided to purge all suspected elements, and there are of course still many Jews who by their push and ability are still to be found in the middle layers of Soviet society." But the coming "tidying and tightening up" was carried out mainly out of fear of what the new Republican U.S. administration would do, Gascoigne postulated. He thought this process of "clearing the decks is somewhat disquieting," though he seemed to empathize with Soviet officials who "feel that they must discard unreliable elements of the population so as to be prepared to deal with any situation which may arise."[54]

Britons like Gascoigne still held the views of those who had introduced the 1939 White Paper, which choked off Jewish immigration to Palestine from Europe on the eve of war. The Americans, who also kept out Jews fleeing the Nazis until the establishment of the War Refugee Board at the end of the war, were no better in helping a threatened people, or in defining the threat. The head of American intelligence, Allen Dulles, carried on the tradition when he wrote in a confidential cable—undated but presumably in January 1953—that while it was now unquestionable that the Soviets were openly using anti-Semitism as a "device . . . we tend [to] regard this aspect [as] still secondary to other considerations." It was not "strict anti-Semitism in [the] usual sense but rather that Jews in [the] Communist world have now begun to feel [the] full force of Stalin's compulsion" to ruthlessly root out all elements with a potential "international" outlook and links with the outside world. Dulles asserted that the Soviet overt propaganda to Arab states "has not widely exploited [the] anti-Semitic potential of [the] Slansky trail or doctors plot."[55]

One of the more perceptive British intelligence gatherers conjectured in a January 16 report that "these strange events must have been touched off by some development which Stalin interpreted as a serious threat to his personal security or to the security of the regime. It may not have been a real plot. But there may have been rumblings." The rumblings he perceived concerned some army leaders such as Marshal Zhukov whom Stalin believed might be plotting against him or his appointed successors. Stalin's best means of forestalling this threat "would be to act as if there had actually been a plot against the lives of those Army leaders who were nearest to him."[56]

In another report, of a *vox populi* conversation between a British diplomat and a Russian taxi driver about the Doctors' Plot, G. Dobbs noted that "in associating the Doctors' Plot with the Jews Stalin had not misjudged the general Russian public." The driver said that he was sure the *Pravda* report was completely true, and that it was common knowledge that this was only the tip of the iceberg. He said that these doctors had run a clinic in his district where they had killed children by wrong injections, and that "it was not the first time that such things had happened." He added that "They" had killed Gorky, sabotaged the Stalin Motor Works, and been in league with the Americans. The Jews were anxious for a return of bourgeois government so that they could make lots of money—everyone knew this. The driver had been in Germany and knew the state that country was in before Hitler had adopted the only way of dealing with "Them." All the Russian people knew that the Jews were their enemies, the taxi driver said. The British diplomat commented that he believed this was representative of the views of the "man in the street" because he and other envoys had heard similar opinions voiced repeatedly.[57]

One British report that reached the Israelis[58] said that signs of a massive purge were clear, and that "the Jews will undoubtedly be placed high on the list though, it should be repeated, not on racial grounds."[59] A subsequent British report said that the daily press accounts from January 13 to the end of February revealed that "a thorough sifting process is going on through the ranks of industry, the administration, the universities and schools and 'liberal' professions." This report's writer also did not think the Zionist-Jewish connection was all that important; he viewed it as simply a part of "Soviet mythology."[60]

But the "sifting" that was going on everywhere should have told the diplomats that the anti-Semitic aspect of the Doctors' Plot was not a peripheral issue; it was relevant also to the non-Jews who were being "sifted" because of their "Jewish characteristics." In Ulyanovsk, Lenin's birthplace, Mandelstam's widow witnessed how it happened at the local teachers' training college where she worked. The refined director, who spoke in a soft, well-modulated voice, conducted the purge of Jewish staff members. He expelled twenty-six teachers—including not only the Jews but anyone who appeared suspiciously intellectual.[61]

It was happening everywhere. Two hundred Jews were dismissed from Odessa University; and all Jewish graduates of medical schools were sent to the remotest areas in the east, such as Kamchatka, and Yakutia in Siberia.[62] The energetic head of the engineering department of a huge state enterprise was called in by the director and told, "You've heard about the doctors. Now tell me yourself—can you people be trusted? My advice to you is to resign."[63] Even in the Gulag sifting was taking place, and the January 13 announcement was taken as a clear sign to the Gulag authorities to do what they wanted with the Jews. The anti-Semitic common criminal prisoners, who often attacked the "politicals," had a field day, saying, "Now we've caught them red-handed. Now their turn has come!" Many of the non-Jewish political prisoners complained about having to serve time together with "fascists who were trying to wreck the Soviet system."[64] The news of the Doctors' Plot hit Siberia like an earthquake, as longtime Gulag resident Eugenia Ginzburg recorded: "Until then, there had been no attempt to single out Jews from others, even during the 1949 Cosmopolitan campaign."[65] The head of the Kolyma Medical Administration, ironically named Shcherbakov, "rushed around the hospital courtyard as if he had suddenly gone out of his mind, exclaiming: 'Isn't Goren a Jew? Isn't Walter a Jew? Well, where are the Jews around here?' "[66]

The isolation from such ominous occurrences of the Western diplomats and journalists in Moscow was paralleled by the seclusion of the Soviet rulers—Stalin, most of all. In his remoteness, including his refusal to see any doctors, he must have been aware of his worsening physical condition. But to submit himself to doctors—most of them Jews, and all of them polluted by Western ideas—was impossible.

Stalin's charge against the doctors was that they were agents of the American Jewish Joint Distribution Committee. Minor details, such as the fact that the Joint's background had been anti-Zionist or at least non-Zionist, would be ignored. There was plenty of material to exploit, including the meetings of JAC leaders Mikhoels and Feffer with Joint officials during the war, and afterward in Moscow.[67]

Within hours of the Doctors' Plot announcement on January 13, the Joint's headquarters in New York told its operatives in Paris to issue a statement emphasizing that for thirty-eight years the organization had engaged in relief and rehabilitation of Jewish victims of war and persecution in sixty countries. The Joint had "never engaged in political activities," it said, and the reports from Moscow about the Joint's espionage or plots against the Soviet government were "fantastic." It also denied the similar accusations against the Joint that had been made at the Slansky trial two months earlier.[68]

Every detail of the Doctors' Plot was planned well in advance of the January 13 announcement, as evidenced not only by Stalin's previously mentioned verbal order instructing that Dr. Vinogradov be linked to the Joint, but also by the Slansky trial "evidence" against the Joint. The latter obviously had been compiled over a long period of time.

Another indication of the methodical planning involved was a detailed January 14 illustrated article about the Joint in the Yiddish-language Warsaw newspaper *Volks Shtimme.* The lengthy article accused the Joint and the agents it had allegedly recruited, such as "Shimelovich and Mikhoels," of attempting "to murder the most devoted leading figures of the Soviet Union within the liberating Soviet army." The "Jewish folk-masses of the capitalist countries" would drive out the "Joint spy-band who strive to confuse the people with the noise of their alms-boxes so that their true espionage-diversionism will not be recognized."[69] Given the slowly grinding mills of the Soviet system, it was clear that the attacks on the Joint had been orchestrated with the Kremlin's East Bloc satellites well in advance. West European Communists were also prepared: An "in depth" six-part series on the Joint by one Pierre Hervé ran in the French Communist paper *Ce Soir* in late January and early February. The wide-ranging "exposé" in this paper founded by poet Louis Aragon grouped together Hitler, American Jewish soldiers in Korea with a grudge against the Soviets, Leon Blum, Guy de Rothschild, Israeli "parasites," the Bund, Ehrlich and Alter, Trotsky, and the Mensheviks.[70] Hervé's series was accompanied by photographs of Jewish children being deported to death camps by the Nazis "thanks to the assistance of the men of the 'Joint.' "[71]

The philanthropists and Jewish professionals of the Joint, such as Honorary Chairman James N. Rosenberg, the wealthy liberal lawyer who had initiated the Jewish farming projects in the Crimea in the 1920s, were stunned by "this strange, hysterical" announcement. Rosenberg called the farm settlement of the Jews in Russia "the greatest effort of my life . . . and the most tragic failure, in final analysis, first destroyed and smashed, in large part, by Hitler and then utterly exterminated by Stalin."[72]

Rosenberg accurately assessed American government reaction to the Soviet anti-Semitic campaign: he said that the pressure would be on Israel to make concessions to the Arabs in order to counteract Soviet advances in the Arab world.[73]

And in fact, U.S. Secretary of State John Foster Dulles had just issued a secret State Department directive regarding the Soviet anti-Semitic activities and the reaction in the Arab world. The directive, which was sent to the American ambassadors in six Arab capitals as well as Tel Aviv, Ankara, Paris, and London, said in the terse language of cables that the State Department would try to channel the expected United Nations debate on the Soviet anti-Semitic campaign "into broadest context of Communist police state based on general denial of basic human rights and persecution of all (repeat all) religious groups. Dept. desires avoid situation in which debate centers on anti-semitism or anti-Zionism."[74] It was a continuation of a longstanding State Department attitude toward the Jews: even at the height of the Holocaust, many American officials said that it was wrong to single out the Jews as Hitler's principal victims; that all persecuted groups should be treated the same.[75]

Among those in America who did not publicly react to the January 13 bombshell was Paul Robeson, who remained quiet about the unknown fate of his friend Itzik Feffer, the defaming of the name of his friend Mikhoels, and the nightmare of his many other Jewish friends in the socialist Fatherland.

French fellow travelers were less cynical. Jean-Paul Sartre, who had just come back from one of Ilya Ehrenburg's peace congresses in Vienna "singing the song of peace and fellowship, has had a rude awakening and is crushed," reported an American diplomat in Paris, who said his émigré contacts had been streaming into his office since the announcement of the plot.[76]

In Israel, when the news of the Doctors' Plot came over the radio, Rabbi Jacob Kolmess, who had left Moscow in 1933 after relatives had paid a large sum of money to bring him out, grasped his chest and died of a heart attack. The January 13 announcement led to stormy debate in the Knesset (parliament), soon resulting in schisms of both the Israeli Communist party and the Leftist Mapam party. On January 19 Foreign Minister Moshe Sharett denounced the libel in a Knesset speech, and all political parties—except the Communists and the fellow-traveling Mapam—united to condemn the accusations and Soviet anti-Semitism. The Israeli Communists accepted the guilt of the doctors, while the Mapam party said it was an "internal Soviet affair" and assailed the Israeli government for "inflating the affair for propaganda purposes."[77]

In London five days after the stormy Knesset debate, Sharett said that the anti-Semitic Soviet campaign was "a clear indication that the Communist leaders have entered a new stage in preparing their countries for war." The purges were part of "a process of blood-letting inside the Soviet system with the aim of strengthening it for war."[78] Many Israeli journalists and Sovietologists also attributed the new anti-Semitic campaign to preparations for World War III, as well as mentioning various other factors: the Malenkov–Beria rivalry, attempts to cut off Soviet Jewry and destroy its cohesion, and a Soviet overture to the Arab world.[79]

Throughout the Communist world—with the exception of Titoist Yugoslavia—the Tass report and *Pravda* editorial were reprinted, with local commentary attached. Hungary's *Szabad Nep* said that the doctors had been paid by the Joint to follow John Foster Dulles's order to "destroy the Soviet Union from within. . . . We also had experiences of this kind. For instance, I. G. Jacobson, the director of the Joint in Hungary, had to be arrested in December 1949 for spying. He was then expelled from Hungary." The paper said that the charge of Soviet anti-Semitism was an American smokescreen to cover up "the anti-Semitic drive all over America in connection with the Rosenberg trial."[80] All the leading Peking dailies splashed the news across their front pages, and the *People's Daily* hailed the exposure as "another victory for all people in the camp of socialism and peoples' democracy in their common fight against American aggression and for peace."[81]

The Chinese had no Jews to arrest, though Beria sent MGB men to arrest Mao Tse-tung's Soviet Jewish doctor.[82] However, East Germany and other Eastern European Communist regimes not only trumpeted the Soviet revelations about the vast Jewish conspiracy, but also began interrogating the leaders of their own tiny Jewish communities that remained after the Holocaust and raiding Jewish homes. Only 2,600 Jews were left in all of East Germany, but having experienced the fury of Hitler's extermination campaign, they felt particularly threatened by the Doctors' Plot. This was true of Holocaust survivors throughout Europe: for example, a thousand Jews in Holland applied for U.S. visas in the month of January 1953, fearing that the Russians might invade from Berlin.

On January 15 four leaders of the East German Jewish community fled to West Berlin with their families and associates, saying they had been under intensive interrogation by state security men. Three days later the secret police swept down on the homes of most of the 2,000 Jews in the Soviet sector of East Berlin. Julius Meyer, who had led the defection to the West, said that the new wave of anti-Semitism did not come from the East Germans but from the Russians. Meyer said that he was constantly questioned about whether the Joint was an agency of the U.S. government, and was asked for the names of all East German Jews who had received food packages from the Joint. His interrogators demanded that he sign a statement saying that the packages contained illegal propaganda material and weapons, but he refused.[83]

This report should have been an ominous piece of news to anyone trying to put together the emerging pieces of the scheduled purge; but no one noticed, not even at the Joint's headquarters. They seemed to have forgotten a major flap over Joint aid packages to Soviet Jews in 1944–45, including the JDC follow-up mission to Moscow a year after the visit by Feffer and Mikhoels. The latter had now been revealed as the departed mastermind behind the whole vast doctors–Joint–Zionist conspiracy. During the war Mikhoels and the Jewish Anti-Fascist Committee had "exposed" a "parcels swindle," saying that the Joint was sending useless items such as "fancy buttons" and tea that tasted like "green poison." Some of these packages were mailed from Jerusalem via Iran, which would make them even more suspicious.[84] But now, in 1953, every Soviet Jew who had ever gotten a Joint package could be accused of receiving subversive materials and arms. The Hungarian newspaper *Szabad Nep* said on January 15, 1953, that the Joint made a practice of "concealing poison and daggers," in the "second-hand clothes" it sent to the Jews. And Czechoslovakia's *Rude Pravo* said on January 16 that the "'gifts' sent by the Joint" were actually "a command to murder."

If the East Germans, who only acted under orders of the Soviet secret police, were compiling a list of Jewish recipients of Joint packages, the same thing was certainly happening on a comparable scale in the USSR. Kaganovich, the great list-maker, was hard at work on this. Every Jew who had ever received a Joint aid package, or for that matter, a letter from a relative abroad was extremely vulnerable. But the West still did not know what was happening in the dark continent of the Soviet empire. Not one of the flood of intelligence reports to the U.S., British, or Israeli government even mentioned the possibility that most Soviet Jews might be deported in the near future, as Stalin had so recently done to eight other Soviet peoples. Nor was there a whisper about the statement then being circulated for the signature of the most prominent Soviet Jews, asking Stalin to send the Jews to "protective camps" for their own security.

CHAPTER 11

The Jews Brace for Exile

Stalin Prepares
His Final Solution

In the last weeks of his life, Stalin's towering rages apparently occurred more frequently.[1] Although he rarely appeared in public or even at Politburo meetings, sensitive ears could pick up the rumblings. In the USSR and among foreign experts on the Soviet Union, many sensed that the Doctor's Plot announced on January 13 marked a possible turning point in world history.

Several dozen of the most prominent and famous Soviet Jews knew that the volcano was roaring and that an epic explosion was near, for after the mid-January announcement was made, they were being told to sign "The Jewish Statement." Stalin's intricate strategem laid a great deal of importance on this "open letter," which was to be published on the front page of *Pravda* following a show trial and public execution of the doctors in Red Square, probably in early April. It would be used to rationalize the deportation of almost all Soviet Jews to concentration camps in Siberia, Kazakhstan, and Birobidzhan. A significant number of "good Jews" like Lazar Kaganovich, who was delegated to draw up the huge lists of names and supervise the deportation, would be allowed to remain in the large Russian cities, where they could serve to counter charges that all Soviet Jews had been exiled.[2]

The Soviet Union has never released the exact text of "The Jewish Statement," which went unpublished because of Stalin's sudden death; but its contents have been described by several of the Jews who saw it. "The statement by the Jews existed and exists," according to Harrison Salisbury, the *New York Times* correspondent in Moscow at the time.[3] From various sources, it is possible to reconstruct the open letter, and an accompanying commentary that was to appear—possibly signed by the newly appointed chief editor of *Pravda,* Dmitri Trofimovich Shepilov, the Party's top propaganda specialist. Shepilov's takeover, on December 17, 1952, of the post once held by Stalin, Kamenev, Bukharin, Molotov, and Suslov, undoubtedly reflected Stalin's immediate need for a polished propagandist. For Stalin knew there would be a world outcry when he openly set about to further the work of the last czar, Nicholas II, who deported the Jews from the Baltic provinces during World War I.

Another major executive change in the Soviet media and government power structure took place around the same time as Shepilov's appointment. A shadowly official, Dmitri I. Chesnokov, became coeditor of *Bolshevik,* as well as head of a mysterious new section of the Central Committee and a junior member of the Presidium.[4] It was Chesnokov who wrote a government pamphlet explaining why the Jews "had to be deported" (one million copies were printed and ready for distribution when Stalin died).[5] The pamphlet, issued by the MVD publishing house, was entitled *Why Jews Must Be Resettled from the Industrial Regions of the Country.*[6] Chesnokov was the Stalin protégé who also suddenly became his point man against détente: in January 1953 he was attacking "concessionists" who tried to "appease the imperialists."[7] Indeed, Chesnokov's two main duties were interrelated, since Stalin's anti-Semitism had become part of Soviet international policy.

Pravda, by far the largest Soviet media outlet, was designated as the major propaganda organ in the coming deportation of the Jews. It still had a number of staffers of Jewish origin, though they were on their way out—even David Iosifovich Zaslavsky, once a trusted Stalin underling who helped to organize the Jewish statement and was one of its signers.[8] Zaslavsky lost his *Pravda* post during the doctor's affair after a colleague said he could no longer work with anyone who belonged to a race of poisoners and traitors.[9] Among those Jews reportedly collecting signatures for the statement were I. S. Khavinson and historian Isaac Izrailevich Mints.[10]

The statement, reconstructed from various sources,[11] read:

We appeal to the government of the USSR, and to Comrade Stalin personally, to save the Jewish population from possible violence in the wake of the revelations about the doctor-poisoners and the involvement of renegade Soviet citizens of

Jewish origin, who were caught red-handed in an American-Zionist plot to destabilize the Soviet government. We join with all Soviet peoples in applauding the punishment of the murdering doctors, whose crimes called for the highest measure. The Soviet people are naturally outraged by the ever-widening circle of treason and treachery and the fact that, to our sorrow, many Jews have helped our enemies to form a fifth column in our midst. Simple, misguided citizens may be driven to striking back indiscriminately at Jews. For this reason, we implore you to protect the Jewish people by dispatching them to the developing territories in the East, where they will be employed in useful national labor and escape the understandably indignant anger prompted by the traitor-doctors. We, as leading figures among loyal Soviet Jewry, totally reject American and Zionist propaganda claiming that there is anti-Semitism in the Soviet Union. It is simply a smokescreen to disguise their own failed attempt to murder Soviet leaders and to deflect world criticism from the issue of American anti-Semitism in the Rosenberg case and American genocidal intentions against the Negro population in the U.S. In the Soviet Union, in contrast, racism is constitutionally forbidden and simply does not exist.

Such "open letters" were a Soviet tradition. Untold numbers of children had signed letters renouncing their parents as "socially harmful elements" and vowing never to talk to them again. Peasants imprisoned in the frozen Siberian wasteland sent collective testimonials praising Stalin for having sent them to the frigid labor camps, where they discovered socialist truth.

Open letters to the press demanding death for innumerable spies and traitors had been a feature of Soviet life since the days of the Great Purges. Boris Pasternak had once refused to sign a collective letter by Soviet writers approving the latest shooting of enemies of the people, but such courage was extremely rare, for the consequences were well known. The executed former economic czar, Voznesensky, for example, had reportedly first fallen into disgrace when he refused to sign a particular death list. But there were always some Soviet intellectuals who were willing to risk their own necks rather than condemn others. Boris Vachtin, son of the famed Russian writer Vera Panova, was told to make a list of the Jews in his huge apartment block in late January 1953 and refused to do so.

The heavy daily diet of media propaganda about Jewish doctors and Jewish spies made Vachtin suspect what the list would be used for, though he certainly did not know that Kaganovich was then immersed in organizing the deportation of the Jews. He did know that at meetings of tenants in countless apartment blocks, demands were voiced that Jews not be allowed to use communal kitchens as a precaution against poisoning. In any event, his was a brave act.[12]

Other Russians risked prison or execution as they stood by the Jews—for example, Justina S. Pokrovskaya, the widow of the great classicist Mikhail Pokrovsky. In a loud voice, she told a group at Moscow University, "What a sorry pass we've come to! Why it's even more horrendous than the Beilis affair."[13]

At least four Jews had the courage, or temerity, to refuse to sign the appeal to deport the Jews: Ilya Ehrenburg, his friend Venyamin Kaverin, Major General Jacob Grigorevich Kreiser, and Bolshoi actor-singer Mark Osipovich Reizen, winner of three Stalin Prizes, mainly for his role as Boris Godunov, Stalin's stage favorite.[14]

Ehrenburg was at his dacha in the Moscow suburb of New Jerusalem on January 13 when he read the announcement of the Doctors' Plot. He had often noticed that most people combined respect for medical science with deep, irrational fear of the doctors healing them. And he knew that Stalin's new conspiracy mixing doctor-poisoners with Jewish and Zionist spies would be a lethal success. He felt he personally was under increasing threat, though he had recently learned at one of the peace conferences in late 1952 that he, along with Paul Robeson, was among the new winners of the Stalin Peace Prize. The two propagandists were old friends, and had collaborated on the 1951 Russian edition of *We Charge Genocide,* a work elaborating on allegations by Robeson, Howard Fast, and others of genocide against American blacks. In his introduction, Ehrenburg had drawn a parallel between American racism and Nazi anti-Semitism and between the extermination of the Jews in German death camps and the ongoing campaign against Negroes in the U.S.A.[15]

Now, fourteen months after Ehrenburg's fantasies of American plans for genocide were published in Moscow, and a few days after January 13, Stalin sent two messengers to Ehrenburg's flat on Gorky Street asking him to sign the statement appealing for the deportation of the Jews.[16] Ehrenburg, who looked like a silvered monkey in his rapidly advancing old age, told Esther Markish in the mid-fifties that it was *Pravda*'s new editor-in-chief, Shepilov, who had asked him to sign the letter, which emphasized the collective responsibility of Soviet Jews for the doctors' crimes. Ehrenburg said he called Stalin's secretary for an appointment and that Poskrebyshev said he would look into it. Three days later Shepilov summoned Ehrenburg and again proposed he sign the letter. Ehrenburg asked him if Stalin knew about the letter. Shepilov handed him a copy, with Stalin's handwritten revisions. "The letter must be published tomorrow," the editor said. But Ehrenburg refused.[17]

Ehrenburg then drafted a letter to Stalin, which he never sent, saying:

> I believe it is my duty to share my doubts with you and to ask your advice. I believe that the only rational solution to the Jewish problem in our socialist state is the assimilation and fusion of people of Jewish origin with the peoples among whom they live. . . . Publishing a letter signed by scientists and composers of Jewish origin is to risk the revival of an ignoble anti-Soviet campaign.[18]

Word of Ehrenburg's refusal to sign spread very quickly among Moscow Jews.[19] He was proud of his action, and he had reason to be. He also was not judgmental about those who did sign. For he understood perfectly the terrible pressures that all prominent Jews were under at this time. They were being called upon to endorse the deportation of their own people to concentration camps, where they would be consumed. The only thing in common among the signers was that they were prominent people identified as Jews. Many of them were dedicated to the Communist cause, and in its name were willing to sacrifice their children as well as urge the execution of all "assassins in white coats." The signers included great artists and scientists, as well as mediocrities, Stalinist sycophants, and people who in their souls were totally opposed to authoritarian ways. One of the latter was Ehrenburg's good friend and collaborator on the JAC and *The Black Book,* Vasily Semenovich Grossman.

Grossman, born in 1905, already had acquired a reputation as one of Russia's greatest writers and journalists. But he was under heavy critical attack at the same time as the papers were full of stories about the Jewish conspirators; and as one of the few survivors of the JAC, he knew he was extremely vulnerable. *Pravda* and

Kommunist attacked both him and the editors of *Novy Mir* (New World) for publishing his Stalingrad novel, *For a Just Cause,* which was "permeated with Pythagorism." What this really meant was that he was part of a "secret society" based on an ancient mystery cult— a typically Soviet, euphemistic way of saying "Jew." Grossman was certain that he faced imminent arrest and possible execution.[20] He simply had to sign. It was perhaps the most difficult decision of his life, though later on he would only refer to it obliquely. In his post-Stalin novel *Forever Flowing,* Grossman's character Ivan (Vanya) asks his cousin Nikolai: "Tell me now, did you sign that letter condemning the doctor-assassins? I heard about it in camp from people who were arrested."

Academician Isaac Mints, too, had been under fire during the recent anti-cosmopolitan campaign, when the famed historian was dismissed from his various academic posts. Now he too was cooperating, asking the Soviet Jewish aristocracy to sign the nefarious document.

Others were even more frightened. Physicist Lev Davidovich Landau, who would become a Nobel laureate in 1962, had been imprisoned during the Great Purges, accused of being a Nazi spy. But he was allowed to work in one of the special "First Circle" prison institutions, since he was conducting nuclear research.[21] Another signer was the second most famous Soviet physicist, Pyotr L. Kapitsa, a JAC stalwart who had won Landau's release by going to the Kremlin and threatening to quit his critically important job as director of the Institute of Physical Problems unless his genius friend was freed.[22] Landau, who had once tried to convince Arthur Koestler that it was a waste of time to read any philosopher predating Marx,[23] was one of the aristocrats who rationalized the existing state of affairs by assuming a cynical posture, saying that humanity never was free of tyranny and violence, and that people were shot everywhere. Before his own imprisonment as a Nazi spy, the future co-father of the Soviet atomic bomb, a haughty, mean-spirited man, testified against fellow physicist Alex Weissberg, saying he was a Gestapo spy and saboteur.[24] Landau's reputation, however, remained one of "brilliance" rather than treachery.

Among the other signers were master violinist David Oistrakh,[25] composer and popular songwriter Matvei Blanter, Stalin Prize–winning poet Yevgeny Dolmatovsky, and director Igor Nezhny,[26] as well as Konstantin Finn (Khalfin), who called himself "the great Russian comedy writer"; Samuel Marshak, the venerated children's

writer and friend of Gorky's whose poems and stories were firmly
in the Russification tradition; writer David Vendrov; and the distinguished historian Eugene Tarlé. There were undoubtedly many
others.

One of the handful who refused to sign, General Kreiser, was a
true Soviet hero, commander of the 51st Army in 1943–45 and a
liberator of the Crimea. Kreiser, born in 1905 and a general at age
thirty-one, had been active in the Jewish Anti-Fascist Committee
and had once told a JAC mass meeting, in August 1942, "My
nation, which has given the world illustrious sages and brilliant
thinkers, is also a nation that fights for its freedom."[27] During the
postwar anti-cosmopolitan campaign, the hero of Smolensk was
stripped of command, which was not restored until the Khrushchev
era.[28]

Ilya Ehrenburg, after taking his stand, became deeply depressed
and once again kept an overnight case packed, fearing he would be
arrested at any moment. Nadezhda Mandelstam came to visit him
at the height of the hysteria. As she was leaving, he told her: "I am
ready for anything." He was certain his turn was coming.[29]

Ehrenburg received a flood of letters in the days after the January 13 announcement, most of them from Jews demanding that he
add his voice to condemn the Jewish doctor-poisoners. A woman in
Baku, Maria Levina, thanked him warmly for his wartime articles,
his pride in being a Jew, and for doing so much about the Nazi
crimes. She herself had lost all of her family in the Holocaust. Now
she was writing to "the representative of the Jewish people" to ask
him to speak out for the death penalty for the doctors, and also the
execution of their children and grandchildren, "so that their ashes
can be thrown to the wind, so that no one can equate them with the
loyal Soviet citizens among the Jewish people."[30] A collective letter
"from Jewish workers in Leningrad" also asked him to condemn
the "murderers in white coats for blotting the name of the Jews"
and to demand the death penalty.[31] D. Aranovich, a member of the
Party and director of an oil factory, called Ehrenburg a "jewel in
the crown of the Jewish people." He was shocked at the treachery
of the exposed Jews, "people belonging to a nation which hasn't
been completely wiped out thanks only to the protection of the
Soviet government. . . . you must say today that the rest of the
Jews aren't like [the criminal doctors]. . . . there are a few elements
who aren't developed, who are anti-Semitic, and they will jump at
this opportunity."[32] A letter signed "the workers" asked him to

publish an article about the "good Jews" like "Kaganovich, Mekhlis, Oistrakh, Sverdlov, Batvinich [a famous weight lifter and Olym-
pic medalist]."[33]

One letter, unsigned and undated, pleaded for Ehrenburg to try
to stem the anti-Semitic tide: "Now is the time to help your people
who are on the edge of destruction, because of an accusation of
treason that is used against the whole people." The writer said that
because she was Jewish, she had just been dismissed from a job she
had held for many years. She looked for another job, but was
refused as soon as it was learned that she was a Jew. "This anti-
Semitism is terrible. Where is the equality between people? Lenin
said that in every nation there are two nations, one progressive and
one not. I beg you to speak out against the general accusations
made against our people."[34]

Another anonymous letter, from a Red Army veteran who had
lost his whole family in the Holocaust, said he was shocked that "all
the Jews will be fired and expelled from Moscow and other places
because all of the Jews are traitors." He was certain he would be
dismissed at any moment. The attitude of all his friends at work
had changed radically. "Some are afraid to talk to me, while others
insult me. . . . I beg you to write an article that will make it clear
that not all Jews are villains, that among us are also heroes and
people of quality and a deep love for our homeland." He added that
"every Jew I know is terribly frightened . . . we are almost certain
that the next stage will be the deportation of all Jews to Siberia."[35]

Just before the January 27, 1953, Kremlin ceremony where he
was to be presented with the Stalin Prize, Ehrenburg was told by a
person called Grigorian that "it would be a good thing if you were
to say a word about the criminal doctors." Ehrenburg refused,
saying that he would relinquish the prize rather than mention the
Doctors' Plot. Grigorian said, "I was only suggesting." At the
ceremony, Ehrenburg's close friend, the famed French Communist
poet Louis Aragon, was among the speakers. Ehrenburg was just
then reading Pierre Hervé's series of articles about the Joint in *Ce
Soir,* Aragon's paper. The articles reminded him of *The Protocols
of the Elders of Zion.*[36]

Ehrenburg's speech that night was brief:

> No matter what his national origin, a Soviet citizen is first and
> foremost a patriot of his country, and he is a true
> internationalist, an opponent of racial and national

discrimination, a fervent believer in the brotherhood of man, a
fearless defender of peace. On this solemn and festive occasion
in the white hall of the Kremlin I want to pay tribute to those
fighters for peace who are being persecuted, tortured and
hounded; I want to call to mind the dark night of prisons, of
interrogations, of trials, and the courage of so many.

At the conclusion of his talk, it was as quiet as death in Sverdlov
Hall. In the press reports the next day, words were added to make
it clear that Ehrenburg was talking, of course, about persecutions
conducted by the forces of reaction.[37] An American embassy dispatch on Ehrenburg's speech said it "may be related to the doctors'
case."[38]

Stalin Prize notwithstanding, Ehrenburg knew he was in trouble. On January 30, he wrote to Politburo ideologist Mikhail Suslov,
asking him to intercede with the official scrutinizers who had ordered alterations in the texts of new editions of his work. He was
also being pressed to change certain surnames in his short novels
The Second Day and *Without Taking Breath*. He was told that
there were far too many "non-indigenous" names mixed in with
the Russian names.[39] The old litterateur, who had been among the
first correspondents to see the full horror of the Nazi death camps,
was shaken to his roots. Ehrenburg, on whose unwilling shoulders
Mikhoels's mantle as leader of Soviet Jewry now seemed to fall,
was as wounded as the Jews who had written to him from all over
the country.

====

Many Jews all over the Soviet Union knew they were about to be
deported. In 1948 and 1949 large numbers of Jews had been transferred to central Siberia.[40] Now, four years later, Jews in urban
centers in the Baltic states, Moldavia, Belorussia, and the Ukraine,
as well as in Moscow and Leningrad, burned their Yiddish books,
avoided going out as much as possible, and stayed close to buildings
and public squares when they did venture out. As Eugenia Ginzburg
noted, it was also the first time that Jews already in the Gulag felt
so threatened simply because they were Jews. Terror engulfed even
the Sephardic Jews of Georgia, where most of them knew nothing
of Yiddish and Ashkenazi culture, and where anti-Semitism had
never been a part of the fabric of life, as it had in Great Russia or
the Ukraine (Little Russia).

At the small synagogue on the second floor of an old building in

Gori, a few hundred meters from Stalin's birthplace, the congregants removed the Torah from its ark and concealed it. "The Jews
of every synagogue in Georgia took their Torah scrolls to hiding
places," one of the congregants who hid the Gori Torah would
recall many years later. "The men who saved them are all dead
today, but they did the greatest thing of their lives."[41] The last
wave of fear had occurred in 1937, when the rabbis in Gori were
arrested. But for the next fifteen years, even through the worst
part of the anti-cosmopolitan campaign, the Georgian Jews had
experienced no anti-Semitism. Then, in February 1953, in the city
of Kutaisi, where most Georgian Jews lived, "the government
brought dynamite into the three synagogues to blow the buildings
up. The Jews told the officials, 'you'll have to blow us up with it.' "
The officials backed down.[42] They thought they could put if off for a
few more weeks, when the Jews would be shipped off to the East.

Stalin's own Secretariat, as well as MGB institutions and Minister Kaganovich, were in charge of planning and logistical preparations for the impending deportation. The ultimate goal was "a real
genocide, Stalin's own extermination of the Jews," according to
Lova Eliav, a writer and Israeli diplomat serving in Moscow in the
1950s, who gathered evidence from hundreds of sources.[43] The
show trial of the Kremlin doctors would include new revelations:
the poisoners' main intended victim was Stalin himself. This would
arouse unprecedented fury among the Soviet people, for it was
another form of the primordial crime that had been the basis for
Russian Judeophobia for centuries: in 1881, for instance, a Jewish
woman, Gesia Gelfman, was tried in the assassination of Czar
Alexander II. The resulting pogroms spread because "the Jews
murdered the Little Father."[44]

Although the animus of the case was anti-Semitic, the fact that a
number of gentiles were among the publicly accused was typical of
Stalin. He had many targets in the Doctors' Plot. His last policy act
was "a calculated effort to demonstrate and dramatize the impossibility of détente," as well as a means of purging his associates and
his countless enemies.[45]

His inclusion of a few gentiles in the plot may have been aimed,
among other things, at deflecting world criticism of Soviet anti-
Semitism; but it backfired. If he had just gone after the Jews, and
not made it clear that he was embarking on another Great Terror,
his associates might have gone along. Instead, they conspired to
put him out of the way.

Under Stalin's master plan, the doctors would be found guilty and sentenced to immediate death, possibly in late March or early April—the Easter season, when the paschal lamb, which Christians associate with Christ, is sacrificed. They would be hanged in Red Square on the *Lobnoye mesto,* a circular stone platform next to the Kremlin which was used in medieval times as a place of execution. Then "incidents" would follow: attacks on Jews orchestrated by the secret police, the publication of the statement by the prominent Jews, and a flood of other letters demanding that action be taken. A three-stage program of genocide would be followed. First, almost all Soviet Jews, 87 percent of whom were concentrated in the big cities in 1939, would be shipped to camps east of the Urals (the majority of Soviet Jews lived in Moscow, Leningrad, Kiev, Odessa, Riga, and Kharkov). Second, the authorities would set Jewish leaders at all levels against one another, spying on each other and engaging in provocations. Also the MGB would start killing the elites in the camps, just as they had killed the Yiddish writers and intellectuals in August of the previous year. The third, and final, stage would be to "get rid of the rest."[46] The Soviet camps would never be turned into efficient Nazi-like death factories; the mortality rate in Stalin's camps was high, but the speed of death was relatively slow, though the lives of almost all the inmates were drastically shortened. Eventually, the "Jewish problem" would disappear by attrition.

Dr. Aryeh Kobovy, who defected from thc East Bloc in November 1952, was, like Eliav, an informed observer whose opinions were studied by the Israeli government. He believed that a systematic extermination policy was out of the question unless a third world war were to erupt; Hitler did not begin his policy of destroying the Jews until after World War II broke out. In the event of a new world war, however, Stalin might very well exterminate millions of Jews.[47] American Jewish leaders also feared the worst. B'nai B'rith president Frank Goldman and Colonel Bernard Bernstein met with State Department officials J. C. H. Bonbright and Walworth Barbour on February 3 and said the developments in the USSR and its satellites led them to believe "the Soviets have decided on a campaign of extermination" similar to Hitler's.[48]

Stalin had already urged high Party and government officials, in his "off-handed" way, to start the pogroms. He told Khrushchev, "The workers at the factories should be given clubs so they can beat the hell out of those Jews."[49] Upon leaving Stalin's dacha at

Kuntsevo, Beria asked Khrushchev, "Well, have you received your orders?" Khrushchev replied, "Yes I have." Khrushchev brought to the dacha two Presidium members, Ukraine first party secretary Melnikov and Ukraine government chief Korotchenko, who were ordered to start pogroms in the Ukraine. Blood was in the air.[50] If any enticement was needed, loyal Soviet citizens should be quietly told that the Jews' property (including apartments filled with "valuable rugs, silver, and musical instruments") would be regarded as legitimate bounty.

In the period between the January 13 announcement and Stalin's death six weeks later, reports circulated that transport to move masses of people was being readied.[51] A few of the small number of Jews remaining in the upper ranks of the police organs, the government ministries, and the army knew specific details about the empty freight cars waiting on the sidings; and this information filtered down to many Jews and their gentile friends.[52] A high-ranking doctor, who had been in charge of checking sanitary conditions on the evacuation trains during the deportations of eight Soviet nationalities, learned in 1952 of the plans for the deportation of the Jews. Transportation was to be arranged along the same lines as in the wartime deportations.[53] In any case, the transport system itself would soon be *judenrein:* a Jewish railway doctor called Izrailit was one of the first to be purged.[54] Stalin reportedly ordered a large number of cattle cars to be readied at major rail centers in February 1953,[55] but this date seems highly doubtful. Given the complexity of his scenario, even if he was speeding up his timetable for the purges, the deportations would probably not have occurred before April or May at the very earliest.

As with the deportation of the Tatars eight years earlier, squads of MGB inventory takers were mobilized to itemize the personal property the Jews would be leaving behind. It is unlikely that there would have been resistance among the security forces to carrying out mass deportations. Every one of them had heard what had happened in the 1930s in the Ukraine and northern Caucasus when some security troops refused to annihilate peasants and were mowed down with them.[56] Now, after the experience of the Great Terror and World War II, the security people would not hesitate to shoot as many individuals as necessary and throw them into clay pits.

There were also indications that the Jews of the East European

satellites would be included. A top Polish Communist official of
Jewish origin told journalist S. L. Schneiderman in 1957 that the
Polish Communist party received orders from Moscow at the end
of 1952 to prepare to assemble the 69,000 Jews still remaining in
the country in order to shut them up in work camps "until further
orders." The proposed way station to Siberia was located along the
Soviet border, between Bialystok, Grodno, and Best in the
Bialowieza forest.[57] But there was strong resistance among Polish
Party leaders.

Transport was also being arranged for the Georgian
Mingrelians. At the end of February, special detachments of Cos-
sack troops reportedly appeared in the Mingrelian center of
Ochanchiri, "frightening people in the streets."[58]

Special barracks were built, "clean and new," according to Jews
who saw the camps after the Stalin years.[59] A Jewish engineer who
worked with the Soviet navy in western Siberia a decade after the
Doctors' Plot saw one never-used camp with row after row of
barracks: "Its vastness took my breath away." This camp was
located in highlands not far from Barnaul, a remote town in the
Kuzbass region, northeast of Kazakhstan and south of Novosibirsk
and the west Siberian oilfields. The general area, as big as Italy and
Yugoslavia combined, was dotted with hundreds of Soviet concentration camps. The camp that the engineer and the navy men
inspected was a sprawling ghost-town with collapsing wooden barracks which covered "at least two square kilometers."[60] In 1956
two similar barracks camps were found *in situ* in Birobidzhan.
These barracks, which were two kilometers long, and others on the
Arctic Ocean island of Novaya Zemlya, northeast of Archangel,
were built on specific orders from Stalin in 1952.[61] At that time
Olga Ivanova Goloborodka, an old Bolshevik who headed the Pen-
sions Department of the Social Security Ministry, accidentally
overheard a conversation in the Council of Ministers building about
the construction of the Birodibzhan barracks for the deported
Jews. "I sat there and thought I would go out of my mind," she
said.[62] Another witness, Ignace Szenfeld, overheard a conversation
between two well-fed police officials in fur coats who were scouting
for camp locations for the Jews in the Kazachinskoye region of
Siberia, near Krasnoyarsk, a few hundred miles from Barnaul.[63]
They were never used. But as Nadezhda Mandelstam wrote,
"There are still barracks waiting for them [the Jews] in some
infinitely remote swamp."[64]

Harrison Salisbury traveled "the length and breadth of Siberia and Central Asia in 1953 (after Stalin's death when travel was opened up) and in 1954" and saw no special new camps. "I do not believe they existed. I think Stalin just planned to ship the Jews into existing camps or the sheer wilderness." The vast unused camps reported by various sources "were the ones where the prisoners were released and returned to European Russia in the [post-Stalin] 50's."[65]

There were also reports of a huge development plan to turn Siberia into an industrial empire. The armies of slave laborers—prisoners and members of the deported nations—would be supplemented by nearly two million Jews, 200,000 Mingrelians, and another two or three million new political prisoners. Together they would build scores of huge plants, like the spirits distillery in Mariinsk. The Gulag administration had been through such experiences many times and the network in the Siberian taiga was already there: commanders, foremen, guards, prisoners' representatives, ration cards, inspection officials, Party and Komsomol representatives, the militia, the MGB and MVD with their rival armies of spies, army men, medical assistants, storehousemen, accountants. The camps were in a high state of readiness for the inflow, as Gulag resident Eugenia Ginzburg noted.[66] Another of the hundreds of thousands of Jews already in the Gulag was Joseph Berger, a founder of the Communist party in Palestine who went back to the socialist fatherland in the early thirties and was enslaved during the Great Purge. Now, as anti-Semitism swept the USSR, Berger became convinced that liquidation of the Jews was planned.[67]

Many Jews were already being rounded up. Some, like Dr. Yakov Rapoport, who was arrested in mid-January 1953, were being directly linked to the Kremlin doctors' case. Others, like Dr. Solomon Nezlin, who was arrested later in the month, were indirectly tied to the plot through a relative; his brother had been among those who viewed Zhdanov's medical records in 1948. The families of executed Jews like Peretz Markish were also arrested in the wake of the January 13 announcement, which had clearly signaled to them that the end was near. "We were waiting. We knew we would be arrested," recalled David Markish, who was fourteen at the time. The whole family was rounded up by the secret police: David; his mother, Esther; his twenty-three-year-old sister, Olga; his twenty-year-old brother, Simon; and their twenty-three-year-old cousin, Yuri, who was arrested only because he lived in the same apartment. The families of other Jewish Anti-Fascist Committee figures were rounded up on January 30 and 31: Zuskin's actress wife, Eda, and their daughter; Leib Kvitko's family; the Bergelsons. The wives of the Kremlin doctors were also arrested.[68]

Esther Markish harbored the hope that she would somehow be able to see her husband now; the family had no idea that Peretz Markish had been liquidated just over five months earlier. She asked the colonel in charge of the police agents, "How is my husband, where is he?" She was told, "That is something you will never know." The family packed what they could as the agents watched, along with the official civilian witnesses: the apartment block's porter and his wife and the maintenance man. The porter's wife asked if she could take some of their left-behind possessions, such as old shoes. Seals were placed on the front door. On February 17, 1953, they were informed that they had been sentenced to ten years in internal exile. They were immediately shipped off in a "Stolypin" sealed rail car to northern Kazakhstan.

A score of other women were in Esther Markish's prison car. She recognized one of them, Maria Yusefovich, wife of a prominent labor official who had been active in the Jewish Anti-Fascist Committee and who had been arrested with the majority of JAC members in 1949.[69]

The Kazakhstan desert region, flat lunar steppe, was where Beria's police troops had transported countless Latvians, Tatars from Crimea, Chechens and Ingushi from the Caucasus, Koreans, Moldavians, Volga Germans, Greeks, Turks, and others. Stalin planned to deport most of the Jews not to Siberia or Birobidzhan, but to the northern regions of Kazakhstan, according to Roy Medvedev.[70] There was certainly room enough for all two million Soviet Jews: Kazakhstan's Karaganda camp alone, which stretched over 300 miles, could accommodate many of them.

After days of travel in the prison coach, the Markish family arrived in the village of Karmachy. The local people thought they were Kremlin doctors and said, "You are Kogan, you are Vovsi." They had heard on the radio about the conspiracy to poison the best sons of Russia, and the name Kogan had become synonymous with "Jew." Their first question was, "Have they begun deporting the Jews, then?" The locals informed them that new camps were being built all along the rail line to distant Birobidzhan, and said they were "waiting for the Jews."[71] The family's incarceration was supervised by the local *komendatura,* run by the Ministry of State

Security. Many other Jews were already in the area, including a whole colony of Bessarabians, who had been exiled when the USSR annexed the Rumanian province in 1940; Bukharan Jews, who spoke a Persian dialect; and residents of Kiev, Odessa, and other cities. On the day of the January 13 announcement, David Markish and countless other Jewish children in Moscow had been beaten by other children and chased by hoodlums. Now, six weeks later, his first encounter with the local youth was no more promising. They chanted, "Kike, kike, on a rope he swings . . . Abraham Jew, the sooner you croak, the better."[72]

CHAPTER 12

A Pack of Wolves

Anti-Semitism Unleashed

In February 1953, as Stalin shipped the families of prominent intellectual Jews to Kazakhstan in the first trickle of the planned mass deportation and ordered the arrest of the last of the old Bolshevik Jews, such as former ambassador to Britain I. Maisky, the media campaign against "alien doctors" and "the pack of mad dogs from Tel Aviv" reached fever pitch.[1] The Moscow Puppet Theater featured grotesque marionettes with ugly Jewish features, and Soviet propagandists were writing essays such as "The Jewish Question Does Not Exist in Socialist Society," by Ladislao Carbajal.[2]

This long essay began naturally enough with a quote from Stalin: "National and racial chauvinism is a moral relic of the cannibalistic period, of man's hatred of man." It emphasized that anti-Zionism had nothing to do with anti-Semitism, for it was simply opposition to a movement that "has its origin in the most decadent bourgeois ideology." That is why "at the time when the imperialists are plunged in the preparation and unleashing of the Third World War, Zionism is there, at the side of the imperialists, in the unenviable role of spies and provocateurs." The writer went on to accuse Prime Minister David Ben-Gurion, Foreign Minister Moshe Sharett, and UN envoy Aubrey [Abba] Eban of Israeli espionage activity on behalf of the U.S.A. and Britain, and said that the Israelis were carrying out genocide, "a brutal war of extermination against the Arab population."[3]

There was no letup in the flood of daily press attacks on Jews that began with the January 13 announcement, or in the reports on the arrest of spies and economic criminals, all of whom had obviously Jewish names. A new peak was reached in mid-February with revelations of Zionist conspiracies in Odessa and the unmasking of espionage rings in Transcarpathia connected to the Joint.[4] American intelligence paid particular attention to the February 6 *Pravda* report on the arrests of spies S. D. Gurevich and Y. A. Taratuta (the latter, a senior employee of the USSR Academy of Sciences, was supposedly lured into spying by the former, an alleged Bundist–Menshevik–Trotskyite U.S. agent). Gurevich, American agents reported, was a close friend of Mikhail Borodin: Lenin's aide, Stalin's man in China, and former editor of *Moscow News*.[5] Now the old Bolshevik Jew was a recent arrival in the Gulag, along with his son, Norman.[6] The Americans were worried that the U.S. embassy would be implicated in the Gurevich case because he had done translations for the Associated Press and the United States Information Service.

In fact, there were reasons to suspect that both Gurevich and Taratuta had been Soviet secret police agents all along. The British embassy said Gurevich was "an extremely shrewd and unscrupulous man" and suggested that the woman called Taratuta, his stated accomplice, had been closely associated with him in Kuibyshev during the war and was implicated in the expulsion of former Associated Press correspondent Robert Magidoff.[7] Gurevich and Taratuta were probably studying their scripts in preparation for the impending trial of the Kremlin doctors, where their testimony would "prove" the existence of the conspiracy linking Soviet Jewish traitors with U.S. spymasters.[8]

Countless other arrests, like that of Maisky or Igor Nezhny, the prewar director of the Moscow Art Theater, went unrecorded in the media. Nezhny, an old friend of Mikhoels, was arrested in February and interrogated by Ryumin himself. He was accused of involvement in the "Zionist Center" of performing artists allegedly orchestrated by pianist Grigory Ginzburg. Ryumin struck Nezhny so hard across the ears that it resulted in deafness. During his interrogation sessions, Nezhny learned some details of Stalin's scenario. After the doctors would be tried and sentenced in the Kremlin's Hall of Columns, a second trial would be staged for the growing number of arrested Zionist artists, writers, and musicians. Like the "poisoner-doctors," the "poisoners of Soviet culture" would be condemned to death.[9]

A study in contrast to the daily diet of reports on Jewish spies and criminals was provided by the multitude of articles praising Lydia Feodosevna Timashuk, the latest winner of the Order of

Lenin. She was described as a "physician" in the ukase of the Presidium of the Supreme Soviet which announced the award of the nation's highest honor for "aiding the government in the unmasking of the doctor-murderers."[10] A lengthy *Pravda* article entitled "Lydia Timashuk's Mail" on February 20 revealed the first biographical details about this ex–secret service agent and "violent anti-Semite," in the words of a non-Jewish former KGB official.[11] The American chargé d'affaires, Jacob D. Beam, considered the eulogistic article an "almost hysterical attempt to whip up enthusiasm for her action" and thought it provided "a revealing indication of the use which the Soviet Government intends to make of her exploit in its internal propaganda."[12]

The article, by Olga Chechetkina, said that because people put so much faith in doctors,

> there is no crime, besides betrayal of the homeland, more monstrous . . . more loathsome than murder covered up with the white smock of a doctor. Now, by the bed of the patient are two people in white gowns. One is a scientist with a great name and degrees, the other is without degrees but has great experience and knowledge accumulated over twenty odd years of working in medicine; and she is filled with a strong sense of duty and regard for the health and life of the Soviet people. Both observe the same symptoms of the disease. But the woman sees that the man with the academic degrees makes an incorrect diagnosis. A wrong diagnosis, incorrect treatment—and that spells death. . . . before her was an enemy, and not one, but a gang of enemies of the Soviet Union, wicked, crafty and well disguised. A struggle began, a very difficult one. After all, those with degrees occupied high positions, and surrounded themselves with "their own people." But the woman fought as one must with enemies of the homeland, in a life-and-death struggle. Perhaps during those days she had a mental image of a burning airplane, and in it, a Soviet flier—her only son. . . . now the name of the doctor, Lydia Feodosevna Timashuk, has become a symbol of Soviet patriotism, of high vigilance, of an irreconcilable and courageous struggle with the enemies of our country. She helped tear the mask from the American hirelings, monsters who used the white coats of a doctor to kill Soviet people.[13]

The article went on to describe some of the great pile of letters received by this "dear daughter of our country," including a collective poem attacking the U.S. hirelings by the pupils of School No. 10 in Sochi, where Stalin often went to bask in the Black Sea sun:

Infamy to you, outcasts of society,
For your black deeds,
And praise for ever and ever
To the glorious, patriotic Russian woman!

The article said that most of the huge number of letters "speak of vigilance" against the Anglo-American "instigators of a new war" and their "filthy agents." A dark threat came from "the workers of Kazan state," who wrote: "It is time for them to understand that our people are vigilant, and that however much they try to undermine the might of our country, the same fate awaits all of them as awaits the apprehended villain murderers."[14]

A similar paean to Timashuk appeared a few days later. The writer noted how "a simple Soviet woman, an ordinary doctor," had caught "the venal vermin who hid a knife and poison under their snow-white frocks . . . these degenerates with serpents' stings in place of hearts." The same theme of a simple but honest doctor catching the venerated celebrity professor was sounded. The question supposedly occurring to Timashuk about the honesty of the unnamed "luminary" clearly referred to his Jewishness: "Is he not alien, is he not an enemy in our Soviet family if he acts thus?"[15] The answer attributed to Timashuk: "Yes, if you are not with my people, not with my Soviet country, then naturally, I am not one of *your* people."

The Soviet campaign did not seem to perturb some of the most prominent American Jewish leaders, in contrast to the heads of B'nai B'rith, who had gone to the State Department to discuss their fears. Rabbi Abba Hillel Silver, the most famous Reform rabbi and American Zionist leader, made a statement in Los Angeles on February 17, 1953, and was dutifully quoted by a New York Jewish Communist magazine: "In the past thirty years of its existence, the Soviet Union has a good record in which no racial or religious intolerance was practiced. I have no evidence that the Soviet Union is launched on an all-out anti-Semitic policy." He said that he was therefore "inclined to give them the benefit of the doubt."[16]

A group of forty-nine prominent Americans, including Eleanor

Roosevelt, Sumner Welles, General Telford Taylor, and Lewis Mumford, were not as sanguine as Rabbi Silver. On February 12 they appealed to President Eisenhower to speak out about the millions of Jews in the Soviet bloc who faced "a new epidemic of pogroms, Communist-inspired attacks on the Jews." The president, they declared, should issue a "solemn public condemnation and warning that this attack against the Jewish people is an incitement to massacre."[17] On February 16 Senator Robert C. Hendrickson introduced Senate Resolution 71, on behalf of himself and two other senators, which compared Communist anti-Semitism to Fascist and Nazi practices.[18] American Fascist organizations, and McCarthyist periodicals like *Common Sense* and *National Renaissance,* commended the Soviets for striking at the Jewish menace.[19]

In Israel, the Jewish Agency Executive did not see any immediate danger. On February 4 it decided to call an international Jewish conference on East European anti-Semitism to be held in Switzerland in mid-March, six long weeks away. World Zionist Organization leader Nahum Goldmann, in an unhurried February 16 cable to his Geneva office, said limpidly that the aim of the conference would be to "repudiate accusations leveled Eastern Europeans against Zionists, JDC and Jews generally." It would also demand "security for Jews in Eastern European countries," which would have fit in perfectly with Stalin's plan to guarantee the Jews safety in Soviet concentration camps.[20] But the Jewish and Zionist leaders' correspondence, or lack of it, during this period indicates that they were not taking Stalin's threats to the Jews very seriously.[21] The Israeli Soviet and East European experts in the Foreign Ministry, as well as Golda Meir, "wanted to make a fuss at the UN General Assembly, but Abba Eban held us back," according to one of the diplomats, Aryeh Levavi. Levavi and Meir wanted to start a campaign immediately.[22]

━━

Though Israeli diplomats had reported in January that the Soviet media attacks were aimed primarily at Jews and "Zionists" and were not focused directly on Israel—other than an occasional reference to Israeli "genocide against the Arabs"—this would all change on February 9. At 10:00 P.M. a violent explosion inside the Soviet legation shook downtown Tel Aviv. Three Soviet citizens were injured, one of them seriously.[23]

The bomb that wrecked the legation was thrown from the backyard of the three-story apartment house where the Soviet officers were located. Moscow immediately charged that the explosion had taken place with the connivance of the police and the government. A Soviet dispatch from Tel Aviv said that "the Zionist press has been carrying on an infamous campaign of slander and lies against the USSR since the Soviet government arrested physicians and other criminal Zionist groups as spies and traitors."[24] The Israeli government at first suspected that the bombing was a provocation. Suspicions were fueled by the diplomats' refusal to allow investigators into the legation until the next day, seventeen hours after the explosion. But a number of Israeli suspects were arrested, and Israel formally apologized to the Soviet Union on February 10. In fact, the bombing had been carried out by followers of Yitzhak Shamir's disbanded Stern group, the smallest and most violent of the pre-state Jewish underground organizations, although this was not known at the time.[25]

Three days after the blast, on February 12, the Soviets broke off diplomatic relations with Israel. Foreign Minister Andrei Vyshinsky summoned Israeli envoy Shmuel Eliashiv to the ministry at 1:00 P.M. and handed him a note, which was broadcast by Radio Moscow an hour later: "Malefactors with the obvious connivance of the police engineered the explosion, wounding the wives of P. I. Yershov and I. G. Grishin." The note rejected Israel's apology and said that the Israelis systematically fanned hatred and enmity toward the USSR and incited hostile actions.[26] The break in ties was played up in the Soviet press. The crowds forming around the public noticeboards where the daily newspapers were on display expressed anti-Semitic sentiments. Golda Meir, in the Israeli pioneer town of Petach Tikva, called it "a black day for Israel, for world Jewry and for the Jews of the Soviet Union. I feel for them in my heart."[27]

Israeli leaders, who had tried hard for four years not to antagonize the Soviets, became increasingly convinced that the Doctors' Plot was a historic watershed, a prelude to the next world war. Ben-Gurion told the Knesset that the Soviet severing of ties was part of a massive defamatory campaign, another scene from the Jews' 4,000-year history of hatred, slanders, torture, destruction, and butchery.

On February 14 *Pravda* discerned a direct link between acts against the USSR organized by Israeli intelligence and the bombing of the legation. It described Israeli leaders as "a pack of mad dogs."[28] *Izvestia* said that the U.S.A. was behind the bombing. An article by L. Vatolina explained that State Department official William Draper, with the aid of the Joint and the banking firms of Dillon, Read and Harriman Bros., was implementing the secret plan of FDR's former secretary of the treasury Henry Morgenthau, Congressman Emanuel Celler, and Senator Jacob Javits to make Israel the main Middle East anti-Communist base. The Joint's staff in Tel Aviv, the article said, included "the dregs of society, Trotskyites, bourgeois nationalists, and all sorts of rootless cosmopolitans who sold their honor, people, and country for dollars."[29]

The Stern group's bombing fit perfectly into Stalin's plans, for it removed Israeli diplomats from Moscow well in advance of the planned deportation of the Jews. A few months earlier Stalin had similarly jumped at the opportunity provided by the U.S. ambassador, George Kennan, when Kennan compared conditions in Moscow to those he had experienced in Nazi Germany. Kennan was declared *persona non grata* in September 1952, and only a chargé d'affaires was left at the American embassy. Stalin did not want perceptive foreigners around, and probably planned to expel the five Western media correspondents sometime in March (Harrison Salisbury, and Henry Shapiro of the Associated Press, were considered especially knowledgeable and thus dangerous). On February 20 the four Israeli diplomats, their wives, and one child left by train for Leningrad and Helsinki, seen off by a large number of Western diplomats.[30]

Ten days later the *Manchester Guardian* reported that Foreign Minister Vyshinsky had invited one of Israel's most hated enemies, the former mufti of Jerusalem, Haj Amin al-Husseini, to visit Moscow from his haven in Cairo. The mufti, the leader of the Palestinian Arabs, had been Hitler's invited guest at Auschwitz and was considered a war criminal by Yugoslavia, where he had headed the SS Muslim legion.[31] The invitation, which happened to be announced on the first day of the Jewish festival of Purim, was made as Nazi collaborators, former Fascist guards, and other war criminals attacked Jewish prisoners throughout the Gulag. "Your end is coming near," Jewish prisoners were told.[32]

Tito's Yugoslavia staged a huge protest meeting against Soviet anti-Semitism on February 27 in Beograd. Representatives of over one hundred Yugoslav organizations and top government officials attended. Speaker after speaker condemned the Soviet suppression of human rights and freedoms; and a resolution read at the rally accused the Kremlin of threatening three million Jews in the USSR and its satellites with "the same possible final consequences" as had so recently occurred under Hitler.[33]

===

The last foreigners to see Stalin alive were two Indians, who were granted separate meetings with the Soviet leader on February 17, 1953. Stalin spoke briefly with the Indian fellow traveller Dr. Saiffrudin Kitchlu and then held a longer meeting with Ambassador Krishna P. S. Menon, a keen-minded, perceptive observer and only the third envoy to be received by Stalin in five years. Both men, who were winners of the Stalin Prize, reported afterward that the Soviet leader seemed in excellent spirits and "good health."[34]

Stalin and Menon, sitting at opposite ends of a conference table with their interpreters, talked about the Korean conflict, Japanese trade, the state of the Indian armed forces, and other subjects, including linguistics. Menon thanked Acting Foreign Minister Malik for the hospitality extended by his ministry, and Stalin commented: "It's only natural. Even shepherds in Russia are hospitable, and we are no more than shepherds. The Soviet people regard all other peoples and races as equal, and there is no trace of condescension in their attitude towards them." Twice he said that it was futile to teach morals to evil people. Stalin was idly sketching throughout their talk, and Menon noticed that he was drawing wolves in various positions—one standing on its hind legs, others about to bite or crouching to attack. He had filled a whole sheet with the drawings.

Menon mentioned that recent American moves regarding the Korean war and Formosa (Taiwan) had been criticized throughout the world, even by the United Kingdom and Canada, and that this should have a restraining effect on American policy. Stalin said: "There's no sign of it yet." Then, suddenly, he added: "Mr. Ambassador, our peasant is a very simple man, but very wise. When the wolf attacks him, he does not attempt to teach it morals, but tries to kill it. And the wolf knows this, and behaves accordingly." Menon, like the rest of the diplomatic community, knew that another bloodbath, a ritual cleansing, or *chistka,* was being prepared on a gigantic scale. He also knew that the Jews were the focus of Stalin's attacks, and that the Kremlin doctors were constantly being referred to as "ferocious beasts in human form" and "Fascist wolves in sheep's clothing."[35] The implications were not lost on him.

＝＝＝

The last half of February was the darkest, most intensely cold month in the memory of Muscovites, with blustery winds and chilling snows that wrapped everyone, living and dead, in the same white shroud. One of these dead, at age sixty-four, was mass executioner Lev Zakharovich Mekhlis, whom Khrushchev characterized as one of the worst of Stalin's "mad dogs."[36] Like Khrushchev, Molotov, Malenkov, Poskrebyshev, and Kaganovich Mekhlis had often played a leading role in the extermination of Party cadres.[37] Mekhlis, the son of a Jewish office worker in Odessa, was an impassioned Bolshevik who had imprisoned his own father and testified against him before a secret police tribunal. In the 1930s, along with Yezhov and Beria, he became the main perpetrator of the purges which wiped out the Soviet officer corps.[38] He was instrumental in the execution of 15,000 Red Army officers. Like Poskrebyshev, Mekhlis had once been Stalin's secretary. And also like Poskrebyshev, he had no personal ambitions other than to be a cog in Stalin's machine, wielding tremendous authority. Along with Kaganovich, he presided mercilessly over the deaths of hundreds of thousands if not millions of people.[39]

Besides Kaganovich, Mekhlis was the last Soviet leader of Jewish origin to serve in the government hierarchy. He had been eased out of his last post, as minister for state control, in October 1950, reportedly because of ill health. He may have been removed as state comptroller, as Yehoshua Gilboa suggests, because it was more expedient for a pure Russian to be at the helm during the welter of exposés of fraud and conspiracy.[40]

Mekhlis was last mentioned in the Soviet press in October 1952, when he was elected at the Nineteenth Congress to the Central Committee. It is not clear whether he played a role in organizing the "Jewish statement" that was to serve as the mandate for the deportation of the Jews. But Mekhlis reportedly feared for his life in the wake of the announcement of the Doctors' Plot, slipping out of Moscow in early February and hiding in the town of Saratov. There he fell "mysteriously ill," according to one rumor, and was brought to Moscow to be treated in the MVD infirmary in Lefortovo prison. Just before his death, he was visited by

Poskbrebyshev, the story goes, who got the dying man to sign a "confession."[41] The historian A. Avtorkhanov claims that Mekhlis was arrested in early February and died in the prison hospital.[42]

His death certificate bore the signatures of Ivan Ivanovich Kuperin, head of the Kremlin Medical Hygiene Administration; Professors P. E. Lukomsky and A. V. Rusakov; and Drs. V. T. Boev and N. I. Kuzmina.[43] But some of the British diplomats in Moscow expressed doubt that Mekhlis's death was due to natural causes, citing the cases of Zhdanov and Dimitrov, who were also greatly honored once safely dead but who had been in disfavor and whose deaths were "widely and plausibly reputed to have been 'assisted.'"[44]

Although Mekhlis may have died as early as February 10, the front page of *Pravda,* on February 14, 1953, announced the time of death as 1:35 A.M. on Friday the 13th, with cause of death given as arteriosclerosis and heart failure. Tass also said he died of a heart seizure following degeneration of the brain and vessels of the heart and nervous systems.

On February 15 thousands thronged for the burial with honors of "Stalin's old comrade-in-arms," but Stalin himself did not attend, and the crowd showed little enthusiasm for the late minister of state control.[45] The guard of honor included Bulganin, Kaganovich, Khrushchev, and Suslov, among the twelve Presidium members attending.[46] They paid their last tributes in the black-draped Hall of Columns, where the body lay in state. The Presidium secretary, A. F. Gorkin, described Mekhlis as a man who "had no other interests in life except the interests of the Communist Party and the Soviet Union."[47] A band played a funeral march as the Kremlin guns sounded. Traffic was snarled throughout downtown Moscow, as the streets around Red Square were roped off by cordons of militiamen, some mounted on horses. The funeral was one of the most lavish since Zhdanov's in September 1948, and stood in sharp contrast to the modest ceremony for former foreign minister Maxim Litvinov, who had died a year earlier. Mekhlis was cremated, and his ashes were interred in the Kremlin wall near Lenin's Tomb.

It seemed obvious, a month after the January 13 announcement, that the Kremlin had staged such a big show because it wished to demonstrate to the outside world that it was not "anti-Jewish," but simply concerned about a "Zionist conspiracy." But behind the death of Mekhlis—if it was "assisted" as seems entirely plausible— there was also a message for internal consumption. Stalin did not pay his personal respects to one of his most loyal associates, though he found the time two days later to talk with an insignificant Indian fellow traveler as well as the Indian ambassador. Most of Stalin's remaining colleagues, especially Beria, Khrushchev, Voroshilov, Molotov, and Mikoyan, were out of favor and possibly faced similar "illnesses" in the coming weeks. The murder of Mekhlis, if such it was, may also have been a sop to the army leadership, who hated him as much as Beria because of his ignominious role in the army purges and in the war.

The January 13 announcement, singling out the military leaders as targets of elimination by the enemies of the Soviet Union, had made it clear that the professional military class was being courted. It was also becoming clear that the attitude of the military hierarchy would have a decisive effect on the struggle to succeed the rapidly aging Stalin. As an American intelligence analysis put it: "Taken together with the consideration shown for the health of high military figures, the current anti-Semitism, both in its internal and external aspects, appears to be an extreme measure and looks as though Moscow was clearing the decks for action." It meant that the Soviets feared "that the United States will place the Soviet Union in a position where war is the only acceptable alternative."[48]

=====

A new world war may well have been part of Stalin's apocalyptic plan. The Israelis believed it, as did a minority of American and English diplomats, as well as some German and Russian émigré Sovietologists. A confidential U.S. dispatch from Munich on January 21, 1953, quoted Konstantin Krylov, an important Soviet defector, and an unnamed Soviet army staff officer as saying that anti-Semitism was being unleashed "as preparation for widespread use during general war. Purpose is to divert people's hatred from regime toward Jews against whom sentiment already strong."[49]

Among themselves Israeli leaders were speculating on the prospects of a world war; and in public, Foreign Minister Moshe Sharett said that the Doctors' Plot "doesn't necessarily mean this is preparation for war but it is part of the preparation for war."[50] But perceptive observers like Harrison Salisbury, after years of pondering the events he had witnessed in Moscow in 1952–53, would disagree.[51] And Salisbury's friend George Kennan, the foremost American Sovietologist, never subscribed to the belief that

the Soviets wanted a world war, and said that the U.S.A.'s possession of the atom bomb had prevented a Soviet invasion of Europe in
1948.[52] But Kennan's belief was based on the fact that there was no
"rational" or political reason for the Soviets to inaugurate a war.
Although Stalin may have been more "rational" than Hitler, and
though he always displayed more cunning and control, in February
1953 he was on the verge of an internal explosion. According to
historian Robert Conquest, the question of whether Stalin intended or feared immediate war "can only be discussed at all if we
at least assume that he was not by now raving mad."[53]

Stalin himself seemed to believe in the inevitability of war, and
he became increasingly sure of it as his condition deteriorated. As
Conquest put it, if it is even partially true that Stalin had become
especially capricious and that "in the last months of the Doctors'
Plot he had lost control in some quite unpredictable way," then the
accepted theory that he was NOT planning war becomes compli-
cated "with an unknown."[54]

The Doctors' Plot certainly was aimed at creating a purge of the
top leadership as well as the middle echelons of Soviet society and
dealing with the "Jewish problem" by deportation. If the third aim
was indeed to prepare the people for war, a possible indication was
published in *Pravda* on February 6, 1953. A major article by Party
official N. Kozev sharply condemned those scholars who disputed
the theory of "capitalist encirclement." They were trying to lull
the people away from the very real threat of attack by the imperialists, he said.

The article, in discussing the Doctors' Plot, also gave the first
Soviet analysis of "what threw these degenerates into the clutches
of American and English espionage": "[h]atred for the Soviet
power, a bourgeois nationalist ideology hostile to our people, grov-
elling before the bourgeois 'way of life' to which they are attracted
with all their being." The article called for vigilance in the face of
external threats by warmongers, and the internal threat of a fifth
column.

The senior members of the Presidium, already under constant
threat, could only look with horror at the web Stalin was weaving,
at his ambitious plan using anti-Semitism as a pivot toward gradually putting the Soviet Union on a full war footing. Solzhenitsyn
would portray Stalin in *The First Circle* as believing that massive
purges must be instituted as a preliminary step toward war—he
had done it in the thirties, and he was doing it now, in 1953.

But a British intelligence gatherer in Moscow argued against this view, reporting to London that "against this theory must be set the fact that there are no outward signs of immediate preparations for war."[55] The expert said that Stalin was "in the second stage of readiness, not the first."[56] But this analysis, written while Stalin was dying or dead, did not take into account the extreme importance of the campaign built around the Doctors' Plot, or the fact that Stalin's conspiracies and "five year" schemes were long-ranging and painstakingly planned. If he was indeed in the "second stage," he was progressing methodically toward the next. As KGB defector Peter Deriabin would put it, because Stalin wished to surpass the Kirov case and the show trials and purges of the thirties, the Doctors' Plot "was an exceedingly long time in production" before the public announcement was made.[57]

Stalin began conjuring up the specter of a third world war as early as February 9, 1946, when he said in a speech that "military catastrophes" were inevitable because of the nature of capitalism.[58] During the war he was suspicious of his allies' intentions once Hitler would be defeated; and undoubtedly, there was good cause for concern.

Toward the end of the war, an NKVD colonel told "Red Orchestra" spy leader Leopold Trepper that Stalin was planning for a possible war with the West in the near future and that this was the reason for the vast scale of the ongoing "purification" of potential internal enemies: "Stalin has also declared that in the long chain of nationalities within the Soviet Union, there were 'weak links'. . . he pointed out those who were suspect to the NKVD: Ukrainians, Belorussians, Ouzbeks, Jews."[59] Stalin was instrumental in setting off the Korean conflict, and by 1950 both sides in the Cold War began to feel that a wider war beyond Korea was on the horizon. And even though the need for coexistence was occasionally voiced by the Kremlin, Soviet domestic policy increasingly took into account the very real prospect of war with the West. This was the backdrop for Zhdanov's 1947–48 psychological and propaganda campaign against Western ways; and the West's most evil embodiment in Soviet society was the rootless cosmopolitans.

The constant harping on the "fifth column" which the Jews supposedly constituted went beyond mere propaganda. Stalin's intentions became clearer at the Nineteenth Party Congress in October 1952, when his anointed successor, Georgi Malenkov, said that a third world war was possible and that it would cause "the collapse of the world capitalist system." In the same speech—ten weeks before the announcement of the Doctors' Plot as the core of an American-orchestrated Zionist design to destroy the Soviet military leaders—Malenkov added that the West was building up Israel as a major base in preparation for the coming world conflict.[60] Four months later, and ten days after Stalin died, Malenkov performed a complete about-face, telling the Supreme Soviet that all international problems could be solved peacefully.[61]

Marxist historian Isaac Deutscher believed that the aim of the Doctors' Plot was to create an atmosphere of war fever and nationalist hysteria, ending in a complete break between East and West. "In such a mood, the 'alien,' the citizen suspected of 'divided loyalties,' is naturally regarded as the worst 'security risk.'. . . And who could be a worse 'security risk' than the Jews with Zionist sympathies or the 'rootless cosmopolitans' whose brothers or cousins lived in the West?"[62]

In notable contrast to the Great Terror of the thirties, the military was not one of the first targets of the Doctors' Plot purges; in fact, the military leaders had been portrayed as the principal targets of the Zionist-Jewish conspiracy organized by the United States. Only the military escaped the new inquisition affecting the entire civilian administration and all other sectors of the society. The reason may have been that Stalin was actively wooing the military leadership at the same time as he served a death notice to his closest vassals, from the insufficiently vigilant Beria to the "British spy" Voroshilov. This time, if war were imminent, he could not afford to unleash terror against the army; that would only come later, at an unspecified point in the Doctors' Plot scenario.

Stalin's ministers had their own contacts with the military leadership, through the "political marshals," Voroshilov and especially Bulganin. The latter saw himself as a liaison between Soviet military and political leaders.

The changes that occurred in the Soviet military leadership during Stalin's last days were not casual ones, though a British diplomat considered the principal change "no more than routine."[63] The Foreign Office also informed Washington that the upheavals throughout Russia and the Eastern Bloc all pointed to a major drive for internal security, and not for war.[64]

As Robert Conquest has observed, from the January 13 list of intended victims of the Jewish poisoners it was possible to discern

that Marshals Konev and Govorov were being honored as the most
loyal "fighting marshals," while Vasilevsky was seen as "a professional rather under the thumb of the politicians . . . and Shtemenko
the political general proper. The most obvious military men missing from the list were Zhukov, Sokolovsky, and Admiral
Kuznetsove."[65] But Marshal V. D. Sokolovsky did not have long to
wait for his redemption. Chief of Staff Sergei Matveyevich
Shtemenko was suddenly replaced within a short period before or
after January 13, though his replacement by Sokolovsky was not
officially revealed until February 21, 1953, a few days before
Stalin's death.[66]

Sokolovsky was close to Zhukov, whom Stalin had banished to
the provinces, and to Bulganin, with whom he had served on the
West Front military council.[67] Zhukov, who would rescue Khrushchev in 1957 in the fight against the old Stalinists, may have
served a similar role in 1953. Within days of Stalin's death, Zhukov
would be named deputy defense minister.

Four days before the change at the top of the Soviet military, on
February 17, *Izvestia* announced the "premature death" of Major
General Pyotr Kosynkin, the Kremlin's chief of security, supposedly the victim of a heart attack. This fanatic Stalin loyalist was
killed, according to KGB defector Deriabin, under the orders of
Beria, Bulganin, and Malenkov, as well as Ignatiev, "who was
working both sides of the street."[68] The Kremlin *komendatura*
which Kosynkin had directed would play a key role in the fall of
Beria eight weeks after Stalin's death: Khrushchev in his memoirs
talks of enlisting the military's help to arrest Beria.

But the military's involvement most likely began weeks earlier,
in February, in a plot which *included* their arch-foe Beria in a
temporary alliance aimed at preventing a vast purge and possible
world war.[69] The rumbles of a conspiracy against Beria by the army
and the circle around Malenkov had been discussed by American
diplomats in mid-January 1953.[70] But no one in the diplomatic,
intelligence, or press circles picked up any hint of a possible plot to
isolate Stalin or to speed along his death. Top Soviet experts believed that the attitude of the military leadership would have a
decisive effect on the struggle for power in the Kremlin, and some
conjectured that the Doctors' Plot was a scheme devised for
Malenkov to obtain the military's backing.[71]

Another key Stalin loyalist who disappeared around the same
time as General Kosynkin was Major General Nikolai Sergeyevich

Vlasik, head of Stalin's personal guard and the longtime major-domo of Stalin's household, whom Svetlana so hated. He, like the other longest-serving Stalin loyalist, Poskrebyshev, was reportedly eased out by Beria, who replaced him with V. Khrustalov.[72]

On February 22 the brakes were suddenly applied to the all-out press campaign against the Jewish spies, poisoners, and wreckers. "Vigilance" was the subject of far fewer articles. Something dramatic had happened.

It is unclear to this day whether Stalin was still alive—or still in control—on February 22, or whether it was he who ordered the changes in the military. What seems undisputed is that an epic struggle was occurring in the Soviet hierarchy over whether to continue with the Doctors' plot, and that the military chiefs were among the major players.[73]

CHAPTER 13

Purimshpiel

Deliverance from Haman

Stalin believed Jews were always trying to penetrate his inner circle, and his conviction was reinforced by the fact that many of his associates were married to Jewish women. He thought that a Jewess married to a gentile ruled the roost, and that Jewry penetrated indirectly where it could not do so directly. The issue of "the Jewish wife" became crucially important during the Doctors' Plot because at least one of Stalin's closest henchmen—Marshal Voroshilov—refused to sacrifice his wife of many years.

During the purges Stalin had arrested President Mikhail Kalinin's Jewish wife, as well as Bukharin's. At the height of the anti-cosmopolitan campaign he had sent Molotov's Jewish wife to Kazakhstan, and he made Poskrebyshev's Jewish wife disappear somewhere in eastern Siberia in 1951.

He had not tolerated the fact that two of his children married Jews, imprisoning his daughter-in-law, Yulia (whom he only referred to as "the Jewish wife"); Svetlana's first love, Kapler; and her father-in-law, Morozov. Stalin had exploded when he confronted Svetlana over her "Jewish problem," screaming and slapping her in March 1943.[1]

It seemed there were Jews wherever he looked. His loyal tin soldier, Marshal Voroshilov, was devoted to his Jewish wife, Catherine. Marshal Bulganin was also happily married to a Jew, Nadezhda. Politburo member Andrei Andreyev, who fell from grace in 1950, was married to Dora Khazan, and Kaganovich the Jew was married to Maria, also one of the tribe. Malenkov, who was suspected of being a bit of a philo-Semite, had a Jewish son-in-law, as, it was said, did Khrushchev. The up-and-coming Leonid Brezhnev was said to have a Jewish wife.

Stalin barred his associates' wives from the long nightly banquets at Kuntsevo; for he knew that foreign intelligence agencies often used women to recruit agents. Malenkov, though he was "uncontaminated by the vile disease" of anti-Semitism, forced his daughter Volya to divorce her Jewish husband, the son of Malenkov's close friend M. A. Shamberg.[2] In the highly charged anti-Semitic atmosphere before and during the Doctors' Plot, all high-ranking Soviet officials were under pressure to divorce their Jewish wives. Marshal Ivan Peresypkin's wife, Roza, a friend of the Markish family, was sent to join Molotov's wife in exile. Even her own sons wanted their father to divorce her, but he refused.[3]

The high rate of intermarriage between Soviet Jews and Russians created agonizing situations, at all levels of Soviet society, in the hysterical atmosphere following the January 13 announcement. Some non-Jews loyally shared the tragic fate of their Jewish spouses. But "there were also incidents of divorces—some of them fictitious, until the storm would blow over."[4] In the Soviet hierarchy, divorce from Jewish mates was a general rule. Marshal Voroshilov, however, simply would not agree to get rid of Catherine.

He had stood up to his master once before, in 1940. The inept marshal, who as people's commissar of defense had totally mishandled the Finnish war, became the object of one of Stalin's white-hot rampages during a dinner at the dictator's dacha. In turn, Voroshilov's blood raced to his head; he jumped up and shouted, "You have yourself to blame for all this! You're the one who annihilated the Old Guard of the army; you had our best generals killed!" He picked up a platter of roast suckling pig and smashed it on the table.[5] Voroshilov was relieved of his duties but kept around as a scapegoat for the next twelve years.

Strangely enough, the former ironworker, who personally observed the executions of the Jews Zinoviev and Kamenev on Stalin's orders, was about to become one of the most unlikely heroes in the annals of Jewish history—though to this day, his courageous stand is virtually unknown.

Marshal Voroshilov loved Stalin, but he loved his Jewish wife even more. He and Catherine owned the biggest and most sumptuous dacha of all the revolutionary grandees, full of Persian rugs, jade vases, silver Caucasian weapons, and Indian silks.[6] He sang, and fancied himself an opera expert. Catherine apparently deferred to his opinions on the subject. Once, when the name of some opera singer came up in general conversation, she looked down into her lap and said: "Kliment Yefremovich doesn't hold a particularly high opinion of her."[7] Along with Molotov and Mikoyan, Voroshilov had become increasingly unwelcome at Stalin's banquet table after the October 1952 encounter at which Stalin suggested that he was a British spy. He was no longer allowed to see many documents, and Stalin insulted him at every opportunity.

Sometime in February 1953 Voroshilov reportedly threatened with a pistol and chased away four MGB agents who had come to his mansion to arrest his Jewish wife; and his devotion to Catherine is what prompted his next, epic defiance of Stalin. It occurred at a Presidium meeting which he was allowed to attend in late February—Stalin's last meeting with his associates, which was called to discuss the expulsion of the Jews.

Stalin's blood pressure had never reached such heights. The histrionics that took place during this encounter between Stalin and at least three members of his Presidium may have been part of a calculated medical conspiracy by Stalin's terrified subordinates.[8] Or Voroshilov's challenge to Stalin may have been totally spontaneous; he would not sit like Molotov when his wife had been arrested.

At the meeting, Stalin revealed details of his plan to combat what he called "a sinister Zionist and imperialist plot" against the USSR. He spoke almost deliriously about "the affair of the Jewish doctors" and said that it necessitated immediate collective deportation to Central Asia and Birobidzhan.[9] When he finished talking, complete silence reigned among the two dozen men sitting around the Kremlin conference table. Then Kaganovich asked in a hesitant voice whether all Soviet Jews without exception were to be deported. Stalin replied, "a certain section," and Kaganovich said nothing more. Another heavy silence followed.[10] Molotov, whose wife was already in the wilderness, broke the long silence in a trembling voice and said that the expulsion of the Jews would have a negative impact on world opinion; Mikoyan shook his head in assent. They were joined, in an outspoken manner, by Voroshilov, who, undoubtedly with Catherine's image in his mind, said that acts like the Doctors' Plot deportation plan had aroused the world against Hitler. In a theatrical gesture, the marshal threw his Party card on the table, saying that the expulsion scheme violated the Party's honor and that he did not want to belong to such an organization. Stalin, his blood rushing to his head, roared: "Comrade

Kliment, it is I who decides at what moment you will no longer be allowed to keep the Party membership card!" Stalin became so enraged that his eyes rolled, and he finally collapsed on the floor—he suffered the fatal stroke then and there. None of the great Kremlin doctors, the leading specialists, could be summoned. Some were dead, others were almost vegetables after weeks of torture. The ordinary doctors who were called arrived fifteen or twenty minutes later. Stalin appeared to be dead. Then Beria did a little dance around the inanimate body, saying: "We are free! Finally, finally! Comrades, the tyrant is dead, rejoice! We can breathe freely!" The others, filled with fear, stood around like stones. Svetlana was summoned. She put her arms around Stalin and cried, "Father, father!" To the consternation of his associates, Stalin opened one eye, then the other, saw his daughter but was unable to utter a word. Beria, seeing that the dictator wasn't dead, threw himself around his knees, crying hysterically for his forgiveness. Minutes later the newly arrived doctors carried Stalin to his private apartment, where he died without regaining consciousness. Khrushchev had the last word: "Tonight, the mice have buried the cat."[11]

There are various versions of the above story, which were leaked in 1957, possibly to show that the Soviet government was not guilty of anti-Semitism, since several of Stalin's associates were described as having stood up to him over the issue of the Jews, thus speeding his fatal attack.[12] But whether the acts of defiance were coordinated and rehearsed among the men Stalin was going to kill remains an unanswered question. Certainly Beria, who knew all about the previous medical murders and who was in charge of the Kremlin medical service and Stalin's medical records, was capable of orchestrating a frontal attack on the ailing Stalin. Certainly the other members of the inner circle, with possible exceptions such as Kaganovich, wanted Stalin dead.

Probably a temporary, emergency alliance had been forged among the six most threatened leaders: Molotov, Mikoyan, Khrushchev, Voroshilov, Bulganin—and their archenemy, Beria. Robert Tucker has suggested that Beria used the Doctors' Plot to deprive Stalin of his doctors, especially Vinogradov, and thereby hasten his end. Although five of Stalin's other top men were threatened, Beria may have been the only one who "had the means and guile to take action, in such a Byzantine way."[13]

Beria alone was in possession of Stalin's medical records, but it is not known if he shared the information with any of Stalin's other associates. All of them could see the Doctors' Plot for what it was, and Beria may very well have conspired with Stalin's other threatened lieutenants to shape and stage the last drama. The united opposition to the deportation of the Jews was agreed upon before the Presidium meeting took place. It surely was not a coincidence that the three of the four most threatened Soviet leaders—Molotov, Mikoyan, and Voroshilov, but not Beria—were the ones who voiced their opposition to Stalin's plans, thereby bringing on his final fit of rage. But suggestions that Stalin was poisoned or otherwise directly murdered remain speculative.[14] Most historians doubt that any of Stalin's lieutenants would have resorted to such a bold maneuver, no matter how terrified they were. At any rate, Stalin's time had come. As Solzhenitsyn put it in a *Gulag Archipelago* footnote about the Doctors' Plot: "This became the first plan of his life to fail. God told him—apparently with the help of human hands—to depart from his rib cage."

=====

On February 22 and 23 there was a sudden lull in the constant press campaign against the Jews and other enemies of the Soviet way of life, and after February 25 no more arrests of Jews were reported. The Doctors' Plot campaign came to a halt on March 1, and *Pravda* the next morning was silent about the doctor-poisoners for the first time since the shock of the January 13 announcement.

Stalin's stroke occurred on Sunday, March 1, according to the official Soviet version of events. In a version of his final hours that differs from the stories of death in the Kremlin, Svetlana Alliluyeva wrote that she learned of her father's condition on March 2, when she was told to go to Kuntsevo. Her brother Vasily was already at the scene, very drunk and screaming at the doctors there, saying that they had killed or were killing his father.[15] Svetlana wrote that Khrushchev and Bulganin were in tears, while an agitated Beria behaved "obscenely," passions playing across his face.[16] Stalin lay on the couch, slowly suffocating as the hemorrhaging affecting part of his brain spread to the rest. His face gradually darkened and his lips turned black. Suddenly, to the terror of everyone, including Svetlana, he lifted his left hand and pointed at them all, as if summoning a curse. His face grew unrecognizable as he literally choked to death.[17] Khrushchev recalled that "a huge man came from somewhere and tried to revive Stalin by administering artificial respiration," until Khrushchev finally shouted at him: "Can't you see the man is dead?"[18]

At least thirty-six hours after Stalin's heart stopped beating, at 7:00 A.M. on March 4, Radio Moscow told the world that the Father of All the Peoples was gravely ill. The announcement was made by a Jew, Yuri Levitan, whose voice, famous throughout the Soviet Union, was now trembling: "The Central Committee of the Communist Party of the Soviet Union and the Council of Ministers of the USSR announce the misfortune which has overtaken our Party and the people—the serious illness of Comrade J. V. Stalin."

Levitan read from a script that said that Stalin had suffered a cerebral hemorrhage affecting vital areas of the brain while in his Moscow apartment on the night of March 1, that he had lost consciousness, and that paralysis of his right arm and leg and loss of speech had followed. "The best medical brains had been summoned for Comrade Stalin's treatment—eight eminent professors," none of whom were eminent, or Jews. It was emphasized that medical treatment was being supervised by "the Central Committee of the Communist Party . . . and the Soviet government," since no Soviet citizen could trust doctors alone.

One indication that Stalin did not die immediately after the stroke was that the MGB interrogators of the imprisoned Kremlin doctors suddenly stopped abusing the "poisoners" and started asking them for medical advice. Dr. Rapoport, the capital's chief pathologist, was taken from his tiny Lefortovo cell and asked, "Which specialist would you recommend for one of our most important people who has just had a stroke?"[19]

In Moscow's embassies, where there had been endless speculation about the meaning of the Doctors' Plot, it was believed now that it had somehow backfired, claiming Stalin himself as its most significant victim. The announcement of the stroke made it obvious to some observers, like the American chargé d'affaires, Jacob D. Beam, that Stalin's morbid mental condition had worsened during the period of the Doctors' Plot, and accounted for the strange air of uneasiness which the January 13 announcement of the great plot had awakened. In a telegram sent from Moscow on March 4, a day before Stalin's death was officially announced, Beam informed the State Department: "If this attack has been approaching for some time, it seems possible that its development has affected Stalin's abnormally suspicious mind and possibly has provided the underlying cause of the alleged doctors' plot against the lives of Soviet leaders."[20]

The official chronology of Stalin's death ignored the fifty-six hours between Stalin's reported cerebral hemorrhage around midnight of March 1 and the public announcement of his illness.

If the actual death date was March 2, as seems likely, it coincided with the occurrence of the Jewish festival of Purim on Sunday, March 1, and Monday, March 2, 1953.[21] Soviet Jews had great cause to celebrate—at least those who knew or sensed that they had been on the verge of destruction when Stalin himself was struck down. A number of Jews had committed suicide in anticipation of the coming events.[22] Never did it seem more appropriate to get drunk—as observant Jews are enjoined to do once a year on this date. Purim, the Jewish sages have said, will be the only festival that will not be abolished when the Messiah comes. Mikhoels and Markish, two of the many murdered Soviet-Jewish leaders, had grown up on the profane and often earthly erotic *purimshpiel*, retellings of the story of Esther and Mordechai, who saved the Jews from the genocide planned by Haman.

Of course, many if not most Soviet Jews did not think of Purim, but genuinely grieved for Stalin. In the government-approved Great Synagogue on Moscow's Arkipova Street, Chief Rabbi Solomon Shliffer led prayers for Stalin's recovery and ordered the Jewish community to fast and pray. At the Vatican, Pope Pius XII, who had been silent while millions of Jews were incinerated in Nazi death camps, prayed for the conversion of the stricken Stalin to "the true faith."

On March 5 at 6:30 P.M., days after Stalin was dead, a bulletin was issued saying that the "end was near." It was a long and detailed report, mentioning dysfunctions of the heart and blood-pumping system and the respiratory system, and making it clear that he would not last through the night. In a later bulletin, the official time of death was given as 9:50 P.M., March 5.

The new government was announced within hours: Stalin's heir was Malenkov. Voroshilov became titular president; Bulganin commissar for war; Molotov, commissar of foreign affairs; Kaganovich, deputy premier; and Beria, commissar of internal affairs. Even before Stalin was buried, his associates had overturned his crucial decision doubling the size of the cabinet, a move they had regarded as their own collective death warrant.

On March 6 Beria's men told the multitude of servants and

bodyguards at Kuntsevo to pack their belongings and get out. Two of Stalin's bodyguard commanders shot themselves.[23]

The speed with which Stalin's successors announced their assumption of power, the reversal of some of Stalin's important changes at the recent Nineteenth Congress, and the offering of gestures toward the army chiefs all indicated that the leaders had worked out an arrangement between themselves before Stalin's death. British intelligence thought so[24], and the Americans concluded that "top Russian leaders as well as Stalin himself may have had some presentiment, possibly in the form of an earlier stroke, of his failing health."[25]

======

Stalin's final exit was relatively hurried, mainly due to the efforts of Nikita Khrushchev, who was suddenly thrust into prominence when he was chosen to head the funeral committee. In contrast to the week's lying-in-state period for Lenin, Stalin's funeral was set four days after his officially reported death. His body was embalmed and the viscera cremated.

Stalin's death unleashed a tremendous wave of emotion, enormous release combined with sorrow or joy. Weeping prevailed in the grief-stricken streets of Moscow on this blackest day of history, when Mother Russia was orphaned. Moscow was still freezing, but the overnight snow had been cleared. On March 6 convoys of trucks carrying Beria's troops quietly moved down Gorky Street and over the Lubyanka hill toward Red Square and other strategic points.

Throughout the country, among the millions who wept were many Jews. In the Ukraine Ida Milgrom, wife of journalist Boris Shcharansky, was one of those who cried uncontrollably—not for Stalin, but because she feared that the Jews would be blamed and that a pogrom was imminent. In the town square of Stalino (Donetsk), where people had gathered to listen to the news, she was horrified to see a man slap an old Jewish woman in the face. "Damn kikes," the man shouted, "you kill our Stalin and now you're crying?"[26]

Esther Markish and her family learned of Stalin's death just after reaching the barren steppes of Kazakhstan, where they had been exiled; they celebrated quietly, still unaware of the fate of Peretz Markish. In the Gulag camps countless prisoners felt the millstone lifted from their necks. Eugenia Ginzburg's body shook and she wept hysterically for two lost decades of her ruined life, for the destruction of her family, and for the millions of other victims. The whole of Magadan was sobbing, asking, "Who will take care of us now?"[27] The entire prison population of the vast camp at Vorkuta got drunk: guards, camp leaders, and prisoners alike. Some religious women in the camps thanked God for delivering them from a false prophet. Chain-gangs of prisoners breaking the Arctic ice yelled, "Stalin croaked!" The sun broke through the clouds, and the prisoners hurled their hats into the frosty air.

In the Moscow prisons, the Kremlin doctors were not informed of Stalin's death. On March 9 a trembling, exhausted Dr. Vovsi was summoned to the interrogation rooms and told to "write the truth." Then for five days, he was left alone. He finally heard of Stalin's death on March 14, when he was summoned once again. They told him that his arrest was a frightful mistake and that he would be freed within days.[28] One of the many other Jewish prisoners in the Lubyanka, General Taukilievich, a former member of the Jewish Anti-Fascist Committee and close friend of Mikhoels, was suddenly freed. He walked home unbelieving, in a state of euphoria. When he knocked on the door of his apartment at 5:30 A.M., his wife asked who it was. He said, "It's me." She thought it was a mistake and told the voice to go away. He knocked again, naming his daughter. "It's me." They thought they were dreaming.[29]

Ilya Ehrenburg had had his great moment when the menace of the Doctors' Plot somehow gave him the strength to refuse to sign the deportation statement. Now, upon the death of Stalin, he reverted to the moral indifference that had kept him alive. He composed a threnody with no hint that the Man of Steel was the destroyer of tens of millions of people, including 600,000 Jews, in his liquidation cellars and concentration camps.[30] Radio Belgrade, on the other hand, entitled its March 5 commentary "Death Rattle in the Throat of World's Greatest Dictator."

At the funeral on Monday, March 9, the crowd of millions stretching for miles around the Kremlin was a terrifying sight. Hundreds of people wedged between army trucks and the walls of buildings were crushed to death. The collective breath of the enormous crowd rose up in a thick white cloud.

The dozen disciples gathered around the body of the Communist Christ. In the official photographs they looked tiny compared to Stalin, who was shot at an angle that made him look huge. Among the pallbearers were the Chinese premier, Chou En-lai, and air force general Vasily Stalin, who was constantly pulling on a flask of vodka and cursing Beria. His sister Svetlana had stood by the coffin, numbly noting the faces of the stream of people walking past, many of them crying, others looking hard to make sure he was dead. She did not kiss the waxen forehead, as she was expected to do.[31] Among the heads of state attending was President Gottwald of Czechoslovakia. His sudden death within hours of the funeral would set off rumors that the man who had four months earlier hanged Slansky and the other Jewish Czech Party leaders was helped along in his journey to the next world, like his mentor, Stalin.

Except for Molotov's personal eulogy—he was the only leader to cry at the funeral—allusions to Stalin were muted and routine. It was widely noted that the speeches by Malenkov and Beria were absent of the usual nasty Stalinist allusions to the Western enemy and stressed a desire for peace and businesslike foreign relations with all states, as well as the need for civil rights and greater prosperity. In the press, the hate-America campaign subsided, though Great Russian nationalism continued to be promoted. The March 5 *Pravda* editorial used the well-known appellation of the Russians as "first among equal peoples," a reassurance that under Stalin's successors they would continue to enjoy primacy in the Soviet Union.

On March 10, the day after the funeral, Harrison Salisbury turned into Hunter's Row from Gorky Street and watched the workmen in front of the Hall of Columns, where Stalin's body had lain in state. Working in the ghostly blue of a carbon-arc floodlight, they loosened the ropes which secured the huge storey-and-a-half painting of Stalin to the facade of the building, and it fell into the street below. "Careful!" one workman shouted. "Never mind," another answered, "They'll not be needing this one again."[32]

======

For two weeks after Stalin's funeral many of the Soviet leaders holed up in their offices in fear of Beria: Molotov at the Foreign Ministry, Khrushchev at Party headquarters, Voroshilov at the Presidium building. But as events would soon prove, it was Beria who had even more reason to fear them.

Although the prevailing theme of press comment was on the collective aspects of the new government, among the leaders themselves the duumvirate of Malenkov and Beria inspired hatred as well as dread; and a plot by Khrushchev and the army to topple them was already well advanced. Unprecedented changes, set off in part by the repercussions of the Doctors' Plot, took place with breathtaking speed.

On March 14 the whole Central Committee held a mysterious meeting that led to Malenkov's resignation a week later, on March 21, after less than three weeks at the top. On March 27 the Presidium broke all precedents and issued a wide-ranging Decree of Amnesty, releasing "from places of detention persons who have committed crimes which do not represent a great danger to the State." Stalin's name was not mentioned in the decree signed by "K. Voroshilov, Chairman of the Presidium of the Supreme Soviet of the USSR." The amnesty included women prisoners with children up to ten years of age, minors up to age eighteen, and convicts suffering from incurable diseases.[33] The most sensational step, however, came a week later, in an extraordinary announcement that indicated a new course, one that would lead to the Twentieth Party Congress in 1956 and the denunciations of Stalin's regime.

On April 3, 1953, Beria's newly organized Internal Affairs Ministry issued a communiqué, published on April 4, saying that the investigation of the doctors accused of "wrecking, espionage and terrorist activities against the active leaders of the Soviet Government" showed that they had been "unlawfully arrested by the former Minister of State Security of the USSR, without any legal basis."[34] The name of Ignatiev, the official who had held this secretive post since 1951, was not given. Stalin's name also was not mentioned in either the announcement or the follow-up reports, as was the case in the amnesty declaration.

The official statement said that the doctors' confessions had been obtained by means of torture (the phrase used was "unacceptable means"). It listed the names of fifteen Kremlin doctors who had been unlawfully detained, and not nine, as had been announced on January 13—but two of the physicians, Etinger and M. B. Kogan, had died long before. This became evident to careful readers in a paragraph further down in the story, which listed doctors who were actually released from custody but omitted their names without explanation. Beria's communiqué also said that "accomplices" were being released.[3] The announcement ignored the charges connected with the "Joint" and the so-called Jewish fifth column, and the entire anti-Semitic nature of the plot.[36] On the same day Dr. Lydia Timashuk's recently awarded Order of Lenin was rescinded by the Presidium of the Supreme Soviet, which declared that it had been "incorrectly awarded."[37]

The official statement disavowing the Doctors' Plot marked a watershed of Soviet history. A U.S. embassy report described the "startling event" of April 4 as concrete evidence "of present regime's break with Stalinism since it must be accepted that Stalin . . . engineered the Doctors' Plot."[38]

Many more than fifteen top doctors had been arrested and tortured, and now they were being released on April 3 and 4, along with their wives. Just before they were freed from their cells, they were all told to "forget everything" and not to talk about their cases. Dr. Rapoport, the chief Moscow pathologist who would have performed the autopsy on Stalin's brain if he had not been incarcerated in Lefortovo, only learned that Stalin was dead when he arrived back at his apartment in the Arbat district on April 4. At that moment he realized the identity of the important patient his interrogators had mentioned about a month earlier, when they had asked him to recommend medical specialists.[39]

Dr. Rapoport had not admitted to being part of the Kremlin plot, though he had "confessed" to being a "bourgeois nationalist" for protesting against quotas on Jews in higher education. Undoubtedly he would have cracked like almost all of his colleagues if the interrogations and torture had continued. Two years after the doctors' release, when Dr. Miron Vovsi was slowly dying of cancer of the leg caused by the torture, he told Dr. Rapoport: "You can't compare my state now with my state then. I've lost my leg, but I'm still a man. Then, I ceased to be a man."[40]

Two days after Beria's startling announcement, on April 6, the leading editorial in *Pravda* hailed the released doctors as "honest and esteemed figures of our State," while extolling Solomon Mikhoels as "that honest public figure and People's Artist of the USSR who has been shamelessly slandered."[41] The editorial revealed that Deputy Minister of State Security Mikhail Ryumin was one of those arrested, accused of torturing the prisoners. His superior, Khrushchev's man, Ignatiev, was dismissed from the Party Secretariat—where he had just been appointed following Stalin's death. Although he was censured, he was still described in the April 6 report as "comrade."[42]

Khrushchev had opposed Beria's unprecedented announcement of a Soviet sin,[43] and the big *Pravda* spread on April 6, whose text was broadcast by Moscow Radio, must also have disturbed him. Beria was not mentioned, but his rivals at the Ministry of State Security were savaged, which could only be to Beria's benefit. Beria himself may have penned a crucial paragraph about his rivals in the security apparatus:

How could it happen that a provocative case, the victims of
which turned out to be honest Soviet citizens, outstanding
representatives of Soviet science, was fabricated within the
precincts of the USSR Ministry of State Security, called upon
to stand guard over the interests of the Soviet State? This
happened first of all because the chiefs of the investigation
branch of this Ministry were not up to their tasks. They
detached themselves from the people, from the Party. They
forgot that they were the servants of the people whose duty
was to stand guard over Soviet legality.[44]

Khrushchev's great worry had been that Beria would be able to
oust Ignatiev from the MGB and regain control of every unit in the
various security ministries. Although this is what happened,
Beria's triumph was short-lived.[45]

Pravda said that "despicable adventurers of Ryumin's type tried
by means of a case they themselves had fabricated to foment in
Soviet society . . . feelings of national hostility, profoundly alien to
Socialist ideology. With this provocative aim they did not shrink
from using base calumny against Soviet people." Ryumin had
"acted as a hidden enemy" who should have aimed his efforts "at
denouncing the real enemies of the Soviet people, the genuine spies
and diversionary agents."[46] Those "guilty of conducting the investigation unfairly have been arrested and brought before the law."
Pravda also said that Ignatiev showed himself to be "under the
thumb" of his subordinate, Ryumin, displaying "political blindness
and gullibility." This was the first time that Western diplomats and
reporters learned that it was Ignatiev who was the minister of
state security.[47]

The Party organ also criticized the medical commission that
"investigated" the charges that the doctors had maltreated
Shcherbakov and Zhdanov. The commissioners had signed "false
accusations against group medical leaders." The "investigators"
had concealed essential details from the medical commission that
showed the doctors' treatment had been correct, *Pravda* said. It
alleged that the commission, instead of studying the case histories
with scientific objectivity, caved in to the fabricators of evidence
and handed down a wrong opinion against the doctors.

British diplomats regarded the *Pravda* article as "an extraordinary step" constituting a drastic repudiation of Stalin's personal
rule.[48] One Foreign Office official said that it was now obvious that

the Doctors' Plot "originated in Stalin's own fears and phobias and that beyond the generals, supposedly destined as victims, was the generalissimo."[49] What neither the foreign specialists nor the Soviet "reformers" themselves said was that there had been an unspoken five-year plan, and that the unmentioned Crimea Affair, the killings of the Jewish intellectuals and JAC leaders the previous year, the Slansky trial, and even the ghost of Trotsky were all part of the same story. As a *New York Times* editorial said thirty-five years later, the Doctors' Plot "was never publicly put in context as the culmination of five years of increasingly vicious official discrimination against Jews."[50]

Throughout these April weeks, the release of the doctors was seen by *Pravda* as an occasion for preaching equality and fraternity and for expounding the Soviet theory of nationalities, constantly repeating that all Soviet peoples and races were equal. Officials were warned that they would be punished for any infringement of rights or preaching of racial hatred.[51]

It was the perfect occasion to begin the long process of de-Stalinization. But it was Beria, not Khrushchev, who was leading the way with the repudiation of the Doctors' Plot. Significantly, the only time that the Doctors' Plot was publicized after Beria's fall in June 1953 was during the trial of Ryumin. One reason may have been that Beria had nothing whatsoever to do with the Doctors' Plot, and wasn't even consulted; indeed the appointment of Khrushchev's ally, Ignatiev, to head the original Doctors' Plot investigation had been a clear sign that Stalin had emasculated Beria, his top security specialist, and planned to destroy him.

The Soviet leaders tried both to downplay the anti-Semitism of the Doctors' Plot and to place the onus on Beria. Mikoyan, for example, told a French interviewer in 1957 that the plot "was not directed against the Jews alone. The majority of the doctors were Russian [sic]. . . . The investigation was a frame-up in all points by Beria's gang."[52] Khrushchev also lied about this, saying that most of the doctors were Russians or Ukrainians, "all honest men who have been rehabilitated," and that Beria was behind it all.[53]

It is probably no coincidence that Mikoyan and Khrushchev are the names that come up most frequently in the various conflicting reports about who actually killed Beria, with whom Khrushchev had been shadow-boxing since Stalin's death.[54] Beria's last meeting with his associates was on June 26, 1953. He may have been strangled to death right there, not executed months later, as the official

Soviet version would have it. Besides Khrushchev and Mikoyan, the executioners have been variously reported to be three Red Army generals, or Voroshilov, Malenkov, and Marshal Konev. That the army played the major role in Beria's arrest and execution seems certain.[55]

Beria, who had exposed the Doctors' Plot as a fabrication, and Ryumin were the main losers in the aftermath of Stalin's death. In the published reports of April 1953, most of the blame was on Ryumin; Ignatiev was blamed to a far lesser degree.[56] A few other Stalin agents were demoted and went into obscurity in the period immediately after the dictator's death, including Chesnokov, the newest Presidium member, who had written the undistributed pamphlet on why the Jews had to be deported; and Zhdanov's son, Yuri (Svetlana's second husband), who was dismissed as head of the Central Committee's Science and Culture Department.[57] Some of Beria's lieutenants were executed along with their chief, but none of them had been tied to the events around the Doctors' Plot.

=====

Among Jews throughout the Soviet Union, the announcements of the first week of April, which happened to occur during Passover, unleashed a tremendous wave of emotion. Until that moment many of them had feared that Stalin's death did not mean the end of the anti-Semitic campaign. The majority of Jews, like their fellow Soviet citizens, could not grasp all that was between the lines.

Although tens of millions of Soviet families had been directly victimized by Stalin, many simply could not imagine that the great man was evil, or draw the logical conclusion that he himself had concocted the scenario which included ridding the USSR of its Jews. That this might have been part of a much more ambitious strategy in preparation for World War III was equally inconceivable.

But observant Jews took to heart the basic message of the Passover freedom festival they were celebrating that week, the memory of the sojourn in Egypt when Israel for the first time became a nation. As the Passover Haggadah (the ritual story read on the first night of Passover) said: "We were slaves to pharaoh in Egypt . . . it was not just one person who rose up against us to destroy us, but, in every generation, men rise against us to destroy us. . . . In every generation it is the duty of each individual to regard himself as though he had gone forth out of Egypt." That message also reached the nonobservant majority among Soviet Jewry: as the last survivor of the Doctors' Plot, the good Communist and nonagenarian nonbeliever Dr. Yakov Rapoport would tell a *New York Times* reporter in 1988, "The generations that follow must know about this."[58]

Ilya Ehrenburg was among those Jews who breathed a sign of relief with the April 4 announcement and the subsequent developments. Immediately upon Stalin's death, he had set about writing his novel *The Thaw*, which gave voice to that newfound ability to breathe.

But even after the exposés, many Jews were still not rehabilitated and most were not taken back into government positions.[59] Khrushchev kept them out. During the Brezhnev era, after a long and difficult struggle, 200,000 Jews were allowed to emigrate, most of them going to Israel. Then the gates were slammed shut. Under Gorbachev, Zionist activists were freed from Soviet prisons, a trickle of emigration was allowed—which after two years became a flood—and the Doctors' Plot was mentioned for the first time since the original "thaw." The authorities permitted publication of the memoirs of Dr. Rapoport and his daughter, Natalia, an eminent chemist. She told an American correspondent that because of Gorbachev's liberal policies, for the first time in her life she was considering joining the Party.[60]

But then the letters reacting to the Rapoports' memoirs began pouring in from all over the Soviet Union. "Most of them were from ignorant anti-Semitic people," Natalia Rapoport told a visitor in February 1989. "But one letter of twelve pages was from a member of the intelligentsia, explaining in the most sophisticated but anti-Semitic terms why the Jews are responsible for the mess Communism is in, why Stalin had the right idea about the Jews."[61] Her desire to become part of Gorbachev's revolution proved ephemeral. In the end, this daughter of the Doctors' Plot decided, along with hundreds of thousands—as many as a million—of the remaining 1.8 million Soviet Jews, to build her future and that of her teenage daughter outside the Russia that had been a home and a prison to Jews for a thousand years.

Epilogue

When the Solomon Mikhoels Jewish Cultural Center was inaugurated in Moscow on February 12, 1989, Nobel laureate Elie Wiesel and other speakers hailed the event as a historic moment, the "final triumph" of the actor Mikhoels and all the other Jews killed by the Stalin regime in its brutal repression of Jewish culture. Among the honored guests were Mikhoels's two daughters and his granddaughter, all of whom had been living in Israel since 1972; they, too, were deeply moved, but felt far more skeptical about the new Soviet Union than did the eloquent Jewish leaders. Like the Russian poet Yevtushenko, they feared that unless a guard was placed permanently over the grave of Stalin, his spirit might once again burst forth to reign over the greatest empire on earth.

To the Soviet Jewish activists who had been harassed, attacked, and arrested for years until the Gorbachev "thaw," everything seemed upside-down. Even an ex–prisoner of conscience, Yuli Edelshtein, had been granted permission to visit from Israel and to take part in the remarkable gathering. The establishment of the center was the result of an unprecedented and much publicized joint effort by the Soviet government, a group of Soviet Jews, and world Jewish organizations. The head of the World Jewish Congress, Edgar Bronfman, hailed the event as the beginning of a "renaissance" of Jewish culture and religion in the USSR, and proudly intoned the words *Am Yisrael hai!* (The people of Israel live!).[1] Also addressing the overflow audience was the head of the recently arrived Israeli diplomatic delegation—the first to be stationed in Moscow since 1967, when the USSR broke off relations with Israel for the second time. The envoy, Russian-born Aryeh Levin, read a message of greeting from Prime Minister Yitzhak Shamir.

Moscow Jews that week were also celebrating the opening of a Jewish studies center attached to no less an institution than the Soviet Academy of Sciences. The renowned Talmudic scholar Adin Steinsaltz had come from Jerusalem to inaugurate the center, where one hundred students would be learning Hebrew, as well as Jewish history, philosophy, and religion, with the Soviet government paying them stipends—quite a change from two years earlier, in 1987, when the teaching of Hebrew was still a crime that carried a five-year prison sentence. Israeli performers Yaffa Yarkoni and Dudu Fischer, meanwhile, were singing Hebrew and Yiddish folk songs and Zionist hymns at Tchaikovsky Hall, where Paul Robeson had performed Yiddish songs forty years earlier with the secret of the doomed Itzik Feffer concealed in his heart. Many of Moscow's Jewish activists cried and applauded as they watched a film of Mikhoels and his GOSET troupe performing Sholom Aleichem's *Tevye the Milkman,* and clips showing Mikhoels and Zuskin in *King Lear.* Mikhoels had been partially rehabilitated under Khrushchev in 1955, as had Markish and the other writers killed in August 1952; but the events of February 14,1989, amounted to a full rehabilitation, while a Kremlin commission on January 26, 1989, completely cleared Markish and his fellow artists and intellectuals.

Kaddish, the prayer for the dead, was recited beneath a large charcoal portrait of Mikhoels, as a Soviet television crew recorded the event. The audience of over one thousand fought to get copies of a slick forty-page program in Russian, Hebrew, and English about the center and about Mikhoels, "King and Knight of Soviet Jewish Culture." In Israel, the *Jerusalem Post* headlined a page-one story from its special correspondent "Mikhoels Triumphs Again in Moscow."[2]

While she was in Moscow Natalie Vovsi-Mikhoels signed a contract with *Novy Mir* to publish a memoir of her father, and she was consulted by Soviet filmmakers about a full-length feature on Mikhoels. She was overwhelmed by the reception her family received, her father's rehabilitation, and the Soviets' announced intention to lead an international UNESCO celebration, on March 17, 1990, of the one hundredth anniversary of his birth.

But she thought the cultural center itself was a "ridiculous" idea and called it "just plain politics—Jewish politics and Soviet politics and people who want money and others who have piles of money and only want credit. They took my father's name without even knowing him or what he stood for. There is no culture, no nothing. I'm totally dissatisfied with it."[3] Despite this, she was encouraged by the sweeping changes Gorbachev had wrought. But she had mixed feelings as well, even regarding the constant revelations about the crimes of the Stalinists. While she was still in Moscow, Vovsi-Mikhoels read in *Literaturnaya Gazeta* that Itzik Feffer, according to just-released KGB files, was indeed a secret police agent. Thus she learned that Feffer did have a direct role in the murder of her father, as the family had suspected for over forty years.[4]

All the events taking place around the opening of the Mikhoels center staggered Soviet Jewish activists, who were no longer being bullied by KGB men as in the recent past. Over twenty Jewish prisoners had been freed in a year's time, including Ida Nudel and Yosef Begun; and thousands of *refuseniks,* whose requests to emigrate to Israel had previously been denied, were allowed to leave the USSR. Furthermore, large numbers of Soviet Jews received permission to visit abroad—something unimaginable even in Gorbachev's first two years in office. By December 1989 Soviet Jews were stampeding to get out, and it was estimated that as many as one million, or more than half of Soviet Jewry, would emigrate by 1992. Vladimir Ze'ev Jabotinsky, the Russian Jew who had founded one of the main streams of Zionism, believed that most of the Jews of Russia would eventually emigrate to the Jewish homeland, and that those who chose to remain in the Diaspora would eventually assimilate completely. That forecast began to assume the shape of prophecy, as the "unbreakable union of free republics" under Great Russian hegemony started to come apart. The process of Soviet decomposition, and the whirlwind of democracy in Eastern Europe, were catalysts for what could become the final Jewish exodus from Russia.

The changing official attitude toward the Jews had become evident with Gorbachev's attack on Stalin on the seventieth anniversary of the Russian Revolution, on November 7, 1987, when he declared that "the guilt of Stalin is enormous and unforgivable."[5] This not only opened the door to a serious reexamination of the Soviet past, but also gave heart to the Soviet nationalities seeking greater independence. As Milovan Djilas put it in an interview in *Encounter* magazine in December 1988, a central tenet of Marxist-Leninist doctrine—the position on nationalities as set down by Stalin in 1913—was being revealed to the world as the Achilles' heel of Communism.

Even the Doctors' Plot was being reexamined for the first time. In September 1987 Pavel Demchenko, a *Pravda* senior editor on a propaganda mission to Israel, told a reporter, "To this day I fail to understand" why the Doctors' Plot took place.[6] Gorbachev himself referred to the case in a speech on Soviet history weeks later; and in April 1988 the memoirs of Dr. Yakov Rapoport and his daughter Natalia Rapoport were published by the Soviets, with revelations that were a shock for Soviet readers.[7]

The Mikhoels center was the brainchild of Australian Jewish leader and longtime activist Isi Leibler; Yuli Kosharovsky, last of the long-term refuseniks who emigrated to Israel shortly after the opening; and Moscow ethnographer Mikhail Chlenov, who had been Anatoly Sharansky's mentor. But despite their euphoria, all these men were aware of the fact that the cultural center could prove to be little more than a "Potemkin village," a showcase model village for positive publicity about Gorbachev's tolerant Russia. One of the groups indirectly sponsoring the center was the Soviet Anti-Zionist Committee, headed by General David Bragunsky, a Jew, who said that it was fine and good for Soviet Jews to "preserve their cultural individuality," but that some people were pretending to develop Jewish culture while in fact "carrying out ideological work among Russian Jews, orienting them to emigrate from the Soviet Union."[8]

Many Soviet Jews, even those who were most enthusiastic about Gorbachev's liberal policy, expressed concern that they would be more vulnerable than ever if a Stalinist backlash resulted from his reforms. Chlenov told a visitor during the week of ceremonies and concerts marking the center's opening that "Jews may be the first victims of the resurgent Russian nationalism. That's why the center, and an organized Soviet Jewry, is essential."[9]

That same week in February 1989, the Leningrad Maly Theater staged readings of Mandelstam, Vasily Grossman, Joseph Brodsky, Vladimir Nabokov, Pasternak, Andrei Platonov, and even Solzhenitsyn—a passage about Stalin from *The First Circle*. Almost every Soviet publication printed stories that no one imagined could ever appear in official Communist media. Even Trotsky was resurrected, if not yet rehabilitated: *Moscow News* featured a long, sympathetic article about his last days in Mexico and interviewed his grandson there.[10]

A February 1989 article by *Krokodil* correspondent Alexander Moralevich, "Call Me a Jew," profiled a falsely accused Jewish chef in Belorussia, Modest Sirotin, who had recently been denounced in a series of anonymous letters to the procurator's office and the People's Control Committee of Belorussia. The writer had accused the Jewish chef of being an Israeli intelligence agent, a "Zionist bandit" who sold the secrets he had overheard in the restaurant where he worked. All one hundred and sixty-five workers in the restaurant collective came to the chef's defense, and the official in charge of local restaurants and canteens said: "The time of anonymous letters has passed."[11]

Such an article would have been inconceivable under previous Soviet rulers. But there were also articles coming from the far right, saying that Stalin had made occasional errors only because of the infuence of Trotsky and other "rootless cosmopolitans." And all the blame for the mass murders of thirty million people was now being placed by the extreme rightists on the Jews Mekhlis and Kaganovich.[12]

The rapid growth of *Pamyat* (Memory), the anti-Semitic mass movement of Great Russian nationalists—which Gorbachev never discouraged—greatly disturbed Soviet Jews. They heard echoes of the czarist Black Hundreds and the dark Stalinist days of 1948–53, The movement's "ideological" leader, Dmitri D. Vasiliyev, a self-styled journalist, is an avid promoter of the *Protocols of the Elders of Zion.* His movement has attracted a great amount of attention and support even among Russian intellectuals, who believe Vasiliyev offers a compelling vision of post-Communist Russia. For years, he has been engaged in a battle with the authorities, alleging that his elderly mother was "killed at the hands of the doctors" as a way of punishing him.[13]

The "environmentalists" of Pamyat blame the Jews for soil erosion and the Chernobyl nuclear disaster, as well as for communism itself. Pamyat, which claims to have a branch in Damascus, also blames the Jews for the destruction of traditional Russian culture in the 1920s and 1930s, and says that Jews in the Soviet arts and media are now "contaminating" what remains of Russian culture.[14] Pamyat's literature includes such questions as: "Who destroyed the Russian nation by means of ideology and alcohol? Who is responsible for the ecological disaster in our country? Who attacks us like a rabid dog with charges of nationalism whenever the word 'Russia' is mentioned?" The answer: Zionists and Masons.[15]

The resurgent Pan-Slavism and Russian nationalism is not the only threat to the Jews. In the spring of 1989 the Muslim fundamentalists in Azerbaijan told leaders of the 100,000 Jews in the city of Baku that they have "three years to get out." Pogroms began: Azeris killed Armenians, perhaps warming up for the Jews, who are considered too close, ethnically and intellectually, to the Armenians.

Pamyat is allowed to exist, though anti-Semitism is proscribed under Soviet law. The Russian nationalists place wreaths on Stalin's grave in Red Square and pray for his resurrection. One leader of the organization, Igor Sechov, preaches against "the danger of cosmopolitanism." He appears at meetings wearing jackboots and surrounded by bodyguards and supporters wearing shirts advertising such slogans as "Down with the occupation of Jewish Nazis" and "We want the decolonization of Russia."[16] In February 1990, Pamyat staged a mass rally in Moscow with the crowd chanting anti-Semitic and anti-Israel slogans. *New York Times* columnist William Safire, commenting on the flow of Jews fleeing the chaotic USSR, wrote: "The nationalists of Pamyat are outspokenly anti-Semitic, recalling the Jews like Trotsky among the old Bolsheviks. The sullen Stalinists speak of the 'Jewish Doctors' Plot' and the purge that followed."[17]

The last major villain connected to the Doctors' Plot, Lazar Moiseyevich Kaganovich, reached the age of ninety-six in 1989; he probably had more blood on his hands than any living person. He stayed indoors during winter days and never answered when his doorbell rang or someone knocked (journalists and writers were always coming to his apartment house on Frunzeskaya Boulevard, according to a maid next door). His relatives brought groceries every day and helped tend to his other needs. He was a prisoner of sorts, listening to the radio, making an occasional phone call, shuffling from room to room. But in the summer months he liked to stroll along Frunzeskaya, and took offense if passersby did not recognize him. The writer Yuli Daniel, son of the Yiddish writer Mark Daniel, called his cat "Lazar Moiseyevich," after Stalin's Jew. Daniel, who was sent to prison with Andrei Sinyavsky in 1968—accused of maligning the Russian nation and in turn accusing it of anti-Semitism—died in 1989. Both the cat and the killer outlived him.

Notes

CHAPTER 1: **The Ossetian Connection**

Books that are not initially cited in the notes for this chapter with title as well as full publishing information appear in the bibliography.

1. The exact date of birth remains unknown, but the Soviets marked Stalin's birthday on December 21.

2. Author interview with Professor Alexander Drushchinsky, Tbilisi, February 24, 1989. The professor, whose Ossetian paternal grandmother knew the Djugashvili family, said: "Keke [Ekaterina] was a common whore—that's why Stalin called her a whore. No one could be sure if Vissarion Djugashvili was the father." Drushchinsky's father, Mikhail Sonakoiyev, was an unusual Ossetian, a member of a former aristocratic family whose people ostracized him because he married a Jew.

3. Rapoport, p. 258ff.

4. Talbott, ed., *Khrushchev Remembers,* 1970, p. 323.

5. Author interview with sexton of the Gori synagogue, Reuben Ben Avraham, and Aharon Ben Daniel, Gori, February 23, 1989. Most Ossetians do not know their ancient language. There is no mention by any biographer that Stalin knew Ossetian, though he did learn the Mingrelian Georgian dialect around the same time that he learned Russian. He would take a special interest in Persian-related languages during his passionate period of interest in linguistics toward the end of his life.

   Although there is no documentary evidence of Stalin's Ossetian roots, the link has been mentioned in passing by many of his biographers, most importantly by Stalin's only childhood friend, Joseph Irmashvili, who was deported from Georgia by Stalin in 1922. Irmashvili described Stalin's father, Vissarion Djugashvili, as "a coarse, uncouth person, like all the Ossetians, who live in the high Caucasian mountains" (Irmashvili, pp. 5–11).

   Stalin's French biographer, Boris Souvarine, writing in the late

1930s, quoted old socialists in the Caucasus who *insisted* that "Catherine Djugashvili is an Osse (Ossetinka) and attach great importance to this detail: not only are the Ossetes less subtle and more crude than the Georgians, but Russia has always recruited among them a strong proportion of gendarmes and of convict-guards" (Souvarine, *Stalin: A Critical Survey of Bolshevism*)—and secret policemen, as well. Under both the czars and the Soviets, an extremely high proportion of secret police agents and prison guards were Ossetians. According to a still-current Georgian joke, "The Ossetians' national instrument is the police whistle." (Drushchinsky interview, February 24, 1989.) Stalin's probable role as a double agent for the czarist secret police during his early years as a revolutionary is consistent with the Ossetian theory.

George F. Kennan, the former U.S. ambassador to the Soviet Union under Stalin, also has referred to Stalin's Ossetian connection: "He had certain well-known characteristics of the Caucasian mountain race to which his father is said to have belonged—an inordinate touchiness, an endless vindictiveness, an inability to ever forget an insult or a slight, but great patience and power of dissimulation in selecting and preparing the moment to settle the score." (Kennan, *Russia and the West under Lenin and Stalin,* p. 248.)

Even a century after Stalin's boyhood, a visitor to the area around Gori, and to the Georgian capital of Tbilisi, could find evidence of Stalin's Ossetian background. Mathematics professor Drushchinsky, of Tbilisi, whose aristocratic Ossete father was a minister in Soviet South Ossetia and Stalin's secret police chief there until he was executed during the early years of the Great Terror, contends that "Djugashvili is a Georgian version of the Ossetian name Jugaev. My father's mother knew everyone. She said that Stalin's father was an Ossete." (Drushchinsky interview, February 24, 1989.)

The elderly sexton of the Gori synagogue, whose grandparents were contemporaries of the Djugashvili family, told a visitor: "The Djugashvilis were Ossetians. Their name was Georgianized. There were many Ossetians in Gori" (author interview with Ben Avraham and Ben Daniel, February 23, 1989). And in fact, the word *djuga,* in the ancient language of the Caucasian mountaineers, meant "iron" (author interview with Nunu Kasayeva, Tbilisi, February 24, 1989). The suffix *vili* in Georgian means "the son of." *Ecce* Stalin.

The greatest Russian poet of the century, the Jewish-born Osip Mandelstam, in the poem about Stalin which cost him his life in the late 1930s, referred to Iosif, "the broad-chested Ossete," the swaggering "Kremlin mountaineer" (Nadezhda Mandelstam, p. 13). Even at the height of Mikhail Gorbachev's renewal of de-Stalinization at the end of the 1980s, Georgians who remained proud of Stalin did not like to mention his Ossetian roots, while those who hated him made a point of saying that he had been a full-blooded Ossetian, the son of a beastly father (Ben Avraham and Ben Daniel interview, February 23, 1989; Drushchinsky interview, February 24, 1989). Tbilisi Intourist official Kasayeva, an Ossetinka in her early fifties, said proudly that her grandparents knew Vissarion Djugashvili, a fellow Ossetian. She called Stalin "a wonderful, wonderful man—a phenomenon. An Ossete" (author interview, February 24, 1989).

6. Kasayeva interview, February 24, 1989.

7. Ainsztein, p. 49.

8. Drushchinsky interview, February 24, 1989.

9. In the eighteenth century the Ossetians, though of Persian origin, joined with their fellow Christian Georgians and sought Great Russian support against the Turks and Persians. According to historian Robert Conquest, "This Christianized Persian people were always pro-Russian" (Conquest, *The Nation Killers: The Soviet Deportation of Nationalities*).

10. Irmashvili, op. cit., p. 12.

11. Alliluyeva, *Twenty Letters to a Friend*, pp. 153–54; Talbott, ed., *Khrushchev Remembers*, 1970, p. 310.

12. Mikhail Lermontov, *A Hero of Our Time*, trans. Vladimir Nabokov, Oxford University Press, Oxford, 1984, p. 16. Buza was a hemp reed drink, or any new wine, from whence the word "booze" may stem. One of Lermontov's characters, a dashing czarist officer, said of the Ossetians, "They can't even say 'bread' in Russian, but they've managed to learn 'officer, give me a tip.' In my opinion, even the Tatars are better: at least they don't drink." In his poem "The Deserter," Lermontov, a Great Russian, ridiculed both Georgians and Ossetians. Not surprisingly, given the pecking order of nationalities, in Georgian translations of this poem, the deserter's nationality is changed to Ossetian.

13. Souvarine, op. cit. In his 1913 nationalities essay, Stalin spoke negatively of the Georgians as having "incited" the Persians and Turks against one another.

14. Drushchinsky interview, February 24, 1989.

15. Smith, p. 21.

16. Gitelman, p. 19.

17. Trotsky, pp. 2–3. Trotsky's preference for northerners is evident in his remarks that "in the countries of the Mediterranean Sea, in the Balkans, in Italy, in Spain, in addition to the so-called Southern type, which is characterized by a combination of lazy shiftlessness and explosive irascibility, one meets cold natures, in whom phlegm

is combined with stubbornness and slyness. . . . It would seem as if each national group is doled out its due share of basic character elements, yet these are less happily distributed under the southern than under the northern sun." This convoluted slap at Stalin also could include Trotsky's own people, for the Jews are of the Mediterranean race.

Trotsky's rational-sounding approach was completely in keeping with Marxist principles. But it was in fact a typical example of rationalist obfuscation. Trotsky wished to pass over the disturbing, atavistic impulses that lay behind Stalin's attitude toward the Jews, and to avoid entirely Stalin's equation of Trotsky with Judas. Stalin's attitude was attributed instead to a streak of coarse, counter-revolutionary anti-Semitism and nothing more. When Trotsky wrote, Stalin was not yet totally possessed by anti-Semitic fervor. But Stalin's personal hatred of Jews, and his use of anti-Semitism as a political weapon, would far exceed the kind of ordinary anti-Semitism to which Trotsky referred.

18. Ben Avraham and Ben Daniel interview, February 23, 1989. According to Aharon Ben Daniel there was a Jewish doctor in the town in his grandfather's time, and "Jews in medicine" have always been in the town, up to present times. The 1893 *Entsiklopedichevsky slovar,* St. Petersburg, gives Gori's population as 7,247. Modern Gori has a population of about 100,000.

19. Anna S. Alliluyeva, *Iz vospominanii,* Sovetska Pisatel, Moscow, 1946, p. 30ff.

20. Smith, op. cit., pp. 26–27.

21. Emil Ludwig, *Stalin,* G. P. Putnam, New York, 1942, p. 19.

22. "Russian priests regularly collaborated with the police (Pipes, *Russia under the Old Regime,* p. 242).

23. Author interview with Mikhail Agursky, July 2, 1989. Agursky's father, Samuel, knew Stalin well, and soon after the Revolution became the top Bolshevik Jew in charge of liquidating Jewish culture and community organization.

24. Deutscher, *Stalin: A Political Biography,* p. 68.

25. Baron, p. 49ff.

26. Norman Cohn, *Warrant for Genocide,* Penguin Books, London, 1970, p. 67. The anti-Semitic circles around the czar began attributing a Jewish plot to take over the world to Theodor Herzl's newly established World Zionist Organization and its first Basel Congress in 1897. G. Butumi, editor of various anti-Semitic tracts, wrote "exposés" of the vast conspiracy involving Herzl, the leftist Russian

Jewish Bund, the Rothschilds, the Freemasons, and the British foreign office. Butumi described this plot in a thin volume called "The Great in the Little: The Imminent Coming of the Antichrist and Satan's Rule on Earth," the seed of the booklet entitled the *Protocols of the (Meetings of the Learned) Elders of Zion.*

27. Cohn, op. cit., p. 115.

28. From its first edition, the *Protocols of the Elders of Zion* was distributed by the army's general staff and by the Okhrana, the czarist secret police. After the Bialystok pogrom of June 14–16, 1906, a Duma investigating committee found that the police had planned and prepared the bloody attacks against Jews, and tried to promote army reprisals against Russian Jews, by linking all Jews to the revolutionary movement and to a great Jewish design to rule the world. The royalist Russian commentator on the so-called *Protocols* urged that "all white peoples" revise their attitudes to the Jews and hit back at them with mass slayings: "We shall make it our task to see that against us such things as plots shall no longer exist."

29. Author interview with Aryeh "Lova" Eliav, September 30, 1987.

30. Gilboa, p. 328.

CHAPTER 2: **Up from the Underground**

1. Victor Serge, *Portraite de Staline,* B. Grasset, Paris, 1940, p. 14.

2. It was said that Karl Marx's father, who converted to the German Lutheran faith when his son was aged six, was a direct descendant of the medieval French Talmudic genius Rashi. Karl's mother was said to be descended from the genius known as the Maharal—Rabbi Low of Prague—creator of the mystical Jewish monster called the Golem.

3. Wistrich, op. cit., p. 6ff.

4. Saul K. Padover, ed., *The Letters of Karl Marx,* Princeton University Press, Princeton, N.J., 1979, pp. 306, 459. Marx remarked on "the nastily Jewish physiognomy" of German socialist leader Ferdinand Lassalle and referred to him as "the Jewish Nigger Lassalle," p. 466.

5. Arthur Hertzberg, *The Zionist Idea,* Jewish Publication Society, Philadelphia, 1960, p. 182.

6. Baron, pp. 73–74, 318–19.

7. Ibid., p. 142ff.

8. Deutscher, *The Prophet Armed: Trotsky 1879–1921,* p. 73ff.

9. V. I. Lenin, Sochinenia (Composition), Ed. 2, Vol. 1, Partizdat, Moscow, 1931, p. 84.

10. Wistrich, op. cit., p. 31ff.

11. Smith, p. 67ff. Stalin's role as a secret agent was the main theme of Smith's biography of the young Stalin. Until the confirmation of many of his findings by Soviet scholars, Smith's extremely detailed book was generally ignored by scholars and Stalinologists, even though it is a painstaking study, based on Okhrana (czarist secret police) documents at the Hoover Institute, Stanford University. Smith, who was the top CIA analyst at the American embassy in Moscow in 1953, understood the mentality and the methodology of the czarist secret police, and "the making of a secret agent" out of Stalin. Two senior Soviet historians, Arochunov and Volkov, who gained access to official Siberian archives, endorsed Smith's theses unreservedly in an article entitled "On Historical Trial," in *Moscovsky Pravda*, March 30, 1989, p. 19 (Wistrich, p. 195).

12. Irmashvili, p. 28.

13. Stalin, *Collected Works*, vol. 1, pp. 21–22.

14. Ibid.

15. Smith, op. cit., p. 87ff.

16. Ibid., p. 97.

17. Deutscher, *Stalin: A Political Biography*, p. 55.

18. Smith, op. cit., p. 76ff.

19. Ibid.

20. Ibid., pp. 122–23.

21. Author interview with Professor Alexander Drushchinsky, February 24, 1989.

22. Baron, p. 169ff. One prominent exception to the trend of revolutionary Jews to deny their origins was the future Soviet foreign minister, Maxim Litvinov, nee Wallach.

23. Wistrich, op. cit., pp. 180–88.

24. Razden Arsenidze, "Iz vospominanii o Staline," *Novy zhurnal*, no. 72, 1963, p. 221.

25. Alliluyeva, *Twenty Letters to a Friend*, p. 159.

26. Trotsky is equated with Judas in Stalin's *History of the Communist Party of the Soviet Union: Short Course*, in Stalin, *Collected Works*, vol. 1.

27. Deutscher, *Stalin*, op. cit., p. 78ff.

28. Quoted in Smith, op. cit., pp. 178–79.

29. David Shub, *Lenin*, Pelican, London, 1966, p. 30.

30. Quoted in Smith, op. cit., p. 188.

31. Trotsky, p. 152; Stalin, *Collected Works,* vol. 2, p. 188.

32. Deutscher, *The Prophet Armed: Trotsky 1879–1921,* p. 167. The Black Hundreds' three-point program ran: "The good of the Fatherland lies in the unshakeable conservation of Orthodoxy and of the unlimited Russian autocracy . . . ; the Orthodox Christian Church must have the predominant and dominating position in the state; and Russian autocracy has sprung from popular reason, it has been blessed by the Church and justified by history." Under the Soviets, the words "Church" and "autocracy" were replaced with the words "Communist Party" and "Soviet state."

33. Smith, op. cit., p. 201ff.

34. Ibid.

35. Wistrich, op. cit., p. 195; Lenin and Beilis in Trotsky, op. cit., p. 154. Despite the Judeophobia that had been whipped up by the authorities, Beilis was found innocent by a jury of simple peasants.

36. Trotsky, op. cit., p. 152ff.

37. Deutscher, *The Prophet Armed: Trotsky 1879–1921,* pp. 209–10.

38. Stalin, *Collected Works,* vol. 2, op. cit., p. 188; idem, "Marxism and the National Question," trans. the British and Irish Communist Organization, London, February 1974.

39. Ibid., p. 2.

40. Ibid., p. 3.

41. Ibid., p. 4. Bauer held that capitalism made it impossible for the Jews to continue as a nation.

42. Ibid., p. 5. To this day, Lenin is praised by "reform" Communists as always having warned against the dangers of Great Russian chauvinism, while all the blame is put on Stalin for concentrating power in the hands of the largest and most powerful nation in the Soviet land. Yet Lenin the editor allowed Stalin to portray the Great Russians as the "welder of nationalities."

43. Ibid., p. 9.

44. *Webster's New International Dictionary,* 1938 edition, p. 1902.

45. Stalin, *Collected Works,* vol. 2, op. cit., p. 9.

46. Ibid., p. 23.

47. Ibid., p. 10.

48. Ibid., p. 11.

49. Ibid., p. 20.

50. Ibid.

51. Ibid.

52. Ibid., p. 24. Stalin wrote: "Social-Democrats strive to secure the right *of all nations* to the use of their own language. But that does not satisfy the Bund; it demands that 'the right of the *Jewish* language' (our emphasis—J.S.) be fought for with 'particular insistence.' . . . Not the *general* right of all nations to use their own language, but the *particular* right of the Jewish language, Yiddish! . . . It is to be expected that the Bund will take another 'forward step' and demand the right to observe all the ancient Hebrew holidays. And if, to the misfortune of the Bund, the Jewish workers have discarded religious prejudices and do not want to observe them, the Bund with its agitation in favor of 'the right of the Sabbath' will remind them of the Sabbath and will inculcate in them, so to speak, 'the Sabbath-day spirit.'"

53. Ibid., p. 25.

54. Ibid.

55. Ibid., p. 30.

56. Ibid., p. 37.

CHAPTER 3: **The Struggle Against "Judas"**

1. Deutscher, *Stalin: A Political Biography,* pp. 120–121.

2. Boris Bazhanov, "Pobeg iz nochi," *Kontinent,* nos. 8–10, 1976, pp. 94–95.

3. Irmashvili, p. 40.

4. Trotsky, p. 173. Stalin's anti-Semitism and his dislike of women—chronicled by his daughter Svetlana—were not incompatible. In Stalin's mind, a close connection existed between femininity, "fake-muscled" intellectualism, and Jewishness. He called his own mother "whore," and would swear at Lenin's widow with the same word. One psychoanalyst's dictum that would seem tailor-made for Stalin went: "The anti-Jew is always an anti-feminist unless he marries a nun, as Martin Luther did" (Rappaport, p. 284).

5. Trotsky, op. cit., p. 173.

6. Smith, p. 304ff. In 1989 Soviet scholars working in Siberian archives found evidence that supports the contention that Stalin broke off his Okhrana connection in 1912 (*Moscovsky Pravda,* March 30, 1989, p. 19).

7. Alliluyeva, *Twenty Letters to a Friend,* p. 69.

8. Cohn, *Warrant for Genocide,* Weidenfeld & Nicolson, London, 1967, p. 112.

9. Baron, p. 159. S. Ansky, the writer of the Yiddish classic *The Dyb-*

buk, eyewitnessed the deportations and wrote about them in *Hurban Ha-yehudim be-polin, Galitsianu u-Bukovina.*

10. Deutscher, *Stalin*, op. cit., p. 125ff. Kamenev's mother was Russian, not Jewish, which made him a gentile in the eyes of observant Jews. But in Russian eyes, half-Jewish, from whatever side, was sufficient to be identified as a Jew.

11. Ibid., p. 139ff.

12. Ibid.

13. Ibid.

14. Alliluyeva, *Only One Year*, p. 168.

15. Deutscher, *The Prophet Armed: Trotsky 1879–1921*, p. 253.

16. Deutscher, *Stalin*, op. cit., p. 146ff.

17. John Reed, *Ten Days That Shook the World*, Random House, New York, 1960, p. 49.

18. Smith, op. cit., p. 361ff.

19. Reed, op. cit. Stalin's name is mentioned twice in Reed's book, and only in passing.

20. Pipes, *Russia under the Old Regime*, p. 54.

21. Author interview with Samuel Agursky's son, Mikhail Agursky, July 2, 1989. Mikhail Agursky emigrated to Israel in the 1970s and became one of Shimon Peres's top advisors on Soviet affairs.

22. *Zhizn Natsionalnostei*, no. 49, December 28, 1919, Statement by Commissariat for Jewish Affairs.

23. Chaim Weizmann, *Trial and Error*, Harper & Row, New York, 1949, p. 88.

24. Baron, p. 169ff.

25. Ibid., p. 170; Conquest, *The Harvest of Sorrow*, p. 24.

26. Payne, p. 233.

27. Author interview with Professor Alexander Drushchinsky, Tbilisi, February 24, 1989.

28. Stalin, *Collected Works*, vol. 5, p. 87ff.

29. Voline [E. K. Eichenbaum], *The Unknown Revolution*, Freedom Press, London, 1955, p. 265ff.

30. Rafail Abramovich, *The Soviet Revolution 1917–1939*, G. Allen & Unwin, London, 1962, p. 42ff.

31. Stalin, *Collected Works*, vol. 4, p. 117ff.

32. The source of these revelations is a report of the Central Committee meeting of October 26, 1923, at which Trotsky told the story of his conversation with Lenin to his Bolshevik colleagues. The document, discovered by Soviet historian Victor Danilov, was published in the

Novosibirsk *Echo* and reported in the London *Observer* on March 25, 1990; it appears in English in the Spring 1990 edition of *History Workshop Journal* (Oxford University Press). Danilov was part of a team of thirty Russian scholars given access to official Soviet archives for a history of the Communist party. The revelations about Trotsky were considered a major step on the part of Mikhail Gorbachev and the Soviet establishment toward the rehabilitation of this controversial figure. Until now, it was assumed that Trotsky had been absent from this meeting because of illness, as Trotsky wrote in his autobiography. But while the authenticity of this conflicting document has yet to be confirmed by independent scholars, other historians have noted Trotsky's faulty memory for many other dates.

33. Deutscher, *The Non-Jewish Jew*, p. 74.

34. De Jonge, pp. 196, 203; Deutscher, *Stalin*, op. cit., p. 290.

35. Medvedev, *Let History Judge*, p. 224; De Jonge, op. cit., p. 202.

36. V. Kravchenko, *I Chose Freedom*, Garden City Publishers, New York, 1947, pp. 275–76.

37. Deutscher, *Stalin*, op. cit., p. 232.

38. Michael Morgan, *Lenin*, The Free Press, New York, 1971, p. 208ff.

39. Payne, op. cit., p. 284.

40. Ulam, p. 26.

41. Lermolo, in her prison memoir, *Face of a Victim*, p. 215, recounts what Lenin's imprisoned chef, Gavriel Volkov, told her were Lenin's last words at the Kremlin rest house in Gorky: "Gavrilushka, I've been poisoned. . . . fetch Nadya [Krupskaya] at once, tell Trotsky, tell anyone you can."

42. Edward H. Carr, *The Triumvirate in Power*, p. 263.

43. De Jonge, op. cit., p. 209.

44. Trotsky, op. cit., p. 418.

45. Ulam, op. cit., p. 210; Antonov-Ovsenko, p. 42.

46. This report remains unverified.

47. De Jonge, op. cit., p. 362.

48. Ulam, op. cit., pp. 285–86.

49. Kennan, *Memoirs*, p. 279.

50. Winston Churchill, *Great Contemporaries*, London, 1937, p. 202.

51. Trotsky, op. cit., p. 411ff.

52. Dostoevsky, *The Unpublished Dostoevsky Diaries and Notebooks*, ed. Carl Proffer, Ardis Books, Ann Arbor, Mich., 1973, pp. 639–45. Many Jews in rural areas in czarist times were restricted in choice of work and forced by economic circumstances to turn their modest

homes into taverns catering to Russian soldiers and travelers, which gave rise to Dostoevsky's prejudiced and inaccurate charge.

53. Conquest, *The Harvest of Sorrow,* p. 20.

54. Ibid., p. 45.

55. George Kennan, *Russia, the Atom and the West,* Oxford University Press, London, 1958.

56. Antonov-Ovsenko, p. 62.

CHAPTER 4:   **The Great Purge**

1. Antonov-Ovsenko, pp. 104–105.

2. Latsis, in the newspaper *Red Terror,* November 1, 1918.

3. The Russian word Alliluyeva, derived from the Hebrew, means "Hallelujah!" Nadezhda means "hope." Nadezhda's parents were revolutionaries who were Stalin's friends before the Revolution.

4. "I am afraid Rosa Kaganovich, Stalin's third wife, did not exist," said Professor Ulam in a letter to the author, September 7, 1988. Sovietologist Mikhail Agursky, the son of Stalin's "Jewish affairs czar," also believes Rosa is a fiction (author interview, July 2, 1989). Stuart Kahan, the American author of a rather questionable 1988 "biography" of his distant relative Lazar Kaganovich, disputes Ulam's widely held view: "Rosa pure invention? I dismiss that. My grandfather confirms Rosa's existence (he grew up with her), as did Lazar himself" (Kahan letter to author, September 28, 1988). Kahan's unsourced book portrayed Stalin as keeping his "ravishing" mistress at 8 Kalinin Prospekt. Kahan stated that Rosa was a doctor, and that Lazar had told her Stalin needed "a physician he could trust." A more apocryphal-sounding line is hard to imagine.

5. Payne, pp. 411–12; Alliluyeva, *Twenty Letters to a Friend,* p. 108ff., makes no mention of this.

6. Antonov-Ovsenko, op. cit., p. 112ff.

7. Ibid.

8. Medvedev, *Let History Judge,* p. 368.

9. Kennan, *Russia and the West,* p. 302.

10. Alliluyeva, *Only One Year,* p. 382.

11. Talbott, ed., *Khrushchev Remembers,* 1970 ed., p. 33.

12. V. Kravchenko, *I Choose Freedom,* Garden City Publishers, New York, 1947, pp. 275–76.

13. Talbott ed., *Khrushchev,* 1970, ed., p. 33.

14. Ibid.

15. Kravchenko, op. cit., pp. 275–76.

16. Alexander Solzhenitsyn, *The Gulag Archipelago: 1918–1956*, p. 193ff.

17. Ibid.

18. Ibid.

19. Ibid.

20. Ibid.

21. Kirov roused Stalin's suspicion because he opposed his demand to liquidate the thousands of "enemies of the people" in the Leningrad Communist party, Kirov's bailiwick. In Politburo meetings in the early 1930s, Stalin would walk out of the room if someone disagreed with him, and anyone with too independent a will had to be eliminated. Kirov was shot to death in his office in the Smolny Institute by Leonid Nikolaev, a disgruntled and distraught ex–Party flunky who had been groomed for the job by the NKVD. Khrushchev, in his 1956 Secret Speech, suggested that Stalin had inspired the murder and vowed to reopen the case, but this was never done.

22. "Monitor," p. 99.

23. Antonov-Ovsenko, op. cit., p. 101.

24. Alliluyeva, *Twenty Letters to a Friend,* op. cit., p. 135ff.

25. Antonov-Ovsenko, op. cit., p. 245.

26. In his book *Mission to Moscow* (V. Gollanez, London, 1942), the American ambassador to the USSR at this time, Joseph Davies, immortalized the portrayal of Stalin as a warm, benign figure who only reluctantly tried the fiendish conspirators of the purge years.

27. Deutscher, *Stalin: A Political Biography,* p. 374.

28. Kravchenko, op. cit., p. 135.

29. Medvedev, p. 348.

30. A. N. Shelepin speech to the Twenty-second Party Congress, quoted in Conquest, *The Great Terror,* p. 222; and Ulam, p. 442.

31. Conquest, op. cit., p. 308.

32. Ibid., p. 209ff.

33. Ibid.

34. Payne, op. cit., p. 334.

35. Reply to an Inquiry of the Jewish Telegraphic Agency of America, January 12, 1931; Stalin, *Collected Works,* vol. 13, p. 30. Though Stalin despised Freud and his followers, his answer, equating cannibalism and anti-Semitism, is consistent with psychoanalytic theory. The anti-Semites represent the forces seeking annihilation of civilization; and the anti-Semitic, paranoid personality is reduced to "the original stage of primitive cannibalism" (Simmel, p. 34).

36. *Pravda* no. 329, November 30, 1937.

37. Ulam, op. cit., p. 396.

38. Payne, op. cit., p. 428.

39. Deutscher, *Stalin,* op. cit., p 350ff.

40. Conquest, op. cit., pp. 96ff. and 190ff.

41. Orlov, *The Secret History of Stalin's Crimes,* p. 350.

42. Conquest, op. cit., p. 117.

43. Ibid., p. 400ff.

44. Alexander Barmin, *One Who Survived,* G. P. Putnam, New York, 1945, pp. 207–208.

45. Conquest, op. cit.

46. Ulam, op. cit., p. 429.

47. Conquest, op. cit., pp. 187–88.

48. Ibid., p. 410; Ulam, op. cit., p. 455. *Pravda,* on June 8, 1937, ran the letter about Pletnev under the headline "Professor—Rapist, Sadist."

49. Though the reference on Pletnev is in one of the many questionable books along the lines of "I Was Stalin's Bodyguard" and the "biography" of Kaganovich (see note 4), it rings true. See N. Romana-Petrovna, *Stalin's Doctor, Stalin's Nurse,* Kingston Press, Princeton, N.J., 1984, pp. vii–viii, p. 5. The Bekhterev reference is in Antonov-Ovsenko, op. cit., p. 254.

50. Solzhenitsyn, *The First Circle,* p. 101.

51. Tucker, *The Soviet Political Mind: Stalinism and Post-Stalin Change,* p. 61ff.

52. Simmel, op. cit., p. 39. The followers of a psychotic leader may not necessarily be suffering from "mass psychosis" but from "dependency on a criminal," according to American psychiatrist Herman von Prag (interview with author, November 1, 1988). Freud in Vienna, Jung in Zurich, and Ferenczi in Budapest all were astonished to have independently discovered a common phenomenon in every single case of paranoid disorder, whether male or female, and regardless of race or social background: "a defense against a homosexual wish" (Freud, p. 162). Stalin became livid over film director Sergei Eisenstein's intimations of homosexual elements in the character of Ivan the Terrible, Stalin's alter ego (Ulam, op. cit., p. 436). Ivan's paranoia reached a fever pitch toward the end of his life, when he was afraid of everything.

53. Conquest, op. cit., p. 400ff.

54. Ibid., p. 403.

55. Trotsky believed that Stalin poisoned Gorky, as well as Lenin; Stalin

had refused to let the great writer visit abroad because of fear he would betray him. Author Isaac Babel, who would soon be among the purge's fatalities, had been extremely close to Gorky in his last years, and told Ilya Ehrenburg that the story he was poisoned was "insane" (Ehrenburg, *Novy Mir,* Moscow, 1962, no. 5, p. 153). But Gorky probably was poisoned—only not by those who died for the crime.

56. Solzhenitsyn wrote that Gorky got what he deserved, since he defended the concentration-camp system even after learning of the widespread torture and killing (*Gulag Archipelago,* p. 191).

57. Conquest, op. cit., p. 403.

58. Ibid., p. 406.

59. Ibid., p. 51.

60. Only a very rough estimate of the number of Jewish victims during the 1930s is possible. My estimate is based on the fact that Jews, although only 1.8 percent of the population in the 1927 Soviet census, officially constituted 4.3 percent of the Party's membership. They also formed an exceedingly high percentage of political commissars, secret police officials, and army officers, while about 11 percent of all Soviet doctors were Jews. This disproportionate representation was true of the intelligentsia as a whole, the art world, and top government bureaucrats. These were the people who were Stalin's main targets. In addition, most memoirs by survivors of the camps note the high percentage of Jewish prisoners throughout the Gulag. According to a February 3, 1953, State Department document (761.00/2-353 Dept # 1332) in The National Archives in Washington, "among certain categories of prisoners the number of Jews was higher than in proportion to their strength in Russia."

61. David J. Dallin and Boris I. Nicolaevsky, *Forced Labor in the Soviet Union,* Hollis & Canter, London, 1948, p. 33.

62. Medvedev, *Let History Judge,* p. 358.

63. *Hitler's Table Talk: Hitler's Conversations Recorded by Martin Bormann,* Oxford University Press, Oxford, 1988, p. 180.

CHAPTER 5: **Rescue Denied**

1. Romain Rolland, the French Jewish intellectual and winner of the Nobel Prize for Literature, had once written a paean to Yagoda, which the revolutionary writer Victor Serge described sardonically as a "handsome article": "The great chief of the concentration camps and of those silent executioners in all the dungeons of the USSR conquered at a stroke the heart of the author of *Jean-Christophe"*

(Serge, 1937, p. 130). The great reformer Nikita Khrushchev said of Yagoda in his memoirs: "I always liked him" (Talbott, ed., *Khrushchev Remembers,* 1970 ed., p. 92).

2. Talbott, ed., *Khrushchev Remembers,* 1970 ed., op. cit.

3. Bortoli, p. 193.

4. Conquest, *The Great Terror,* p. 431.

5. Cang, p. 76.

6. Author inteview with Mikhail Agursky, July 2, 1989.

7. Conquest, op. cit., p. 430; Shostakovich, p. 97.

8. Redlich, "The Jews under Soviet Rule During World War II," p. 20ff.

9. Arthur Koestler, *The Yogi and the Commissar,* Hutchinson, London 1983, ed., p. 186. But Koestler was inaccurate: the deportations of kulaks, Cossacks, and others in the earlier part of the 1930s had been on a bigger scale.

10. Solomon M. Schwartz, *The Jews in the Soviet Union,* Syracuse, 1951, p. 310.

11. Goldberg, pp. 51–52.

12. Medvedev, *Let History Judge,* p. 493.

13. Gilboa, pp. 7–8.

14. Deutscher, *The Non-Jewish Jew,* pp. 77–78.

15. Antonov-Ovsenko, p. 248; Alliluyeva, *Twenty Letters to a Friend,* p. 158ff; Ulam, pp. 548–549.

16. Yulia was released from prison in 1943.

17. Alliluyeva, op. cit., p. 172ff., and *Only One Year* pp. 150–154; De Jonge, p. 404. Kapler remained in the Gulag for ten years, until after Stalin's death.

18. Alliluyeva, *Twenty Letters to a Friend,* op. cit., p. 181.

19. Gilboa, op. cit., p. 32.

20. The late Israeli historian Aryeh Tartakower estimated that no more than half a million Jews were evacuated from war areas, though others have said the figure was twice that (Shivtey Yisrael, *European Jewry in Present Times,* vol. 2, Tel Aviv, 1966, p. 24. See also Schwartz, *The Jews in the Soviet Union,* Appendix: "Evacuation and Re-Evacuation of the Jews in the War." These were either Jews who could go off with their factories, Jews who had money, or Jews who were shipped to Siberian prison camps because they might awaken Jewish nationalism among Soviet Jewry. At the same time, massive numbers of "unreliable" Poles and Balts were deported into Asian Russia. It was not a question of priorities, or a logistical

problem: for example, two million people were evacuated or fled from Moscow in two weeks of October 1941; and while the small number of inhabitants at some Jewish collective farms in the Crimea were evacuated, over a million Jews in similar settlements in the Ukraine were abandoned to the Nazis and their nationalist Ukrainian allies. Jews were beaten back by the police when they sought to rush evacuation trains (J. L. Teller, *The Kremlin, the Jews and the Middle East,* New York, 1957, p. 75).

21. Historian S. Schwartz, quoted in Redlich, op. cit., p. 112.

22. Gilboa, op. cit., p. 3; Gitelman, p. 198.

23. Cang, op. cit., p. 87.

24. The number of Jews holding the highest military honor—Hero of the Soviet Union—was second only to that of the Great Russians. On a per capita basis, they were the highest by far (Redlich, op. cit., pp. 129–30).

25. Deutscher, *Stalin: A Political Biography,* p. 471.

26. Redlich, op. cit., p. 116ff. Stalin's set of priorities in evacuation was typically totalitarian. Taganrog, an expanding industrial city of 190,000 people near the Azov Sea, was an example. Taganrog, once a town of spacious gardens and orchards, had been transformed by the Soviets into a sooty industrial city whose canneries and metallurgical and aviation plants were partially run by slave labor. The Nazi advance in October 1941 was so rapid that many of the political, criminal, and "security" prisoners were stranded in cattle cars at the rail station where they had been brought to be evacuated. Only part of the aeronautics plant was dismantled and evacuated in time, because train traffic was tied up by the deportation of prisoners. Beria's men rushed tank trucks to the rail depot, drenched the jammed cattle cars with oil and set them on fire, burning the prisoners alive (Solzhenitsyn, *The Gulag Archipelago,* p. 31). As soon as the Nazis entered Taganrog, they rounded up the city's 15,000 to 20,000 Jews—mostly women, small children, and the elderly—and marched them to a ravine, Petrushin Gully, where they were slaughtered (Ainsztein, p. 226). Like the Jews of Kiev slaughtered at Babi Yar, the Taganrog Jews were described by the Soviet media only as "Soviet citizens." (Soviet Government Statements on Nazi Atrocities, Hutchinson & Co., London, 1946, pp. 136–43).

27. The Allies, at the Moscow Conference which ended on November 1, 1943, did not mention the extermination of the Jews among a long list of atrocities which the Germans would be held responsible for: Czechs, Greeks, Serbs, French hostages, Polish officers, and Cretan peasants were specified. But not Jews. This was the heart of the

matter: the Jews were not regarded as a nation by the Allies. Even the Soviets, who had officially recognized the Jews as a Soviet nationality, and entered the word "Jewish" under the nationality category on internal identity documents, refused to accord them the status of a people when it came to their extermination.

28. Talbott, *Khrushchev Remembers,* 1920 ed., op. cit., p. 274.

29. Redlich, op. cit., p. 29.

30. Conquest, op. cit., pp. 483–84; Redlich, *Propaganda and Nationalism in Wartime Russia,* p. 29ff.

31. Redlich, *Propaganda,* op. cit., Gitelman, op. cit., p. 226.

32. Conquest, *Propaganda,* op. cit., p. 513.

33. Baron, p. 261.

34. Leneman, op. cit., p. 103ff.; Gitelman, op. cit., p. 226.

35. Redlich, *Propaganda,* op. cit., p. 29.

36. Conquest, op. cit. Alter's book *Man in Society,* published just before the war, had had a profound impact on his fellow socialists, including French leader Léon Blum, a close personal friend of both men (Leneman, op. cit., p. 109).

37. Stanislav Kot, *Conversations with the Kremlin and Despatches from Russia,* Oxford University Press, London, 1963, p. 159.

38. Leneman, op. cit.

39. Redlich, *Propaganda,* op. cit. Ambassador Kot's attempt to worry Vyshinsky about the "hullabaloo" American Jewish organizations would raise was probably no more than a ploy. He knew the Soviets regarded American Jews as potential allies in pushing for the rapid opening of a second front. But he probably did not realize how cynical most of these organizations would be about raising a fuss over the fate of just two Jews, no matter how prominent, at a point in time when Hollywood was portraying a benign Uncle Joe Stalin in *Mission to Moscow,* an apologia for the Great Terror. Only a few exceptional leaders opted out of the pro-Stalin chorus: Dubinsky, though a left radical, had been a firm critic of the show trials, and rebuffed pressure from the State Department and Jewish and gentile liberals who tried to dissuade him from protesting against the executions (Conquest, op. cit.). Among the American Zionists, the only leader who openly condemned the executions was Chaim Greenberg, head of the American Zionist Emergency Council—a former Soviet Jew who had been arrested by the Communists several times for Zionist activity.

40. Talbot, ed., *Khrushchev Remembers,* 1970 ed., op. cit., p. 183. Khrushchev said Shcherbakov died of drink, trying to please Stalin. On

one occasion Shcherbakov exposed a ruse by Beria, Malenkov, and Mikoyan of drinking colored water instead of wine during the nightly heavy eating and drinking sessions at Stalin's table. The dictator raised a terrible uproar when he learned of it (Ibid., p. 322). George Kennan, in a dispatch from Moscow upon the death of Shcherbakov, described him as "the center of those currents of hostility toward the Western world in general and the United States in particular" in the Soviet hierarchy. He noted that his latest function as propaganda chief was "one of almost unparalleled importance" (National Archives, 861.44 Shcherbakov/5–1145, May 11, 1945, telegram 58592).

41. Ehrenburg, *Men, Years, Life.* One of Shcherbakov's assistants, Kondakov, rejected Ehrenburg's draft of a message from the JAC to American Jews about Nazi atrocities, in which he mentioned the 500,000 Red Army Jews battling the Soviets. "There's no need to mention the exploits of Jews in the Red Army. It's bragging," Kondakov said.

42. "An actor . . . tribune," quoted in Redlich, *Propaganda,* op. cit., p. 81. Vovsi-Mikhoels, *Avi Shlomo Mikhoels* (in Hebrew), p. 102.

43. "I am a Jew," lines translated by Joseph Leftwich, YIVO Institute, New York. Other verses quoted in Gilboa, op. cit., pp. 120–121.

44. Author interview with Esther and David Markish, July 11, 1988; Esther Markish, *The Long Return,* p. 142ff.

45. Baron, p. 262.

46. See, for example, Redlich, *Propaganda,* op. cit., p. 29ff.; author interview with Natalia Vovsi-Mikhoels, February 11, 1988.

47. Esther Markish interview, July 11, 1988.

48. Howard Fast, *The Naked God,* The Bodley Head, London, 1955.

49. Gitelman, op. cit., p. 230.

50. Goldmann to Henderson, May 11, 1943, Z5/371, Zionist Archives, Jerusalem.

51. Wise and fellow Zionist leader and Reform rabbi Abba Hillel Silver hoped to persuade the Soviets to reconsider their hostility to Zionism and Hebrew, and this was reportedly the main reason they so warmly welcomed Mikhoels and Feffer. Baron, op. cit., p. 421, note 22.

52. Redlich, *Propaganda,* op. cit., p. 118ff., p. 190 (note 45).

53. FBI documents obtained under FOIPA No. 100-225072-1,3.

54. Leneman, op. cit. The author gives a figure of $3 million raised, but it was probably half as much.

55. "Calling All Jews to Action," London, Jewish Fund for Soviet Russia, 1943, pp. 96–97.

56. Baron, op. cit., p. 421, note 22.

57. The Joint's liberal creed viewed Judaism as a religion without a nationalist content. To its founders, Palestine was just another refuge.

58. American Jewish Joint Distribution Committee (JDC) Archives, New York, file 431; Paul Baerwald letter to Louis Levine, April 23, 1945.

  In 1953 the Joint launched a pilot project with a group of twenty-one Jewish-German doctors, most of whom were brought to the USSR from French refugee camps. The climate in the Soviet Union, however, was not a healthy one for foreigners. Many of these doctors, who were soon joined by some seventy others, would be destroyed. Some would be accused in 1936 of being Gestapo agents (Bauer, pp. 96–97). In 1937 fourteen of the doctors were arrested, as well as most of the Joint's senior staff, including Samuel Lubarsky, Ezechial Grower, and Aaron Zaichik. They were sent to the Gulag, liquidated, or disappeared. The former Soviet minister of health, Grishka M. Kaminsky, a non-Jew who was officially responsible for giving the German-Jewish doctors a haven in the USSR, also was liquidated. Kaminsky had to be disposed of in any case, for he was one of those who had signed the "natural death" certificates of Stalin's friends and victims V. V. Kuibyshev and Sergo Ordzhonikidze (Talbott, ed., *Khrushchev Remembers,* 1970 ed., op. cit., pp. 36–37.

59. Leneman, op. cit., p. 269.

60. Yehuda Bauer, *American Jewry and the Holocaust,* Wayne State University, Detroit, 1981, p. 297ff.

61. Baron, op. cit., p. 266.

62. Ibid.

63. Schwartz, op. cit., p. 217, note 31.

64. Baron, op. cit., p. 262.

65. Redlich, *Propaganda,* op. cit., p. 125ff.

66. *Einikeyt,* April 5, 1943; July 13, 1944.

67. Ibid., March 15, 1945.

68. Redlich, *Propaganda,* op. cit., p. 112.

69. Gilboa, op. cit., p. 50.

70. Author interview with Natalia and Nina Vovsi-Mikhoels, February 22, 1988.

71. Redlich, *Propaganda,* op. cit., p. 169.

72. Leneman, op. cit., p. 188. Both the Karaites and the Krimsheg sect in the Crimea had presented a racial problem for the Nazi extermi-

nators, until finally Reinhard Heydrich ruled that the Krimshegs, Muslims of Jewish "race," should be massacred, while the Karaites, who were Tatars by race and "pseudo-Jews" by religion, should be spared (Gerald Reitlinger, *The Final Solution,* Sphere Books, London, 1971, p. 257). But some Karaites were treated as Jews by the Nazis (Leneman, op. cit.).

73. See Nikolai Deker and Andrei Lebed, eds., *Genocide in the USSR: Studies in Group Destruction,* Institute for the Study of the USSR, Munich, 1958. According to one report, Mikhoels told three Jewish Red Army officers who visited him during this period that he had also failed to get the government to mention in any official communication or state media the tragedy of the Jews in the areas occupied by the Nazis (Leneman, op. cit.). What casts doubt on this report is the unlikelihood of Mikhoels or any other prominent Soviet citizen talking so frankly to three people. Everyone knew the odds were that at least one of them would turn out to be an informer.

74. Redlich, *Propaganda,* op. cit., p. 52.

75. Stalin, "Marxism and the National Question," trans. the British and Irish Communist Organization, London, February 1974.

76. *The Unpublished Dostoevsky Diaries and Notebooks,* Carl Proffer, ed., Ardis, Ann Arbor, Mich., 1973, pp. 646–50.

77. Talbott, ed., *Khrushchev Remembers,* 1970 ed., op. cit., p. 274, p. 281 (footnote by Edward Crankshaw).

78. Medvedev, *Let History Judge,* op. cit., p. 493ff.

79. Cited in Deker and Lebed, eds., *Genocide in the USSR,* op. cit., pp. 104–105.

80. Conquest, *The Nation Killers: The Soviet Deportation of Nationalities,* p. 50ff.

81. G. A. Tokaev, *Betrayal of an Ideal,* London, Harvill Press, 1954, and *Comrade X,* London, Harvill Press, 1956. Tokaev's two books are among the many Soviet memoirs whose authenticity is questioned by scholars.

82. Conquest, *The Nation Killers,* op. cit., p. 101ff.

83. Ibid., p. 50ff.

84. Ibid., p. 105.

85. Dzhirkvelov, p. 26. This memoir by a "defector" appears to have been sanctioned by the KGB.

86. The allegation that all these people as a nation collaborated with the Nazis was basically untrue, though many individuals among them did aid the Nazis. The percentage of Ukrainians who supported the Nazis was higher than that of the deported nationalities, yet the

Ukrainians avoided such a fate because there were too many of them, as Khrushchev said in his 1956 Secret Speech.

87. Conquest, *The Nation Killers,* op. cit., p. 62. These Soviet citizens were descended from German settlers invited to Russia by Catherine the Great.

88. Ibid., pp. 54–55. In the war, 20,000 Kalmyks fought valiantly at Rostov in 1942, and were still being praised by the Soviets even after the Germans finally withdrew from the area in January 1943. Then they suddenly disappeared. No public statement was ever made about the deportation of this nation.

89. Antonov-Ovsenko, op. cit., p. 280.

90. Talbott, ed., *Khrushchev Remembers,* 1970 ed., op. cit., p. 69.

91. Conquest, *The Nation Killers,* op. cit., pp. 68–70.

92. Ibid., p. 291.

93. Talbott, ed., *Khrushchev Remembers,* 1970 ed., op. cit., p. 312.

94. Charles E. Bohlen, *Witness to History 1929–1969,* W. W. Norton, New York, 1973, p. 203.

95. Alliluyeva, *Only One Year,* op. cit., pp. 152–53.

96. Ibid.

97. Redlich, *Propaganda,* op. cit., pp. 211–12.

98. Roy Medvedev interview, *Arguments and Facts Magazine,* Moscow, February 4, 1989.

99. Goldberg, op. cit., p. 59.

100. Baron, op. cit., pp. 262–63; Ehrenburg and Grossman, *The Black Book.*

101. Baron, op. cit.

CHAPTER 6: **An Actor's Tragedy**

1. Author interviews with Natalia and Nina Vovsi-Mikhoels, February 4–22, 1988. Mikhoels's first wife, the actress Zhenya Levitas, died in 1934, leaving him with their two small girls.

2. Stalin personally ordered Meyerhold's theater to be closed, according to Shostakovich, p. 48.

3. Author interview with Mikhail Kalik, February 21, 1988.

4. Benjamin Pinkus, *The Soviet Government and the Jews, 1948–1967: A Documented Study,* Cambridge University Press, Cambridge, Enland, 1984, pp. 183–84.

5. Kalik interview, February 21, 1988. Stalin was an avid movie fan, and there were almost nightly showings in his private screening

room. He liked Tarzan films, Charlie Chaplin's work (presumably not *The Great Dictator*), and Soviet films about how he had led the Revolution and won World War II almost single-handedly. The actors in these films assumed heroic but diffident poses as they played Molotov or Beria, clicking their heels and saying, "That's right, Iosif Vissarionovich!" In the 1949 film *The Fall of Berlin*, the actor playing Marshal Zhukov, who took the city, appears for only a few seconds—to take orders from the military genius at the helm. Stalin is the only one capable of taking action. He issues orders, and only Poskrebyshev, his personal secretary, reports to him. Stalin acts for everyone.

6. Alliluyeva, *Twenty Letters to a Friend*, p. 184ff.

7. Ibid., p. 196.

8. Such sentiments were not confined to Stalinist Russia. American writers Truman Capote and Jack Kerouac said similar things about American-Jewish writers and publishers.

9. Shostakovich, op. cit., pp. 108, 180, 197. Stalin took a keen interest in the arts; and he was not always the complete boor as he has been portrayed by Shostakovich and many others. Despite his perverse remarks about Shakespeare, or his foolish forays into the worlds of classical music and film, or his preference for the mundane, he was extremely well read and was also capable of showing good taste: he liked Saltykov-Shchedrin's satires, Gogol and Bulgakov, and Verdi's operas, for example. Bulgakov's brilliant *The White Guard* was his favorite contemporary play. Before the war, he often took Svetlana to the Moscow Art Theater, the Maly, and the Bolshoi. He saw *Boris Gudonov* over and over again, entranced by this late sixteenth century drama of personal ambition. Stalin must have delighted in the elements of the story: threatening German troops, a wicked monarch, hard-drinking monks, Red Square as a place of execution, poison and intrigue, a character named Khrushchev who calls the would-be czar "our father," and lines such as "Thou wilt not escape the judgment even of this world,/As thou wilt not escape the doom of God." The ethical essence of the Pushkin play set to Mussorgsky's music is that the blood of the innocent will one day rise from the soil, demanding and receiving justice.

10. Ulam, pp. 643–44.

11. Pinkus, op. cit. The "patriotic theater critics," in contrast to the "aliens," rhapsodized about the stilted anti-American plays that were the hallmark of postwar Soviet drama—such as *Uncle Tom's Cabin,* and *The Mad Haberdasher*, about President Truman. Simonov's *The Russian Question* portrayed degenerate American journalists who sell their souls for greenbacks.

12. Shostakovich, op. cit., p. 117ff.

13. Koestler, p. 42. Koestler attacked Brecht's 1931 play *Die Massnahme* (The Punitive Measure), in which a young Communist acquiesces in his own liquidation. Koestler commented on the fact that Brecht during the Stalin purges similarly acquiesced in the extermination of his mistress and closest friend, the actress Carola Weher.

14. Sergei M. Eisenstein, *Ivan the Terrible,* trans. and ed. Ivor Montagu, New York, Simon and Schuster, 1962, p. 7. In Shostakovich's estimation, Eisenstein had sunk to the lowest depths when he made the film *Bezhin Meadow,* glorifying Pavlik Morozov, the Kulak boy who had denounced his parents in the early thirties and was murdered for it. The composer was not saddened when the film was destroyed on Stalin's command (Shostakovich, op. cit., pp. 192–93).

15. *Moscow News* no. 32, 1988.

16. Eisenstein, op. cit., p. 16.

17. *Moscow News,* op. cit.

18. Ibid.

19. Shostakovich, op. cit., p. 99.

20. Critics hailed Mikhoels, who began playing Lear in the early 1930s in writer Samuel Halkin's superb Yiddish translation, as the "best Lear of the century," The celebrated English director Gordan Craig, who was not in the habit of giving compliments, was mesmerized by Mikhoels's Lear, and said that the English theater could not really do justice to Shakespeare "because we don't have an actor like Mikhoels." One GOSET performance of King Lear was also recorded on film, only a snippet of which survives (Hebrew University Film Archives, Mount Scopus, Jerusalem): The Fool, played by Zuskin, stretches his limbs as Lear's favorite daughter, Cordelia, holds one of his hands. Suddenly the jester becomes stiff and formal as he hands the crown to the daughter. Laughter among the players—and the Fool crowns himself.

21. Redlich, *Propaganda and Nationalism in Wartime Russia,* p. 78.

22. Author interviews with Natalia and Nina Vovsi-Mikhoels, February 4–22, 1988. Yet another prevalent myth is that Kaganovich attended a performance of Lear by Mikhoels and scrutinized the actor's every gesture. Kaganovich supposedly became agitated as Lear exclaimed, "Tremble, then, monster, for all these crimes you have committed which you hold secret." The minister then was said to have stormed out of the theater, saying, "This Mikhoels isn't doing theater! It's simply agitation, and of a most dangerous kind!" Leneman, p. 127ff., is one of many accounts that portrays Mikhoels as a kind of court jester to Stalin whose all-night performances were

said to have thrilled the dictator. This was pure fiction, according to Mikhoels's daughters. GOSET actress Nina Sirotina told the Wiener Oral History Library that Kaganovich attended a Mikhoels play in 1930, came to his dressing room, banged on the table and said, "My people are not like this."

23. Natalia and Nina Vovsi-Mikhoels interviews, February 4–22, 1988.
24. Markish, p. 83.
25. Ehrenburg, *Men, Years, Life.*
26. Author interview with Natalia Vovsi-Mikhoels, April 4, 1988.
27. Shostakovich, op. cit., p. 65.
28. Ibid.
29. Ulam, p. 470; Tucker, *The Soviet Political Mind: Stalinism and Post-Stalin Change,* pp. 95–96, 110; Kennan, *Russia and the West,* p. 248.
30. Author interview with actress Etel Kovinskaya, May 2, 1988; GOSET actor quoted in B. Z. Goldberg, *The Jewish Problem in the Soviet Union,* p. 152.
31. Vovsi-Mikhoels sisters interviews, February 4–22, 1988. One of Mikhoels's last film appearances was in Alexandrov's *The Circus,* about a young American woman with a mulatto child who comes to Russia, where the Soviet peoples serenade the persecuted child. Mikhoels did so in Yiddish. In 1948, soon after his death, he would be sliced out of the film. His American black friend, Paul Robeson, would learn the truth about Mikhoels's fate, and that of Feffer, as well. Robeson sang songs in Yiddish, too. But out of loyalty to Stalin and communism, he would refuse to sing out about the murders of his friends, or the persecution of tens of millions of Soviet citizens.
32. Author interview with Esther Markish, July 11, 1988. Redlich, p. 55.
33. Natalia Vovsi-Mikhoels interview, February 11, 1988. Critics, along with actors, writers and artists, were watched by a special division of Stalin's secret police (Dzhirkvelov, pp. 66–67).
34. Vovsi-Mikhoels sisters interviews, February 4–22, 1988.
35. "So What if I'm Circumcised," by Itzik Feffer, in *A Treasury of Yiddish Poetry,* edited by Irving Howe and Eliezer Greenburg, Schocken Books, New York, 1972.
36. Vovsi-Mikhoels sisters interviews, February 4–22, 1988. Alliluyeva, *Only One Year,* pp. 153–54. Stalin kept the coat with similar gifts, according to Svetlana.
37. The Chekists frequently staged car accidents to cover up murder. Around the same time as the alleged "accident" in which Mikhoels

and Golubov died, the secret police arranged a similar car mishap to eliminate a leader of the aborted Soviet-inspired attempt to detach Azerbaijan from Iran and join it to the USSR (Dzhirkvelov, pp. 66–67).

38. Gilboa, pp. 82–83.

39. G. Reitlinger, *The Final Solution,* Sphere Books, London, 1971, p. 23.

40. Alliluyeva, *Only One Year,* op. cit., p. 154.

41. Vovsi-Mikhoels sisters interviews, February 4–22, 1988.

42. Interviews, as note 41. Because Mikhail Kaganovich was still in jail at that point, it was obviously extremely risky for Lazar Kaganovich to send such a message, and it seemed entirely out of character, as well.

43. Redlich, *Propaganda,* op. cit., p. 218.

44. Vovsi-Mikhoels sisters interviews, February 4–22, 1988.

45. Goldberg, op. cit., p. 101.

46. Esther Markish interview, July 11, 1988. Eight years later, after Esther returned from exile in Kazakhstan, another general who had served under Trofimenko in Minsk told her that Beria and the MGB had killed Mikhoels on the personal orders of Stalin.

47. Smith report to State Dept., 861.00/1-2748, January 27, 1948, National Archives, Washington, D.C.

48. Ibid. The most authoritative account, the report said, was that Mikhoels and Golubov, on the evening of "January 11 or 12 . . . visited the home of another friend of Mikhoels, I. G. Pfeffer [sic], a poet of some renown and vice-president of the Jewish Anti-Fascist Committee. On their way home Mikhoels and Golubov were attacked by persons unknown and both killed, although Mikhoels lived long enough to tell the story. . . . a number of various rumors attributed anti-Semitic feeling to the attackers, and such a motive cannot, indeed, be completely discounted. On the contrary, however, the murderers may have been Jews themselves, for Mikhoels has been known as anti-Zionist and Byelorussia has been mentioned as a center of Zionist feelings in the USSR." The embassy dispatch erroneously reported that Feffer lived in Minsk. But there was no mistake in placing Feffer in Minsk at the time of the premeditated murders. The Jews involved in Mikhoels's killing were not Zionists, but Stalinists.

49. Vovsi-Mikhoels sisters interviews, February 4–22, 1988.

50. Interview, as note 49.

51. GOSET actress Nina Sirotina (Wiener Oral History Library, Amer-

ican Jewish Committee, New York) remembered it somewhat differently: "His eyes were bulging . . . he was completely disfigured. . . . The hand, which had been wrenched out of joint, they also somehow put it so that he had his famous gesture with the index finger pointing. . . . He had extremely expressive hands, hands such as not a single actor in the world ever had. . . . There was a great deal he didn't have to say, his hands could say a great deal."

52. All quotes from Markish's poem are from a translation by Herbert Paper. Ehrenburg in his memoirs recalled these lines as: "Your disaster has riven the heart of the whole nation. The six million arise in their graves to honor you, as you honored their memory when you fell among the ruins of Minsk."

53. The two direct references to murder are: "With hurt and murder-scars upon my face" and "Oh, the hand of murder did not silence you."

54. Ehrenburg, *People, Years, Life;* Esther Markish interview, July 11, 1988.

55. "Be not ashamed of your wounded ancient face, /Of your smashed and broken kingly pate," Markish read. "/This is your word in blood, your noblest paint, /In which, a corpse, you outlive the stage. . . . Be not ashamed of your defilement and your pain, /—Let eternity be ashamed!" The poem ended with a reference to what could be interpreted as the Soviet homeland, or to the Promised Land of the Jewish people: "And beyond—with the dreams of our land /On high. . . ."

56. Vovsi-Mikhoels sisters interviews, February 4–22, 1988.

57. The prayer's message was that Jews and Judaism would always survive the Deluge, and the continuing flood of foreign ideologies and cultures.

CHAPTER 7:   **The Crimea Affair**

1. Author interview with Natalia and Nina Vovsi-Mikhoels, February 4, 1988.

2. Interview, as note 1.

3. Author interview with Natalia Vovsi-Mikhoels, April 4, 1988.

4. Nina Sirotina, oral history, William Wiener Oral History Library, American Jewish Committee, New York.

5. Natalia Vovsi-Mikhoels interview, April 4, 1988.

6. Interview, as note 5.

7. Author interview with Esther Markish, July 11, 1988; Markish, p. 160ff.

8. The Mikhoels sisters were afraid to talk to friends. Once when Natalia visited a composer, she saw the "tail" write down his address, so she stopped her social life entirely. People she knew would cross the street to avoid saying hello. "We would thank God every morning when we woke up in our own beds, but never knew if we would be taken to prison that night." Interview with Natalia Vovsi-Mikhoels, February 11, 1988.

9. Nina Sirtona, oral history, as note 4.

10. Hahn, p. 94ff.

11. Talbott, ed., *Khrushchev Remembers,* 1970 ed., p. 304; Djilas, p. 155.

12. Alliluyeva, *Only One Year,* p. 384.

13. Public Record Office, Kew, England, FO371/71640 XP9597 February 16, 1948, letter from E. R. Warner.

14. Author interview with Dr. Solomon Nezlin, December 18, 1988. Solomon Nezlin, one of the physicians arrested after most of the Kremlin doctors were already in prison, was apparently held because his brother, Binyamin, had been among the physicians consulted in 1948 about Zhdanov. At age ninety-six, Solomon Nezlin immigrated to Israel with his wife, son, and grandson.

15. Author interview with Dr. Yakov Rapoport, February 19, 1989.

16. Interview, as note 15. The nonagenarian former head of Moscow University's pathology department, whose memoirs of the Doctors' Plot were published in the glasnost USSR of 1988, said he was certain that Zhdanov and Shcherbakov died naturally—of drink.

17. It was a custom among the various peoples in Georgia to spend a great deal of time at the dinner table, and Georgian artists like Gudiashvili and Pirosmani depicted this tradition in many of their paintings. Stalin ate huge quantities of meat, which Djilas thought "reflected his mountaineer origins" (Djilas, op. cit., p. 77).

18. Ibid., p. 154. Stalin knew very well that there were still several Jews on the Central Committee, including Paulina Zhemchuzina and Lozovsky, as well as henchmen Kaganovich and Mekhlis.

19. Antonov-Ovsenko, p. 282.

20. Gromyko quoted in Walter Laqueur, *A History of Zionism,* New York, Schocken, 1976, p. 528.

21. American policymakers were worried about Soviet gains in the Middle East. Diplomat and Sovietologist George Kennan, who at that time devised the famed "containment" policy that was in effect until Gorbachev's "revolution," presented a plan to Secretary of State George Marshall which dealt with the Soviet expansionist threat in this area. He believed that the establishment of the state of Israel

("American military support for which I resolutely opposed") was heightening "the danger of Communist infiltration in the Arab countries" (Kennan, *Memoirs 1925–1950,* p. 380).

22. Dzhirkvelov, pp. 246–47.

23. Jewish Labor Committee Report, "Plight of Jews in Countries Behind the Iron Curtain," New York, March 12, 1950.

24. Soviet orientalist Vladimir Lutskii's remarks at Moscow University in June 1949 reinforced this view: "The Zionist bourgeoisie [in Israel] serves as a support for the implementation of the Anglo-American imperialist plans. . . . It was easy for the U.S.A. to convert the Zionist leaders into American agents" (Ro'i, p. 77).

25. Jonathan Frankel, Study Paper, Hebrew University Library, Jerusalem, p. 14. But the Soviets were still supporting some Israeli positions at the United Nations as late as November 1948, according to Ro'i, p. 61.

26. Deutscher, *The Non-Jewish Jew,* p. 81.

27. One of the many arrested was the violinist Pinke, concertmaster of the Moscow Opera.

28. National Archives, Washington, D.C., 861.00/1–1348, Confidential no. 60, from W. J. Stoessel, Moscow, January 13, 1948.

29. The allegation is still presented as fact by several of the leaders of the Soviet Jewry emigration movement who came to Israel in the 1970s and 1980s.

30. Author interview with Lou Kadar, March 8, 1989.

31. Author interview with Aryeh Levavi, March 13, 1989. Levavi, Israeli first secretary and later consul during his 1948–50 stint in Moscow, believes the rebuke was delivered by Deputy Minister Valeri Zoron.

32. Professor Edith Frenkel, of Hebrew University, was personally familiar with two such cases (author interview by telephone, March 8, 1989).

33. Author interview with David Markish, July 11, 1988.

34. Gitelman, p. 241.

35. Golda Meir, *My Life,* New York, Putnam, 1975, p. 253.

36. Ibid.

37. Aryeh Levavi interview, March 13, 1989.

38. Alliluyeva, *Twenty Letters to a Friend,* p. 194.

39. Alliluyeva, *Only One Year,* op. cit., p. 409.

40. *New York Times,* March 29, 1953, 30:1.

41. Alliluyeva, *Only One Year,* op. cit.

42. Meir, op. cit.; Marie Syrkin, *Golda Meir, Woman with a Cause: An Authorized Biography,* New York, Putnam, 1963, pp. 230–231.

43. Syrkin, *Golda Meir.*

44. Namir, pp. 83–84.

45. Ibid., p. 89ff. Ehrenburg once again appeared to be deep in his cups at this encounter. He spoke of the USSR as being glacially indifferent to the internal matters of foreign states. "The very fact of its existence upon the earth is enough to assure its influence—in the same way that it is not necessary for the Gulf Stream to 'interfere' with cold water; the very fact of its existence warms it."

46. Goldberg, p. 104; Gilboa, p. 109.

47. Leneman, p. 80. Ehrenburg even criticized Stalin's favorite novelist, Mikhail Sholokhov, the celebrated author of *And Quiet Flows the Don,* for not mentioning Jews in a book about those who fought for the Soviet fatherland. Sholokhov answered that "at the battlefronts, I didn't encounter any Jewish soliders."

48. Author interview with Simon Chertok, February 11, 1988. In the years immediately following the war, Ehrenburg included many sympathetic portrayals of Jews in his novels. In *The Storm,* for example, the honest dogmatist Osip and the lighthearted Frenchman Leon were the author's Jewish alter-egos. But because of Zhdanov's policies, Ehrenburg destroyed the original manuscript and cut out most of the pro-Jewish references (Gleb Struve, *Soviet-Russian Literature 1917–1950,* Oklahoma University Press, Oklahoma City, 1951). On the other hand, when he referred to the famous Jewish painters he knew, he never referred to them as Jews, but as, for example, "the Russians Chagall and Soutine."

49. George F. Kennan, letter to author, February 26, 1988.

50. Namir, p. 225ff. Namir, like all diplomats in the Israeli foreign ministry, was required to take a Hebrew name.

51. Ibid., p. 263.

52. Aryeh Levavi interview, March 13, 1989.

53. Goldberg, op. cit., p. 101.

54. Antonov-Ovsenko, op. cit., p. 290.

55. Jewish Labor Committee report, "Plight of Jews in Countries Behind the 'Iron Curtain,'" op. cit. National Archives, Washington, D.C., 861.411/3–2150, cover letter from Adolph Held to Secretary of State Dean Acheson. *New York Times* correspondent Harrison Salisbury also confirmed that many Jews were shipped east from Odessa and other Black Sea regions in 1949. My own rough estimate

is that as many as 150,000 Jews were arrested during the last five years of Stalin's regime.

56. Aryeh Levavi interview, March 13, 1989.

57. Namir, op. cit., p. 230.

58. Esther Markish interview, July 11, 1988; Markish, *The Long Return,* p. 142. Markish says Feffer was arrested on December 24, 1948, but another source, in Moscow, said Feffer was arrested in late November.

59. David Bergelson, *Yidn un de Foterland Milkhoma,* Moscow, 1941, p. 23.

60. Esther Markish interview, July 11, 1988.

61. Ibid.

62. Ibid.

63. Namir, op. cit., p. 215.

64. Roman Brackman, "Stalin's Failed Massacre," *Midstream,* December 1987, p. 16.

65. Interview with Esther Markish, July 11, 1988; Markish, *The Long Return,* p. 166ff.

66. Talbott, ed., *Khrushchev Remembers,* 1970 ed., pp. 276–77.

67. Alliluyeva, *Only One Year,* op. cit., p. 407.

68. Esther Markish interview, July 11, 1988.

69. David Markish interview, July 11, 1988.

70. Goldberg, op. cit., p. 142.

71. Howard Fast, *The Naked God,* The Bodley Head, London, 1958, p. 78.

72. Fadeyev, after Khrushchev's 1956 speech, drank himself into a stupor for twelve days and then shot himself in the head.

73. Mary McCarthy, letter to author, October 27, 1988.

74. Gilboa, op. cit., p. 206.

75. Leneman, op. cit., p. 86; Goldberg, op. cit., p. 112.

76. Goldberg, p. 112.

77. According to Harrison Salisbury, who translated and edited some of Ehrenburg's literary essays, "There is a large, unpublished but I hope still existing portion of his memoir which did not pass the censor in the 50s. I hope it may now be published. It will cast light on a lot of things." Salisbury thought Ehrenburg "a prickly man. But I respected him" (Salisbury, letter to author, June 27, 1988).

78. Paul Robeson, Jr., "How My Father Last Met Itzik Feffer," *Jewish Currents,* November 1981, p. 4. Until Paul Robeson, Jr.'s revelation, the most common version of the story, published in many books

and periodicals, was that Feffer and Robeson met at the Metropole Hotel restaurant, joined by two of Feffer's "friends," MGB men in civilian clothes. They all had an amiable conversation, in which Feffer assured Robeson that all was well with him and all the other Jewish writers, who were busy churning out their work. Feffer reportedly kept his hands below the table, to conceal the fact that his fingernails had been pulled out (author interview with Natalia and Nina Vovsi-Mikhoels, February 11, 1988).

79. Paul Robeson, Jr., op. cit. He maintains (interview with author, October 17, 1988) that the efforts of his father, Fast, and others "kept Feffer alive for three more years. Why is it difficult for liberal Americans to understand that? My father had better things to worry about with black people in America. . . . My father raised the issue in the Soviet Union. He, Joliot Curie, and Howard Fast wrote letters to Stalin not to kill these people. Our agenda then and now is black interests first." Paul Robeson, Jr.'s revelation about the true Robeson-8Feffer meeting created an uproar in the American Communist world, with Robeson biographer Lloyd L. Brown terming the report a "lie" which "gravely impunged the honor of one of the greatest Americans of our era" "Reply to 'How My Father Last Met Itzik Feffer'" (*Jewish Currents*, February 1982). It wasn't a lie, but it did gravely impugn Paul Robeson's honor to the handful of people who now know of Robeson's cover-up.

80. Robeson, "How My Father Last Met Itzik Feffer," op. cit., author interview with Paul Robeson, Jr.

81. Paul Robeson, Jr., interview.

82. *Soviet Russia Today,* August 1949.

83. Author interview with A. B. Magil, October 13, 1988.

84. Shostakovich, op. cit., p. 152.

85. Fast, op. cit., p. 105. Fast was not alone in trying to impugn Ehrenburg. One journalist, Bernard Turner, who had been Moscow correspondent of *Davar* of Tel Aviv and the *London Daily Herald* during the war and was imprisoned in the Gulag for "espionage" in 1943, claimed that he met Feffer and Bergelson in a Siberian transit camp in 1950 and that they told him Ehrenburg had been the chief witness against the Jewish writers, and giving "crushing testimony" against his close friend Solomon Lozovsky. The writers allegedly asked Turner, should he ever meet Ehrenburg, to "demand in our name that he lay a wreath on the graves of the innocents who were murdered and that he beg for their forgiveness" (Leneman, p. 78). The Turner story cannot be true, according to Peretz Markish's widow, Esther, for none of the imprisoned writers ever left the

Moscow prisons (author interview Markish, July 11, 1988). "Turner lied," said Esther Markish. "We know that the writers were never in any camp; they never left Moscow." Ehrenburg totally denied Turner's charges in August 26, 1957, interview in *Le Monde*.

86. Goldberg, op. cit., pp. 60, 141. The JAC's American counterpart managed to snare Albert Einstein into serving as its honorary president. But Moscow, which opposed any themes of Jewish unity, suppressed Einstein's preface to the JAC's English edition of *The Black Book* (Gilboa, op. cit., p. 74).

87. Goldberg, pp. 60, 141. Paul Robeson headed another pro-Soviet group, the National Council of American Soviet Friendship, with Communist sympathizers Rockwell Kent and Joseph Davies (Davies, the former U.S. envoy to the USSR, had glorified the show trials). Among the group's Jewish supporters were Joseph Rosen of the Joint Distribution Committee and Philip Klutznik of B'nai B'rith.

88. Talbott, ed., *Khrushchev Remembers*, 1970 ed., p. 279.

89. "Linguistics in the Stalinist Epoch," *Russkii yazyk v shkole* (Russian Language in the School), no. 6, 1949, trans. Joint Press Reading Service, Moscow. The writer hailed Stalin for gathering "vast linguistic materials. . . . Soviet linguistics is wholly obliged to the great coryphaeus [chorus leader] of Soviet science, J. V. Stalin."

90. K. P. S. Menon, *The Flying Troika,* London, 1963.

91. Ibid.

92. *Soviet Affairs Notes,* no. 104, February 24, 1950.

93. National Archives, Washington, D.C., 861.412/5–1950 May 19, 1950 letter from First Secretary John Evarts Horner, embassy dispatch no. 638.

94. *Pravda,* June 20, 1950. Stalin modestly disclaimed any expertise in linguistics and said he would only discuss Marr's theories in Marxist terms.

95. Ibid., August 2, 1950.

96. *Pravda,* June 21, 22, 1951.

97. *Voprosy filosofii* (Problems of Philosophy), no. 3, 1950.

98. Gilboa, op. cit., pp. 78, 229.

99. Jerusalem University Collection of Documents on Soviet-Jewish Relations, ed. J. Frankel, Jerusalem, 1965, pp. 88, 97, 168.

100. Memorandum re Mr. Rosenberg's statement of Sept. 13, 1944, file no. 431, JDC Archives, New York. The JDC, which characterized its past work in the Crimea as "one of the most notable activities in the entire history" of the Joint, also suggested to the Soviets to increase aid to the Jews in the light of the British White Paper restricting

Jewish immigration into Palestine during the war (file no. 431, The Crimea, pt. 6).

101. Redlich, *Propaganda and Nationalism in Wartime Russia,* p. 53.

102. Ibid.

103. JDC Chairman Paul Baerwald letter of April 23, 1945, to Louis Levine; Pavel Mikhailov letter to Baerwald, May 5, 1945; Baerwald to Mikailov, July 24, 1945—all JDC Archives, op. cit., file no. 431.

104. Esther Markish interview, July 11, 1988; Redlich, p. 55.

105. Dzhirkvelov, op. cit., p. 250.

106. Gilboa, op. cit., p. 237; Redlich, pp. 54–55.

107. Esther Markish interview, July 11, 1988; Markish, *The Long Return,* p. 143.

108. Ulam, p. 479.

109. Talbott, ed., *Khrushchev Remembers,* 1970 ed., p. 276.

110. Dzhirkvelov, op. cit., pp. 256–57.

111. Conquest, *The Nation Killers,* p. 110.

112. Talbott, ed., *Khrushchev Remembers,* 1970 ed., p. 262.

113. Roy Medvedev, *Let History Judge,* p. 495.

114. Baron, p. 271.

115. Simon Chertok interview, February 11, 1988.

116. Zhores Medvedev, *Gorbachev,* Norton, New York & London, 1988, p. 34ff.

117. Shtern related this conversation to Esther Markish in November 1955 (Markish interview, July 11, 1988; Markish, *The Long Return,* p. 240ff).

118. Markish interview, July 11, 1988; Markish, *The Long Return,* p. 243.

119. Talbott, ed., *Khrushchev Remembers,* 1970 ed., p. 275.

120. The poet David Hofshtein returned to the USSR from Palestine in the 1920s, where he had considered settling on a kibbutz. When the Soviets backed the establishment of Israel, Hofshtein was deluded enough to suggest that the Education Ministry introduce the teaching of Hebrew in Soviet schools (Baron, op. cit., p. 268).

121. The number of victims has generally been given as twenty-five, but this is definitely incorrect. The confusion stems in part from the fact that several of the intellectuals died during detention before the August 12, 1952, mass execution. According to one researcher, Haifa University lecturer Avraham Greenbaum, only eight were killed on August 12 (author interview with Greenbaum, March 21, 1989). But shortly after the Central Committee under Mikhail Gorbachev issued a decree in January 1989 totally clearing the

executed Jews, Major General Petukhov of the Supreme Soviet said that the number executed on August 12 was fourteen (*Nedalia* weekly, February 13–19, 1989). His list did not include Greenburg, Nusinov, Levin, or Dobruchin, but did include two others, Teumin and Ostrovskaya.

122. Esther Markish interview, July 11, 1988; Markish, *The Long Return,* p. 240ff.

123. Ibid.

124. Ibid.

125. Ibid.

126. Ibid.

127. Lena Shtern's position in the Academy was restored after Stalin's death. The Lithuanian-born Communist had lived in the U.S.A. for many years and acquired American citizenship before immigrating to the USSR in the 1920s. The FBI file on "Lena Stern"—100–829–833—remained classified *in toto* in 1989. She died in 1968.

128. Leneman, op. cit., p. 74ff.

129. *Nedalia* weekly, op. cit. Abakumov was dismissed by Stalin in July 1951, over a year before the trial and execution of the Jewish writers. The tall jujitsu expert personally took part in many torture sessions, and was adept at breaking spines (Solzhenitsyn, *Gulag Archipelago,* p. 60; *First Circle,* pp. 82–83).

CHAPTER 8: **The Slansky Trial**

1. According to Jewish legend, Moses himself was the inventor of "modern" medicine (Louis Ginzberg, *The Legends of the Jews,* Philadelphia, Jewish Publication Society, 1968, vol. 5, p. 403) and Jews have a special calling to the profession.

2. "To employ Jewish doctors means nothing else than to cuddle serpents in our bosom and to raise wolves in our home," the clergy of Frankfurt declared in 1652 (Joshua Tractenburg, *The Devil and the Jew,* Harper & Row, New York, 1966, p. 94).

3. Cang, pp. 112–13.

4. Shostakovich, p. 147.

5. Baron, p. 94.

6. Gilboa, p. 81.

7. Author interview with Dr. Yakov Rapoport, February 19, 1989.

8. Ginzburg, *Within the Whirlwind,* p. 248. Dr. Walter Anton, husband of the author of this transcendent memoir, died of a trophic ulcer after release from the camps.

9. Emiot, 1981.

10. Solzhenitsyn, *The Gulag Archipelago,* p. 226.

11. Ibid., pp. 309–10.

12. Ginzburg, op. cit., p. 142.

13. Ibid, p. 271.

14. Ibid, p. 279.

15. Ibid, p. 314.

16. Ibid., pp. 190–91.

17. Gilboa, op. cit., p. 299.

18. Author interview with Vovsi-Mikhoels sisters, February 11, 1988.

19. The press did trumpet the story of two other traitorous doctor-scientists, the Jew Roskin and his Russian wife Klyuyeva, microbiologists engaged in cancer research. According to the reports, their discovery of a preparation called "KR" had filtered through to the West, and the couple was soon under attack for treason. A writer of Jewish origin, Alexander Shtein, won a Stalin Prize for his play about the affair, *The Court of Honor,* which drew huge audiences.

20. Author interview with Dr. Solomon Nezlin, December 18, 1988.

21. During his long career, Dimitrov had headed the Comintern, the Communist International, and the Popular Front in the 1930s. He gave up his Soviet citizenship after the war and became premier of Bulgaria in 1946.

22. Gilboa, op. cit., p. 299. The other signers were V. N. Vinogradov, Mayorov, Fiodorov, and Vasilenko.

23. Solomon Nezlin interview, December 18, 1988.

24. Solzhenitsyn, *First Circle,* p. 84.

25. David Gai, "The 'Doctors' Case,'" *Moscow News Weekly,* no. 6, 1988.

26. Author interview with Esther Markish, July 11, 1988; Markish, *The Long Return,* p. 169.

27. Solomon Nezlin interview, December 18, 1988.

28. Interview, as note 27.

29. Interview, as note 27.

30. Vovsi-Mikhoels sisters interview, February 11, 1989. At the hamlet, the widow of Dr. Sherishevski, one of the prominent Jewish doctors slain by Stalin during the Great Terror, tended a very special two-story dacha, built of stone instead of wood, where she lived year-round. When there was no answer at Dr. Etinger's neighboring dacha, the Mikhoels sisters assumed he had been arrested as part of the anti-cosmopolitan campaign.

31. Solomon Nezlin interview, December 18, 1988.

32. Interview, as note 31.

33. *Moscow News Weekly,* op. cit.

34. Alliluyeva, *Twenty Letters to a Friend,* p. 20.

35. Talbott, ed., *Khrushchev Remembers,* 1970 ed., p. 329.

36. Ibid., pp. 329–30.

37. Ibid., p. 223.

38. Tucker, p. 156.

39. The program was announced in 1948, but projects did not begin until the summer of 1950.

40. Author interview with Alexander Chakovsky, October 18, 1988.

41. Antonov-Ovsenko, p. 638.

42. De Jonge, p. 499.

43. Victor Alexandrov, p. 311.

44. Solzhenitsyn, *First Circle,* p. 125; Talbott, ed., *Khrushchev Remembers,* 1970 ed., p. 320.

45. Talbott, ed., *Khrushchev Remembers,* 1970 ed., p. 321.

46. Chakovsky interview, October 18, 1988.

47. The article "Is It Possible to Prolong Life?" by Abdulla Karaev reported on three hundred people in Baku, one of Stalin's pre-revolutionary stomping grounds, who "are distinguished by extraordinary old age."

48. National Archives, Washington, D.C., 861.2614/1–2150 File 1950–54, Box 5164.

49. Talbott, ed., *Khrushchev Remembers,* p. 285.

50. Gilboa, op. cit., p. 250.

51. *Pravda,* October 13, 1952. Stalin's only speech at the Congress, just seven minutes long, did not include bellicose language. He posed as the cool economic thinker discussing the socialist versus the capitalist market, and prophesying that England and France would come into conflict with the United States.

52. Author interview with Leonid Koriavin, October 18, 1988.

53. Talbott, ed., *Khrushchev Remembers,* 1970 ed., p. 297.

54. Ibid., appendix 4, p. 674.

55. Ibid., p. 298.

56. Ibid., p. 279.

57. Ibid., p. 300.

58. Ibid., p. 332.

59. Ibid., p. 293.

60. Author interview with David Markish, July 11, 1988.

61. The fate of Poskrebyshev's Jewish wife goes unrecorded. As

Khrushchev noted, Poskrebyshev certainly would have been executed had Stalin lived another few weeks. A friend of the Markish family, the late Professor Yakov Bruskin, met Posbrebyshev in the street during the Khrushchev years, carrying a big bundle under his arm. Poskrebyshev said it was his memoirs, and that he was on his way to donate it to the Marxist-Leninist Institute. Poskrebyshev died in a hospital in 1966, where "he was still boasting of his treacheries" until his last breath (Harrison Salisbury, letter to author, June 27, 1988).

62. Conquest, *Power and Policy in the USSR: The Study of Soviet Dynasties,* p. 173.

63. Roy Medvedev, *Let History Judge,* p. 477.

64. Cotic, p. 23ff. Otto Sling, a Jew who headed the second largest Party district in Czechoslovakia and was a veteran of the International Brigade in Spain, was the first to be arrested, in October 1950. His interrogator, Bohumik Doubek, told his men to "turn Sling into a pile of cowshit," which is what they did.

65. Ibid., pp. 78–79.

66. Gilboa, op. cit., p. 280.

67. Talbott, ed., *Khrushchev Remembers: The Last Testament,* p. 186.

68. Cotic, op. cit., p. 144.

69. *Rude Pravo,* November 30, 1952, quoted in Cotic.

70. Gilboa, op. cit., p. 269.

71. Cotic, op. cit., p. 115ff.

72. Ibid., p. 100ff.

73. Cotic, op. cit., p. 168.

74. Ibid., pp. 78–79. Slansky had once told Avriel, "When it comes to Jewish affairs, I must think twice in order to restrain my anti-Jewish feelings."

75. *Rude Pravo,* November 22, 1952, quoted by Cotic, p. 79.

76. Cotic, p. 85.

77. Gilboa, op. cit., p. 281. The two Israelis would stand trial themselves in August 1953 for alleged involvement in an American-Israeli plot against the Communists. Israeli Communists stuck to the party line. Meir Wilner, then and now a Knesset parliamentarian and leader of the Israeli Communist party, denied that there was any anti-Semitism in the socialist world and said: "It is not in Prague but in Tel Aviv that a campaign of anti-Jewish incitement is being conducted, by those who identify that filthy gang of spies with the Jewish people" (Cotic, p. 184).

78. Cotic, op. cit., p. 134.

79. Ibid., p. 150ff., p. 191.

80. Chakovsky, looking back from a 1988 perspective, would say that this "hyperbole" was simply reflective of the times, and that the cult of personality was only "an aberration" in Soviet history (Chakovsky interview, October 18, 1988). Chakovsky was finally dismissed in 1989 as editor of the multimillion-circulation literary journal and head of the Soviet Writers' Union.

81. *New Republic,* November 27, 1952.

82. *Ha'aretz,* December 18, 1952.

83. *New York Times,* November 23, 1952.

CHAPTER 9:   **The Arrest of the Kremlin Doctors**

1. David Gai, "The Doctors' Case," *Moscow News Weekly,* no. 6, 1988.

2. S. Badasch, letter to author, February 18, 1988.

3. Gai, "Doctors' Case," op. cit.

4. Ibid.

5. National Archives, Washington, D.C., 350USSR Secret Security Information no. 1033, January 14, 1953, from Beam to Secretary of State.

6. Talbott, ed., *Khrushchev Remembers,* 1970 ed., p. 302.

7. Ulam, p. 725.

8. Talbott, ed., *Khrushchev Remembers,* 1970 ed., p. 306.

9. Author interview with Natalia and Nina Vovsi-Mikhoels, February 4, 1988; Gai, "Doctors' Case," op. cit.

10. Vovsi-Mikhoels sisters interview, February 4, 1988.

11. Author interview with Dr. Yakov Rapoport, February 19, 1989.

12. Gai, "Doctors' Case," op. cit.

13. Roy Medvedev, *Let History Judge,* p. 494; and Khrushchev's Secret Speech, 1956. Khrushchev, Ignatiev's patron (some would view their relationship as more of a partnership between conspirators), recalled that "Stalin used to berate him viciously over the phone in our presence."

14. The account of Vovsi's interrogation has been drawn primarily from Vovsi-Mikhoels sisters interview, February 22, 1988; and from Dr. Rapoport's memoirs and his interview, February 19, 1989.

15. Dr. Vovsi would only relate details of his arrest and imprisonment to his family and close friends after Khrushchev's Secret Speech in 1956.

16. Gai, "Doctors' Case," op. cit.

17. Author interview with Alexander Chakovsky, October 18, 1988. Chakovsky, who held the same top post under Gorbachev until the spring of 1989, denied that there ever was such a letter: "You don't

know what you're talking about," he told me. Chakosky, though well tanked up after a literary reception in Boston followed by a steak dinner at the Harvard Club, was not about to confess to me that he was an accomplice in Mikhoels's murder and in Vovsi's torture, especially since he was a reluctant but leading conductor of Gorbachev's perestroika policy. To some minds, he is one of tens of thousands of old Stalinists—from the doddering Kaganovich down to the ex–torturers and executioners who worked in the Lubyanka basement—who should be put on trial, as Nazi war criminals have been. Harvard's Russian Studies Department debated whether to invite the old Stalinist to speak during his October 1988 visit, deciding to do so in the end.

18. Gai, "Doctors' Case," op. cit.

19. Vovsi-Mikhoels sisters interview, February 4, 1988.

20. In 1955, two years after Dr. Vovsi' release, one leg was amputated; in 1960 he died at age sixty-three of sarcoma of the leg, a cancer that was caused by the beatings.

21. Vovsi-Mikhoels sisters interview, op. cit.

22. Interview, as note 21.

23. Natalia Vovsi-Mikhoels interview, February 11, 1988.

24. Roy Medvedev, op. cit., p. 494; and Khrushchev's Secret Speech, 1956.

25. Talbott, ed., *Khrushchev Remembers,* 1970 ed., pp. 306–307.

26. Bortoli, p. 117ff. According to Khrushchev, Stalin said this in January or February 1953.

27. Talbott, ed., *Khrushchev Remembers,* 1970 ed., p. 305.

28. Ibid., p. 307.

29. Crankshaw's note in ibid., p. 302.

30. Talbott, ed., *Khrushchev Remembers,* p. 307.

31. Deutscher, *Stalin,* p. xvi.

32. Author interview with Lova Eliav, September 30, 1987.

33. Talbott, ed., *Khrushchev Remembers,* 1970 ed., p. 306; Seaton, pp. 167–68.

34. Gai, "Doctors' Case," op. cit.

35. Talbott, ed., *Khrushchev Remembers,* 1970 ed., p. 306.

CHAPTER 10: **Assassins in White Coats**

1. Author interview with Natalia Vovsi-Mikhoels, February 4, 1988.

2. *Pravda,* January 13, 1953.

3. Author interview with Alexander Chakovsky, October 18, 1988.

4. *Pravda,* op. cit.

5. Ibid.

6. Ibid.

7. *Izvestia,* January 13, 1953.

8. *Trud,* January 13, 1953.

9. *Literaturnaya Gazeta,* February 21, 1953.

10. *Pravda,* February 6, 1953.

11. *Meditainski Rabotnik,* January 30, 1953.

12. *Soviet Lithuania,* January 20, 1953.

13. *Krokodil,* January 30, 1953.

14. *New Times,* no. 4, January 21, 1953.

15. *Izvestia,* January 24, 1953.

16. *Pravda,* January 25, 1953.

17. *Kommunist,* January 14, 1953, pp. 46–58.

18. *Pravda Ukrainy,* January 16, 1953.

19. Vasiliyev was a top official in the Writers' Union, who made it almost impossible for Jewish writers to publish after 1949.

20. Boris Shcharansky's private papers, Jerusalem. Access granted to author by his widow, Ida Milgrom, and son, Natan Sharansky. Both the Donetsk newspaper and the *Pravda Ukrainy* in Kiev went after local Jewish doctors: chief gynecologist Lurie was condemned for not wanting to study complaints; Drs. Vasserman, Ravich, and Leertzman allegedly used the Nikolayev hospital as if it were their private clinic; Drs. Zaslavsky and Gendelman of the First Podolsk Hospital were negligent and harassed patients; Jewish doctors would only help patients if they were bribed; Drs. Rapoport and Kogan at the Donetsk tuberculosis hospital had given wrong treatment; Dr. Lattman at Lurie's clinic defended the right to make mistakes; medical professors like Kagan and Ehrlich at Kiev University did not have proper degrees, nor did Goredensky, Shvatberg, Poznonsky, etc. Once again, the doctors were all Jews; the victims were all Ukrainians or Russians.

21. Ehrenburg, vol. 6.

22. Author interview with Etel Kovinskaya, March 2, 1988.

23. Nadezhda Mandelstam, *Vtoraya kniga,* Paris, 1972, p. 432, quoted in De Jonge, p. 502.

24. Author interview with Ina Rubin, January 25, 1988.

25. Irina Kirk, *Profiles in Russian Resistance,* New York, Quadrangle, 1975, p. 166.

26. Author interview with the pharmacologist's daughter, Dina Beilin,

February 4, 1988. Dina Beilin, along with Anatoly Sharansky, became a leader of the Jewish emigration movement in the 1970s.

27. Gitelman, p. 240.

28. Author interview with David Yoffe, February 23, 1989.

29. Interview, as note 28.

30. Natalia Vovsi-Mikhoels interview, February 4, 1988.

31. Quoted in Gilboa, p. 308.

32. Natalia Vovsi-Mikhoels interview, February 4, 1988.

33. Public Record Office, Kew, England, FO371/106513 DO9553, January 27, 1953.

34. National Archives, Washington, D.C., 350USSR, January 18, 1953, letter from George Lister, Regensburg, Germany.

35. Ulam, pp. 634–35.

36. Djilas, p. 159.

37. Author interview with film director Mikhail Kollik, March 21, 1988. A close woman friend of Kollik's told him that her previous lover, Beria, was not perverted as far as she knew, but that it served Khrushchev's interests to portray him as a sexual maniac.

38. Interview, as note 37.

39. National Archives, Washington, D.C., 350USSR, Dispatch no. 202 from Dunn in Paris, Dept. no. 4008, January 16, 1953.

40. *Pravda,* January 13, 1953.

41. *Voprosy Leninizma,* 11th edition, p. 605; quoted by Andrei Vyshinsky, *Ucheniye Lenina-Stalina o proletarskoi revolyutsiy i gosudarstve,* Moscow, 1947, p. 89.

42. National Archives, Washington, D.C., 350USSR, Dispatch no. 13, from Thayer in Munich, Dept. no. 381, January 21, 1953.

43. Dzhirkvelov, p. 141.

44. National Archives, Washington, D.C., 350USSR, Dispatch no. 12, from Thayer in Munich, Dept. no. 3801, January 21, 1953.

45. Public Record Office, FO371/106513 DO9553.

46. National Archives, Washington, D.C., 761.00/10–251 XR601.84a61, from George Lister in Moscow, October 2, 1951.

47. Prime Minister's Office Archives, Jerusalem, Source 41112/aleph, File 2410/19, "Doch 3/53, Inyan Ha'rofim vparashat ha'iranut."

48. Prime Minister's Office Archives, Jerusalem, Source 4115/aleph, File 2410/21/aleph, February 4, 1953, message from Gideon Raphael, New York; and "Notes of a Conversation Between Mr. William Epstein and Mr. Pavel F. Shakov, both of the U.N. Secretariat"; Harrison Salisbury, letter to author, June 27, 1988.

Israeli intelligence would become effective in the USSR only after Stalin's death and the "thaw" under Khrushchev.

49. Ibid., Source 41112/aleph, File 2410/19, February 10, 1953.

50. *Kommunist,* January 14, 1953, p. 46ff; and "Soviet Warning on Security," *London Times,* January 23, 1953.

51. National Archives, Washington, D.C., 350USSR, January 14, 1953, Dispatch no. 181, from Bonn, Dept. no. 3240.

52. Public Record Office FO371/1063513 DO9553, January 16, 1953, Gascoigne to Eden, Confidential no. 13.

53. Ibid., January 13, 1953, Minutes.

54. Ibid. But Gascoigne's British colleagues continued to disagree with his analyses, albeit in the most polite tones, saying that "like ourselves, Sir A. Gascoigne still has an open mind about the real motives behind the arrest of these doctors."

55. National Archives, Washington, D.C., 350USSR, Dulles, Dept. no. 622, undated, but presumably in January 1953.

56. Public Record Office FO371/106513 DO9553, January 16, 1953, no. 13, 101.7/3/53.

57. Ibid., January 15, 1953, no. 13, 101.7/2/53.

58. There was some exchange of information between the British and Israeli foreign ministries over the affair, agreed upon by Anthony Eden and Dr. Walter Eytan, including one of Harry Hohler's reports, "Attacks on Jews Behind the Iron Curtain."

59. Prime Minister's Office Archives, Jerusalem, Source 41112/aleph File 2410/19, February 4, 1953.

60. Public Record Office FO371/106513 DO9553, March 3, 1953, Grey to Hohler.

61. Mandelstam, p. 313.

62. Gitelman, p. 239ff.

63. Goldberg, p. 147.

64. Emiot, p. 126ff.

65. Ginzburg, *Within the Whirlwind,* p. 350ff.

66. Ibid., p. 345.

67. The Joint's director of relief activities, David Weingard, for example, had met with Mikhoels and Feffer in Moscow in August and September 1945, to discuss Soviet complaints that Soviet Jews were getting preferential treatment in receiving aid packages (JDC Archives, New York: Russian Food Packages File no. 426, letter from Weingard to James Rosenberg, November 20, 1945).

68. JDC Archives, New York, AR4564.3280.

69. A caricature that illustrated the January 14 *Volks Shtimme* article portrayed a Jewish doctor with a gun labeled "U.S." in his belt and a vial of poison in one hand, holding in the other hand a dummy with a Joint collection box around his neck. The caption read, "With the song 'Good-hearted Jews, help!' the Joint wanted to mask its murderous practice of poisoning people and spying." At the top of the drawing appeared a paragraph from the *Pravda* report that tied the majority of the arrested doctors to the Joint (JDC Archives, New York, AR4564.3280–1).

70. This was the first mention of Ehrlich and Alter, executed a dozen years earlier, in the Communist press reports about the vast conspiracy.

71. The Eastern Europeans followed the cues of the Soviet media, whose focus on the Joint included an article in *New Times* of January 21 headlined, "The Zionist Agency of the American Intelligence Service." It said that in addition to the Kremlin doctors' espionage ring, the Joint ran extensive spy operations in Hungary. In actual fact, the Joint's welfare work in Hungary included large-scale aid to 10,000 Hungarian Jews (JDC Archives, New York, AR4564.3280).

72. JDC Archives, Gen. Moscow, Attacks on JDC, Rosenberg to Warburg, January 23, 1953.

73. Ibid.

74. National Archives, Washington, D.C., 761.00/2–1753, Box 3806, February 17, 1953, Dulles 06413.

75. The tale has been told best by David Wyman, *The Abandonment of the Jews,* Pantheon, New York, 1985, and Arthur Morse, *While Six Million Died,* Random House, New York, 1967.

76. Sartre and his associates "expressed bewilderment" at Moscow's action, which had "kicked the fellow travelers at Vienna in the face" (National Archives, Washington, D.C., 350USSR, January 16, 1953, Message no. 17, to Walworth Barbour). Sartre's newspaper, the fellow-traveling *Liberation,* was unusually cautious, a British diplomat noted. The paper said that if the accusations against the doctors were false, then those making them must be judged severely, but if they were true, then the doctors were guilty of a crime comparable to the use of biological warfare in Korea—which the Communists and their supporters claimed the West was engaged in. The paper said accusations of anti-Semitism in Russia were groundless (Public Record Office FO371/106513 D09553, Outward Telegram no. 14, January 15, 1953).

77. Mapam split on the Israeli Communist party motion to take no action on the issue, which was supported by the pro-Communist

Sneh faction and opposed by the Chazan-Yaari and Achdut Avoda factions. Most Israeli Communists, devoted Stalinists, repeated Moscow's line that "Israel is the new land of the dollar, where Yankee banking and financial interests control the reins of the economy, and the Israeli Zionist organizations find it simple to direct their espionage and sabotage activities against the world of socialism" (Prime Minister's Office Archives, Jerusalem, Source 41112/aleph File 2410/19).

78. *London Times,* January 24, 1953.

79. The Arabs obviously saw it differently. Arab diplomats in Washington told the State Department that they were worried that the Soviet purges would damage Arab-Western relations "through increased sympathy on part of West for Israel" (National Archives, Washington, D.C., 761.00/2–1953, Box 3806, Airgram 2699, February 27, 1953). The press and radio in much of the Arab world saw a Zionist hand behind the Soviet purge of Jews: the Iraqi newspaper *Ad Difaa* said on February 7 that the Doctors' Plot was the result of "a Zionist conspiracy to force the Soviets to persecute Jews in order to make Jews flee Russia and swell the number of refugees for Israel." Radio Damascus, in a January 27 broadcast to Israel, said that the recent purges directed against Jews were actually Western and Jewish devices to save Israel from bankruptcy. The well-known Syrian statesman Faris al-Khuri, speaking on Jordanian radio, said that all acts committed by the Jews so far showed the world "their bad intention wherever they are and wherever they settle." He added that "these Jewish criminal acts aim at destroying the world and at strengthening world Jewry" (National Archives, Washington, D.C., 761.00/2–1953, Box 3806, Airgram 2699, February 27, 1953).

80. *Szabad Nep*, January 15, 1953.

81. Quoted by the B.B.C. on January 16, 1953. Public Record Office FO371/106513 D09553.

82. Deriabin, p. 323.

83. UPI dispatch from Berlin, January 27, 1953, by Joseph W. Grigg: "East German Jews Fear Worse Red Terror."

84. JDC Archives, New York: Russian Food Packages File no. 426, October 4, 1944, letter to Joseph Hyman from J. A. Rosen; October 23, 1944, cable for Judah Magnes, Jerusalem—JDC Russian file 2100.

CHAPTER 11: **The Jews Brace for Exile**

1. Author interview with Dr. Yakov Rapoport, February 19, 1988.

2. Interview, as note 1; Antonov-Ovsenko, pp. 290–91; Roy Medvedev, *Let History Judge,* p. 496.

3. Harrison Salisbury, letter to author, June 27, 1988.

4. Hahn, p. 153

5. Alexander Nekrich, *Otreshis ot strakha,* London, Overseas Publications Interchange, 1979, p. 114. Nekrich, the highly respected Harvard historian, worked at the Moscow History Institute at the time of the Doctors' Plot. In 1949 Chesnokov had been chief editor of the Institute of Philosophy's journal *Voprosy filosofii,* which was a major organ in Stalin's battle against thought. Chesnokov lost all his posts upon Stalin's death.

6. Antonov-Ovsenko, op. cit., p. 291.

7. Tucker, p. 97.

8. In pre-revolutionary days, Zaslavsky (who was seventy-two in 1953) had once been labeled by Lenin as a "notorious slanderer" and "a blackmailing pen for hire."

9. Baron, p. 324.

10. Antonov-Ovsenko, op. cit., p. 325; Medvedev, op. cit., p. 496.

11. The main sources are Ehrenburg's conversations with Mikhoels's daughters and Esther Markish (author interviews, cited throughout). There is also a scanty version in Ehrenburg's memoirs (Ehrenburg, *Men, Years, Life,* vol. 6).

12. Author interview with Professor Ilia Serman and Ruth Serman, March 3, 1988.

13. Author interview with Esther Markish, July 11, 1988; Markish, *The Long Return,* p. 175.

14. Ibid. In many interviews, the same question was posed: Who signed and who didn't? Perhaps there were more than four Jews who refused to sign, but it is doubtful.

15. Ewa Berard-Zarzycka, "Ehrenburg in Post-War USSR," *Soviet Jewish Affairs,* vol. 17, no. 1, Spring, 1987, p. 45.

16. There are conflicting stories about the way Ehrenburg refused to sign, and who the messengers were. "Mints and Marinin," according to Berard-Zarzycka (ibid.); the ailing Lev Mekhlis or the editor of *Pravda,* according to others. Yet another version says that propaganda chief M. B. Mitin presented the draft statement to Ehrenburg with a list of some of the signatures that had already been obtained. He supposedly pointed to Kaganovich's name, which was crossed out in red pencil, and hinted that Stalin had done this to exempt his pet Jew (Roman Brackman, "Stalin's Failed Massacre," *Midstream,* December 1987).

17. Esther Markish interview, July 11, 1988. Khrushchev offered yet another version of Ehrenburg's role in his taped memoirs—in which he often confused or obfuscated names, facts, and dates. He recalled that "at one point Stalin wanted to have a statement published in

the press to the effect that there was no anti-Semitism in the Soviet Union. He ordered Kaganovich and Ehrenburg to join in drafting the statement. He particularly wanted their signatures on it, even though he had no shortage of people to sign it. Kaganovich squirmed around a lot but of course ended up signing, since he did everything Stalin told him. But to the best of my recollection—and I don't want to make a mistake here—Ehrenburg categorically refused to sign" (Talbott, ed., *Khrushchev's Remembers: The Last Testament,* pp. 77–78). Khrushchev's blurring of the statement's contents seems intentional.

18. Berard-Zarzycka, op. cit., p. 47. The writer of the article said that the original letter is in a private archive.

19. Serman interview, March 3, 1988.

20. *Kommunist,* February 16, 1953.

21. Ulam, pp. 439, 443.

22. *Komsomolskaya Pravda,* July 8, 1964.

23. Koestler, p. 65.

24. Ibid.

25. Antonov-Ovsenko, op. cit., p. 291. According to Yakov Soroker's biography of Oistrakh, published in Jerusalem in 1982, the violinist, though he once performed at a memorial for Mikhoels, played down his Jewish origins and married a Russian woman. But he did sign several JAC appeals during the war years. In 1953 he was awarded the title People's Artist of the USSR.

26. Esther Markish learned from Ehrenburg that Blanter, Dolmatovsky, and Nezhny signed; interview with author, July 11, 1988.

27. Gilboa, p. 49. The Nazis had warned Soviet soldiers, in effective radio broadcasts, not to entrust their lives to "Yankel Kreiser."

28. Khrushchev described Kreiser as a personal friend, according to Leneman, p. 227. In 1956 the ex-general signed a similar kind of Jewish statement, a "public protest" against Israel's actions during the Suez crisis.

29. Mandelstam, p. 115.

30. Yad Vashem Archives, Jerusalem, Ehrenburg Collection, Letter 473. Ehrenburg died in 1967, but the existence of the letters, and the fact that he had arranged for them to be brought to the archives at the Holocaust Memorial in Israel, were not revealed until 1988. The choice of the letters he left shows his wish not only to preserve something of the spirit of the times, but also to indicate how difficult it was for him to refrain from adding his voice to the condemnations.

31. Ibid., Letter 471.

32. Ibid., Letter 474.

33. Ibid., Letter 483.

34. Ibid., Letter 480.

35. Ibid., Letter 482.

36. Ehrenburg, *Men, Years, Life,* op. cit., vol. 6.

37. Ibid.

38. National Archives, Washington, D.C., 350 USSR, Telegram no. 1089, from Beam to Secretary of State, January 28, 1953.

39. Ehrenburg, *Men, Years, Life,* op. cit.

40. Harrison Salisbury, *An American in Russia,* Harper, New York, 1955, p. 284.

41. Author interview with Aharon Ben Daniel, February 23, 1989. The sexton, Reuben Ben Avraham, and congregants of the Gori synagogue would only identify themselves by their Hebrew names.

42. Interview, as note 41.

43. Author interview with Lova Eliav, September 30, 1987. Eliav's information about the genocide plan came during the Khrushchev era from veteran Communist officials who were Jews, including former high-ranking servicemen. "They were less afraid to talk in places like Yalta than in Moscow or Leningrad. Those who had links to the military-industrial complex spelled out to me the designs and actual plans for genocide. No one gave me a full picture; it came in bits and pieces. At first I thought it exaggerated, but *hundreds* told me, from so many walks of life. It was no rumor. Plans were in various stages of implementation."

44. Gitelman, op. cit., p. 5.

45. Tucker, pp. xii, 43.

46. Eliav interview, September 30, 1987.

47. Prime Minister's Office Archives, Jerusalem, Source 41112/aleph, File 2410/19.

48. Goldman suggested coordination between B'nai B'rith and the government "to prevent or deter a Soviet campaign in that direction." But the State Department officials explained that since the Soviets were charging that the U.S.A. used Jewish organizations for espionage, such a joint effort "might be counter-productive in tending to suggest confirmation of such a relationship" (National Archives, Washington, D.C., FW 761.00/2–353, Box 3806, Dept. of State Memo of Conversation, February 3, 1953).

49. Talbott, ed., *Khrushchev Remembers,* 1970 ed., p. 258ff.

50. Ibid.

51. Historian Robert Conquest, though conceding that "the plan to deport the Jews to Siberia is very sketchily evidenced," believes the plan "seems true enough" (letter to author, February 11, 1987).

52. Eliav interview, September 30, 1987.

53. Goldberg, pp. 148–49.

54. *Trud,* February 14, 1953.

55. Brackman, "Stalin's Failed Massacre," op. cit.

56. One squadron, which refused to strafe Cossack villages, was disbanded and half its members executed. An entire OGPU regiment was annihilated and thousands of bodies floated down the rivers (Conquest, *Harvest of Sorrow,* pp. 156).

57. Leneman, pp. 137–38.

58. Brackman, "Stalin's Failed Massacre," op. cit.

59. Author interview with Professor Edith Frenkel, October 25, 1987.

60. Author interview with Vladimir Lifshitz, November 9, 1987. Lifshitz would revisit Siberia twenty years later, not as a touring engineer, but as a Jewish prisoner of conscience.

61. Antonov-Ovsenko, op. cit., p. 325ff.

62. Ibid.

63. Bortoli, p. 115.

64. Nadezhda Mandelstam, *Hope Abandoned,* Penguin, London, 1976, p. 501.

65. Harrison Salisbury, letter to author, June 27, 1988.

66. Ginzburg, *Within the Whirlwind,* p. 345ff.

67. J. Berger, *Shipwreck of a Generation,* Harvill Press, London, 1971, pp. 131–32.

68. Author interview with Esther and David Markish, July 11, 1988.

69. Interview, Esther and David Markish, July 11, 1988.

70. Medvedev, *On Stalin and Stalinism,* p. 148.

71. Esther and David Markish interview, July 11, 1988.

72. Ibid.

CHAPTER 12:   **A Pack of Wolves**

1. *Pravda,* February 14, 1953, article by Yuri Zhukov.

2. Prime Minister's Office Archives, Jerusalem, Source 41112/aleph, File 2410/19.

3. Ibid.

4. *Pravda Ukrainy,* February 12, 13. *Pravda Ukrainy's* February 13 article, under the heading "Zionists Are the Accursed Foes of the Working People," went to fantastic lengths to implicate Jewish lawyers, rabbis, and American and Joint officials in a scheme supposedly financed by "Tomashoff Baruch, a relative of the wealthy

American 'atom-monger' [presidential adviser Bernard] Baruch,"
in a hoary incident that was now linked to the Slansky case and the
affair of the doctors. A February 16 article in the same paper attacked Ukraine health minister Shupik and numerous Jewish doctors for "carelessness and unprincipled administration."

5. National Archives, Washington, D.C., 350USSR EMBTEL 1129,
   Moscow Embassy to SECSTATE from Beam, February 6, 1953.

6. Dzhirkvelov, p. 255ff.

7. Public Record Office, Kew, England, FO371/106513 D09553
   Ns1017/16, no. 63, February 10, 1953, from Moscow to Foreign
   Office.

8. Gilboa, pp. 316–17.

9. Author interview with Esther Markish, July 11, 1988; Markish, *The
   Long Return*, pp. 235–36.

10. *Pravda*, January 21, 1953.

11. Dzhirkvelov, op. cit., p. 252.

12. National Archives, Washington, D.C., 350 USSR, Embassy Tele-
    gram no. 1203, February 20, 1953; *Pravda*, February 20, 1953.

13. *Pravda*, February 20, 1953.

14. Ibid.

15. From the article, which appeared in *Medical Worker* on February
    24, it could be learned that Lydia's heroic pilot son did not die, as the
    Pravda article had intimated. The writer, Elena Kononenko, also
    described some of the thousands of letters and telegrams pouring
    into Moscow in praise of Timashuk. The article vilified the criminals
    in white coats who ganged up to "coldly ridicule the medical conclu-
    sion of Lydia Feodosevna and call into question her political matu-
    rity and even honor."

16. Louis Harap, "Stalin and the Jewish People," *Jewish Life* maga-
    zine, April 1953.

17. National Archives, Washington, D.C., 761.00/2–1753, Box 3806.
    They said that "the potential danger of physical violence to the
    3,000,000 Jews in these countries is a real one. . . . During the Hitler
    period the civilized world, caught by surprise, unable to believe that
    mass extermination could be a realizable objective, did little to stop
    it. Today, with that ghastly record in mind, we have no excuse for
    procrastination."

18. National Archives, 761.00/2–1753, Box 3806, Hendrickson resolu-
    tion.

19. National Archives, 761.00/2–1453, Box 3806, Cable 1171, February
    14, 1953.

20. Zionist Archives, Jerusalem, File Z6/758.

21. Nahum Goldmann's letters from this period show he was far more concerned about collecting press clippings that mentioned him, and writing to British publisher George Weidenfeld about his autobiography (Zionist Archives, Jerusalem, File Z6/758, vols. 1 and 2).

22. Author interview with Aryeh Levavi, March 13, 1989. American Jewish organizations were more attuned to the realities and decided to act quickly, staging a mass protest rally in New York on February 17, in which they demanded that the Soviets end the anti-Semitic campaign and allow Soviet Jews to emigrate to Israel (*New York Times,* February 18, 1953).

23. A week earlier, a Soviet bookshop in Jerusalem had been fire-bombed; but the Soviet minister in Tel Aviv, Pavel Ivanovich Yershov, had refused the Israeli government's offer of a police guard. The Soviets fired all Jewish staffers at the legislation on February 2.

24. Prime Minister's Office Archives, Jerusalem, Source 41112/aleph File 2410/19, "Israel Government an Accomplice in the Crime Against the Soviet Embassy in Tel Aviv," February 11, 1953, Soviet dispatch.

25. The ideological head of the former supernationalist terror group, Israel Eldad, helped plan the operation, according to Tel Aviv lawyer Ya'acov Heruti, who served three years in prison for his role in the bombing (author interview with Heruti, March 29, 1989). Heruti, who was in his early twenties in 1953, says he never regretted his action. The explosives were manufactured by the Stern group veterans: "We had loads of them." Eighteen Israelis, all members of the "Anti-Communist League," were charged on February 15 with planting the bomb or with conspiracy.

26. *Jerusalem Post,* February 13, 1953.

27. Ibid.

28. *Pravda,* February 14, 1953.

29. *Izvestia,* February 24, 1953.

30. Dr. Eliashiv, the head of the mission, told Scandinavian reporters that although Soviet anti-Semitism could in no way be compared to the Nazi type, the Jews were the only Soviet nationality whose national and cultural life had been stopped entirely, putting them in a highly vulnerable position (Prime Minister's Office Archives, Jerusalem, Source 41112/aleph File 2410/19). Of course, neither he nor any other Israeli diplomat had heard a word about the frantic preliminary preparations for the deportation of the Jews (Levavi interview, March 13, 1989).

31. *Manchester Guardian,* March 2, 1953.

32. Gilboa, op. cit., p. 318.

33. JDC Archives, New York, AR4564.328; Zionist Archives, Jerusalem, S41/447, March 5, 1953, letter from Solomon Kalderon and Dr. Albert Vaja to Zionist Central Archives.

34. Menon recounts this singular meeting in detail in his memoir *The Flying Troika,* London, 1963.

35. As in P. Simonov's play *The Russian Question,* in which American spies and "bourgeois nationalists" are shown trying to kill the noble leader of a collective farm.

36. Talbott, ed., *Khrushchev Remembers,* 1970 ed., p. 174.

37. Medvedev, *Let History Judge,* p. 345.

38. Ulam, p. 447.

39. In the 1930s this coarse, ignorant man succeeded the cultured Bukharin as editor of *Pravda;* his main qualification was that in 1927 he wrote an article entitled "Under the Wise Direction of our Great Genius Leader and Teacher Stalin." In 1937 he added the editorship of *Izvestia* to his journalistic achievements. Stalin sent him to Nazi Berlin in May 1937 to obtain documents used to condemn and execute Marshal Tukachevsky and his associates. Whether in his capacity as *Pravda*'s editor, or as chief army political general during World War II, he had "a particularly strong influence on Stalin" and had caused uncountable deaths as one of the tyrant's chief instruments of death, according to Khrushchev's memoir (1970 ed., p. 174). He was a dangerous, ill-natured man "of a destructive turn of mind" (Seaton, p. 116). Ulam writes that Mekhlis in the Crimea "terrorized the local commander, issued conflicting orders and greatly contributed to the Soviet debacle" (p. 566). Only one source, the Jewish historian Ainsztein, disagrees with the general assessment of Mekhlis's military abilities, contending that "he played a most important role in preventing the collapse of the Red Army" (Ainsztein, p. 200).

40. Gilboa, p. 251.

41. Payne, p. 668; Alexandrov, p. 325. However, Poskrebyshev himself had already fallen into disgrace before this time, and was not likely to have been sent on any mission at all.

42. Avtorkhanov, *The Reign of Stalin,* p. 197.

43. *Pravda,* February 14, 1953.

44. Public Record Office, Kew, England, FO371/10116576 009552, Minutes to S1571/2, February 14, 1953. Other diplomats thought Mekhlis probably died a natural death.

45. Public Record Office, FO371/106576 009552, Dispatch 1853/2/53 Ns 1571/3, February 18, 1953.

46. *Pravda,* February 16, 1953.

47. Public Record Office, Kew, England, FO371/106576 009552 Dispatch 1853/2/53 Ns 1571/3, February 18, 1953.

48. National Archives, Washington, D.C., 350 USSR, Foreign Service Dispatch 2283, from George L. West, Bonn, to Dept of State, February 4, 1953.

49. National Archives, Washington, D.C., 350 USSR, Dispatch no. 13, from Thayer in Munich to State Dept., January 21, 1953.

50. *Jerusalem Post,* February 14, 1989.

51. "I don't think that the Third World War theory makes much sense. Stalin was crazy all right but crazy like a fox" (Harrison Salisbury, letter to author, August 2, 1988).

52. Kennan, *Russia, the Atom and the West,* Harper, New York, 1958, p. 53.

53. Conquest, *Power and Policy in the USSR,* p. 170.

54. Ibid., p. 172.

55. Public Record Office, Kew, England, FO371/106513 D09553, March 3, 1953, Paul Grey to H. A. F. Hohler.

56. Ibid.

57. Deriabin, p. 318. French intelligence reports closely paralleled British Foreign Office thinking, saying, "There is no (repeat no) evidence of military dispositions or stockpiling indicating that the Kremlin is planning any new aggressive moves" (National Archives, Washington, D.C., 761.00/3-353, Telegram 4879 from Paris to Secretary of State, March 3, 1953). But if Stalin was planning war, he was not about to jeopardize the Soviet population by any obvious maneuvers. He was paving the way slowly, in his usual manner. The war would come in its time.

58. *Pravda,* February 10, 1946.

59. Trepper, *The Great Game: The Story of the Red Orchestra,* p. 356.

60. Yitzhak Ro'i, p. 104ff.

61. Ibid.

62. Issac Deutscher, *Russia—What Next?,* New York, Oxford University Press, 1953, p. 192.

63. Public Record Office, Kew, England, FO371/106513 DO9553.

64. National Archives, Washington, D.C., 350 USSR, Dispatch 184 from London to State Dept., January 21, 1953. Harrison Salisbury believes that "those army changes in February 1953 are of course

significant. Unfortunately I do not possess the key. Maybe in today's Moscow the puzzle will be made public" (Salisbury, letter to author, June 27, 1988).

65. Conquest, *Power and Policy in the USSR,* op. cit., p. 168.
66. Sokolovsky's appointment was divulged in a typical Soviet manner—in the title he was given on invitations that foreign attaches received on February 21 to Armed Forces Day celebrations set for February 23 (National Archives, 350 USSR, Dispatch 1206, February 21, 1953, from Beam in Moscow to Secretary of State).
67. Seaton, p. 127.
68. Deriabin, p. 239.
69. Talbott, ed., *Khrushchev,* 1970 ed., p. 363ff.
70. National Archives, 350 USSR, Dispatch 8, from Thayer in Munich, January 19, 1953.
71. National Archives, 350 USSR, Dispatch 2283, from George L. West, Jr., Bonn, to Dept. of State, February 4, 1953.
72. De Jonge, pp. 146, 497.
73. Conquest, *Power and Policy in the USSR,* op. cit., p. 167.

CHAPTER 13: *Purimshpiel*

1. Ulam, p. 582.
2. Talbott, ed., *Khrushchev Remembers,* 1970 ed., p. 313.
3. Author interview with Savely Dudakov, July 13, 1988. Even long after Stalin's death, the particular prejudice against Jewish women was widespread in the Soviet Union. The popular anti-Semitic novel *Nabat* (Tocsin), by Ivan Shevtsov, "revealed" the existence of a secret spy school in Tel Aviv that trained beautiful Jewish girls to become the wives of prospective leaders in the Third World. In an earlier book, the same author said that such a network existed in the USSR and that Brezhnev was one of its victims (Mikhail Agursky, "The 'Demon Jew' and the Soviets," *Jerusalem Post,* February 2, 1989).
4. Gilboa, p. 329.
5. Talbott, ed., *Khrushchev Remembers,* 1970 ed., p. 163.
6. Alliluyeva, *Only One Year,* p. 401.
7. Ibid., p. 170.
8. Roy Medvedev leads the school of thought that believes there was no evidence of a plot against Stalin. Aleksandr M. Nekrich and Mikhail L. Heller agree: "Stalin died a natural death" (Heller and Nekrich,

p. 507). Professor Robert Tucker leads the school that believes Stalin's death was speeded by human hands.

9. The main version of the story was revealed on June 7, 1957, in an article by Michel Gordey in *France-Soir,* based on information from a former Stalin aide and key Khrushchev protégé, Panteleimon Ponomarenko. During the war Ponomarenko headed the Central Committee in White Russia. He and Khrushchev had been ordered to work out an exchange of populations with the Polish provisional government toward the war's end. He was then appointed Soviet ambassador in Warsaw. After Khrushchev revealed some of Stalin's crimes at the 1956 Twentieth Congress, Ponomarenko served as the Soviet ruler's main source for leaks to the West about Stalin's last days. Khrushchev made sure that Beria, who was executed a few months after Stalin's death, would share the opprobrium for the tyrant's last plot.

10. *France-Soir; New York Times,* June 8, 1957. Both Ponomarenko and Khrushchev attended the last meeting with Stalin. Khrushchev, the original source of the *France-Soir* story, had already offered a variation on the same theme as the Ponomarenko story—also in an indirect manner. The *Times* of London reported in April 1956 that shortly after the Twentieth Congress, Khrushchev told a smaller Party meeting about the Doctors' Plot and Stalin's deportation plans for Soviet Jewry. Stalin had become more and more inflamed against the Jews, Khrushchev reportedly said. "His rage grew until, just before his stroke in March, he told a meeting of Soviet leaders that he had decided to gather all the [Jewish] community together and transport them to a northern region within a new pale. Mikoyan and Molotov both protested, saying that such an act would cause indignation abroad. Marshal Voroshilov declared that the proposal was criminal, the kind of outrage that had roused the world against Hitler. Stalin worked himself into a fury and the next that was known was that he had his stroke." The *Times* correspondent thought the story significant because it was being passed along to East European Communist leaders. A major difference between the first two versions of the story was the timing of Stalin's attack—at the meeting itself or shortly afterward. Another variation was the location where the Jews were to be exiled—Central Asia and Birobidzhan or Siberia. According to both reports it was Voroshilov's brave, defiant move that brought on Stalin's apoplexy.

11. Khrushchev tried a third time to get the story out. Three months after the *France-Soir* story appeared, he told a visiting American Christian sociologist, Dr. Jerome Davis, that he had "saved" the Jews from exile in Siberia and that by his opposition, together with

other members of the Party Politburo, he had "forced Stalin to stay his hand" (London *Times,* September 8, 1959, p. 11).

12. *France-Soir,* June 7, 1957.

13. Robert Tucker, letter to author, September 14, 1988.

14. The means were there, despite all of his food tasters and thousands of bodyguards. The technical department of the secret police supplied its operatives and agents with a variety of items like pens or fake cigarettes which could fire lethal doses of poison. The poison used left no traces in the body of the victim and produced the effect of a stroke, a heart attack, or suffocation (Dzhirkvelov, p. 51).

15. Alliluyeva, *Twenty Letters,* p. 212.

16. Ibid., pp. 6–7.

17. Ibid., p. 10.

18. Talbott, ed., *Khrushchev Remembers,* 1970 ed., p. 341ff.

19. Author interview with Dr. Yakov Rapoport, February 19, 1989.

20. National Archives, Washington, D.C., 350USSR, 370.31, Box 178, Beam to SECSTATE, March 4, 1953.

21. The Purim festival is marked for one day in the Diaspora, and two in walled Jewish cities like Jerusalem.

22. Gilboa, p. 330.

23. Alliluyeva, *Twenty Letters,* op. cit., p. 23.

24. As a British intelligence gatherer in Moscow put it: "The rapidity with which an agreement was reached, even on details, suggests . . . that when it came to the point there was no serious difference of opinion between Malenkov, Beria, Molotov, and other principals . . . including, incidentally, Kaganovich, the Jew" (Public Record Office, Kew, England, FO371/106513 Ns 1017/26, from Paul Grey to Hohler, March 12, 1953).

25. National Archives, Washington, D.C., 350USSR, May 21, 1953, Dispatch no. 480, Elim O'Shaughnessy to Dept. of State.

26. Anatoly Sharansky, *Fear No Evil,* New York, Random House, 1988, p. x.

27. Ginzburg, *Within the Whirlwind,* p. 352ff.

28. Author interview with Natalia Vovsi-Mikhoels, February 22, 1988.

29. Interview, as note 28.

30. Ehrenburg wrote: "The buildings of Warsaw, reduced to ashes and now reborn, donned mourning: In New York upright people, surrounded by police, informers and ruffians, spoke with sadness: 'The friend of peace has died. . . . Our grief has become the grief of mankind. . . . It was he who helped the people prevent a new war, he

who protected millions of children, thousands of cities" (*Pravda*, March 11, 1953).

31. Alliluyeva, *Only One Year,* p. 156.

32. Salisbury, *Stalin's Russia and After.*

33. *Pravda,* March 28, 1953.

34. Ibid., April 4, 1953.

35. The list of Kremlin physicians read: Professors M. S. Vovsi, V. N. Vinogradov, M. B. Kogan, B. B. Kogan, P. I. Yegorov, A. I. Feldman, Y. G. Etinger, V. H. Vasilenko, A. M. Grinshtein, V. F. Zelenin, B. S. Preobrazhensky, N. A. Popova, V. V. Zakusov, N. A. Shereshevsky, and Dr. G. I. Mayorov. Of the six doctors whose arrest had not been previously reported, four—Vasilenko, Zelenin, Preobrazhensky, and Zakusov—were members of the Academy of Medical Sciences. Professor Vasilenko was one of those who had signed the bulletin announcing Zhdanov's death. Professor Zakusov had been a Soviet delegate to the UN Social and Economic Commission.

36. Gilboa, p. 334.

37. According to one of the released "accomplices," Dr. Solomon Nezlin (author interview, December 18, 1988), Timashuk was still alive in the early 1980s and living in Moscow.

38. National Archives, Washington, D.C., 350 USSR, Cable no. 1418 to SECSTATE, April 4, 1953.

39. Rapoport interview, February 19, 1989. The *New York Times,* in an editorial on Sunday, May 15, 1988, commenting on the publication in Moscow of Dr. Rapoport's memoirs, noted the "macabre sequence" in which the doctor-poisoners were "seized, tortured, then asked for advice about the illness of the dictator."

40. *New York Times,* May 13, 1988, p. 1, and Sunday, May 15, 1988.

41. *Pravda,* April 6, 1953.

42. Khrushchev would protect Ignatiev in the coming purges and executions of Beria's men in the second half of 1953, and he was instrumental in installing another person loyal to him, Ponomarenko, as Central Committee secretary in the semi-disgraced Ignatiev's place in late May or early June.

43. Dzhirkvelov, p. 143.

44. *Pravda,* April 6, 1953.

45. Talbott, ed., *Khrushchev Remembers,* 1970 ed., p. 340.

46. *Pravda,* April 6, 1953. The article said that "capitalist encirclement" still existed and that the capitalists would continue to send spies and diversionists to undermine the USSR.

47. Public Record Office, Kew, England, FO371/106513 D09553 Ns1017/25 Minutes no. 220, April 7, 1953. *Pravda*'s, April 6 article cited Ryumin and Ignatiev's other MGB subordinates as having "tried to kindle feelings of racial hatred. . . . such a criminal acts of hidden enemies of the people could not remain and shall not remain unpunished." The paper said that the Soviet people had greeted the reversal with great satisfaction, certain that the government, by "boldly revealing deficiencies in the state machinery" and owning up to them, had proven the "great strength of the Soviet State, of the socialist system." *Pravda* declared that "the Soviet Government openly and directly speaks about [shortcomings] to the people."

48. One Foreign Office official wrote: "The only logical inference which the Soviet people can draw is that the arrest of the doctors came on Stalin's direct orders, and as a result of some persecution mania" (Public Record Office, Kew, England, FO371/106513, D09553, Ns1017/25, April 7, 1953, Minutes no. 220, from H. T. Morgan).

49. Ibid., Ns1017/23, April 13, 1953, from H. T. Morgan.

50. *New York Times* editorial, May 15, 1988.

51. *Pravda,* April 6–8, 11, 17, 19, 1953.

52. *Réalités,* May 1957.

53. Goldberg, pp. 145–46.

54. In 1956 Khrushchev reportedly said that Mikoyan had killed Beria; and Boris Nicolaevsky, formerly of the Marx-Engels Institute in Moscow, also said that it was Mikoyan who had slain him (*Facts on Communism*, vol. 2, *The Soviet Union from Lenin to Khrushchev*, Committee on Un-American Activities, House of Representatives, 86th Congress, U.S. Govt. Printing Office, Washington, D.C., 1961. Others have said that Beria was shot by Marshal K. S. Moskalenko, one of Khrushchev's wartime associates in the Ukraine, who replaced Beria's man, P. A. Artemev, as commander of the vital Moscow military district after Stalin's demise.

55. A sign was given at the July 10, 1953, plenary meeting of the Central Committee, which denounced Beria and at the same time elevated Marshal Zhukov from candidate to full member of the committee.

56. Khrushchev would speak kindly of Ignatiev in his 1956 Secret Speech (Talbott, ed., *Khrushchev Remembers*, 1970 ed., appendix, p. 657): "Present at this Congress as a delegate is the former Minister of State Security, Comrade Ignatiev. Stalin told him curtly, 'If you do not obtain confessions from the doctors we will shorten you by a head.'"

57. Conquest, *Policy and Politics in the USSR*, p. 182.

58. *New York Times,* May 13, 1988, p. 1.

59. Dzhirkvelov, p. 254.

60. *New York Times,* May 13, 1988, p. 1.

61. Author interview with Natalia Rapoport, February 19, 1989.

Epilogue

1. *Jerusalem Post,* February 13, 1989.

2. Ibid., February 15, 1989.

3. Author interview with Natalia Vovsi-Mikhoels, May 7, 1989.

4. Article by Arkady Waxsberg, *Literaturnaya Gazeta,* March 15, 1989.

5. *New York Times,* November 8, 1987.

6. *Jerusalem Post,* September 29, 1987.

7. Dr. Rapoport's memoirs were published in the monthly *Druzhba Narodov* (Friendship of the Peoples), April 1988; Natalia Rapoport's memoir was published at the same time by the monthly *Yunost.*

8. *Jerusalem Post,* February 15, 1989.

9. Author interview with Mikhail Chlenov, February 15, 1989.

10. *Moscow News,* no. 7, February 7, 1989.

11. *Sputnik,* (reprint of *Krokodil* article) Moscow, February 1989.

12. Walter Laqueur, "Buying Books in Moscow," *Encounter,* September-October 1988.

13. Vasiliev interviewed by Walter Ruby, *Jerusalem Post,* March 7, 1989. Vasiliev is a monarchist and "reborn Christian" who blames Western entrepreneurs like the Jew Armand Hammer, Lenin's friend, for "pollution"—poisoning the air, as he told a Jewish reporter in February 1989 (from tape of interview by Walter Ruby, February 15, 1989).

14. Pamphlet, "Pamyat: Hatred under Glasnost," 1989, Anti-Defamation League of B'nai B'rith, New York, p. 4.

15. Ibid., pp. 19–20.

16. *International Herald Tribune,* March 7, 1989.

17. Ibid., February 13, 1990.

Dramatis Personae

V. S. Abakumov, born about 1897, was a Cheka official and head of the Soviet secret police (SMERSH) during the war. He became minister of state security and Beria's chief aide until his deposition just before the Doctors' Plot announcement. He was tried for treason and executed in 1954.

Samuel Agursky, a former anarchist and member of the Jewish Bund, became co-head with Stalin of the Jewish Commissariat after the Revolution. Agursky headed Stalin's early campaign against Jewish political, religious, and cultural organizations.

Nadezhda Alliluyeva was Lenin's secretary and became Stalin's second wife. She was the mother of two of Stalin's three children, Vasily and Svetlana. Although apparently a suicide, Nadezhda is thought to have been murdered by Stalin in November 1932 following an argument.

Svetlana Alliluyeva, Stalin's daughter, was his favorite child. But her relationships with Jewish men, one of whom she married, aroused the paranoid suspicion that the Jews were trying to penetrate his family. Svetlana's memoirs are a frightening look at Stalin's domestic life and testify to some of his worst crimes.

Viktor Alter, born in 1890, was active in both the Russian and the Polish Jewish Bund and was an internationally respected socialist leader. He and colleague Henryk Ehrlich first proposed the idea of a Jewish Anti-Fascist Committee. Both were arrested and killed in December 1941.

Isaac Emanuilovich Babel, born in 1894, was one of Russia's greatest writers. A Jew who fought in the Red Army during the civil war and worked for the Cheka as well, Babel became disillusioned with communism and was eventually arrested in the purges of the 1930s. He died in the Gulag around 1940.

David Bergelson, born in 1894, was a distinguished Yiddish poet and Communist believer who wrote lavish encomiums to Stalin. A member of the JAC, Bergelson was among the many victims of the purge of August 1952.

Lavrenty Pavlovich Beria, a Georgian-Mingrelian born in 1899, succeeded Yezhov in 1938 as head of the secret police. Deputy prime minister in charge of security from 1941 to 1953, Beria was one of Stalin's key targets in the Doctors' Plot. He was arrested in June 1953 and executed soon after.

Nikolai Ivanovich Bukharin, born in 1888, was a leading Bolshevik theoretician—"the favorite of the whole party," in Lenin's words. Bukharin supported Stalin against Trotsky and later against Zinoviev and Kamenev. As leader of the "Right opposition," Bukharin was, ironically, prosecuted as a "Trotskyite" during the principal show trial and executed in 1938.

Nikolai Alexandrovich Bulganin, born in 1895, was a Soviet marshal and minister of defense from 1947 to 1949. Like a surprising number among Stalin's inner circle, Bulganin had a Jewish wife, who was also a physician.

Felix Edmundovich Dzerzhinsky, born in 1877 of Polish origin, founded the Soviet secret police network in 1917 and was its head until his death in 1926.

Ilya Grigoriovich Ehrenburg, born in 1891, was a Jewish writer and intellectual whose dispatches from the front in World War II made him the Soviet Union's best-known journalist. A committed Communist who publicly attacked Zionism, Ehrenburg somehow managed to stay alive, despite his refusal to sign an open letter endorsing Stalin's plan to deport the Jews. He died in 1967.

Henryk Ehrlich, born in 1882, was a leader of the Polish Jewish Bund who was shot, along with Viktor Alter, on Stalin's orders in late 1941. Their deaths were revealed only two years later, after an international outcry; Molotov claimed they had been executed as Nazi agents.

Sergei Eisenstein was a Soviet Jewish filmmaker whose epic *Ivan the Terrible* annoyed Stalin for its portrayal of the czar as corrupt and effeminate. Eisenstein was summoned to the Kremlin for a lecture on history and film aesthetics from Stalin himself, and wrote a public apology for his "errors."

Dr. Yakov Etinger, the first of the Kremlin doctors to be arrested, died under torture several months before the Doctors' Plot announcement.

Alexander Alexandrovich Fadeyev, born in 1901, was a novelist whose work was considered a model of socialist realism. As head of the Writers' Union, he helped conceal the disappearances of leading Jewish writers in the 1940s and 1950s. Fadeyev committed suicide in 1956 after Khrushchev's Secret Speech denouncing Stalin.

Itzik Feffer, a well-known Yiddish poet, was a colonel in the Red Army and a member of the JAC. A close associate of Jewish actor Solomon Mikhoels, the two were sent on an extended wartime mission to the West, where they met with many leading Jewish figures. Feffer, who was also a secret police agent, is thought to have conspired in Mikhoels' murder. He himself was executed in 1952 along with many other Jewish intellectuals.

M. V. Frunze was Trotsky's successor as Red Army commander and a probable victim of "medical murder," after Stalin personally ordered him to undergo an unnecessary operation in 1924.

Maxim Gorky, born in 1868, was the best-known Soviet writer of his generation and, as chairman of the Writers' Union, the chief proponent of socialist realism. Gorky died in 1936, a probable victim of medical murder during the purges. Secret police chief Yagoda and Dr. Levin were later accused of his murder and executed.

Vasily Grossman, a leading Jewish writer and journalist and a member of the JAC, was attacked in the Soviet press at the time of the Doctors' Plot and was one of many Jewish cultural figures who signed an open letter asking Stalin to deport the Jews.

S. D. Ignatiev was Ryumin's superior, Beria's rival, and Khrushchev's key secret police ally after replacing Abakumov as minister of state security. Ignatiev was instructed to fabricate evidence against the Kremlin doctors.

Joseph Irmashvili, a boyhood friend of Stalin, was exiled in the early 1920s. He provided much information about Stalin's early life.

Lazar Moiseyevich Kaganovich, born in 1893, was the highest-ranking Jew in the Soviet Union, holding several ministerial positions under Stalin. Kaganovich drew up extensive lists of state enemies—many of them Jews—for execution in the purges. The aged Bolshevik was still alive in Moscow in 1990.

Lev Borisovich Kamenev, born Rosenfeld in 1882, a half-Jew who was also Trotsky's brother-in-law, was one of the five top Bolshevik leaders and after Lenin's death served in the ruling troika with Stalin. Kamenev was killed in 1936 during the Great Terror.

Dr. Boris Borisovich Kogan, born in 1896, was linked by Stalin himself to the "medical murder" of Zhdanov and other Communist leaders.

Dr. M. B. Kogan, a Jewish physician who worked in the Kremlin Hospital, died under torture in November 1951.

Jacob Kreiser, a Jewish general, was the hero of the battle of Smolensk and the struggle for the Crimea. A JAC activist, Kreiser was one of the few who refused to sign the open letter recommending deportation of the Jews.

V. V. Kuibyshev, Kirov's ally in the Politburo, died suddenly in 1935 and may have been killed on Stalin's orders. Kremlin doctors Levin and Pletnev were charged with his "medical murder" during the show trials of 1938.

Leib Kvitko, a leading Jewish writer and JAC activist, was arrested in December 1948 and killed in August 1952.

Dr. Lev Grigorievich Levin, born in 1870, was a Jewish physician who attended both Lenin and Stalin. Levin was prosecuted during the show trials for the "medical murder" of Gorky and Kuibyshev, and executed in 1938.

Maxim Maximovich Litvinov, born in 1876 as Meir Wallach, was a Polish Jew who served as Trotsky's secretary and later became Soviet foreign minister, until just before the pact with Hitler was announced. Litvinov died in 1952.

Solomon A. Lozovsky, born in 1878, served as vice commissar for foreign affairs and was the chief wartime Soviet spokesman. A JAC official, Lozovsky was marked as a "cosmopolite" during the purges and killed in 1952.

Georgi Maximilianovich Malenkov, born in 1902, was Stalin's last chief aide. A Politburo member from 1946, he held power for nine days after Stalin's death and then resigned as secretary of the Central Committee.

Peretz D. Markish, born in 1895, was a leading Yiddish poet, playwright, and novelist. Also a JAC activist, Markish, arrested in January 1949, was among those killed in August 1952.

Julius Martov, born Zederbaum in 1873, was leader of the losing Menshevik faction of the Russian Social Democratic party. The Mensheviks were heavily dominated by revolutionaries of Jewish origin who, like the Bolshevik Jews, were strongly opposed to the Jewish Bund or any other manifestation of Jewish nationalism or religion. Martov died in 1923.

Lev Z. Mekhlis, a high-ranking Soviet Jew and sometime editor of *Pravda,* was an NKVD general who purged the officers' corps and later became minister of state control. Mekhlis left the Politburo in 1950 and died under suspicious circumstances two weeks before Stalin's death.

Vsevolod Emilievich Meyerhold, born in 1874, was a leading Jewish actor and theater director. A friend of Mikhoels and Babel, Meyerhold was arrested in 1939 and perished in the Gulag shortly afterwards.

Solomon Mikhailovich Mikhoels (Vovsi), born in 1890, was Russia's greatest Jewish actor and director. Mikhoels, who directed the popular Moscow Yiddish Theater (GOSET) and headed the Jewish Anti-Fascist Committee, was killed on Stalin's orders in January 1948. Five years later, he was named as mastermind of the Doctors' Plot.

Vyacheslav Mikhailovich Molotov (Scriabin), born in 1890, was Soviet minister of foreign affairs from 1939 until 1949, when he fell from Stalin's favor. Although his wife Paulina, a JAC activist, was arrested in 1948 and shipped to Siberia, Molotov never dared inquire about her fate.

Grigori (Sergo) K. Ordzhonikidze, born in 1886, was a fellow Georgian who became Stalin's close aide, though as a Politburo member he reportedly tried to limit the scope of the purges. He was shot or committed suicide in 1937.

Alexander Poskrebyshev, born in 1891, was Stalin's personal secretary.

Married, like many other Kremlin officials, to a Jewish woman, he divorced her on Stalin's orders.

Dr. Yakov Rapoport, chief Moscow pathologist, was arrested in January 1953 as a suspect in the Doctors' Plot. Released after Stalin's death, Rapoport was still living in Moscow in 1990.

M. D. Ryumin, chief of the secret police branch in charge of investigating the Doctors' Plot allegation, was an anti-Semite who believed the JAC harbored "spies and traitors." Ryumin was among those executed in the wake of Stalin's death.

Alexander Sergeyevich Shcherbakov, born in 1901 and termed a "poisonous snake" in Khrushchev's memoirs, was the most anti-Semitic Politburo member after Stalin and was expected to succeed him. His death in 1945 was later blamed on Jewish Kremlin doctors.

Dr. Boris Shimelovich, a prominent Jewish physician and chief of Moscow's Botkin Hospital, was active in the JAC and a close friend of Mikhoels. Shimelovich was named by *Pravda* as a key conspirator in the Doctors' Plot.

Lena Solomonovna Shtern, born in 1878, known as "Einstein in skirts," was Russia's most distinguished female scientist. Admitted to the Academy of Sciences as the discoverer of "Soviet penicillin" and a prominent JAC activist, Shtern was among the leading Jewish intellectuals secretly tried in July 1952. She alone was spared.

Rudolph Slansky, the Jewish-born head of the Czech Communist party and an extreme anti-Zionist, was tried in Prague with thirteen other top officials, most of them Jews, and executed in 1952.

Jacob Sverdlov, born in 1883, a Bolshevik of Jewish origin, shared a period of Siberian exile with Stalin before the Revolution. Sverdlov, who became the first Soviet head of state, died in 1921.

Lydia Timashuk was an informer in the Kremlin Hospital who denounced the Doctors' Plot to the secret police. Awarded the Order of Lenin, Timashuk become a national heroine, but was discredited after the release of the doctors in April 1953.

Dr. Vladimir N. Vinogradov, born in 1882, an eminent physician who personally attended Stalin, was head of the Kremlin Hospital and a leading figure in the Doctors' Plot affair. He died in 1964.

Kliment Yefremovich Voroshilov, born in 1882, was Stalin's longtime associate and the leading "political marshal" of the Red Army. Relieved as commissar of defense in 1940, he was entirely out of favor by 1952. Voroshilov, whose wife was Jewish, defied Stalin when he announced his plan to deport the Jews.

Dr. Miron Vovsi, a cousin of Solomon Mikhoels, was the Red Army's chief physician during the war and the Kremlin's highest-ranking Jewish doctor. Vovsi, accused of the leading role in the Doctors' Plot, was arrested and tortured on Stalin's orders. Later released, he died of his injuries in 1956.

Natalia and Nina Vovsi-Mikhoels, the two daughters of murdered Jewish actor Solomon Mikhoels, emigrated to Israel during the Brezhnev era.

Genrikh G. Yagoda, born in 1891, was a Jewish pharmacist who became a Cheka agent in 1920. Known as Stalin's master poisoner, he headed the secret police until 1936. Yagoda was tried with Bukharin in the last great show trial and executed in 1938.

Nikolai Ivanovich Yezhov, born around 1894, succeeded Yagoda as chief of the NKVD in 1936. Yezhov oversaw the Great Terror until his own removal and execution in 1938 or 1939.

Andrei Alexandrovich Zhdanov, born in 1896, was a longtime Stalin aide who directed the official campaign against "formalist" and "cosmopolitan" culture. His death in 1948 was later blamed on Jewish doctors.

Paulina S. Zhemchuzina, born in 1896, was Molotov's Jewish wife and a high-ranking Soviet official. She was also active in the JAC. A Stalin loyalist, she was arrested and exiled in 1948.

Grigory Evseevich Zinoviev, a Jew born Radomisky in 1883, was a member of the ruling troika after Lenin's death and headed the Comintern, charged with promoting world revolution. Stalin had him executed along with Kamenev following a major public trial.

Benjamin Zuskin, a Jewish actor and co-director of the Moscow Yiddish Theater, was arrested a year after the murder of Mikhoels and executed in 1952 along with many other Jewish cultural figures.

Bibliography

AINSZTEIN, REUBEN. *Jewish Resistance in Nazi-occupied Eastern Europe*. London: Paul Elek, 1974.

ALEXANDROV, VICTOR. *The Kremlin*. London: Allen & Unwin, 1963.

ALLILUYEVA, SVETLANA. *Twenty Letters to a Friend*. New York: Harper & Row, 1967.

————. *Only One Year*. New York: Harper & Row, 1969.

ANTONOV-OVSENKO, ANTON. *The Time of Stalin*. New York: Harper & Row, 1981.

AVTORKHANOV, ABDURAKHMAN. *The Reign of Stalin*. London: Bodley Head, 1953.

BARON, SALO W. *The Russian Jews under Tsars and Soviets*. New York: Schocken, 1987 edition.

BAUER, YEHUDA. *My Brother's Keeper: A History of the American Joint Distribution Committee*. Philadelphia: Jewish Publication Society, 1974.

BORTOLI, GEORGES. *The Death of Stalin*. London: Phaedon, 1975.

CANG, JOEL. *The Silent Millions: A History of the Jews in the Soviet Union*. New York: Taplinger, 1970.

CONQUEST, ROBERT. *The Nation Killers: The Soviet Deportation of Nationalities*. London: Macmillan, 1970.

————. *The Harvest of Sorrow: Soviet Collectivization and the Terror-Famine*. New York: Oxford University Press, 1986.

————. *Power and Policy in the USSR*. New York: Phaeton, 1975.

COTIC, MEIR. *The Prague Trial: The First Anti-Zionist Show Trial in the Communist Bloc*. New York: Herzl Press, 1987.

DE JONGE, ALEX. *Stalin and the Shaping of the Soviet Union*. London: William Collins, 1986.

DERIABIN, PETER. *Watchdogs of Terror: Russian Bodyguards from the Tsars to the Commissars*. New York: University Publication of America, 1984.

DEUTSCHER, ISAAC. *Stalin: A Political Biography*. New York: Vintage, 1960.

———. *The Non-Jewish Jew and Other Essays*. New York: Hill & Wang, 1968.

———. *The Prophet Armed: Trotsky 1879–1921*. New York: Vintage, 1965.

———. *The Prophet Unarmed: Trotsky 1921–1929*. New York: Vintage, 1965.

DJILAS, MILOVAN. *Conversations with Stalin*. New York: Harcourt Brace, 1962.

DZHIRKVELOV, ILYA. *Secret Servant: My Life with the KGB and the Soviet Elite*. New York: Harper & Row, 1987.

EHRENBURG, ILYA. *Men, Years, Life*. 6 vols. London: MacGibbon & Kee, 1966.

———, and GROSSMAN, VASILY, eds. *The Black Book*. New York: Holocaust Library, 1981.

EMIOT, ISRAEL. *The Birobidzhan Affair: A Yiddish Writer in Siberia*. Philadelphia: Jewish Publication Society, 1981.

FAINSOD, MERLE. *Smolensk under Soviet Rule*. Cambridge, Mass.: Harvard University Press, 1958.

———. *How Russia Is Ruled*, Cambridge, Mass.: Harvard University Press, 1953.

FREUD, SIGMUND. *Three Case Histories*. New York: Macmillan, 1963.

GILBOA, YEHOSHUA A. *The Black Years of Soviet Jewry 1939–1953*. Boston: Little, Brown, 1971.

GINZBURG, EUGENIA SEMYONOVNA. *Journey into the Whirlwind*. New York: Harcourt Brace Jovanovich, 1967.

———. *Within the Whirlwind*. New York: Harcourt Brace Jovanovich, 1981.

GITELMAN, ZVI. *A Century of Ambivalence: The Jews of Russia and the Soviet Union, 1881 to the Present*. New York: Schocken, 1988.

GOLDBERG, B. Z. *The Jewish Problem in the Soviet Union: Analysis and Solution*. New York: Crown, 1961.

GROSSMAN, VASILY. *Life and Fate*. London: Collins Harvill, 1985.

HAHN, WERNER. *Postwar Soviet Politics: The Fall of Zhdanov and the Defeat of Moderation, 1946–53*. Ithaca: Cornell University Press, 1982.

HELLER, MIKHAIL I., and Nekrich, Aleksandr M. *Utopia in Power: History of the Soviet Union from 1917 to the Present*. New York: Summit Books, 1986.

HOFSTADTER, RICHARD. *The Paranoid Style in American Politics*. Chicago: University of Chicago Press, 1979 edition.

IRMASHVILI, J. *Stalin und die Tragodie Georgiens.* Berlin: Volksblatt-Druckerei, 1932.

JORAVSKY, DAVID. *The Lysenko Affair.* Cambridge, Mass.: Harvard University Press, 1970.

KENNAN, GEORGE F. *Russia and the West under Lenin and Stalin.* Boston: Little, Brown, 1961.

―――. *Memoirs, 1925–50.* Boston: Little, Brown, 1967.

KOESTLER, ARTHUR. *The Invisible Writing.* London: Collins & H. Hamilton, 1954.

LENEMAN, LÉON. *La Tragédie des Juifs en URSS.* Paris: Desclée de Brower, 1959.

LERMOLO, ELIZABETH. *Face of a Victim.* New York: Harper & Brothers, 1955.

LEVINE, ISAAC DON. *Stalin's Great Secret.* New York:; Coward-McCann, 1956.

LEVINE, NORA. *The Jews in the Soviet Union Since 1917: Paradox of Survival.* 2 vols. New York and London: New York University Press, 1988.

MANDELSTAM, NADEZHDA. *Hope Against Hope.* New York: Atheneum, 1970.

MARKISH, ESTHER. *The Long Return.* New York: Random House, 1978.

MEDVEDEV, ROY A. *On Stalin and Stalinism.* Oxford: Oxford University Press, 1979.

―――. *Let History Judge: The Origins and Consequences of Stalinism.* New York: Knopf, 1971.

"Monitor." [pseudonym] *The Death of Stalin Investigated by Monitor.* London: H. Wingate, 1958.

NAMIR, MORDECHAI. *Shlichut B'Moscava* (Mission in Moscow). Tel Aviv: Am Oved Publishers, 1961.

NICOLAEVSKY, BORIS I. *Power and the Soviet Elite.* London: Pall Mall Press, 1966.

ORLOV, ALEXANDER. *The Secret History of Stalin's Crimes.* London: Jarrolds, 1953.

PAYNE, ROBERT. *The Rise and Fall of Stalin.* London: Pan Books, 1968.

PIPES, RICHARD. *Russia under the Old Regime.* London: Penguin, 1984.

―――, ed. *The Russian Intelligentsia.* Hamilton, N.Y.: Colgate University Press, 1961.

RAPPAPORT, ERNEST A. *Anti-Judaism: A Psychohistory.* Chicago: University of Chicago Press, 1975.

REDLICH, SHIMON. "The Jews under Soviet Rule During World War II." Ph.D. diss. New York: New York University, 1968.

————. *Propaganda and Nationalism in Wartime Russia: The Jewish Antifascist Committee in the USSR, 1941-1948*, East European Monographs No. CVIII, East European Quarterly, Boulder, Colo., 1982.

RO'I YAACOV. *From Encroachment to Involvement: A Documentary Study of Soviet Policy in the Middle East*, 1945-1973. New York: John Wiley, 1974.

SALISBURY, HARRISON. *Moscow Journal*. Chicago: University of Chicago Press, 1961.

————. *Stalin's Russia and After*. London: MacMillan, 1955.

————. *The 900 Days: The Siege of Leningrad*. New York: Harper & Row, 1969.

SEATON, ALBERT and JOAN. *The Soviet Army 1918 to the Present*. New York: New American Library, 1986.

SERGE, VIKTOR. *From Lenin to Stalin*. New York: Pioneer, 1937.

SHOSTAKOVICH, DMITRI. *Testimony: The Memoirs of Shostakovich,* ed. Solomon Volkov. London: Faber & Faber, 1981.

SIMMEL, ERNST, ed. *Anti-Semitism: A Social Disease*. New York: International Universities Press, 1946.

SMITH, EDWARD ELLIS. *The Young Stalin: The Early Years of an Elusive Revolutionary*. London: Cassell, 1967.

SOLZHENITSYN, ALEXANDER. *Cancer Ward*. New York: Bantam, 1969.

————. *The First Circle*. New York: Bantam, 1971.

————. *The Gulag Archipelago: 1918-1956*. London: Collins Harvill, 1988.

SOUVARINE, BORIS. *Stalin: A Critical Survey of Bolshevism*. New York: Longmans, Green, 1939.

STALIN, JOSIF [JOSEPH]. *Collected Works. vols. 1-13*. Moscow: Foreign Language Publishing House, 1949-55.

STERN, FRITZ. *The Politics of Cultural Despair*. Berkeley: University of California Press, 1961.

SWAYZE, HAROLD. *Political Control of Literature in the USSR, 1946-59*. Cambridge, Mass.: Harvard University Press, 1962.

TALBOTT, STROBE, ed. *Khrushchev Remembers*. Boston: Little, Brown, 1970.

————. *Khrushchev Remembers: The Last Testament*. Boston: Little, Brown, 1974.

TREPPER, LEOPOLD. *The Great Game: The Story of the Red Orchestra*. London: Michael Joseph, 1977.

TROTSKY, LEON. *Stalin: An Appraisal of the Man and his Influence*. New York: Stein & Day, 1967 edition.

TUCKER, ROBERT C. *The Soviet Political Mind: Stalinism and Post-Stalin Change*. London: George Allen, 1972.

ULAM, ADAM B. *Stalin: The Man and His Era.* New York: Viking, 1973.

VOVSI-MIKHOELS, NATALIA. *Avi Shlomo Mikhoels* (My Father Solomon Mikhoels). Israel: Kibbutz Hameuchad Publishers, 1982.

WERTH, ALEXANDER. *Russia: The Post-War Years.* London: Robert Hale, 1971.

WISTRICH, ROBERT S. *Revolutionary Jews from Marx to Trotsky.* London: Harrap, 1976.

WOLFE, BERTRAM. *Khrushchev and Stalin's Ghost.* New York: Praeger, 1957.

Index